# Richard Flanagan

# SYDNEY STUDIES IN AUSTRALIAN LITERATURE

Robert Dixon, Series Editor

---

The **Sydney Studies in Australian Literature** series publishes original, peer-reviewed research in the field of Australian literary studies. It offers engagingly written evaluations of the nature and importance of Australian literature, and aims to reinvigorate its study both locally and internationally. It will be of interest to those researching, studying and teaching in the diverse fields of Australian literary studies.

*Alex Miller: The Ruin of Time*
Robert Dixon

*Australian Books and Authors in the American Marketplace 1840s–1940s*
David Carter and Roger Osborne

*Colonial Australian Fiction: Character Types, Social Formations and the Colonial Economy*
Ken Gelder and Rachael Weaver

*Contemporary Australian Literature: A World Not Yet Dead*
Nicholas Birns

*Elizabeth Harrower: Critical Essays*
Ed. Elizabeth McMahon and Brigitta Olubas

*The Fiction of Tim Winton: Earthed and Sacred*
Lyn McCredden

*Richard Flanagan: Critical Essays*
Ed. Robert Dixon

*Shirley Hazzard: New Critical Essays*
Ed. Brigitta Olubas

# Richard Flanagan

## Critical Essays

Edited by Robert Dixon

SYDNEY UNIVERSITY PRESS

First published by Sydney University Press
© Individual contributors 2018
© Sydney University Press 2018

**Reproduction and Communication for other purposes**
Except as permitted under the Act, no part of this edition may be reproduced, stored in a retrieval system, or communicated in any form or by any means without prior written permission. All requests for reproduction or communication should be made to Sydney University Press at the address below:

Sydney University Press
Fisher Library F03
University of Sydney NSW 2006
AUSTRALIA
sup.info@sydney.edu.au
sydney.edu.au/sup

 A catalogue record for this book is available from the National Library of Australia.

ISBN 9781743325827 paperback
ISBN 9781743325964 epub

Cover image by Joel Saget.
Cover design by Miguel Yamin.

# Contents

The Novels of Richard Flanagan: An Introduction    1
   *Robert Dixon and Liliana Zavaglia*

1   Circles of Violence: Historical Constellations in *Death of a River Guide* and *The Sound of One Hand Clapping*    21
   *Robert Dixon*

2   Greening a Narrative Mode: Antipodean Magical Realism and Ecocriticism in Richard Flanagan's Fiction    43
   *Ben Holgate*

3   "Smashing and singing and sobbing and howling": Sound and Richard Flanagan's Tasmania    59
   *Joseph Cummins*

4   Spatial Anxieties: Tourists, Settlers and Tasmania's Affective Economies of Belonging in *A Terrible Beauty*, *Death of a River Guide* and *Gould's Book of Fish*    73
   *Laura A. White*

5   Rewriting History: *Gould's Book of Fish*    87
   *Bill Ashcroft*

6   Richard Flanagan's "Post-post" and the Mapping of the Altermodern    103
   *Salhia Ben-Messahel*

7   Contestations of Authority: Richard Flanagan's Australian Biofictions    119
   *Marc Delrez*

8   The Genealogy of Wanting    135
   *Margaret Harris*

9   Terror, Paranoia and Manipulation: The Politics of Fear in *The Unknown Terrorist*    155
   *Nathanael O'Reilly*

10   Sydney, a City without Love: The Unknown Terrorist in *The Unknown Terrorist*    169
   *Theodore F. Sheckels*

| | | |
|---|---|---|
| 11 | "Fireless flame gone amorous": War amid Love in *The Narrow Road to the Deep North*<br>*Nicholas Birns* | 179 |
| 12 | "Out of the tear-drenched land": Transnational Sites of Memory in *The Narrow Road to the Deep North*<br>*Liliana Zavaglia* | 193 |

Contributors 221

Index 223

# The Novels of Richard Flanagan: An Introduction

Robert Dixon and Liliana Zavaglia

On 14 October 2014, Richard Flanagan was awarded the Man Booker Prize for *The Narrow Road to the Deep North* (2013). It was a signal moment not only in his own career but also in the international reception of Australian literature. In his acceptance speech and in media interviews in London, however, Flanagan identified with Tasmania rather than Australia, explaining, "I do not come out of a literary tradition. I come from a tiny mining town in the rainforest on an island at the end of the world."[1] Echoing Salman Rushdie in the wake of his own Booker win for *Midnight's Children* in 1981, Flanagan went on to claim that "Literary culture … is the vengeance of the edges on the centre".[2]

Alluding to the second of the *Star Wars* films, Rushdie's famous article, "The Empire Writes Back with a Vengeance", was meant to suggest the role of literature in resisting the legacies of British imperialism;[3] by 2014, however, the postcolonial world had been swept up, in turn, by the economic, political and cultural cross-currents of globalisation, with its complicated interplay between the local, the national and the global.[4] According to Stephen Romei, Flanagan "does not see literature in terms of homeland or nationality",[5] while Geordie Williamson describes him as a regional writer who has "broken through to a global readership", locating Tasmania not as the "benighted outpost" of popular imagination but "a distinct region awaiting its voice".[6]

What we are dealing with here are questions of scale. What scale of the knowable community is an appropriate frame for Flanagan's fiction? At what scale – from the local, through regional, national and transnational to world and planet – do his novels ask to be read? What are the consequences of approaching a regionally identified author like Flanagan from the scale of the nation, or a national literature like that of Australia from the

---

1   Richard Flanagan, interviewed by Alan Yentob in *Richard Flanagan: Life after Death*, dir. Jack Cocker (BBC Scotland, 2015). https://vimeo.com/135694839.
2   Richard Flanagan cited in Geordie Williamson, "Literary Masterpieces from a Small Island", *Weekend Australian*, 18–19 October 2014, 17.
3   Salman Rushdie, "The Empire Writes Back with a Vengeance", *Times*, 3 July 1982, 8.
4   Patrick Bixby, "From the Postcolonial to Contemporary Reality of Globalization: Rushdie's Later Novels", in *Salman Rushdie's Midnight's Children*, ed. Reena Mitra (New Delhi: Atlantic, 2006), 119.
5   Stephen Romei, "Man Booker Winner Richard Flanagan's Triumph Against Odds", *Australian*, 16 October 2014, 11.
6   Williamson, "Literary Masterpieces from a Small Island", 17.

scale of the world? This is another way of asking, where is the work of a writer like Richard Flanagan best located? The answers to these questions lie in Flanagan's own genesis as a distinctly Tasmanian writer who was shaped, in his own words, by "the remotest island of the remotest continent".[7] It is the specific history and insights forged in the island space of Tasmania, by its remarkable landscapes and cross-cultural communities, which have in turn shaped the preoccupations of his literary fiction.

Richard Flanagan was born in Tasmania in 1961 and grew up in the west coast mining town of Rosebery, twenty-five kilometres northeast of Zeehan. His father, Arch Flanagan, a primary school teacher and former prisoner of war on the Thai–Burma Railway, was the only member of his family to finish high school. The fifth of six children, Flanagan left school at sixteen to work in the bush. After returning to his studies, he graduated in 1982 with first-class honours in history at the University of Tasmania. His honours thesis was later published as *A Terrible Beauty: History of the Gordon River Country* (1985). In it he traces the Aboriginal occupation of the area from ancient times until after the invasion, revealing its silenced histories and disputing the prevailing view that the early white explorers and bushmen had a confrontational and uncaring attitude towards the region and its people. Flanagan is equally critical of today's pro-development and pro-conservation lobbies, each of which seeks legitimacy in its own version of the wilderness myth, promoting the view that Tasmania is and has always been an "empty" land rather than one of sustainable, long-term human cultivation, first by its Indigenous population and then by its working-class rural settlers.[8] As a number of contributors to this volume observe, Flanagan chooses to see Tasmanian history as one of indigenisation and cross-cultural intermingling, and not solely a narrative of colonisation, with its entailing myth of Indigenous extinction.

In 1982, Flanagan was awarded a Rhodes Scholarship at the University of Oxford, where he has said that he was introduced, "in a single, small town", to "all that is worst and most contemptible about English society". According to Flanagan, "Oxford is a place that makes people ashamed of who they are and where they come from, and strive to be like people who will never accept them".[9] At Oxford, Flanagan researched and wrote his MA dissertation in the field of labour history, later published as *"Parish-Fed Bastards": A History of the Politics of the Unemployed in Britain, 1884–1939*.[10] After returning to Tasmania in 1989, he co-edited with fellow-historian Cassandra Pybus *The Rest of the World Is Watching: Tasmania and the Greens* (1990), an anthology of essays on the history and politics of the conservation movement. The second of Flanagan's two essays in that collection, "Return the People's Pedder!", begins with a quotation from Walter Benjamin, whose distinctive brand of historical materialism has had a formative influence on Flanagan's own philosophy of history: "To articulate the past historically … means to seize hold of a memory as it flashes up at a moment of danger … In every era

---

7   Richard Flanagan, *Death of a River Guide* (1994; Ringwood, Vic: Penguin, 1996), 149.
8   Richard Flanagan, *A Terrible Beauty: History of the Gordon River Country* (Melbourne: Greenhouse Publications, 1985).
9   Richard Flanagan cited in Rex Direen, "Two Rhodes Scholars: Is Tasmania Ridiculous or Sublime?", an unpublished essay on Flanagan and Peter Conrad, Richard Flanagan Papers, NLA, Box 19.
10  Richard Flanagan, *"Parish-Fed Bastards": A History of the Politics of the Unemployed in Britain, 1884–1939* (New York: Greenwood Press, 1991).

the attempt must be made anew to wrest tradition away from a conformism that is about to overpower it".[11]

Flanagan's preoccupations as a novelist have been remarkably consistent since this early co-edited book, which reverses the point of view of the "storyteller" – another signature Benjaminian phrase[12] – from that of the world/empire/nation to that of the island/edge/province. This visual and aesthetic but also intensely political reorientation, which already recalls Rushdie's idea of "writing back", is associated with the goal of recovering the small-scale local histories otherwise marginalised by triumphal narratives from the metropolitan centres. *The Rest of the World Is Watching* implies a consciously antipodean perspective that often recurs in Flanagan's later writings, indicating a strong spatial awareness of Tasmania as an island community located at the ends of the earth whose fortunes have been variously shaped by the legacies of imperialism, nationalism and globalisation:

> It is no happy accident that the most potent force in current Australian politics should come from the periphery rather than the perceived centres of power, or that this remote place should prove to be a paradigm for political change internationally. In a world where the political–economic complex is concentrated at the centre – Tokyo, New York, Sydney – it is inevitable that challenge ... will come from the periphery.[13]

In this literally eccentric but principled point of view, island Tasmania is recognised as a source of innovation sufficient to transform the distant centres of world culture and power, reversing its own dark inheritance as Europe's antipodes to become the originary point for a new "ecocentric philosophy". In another early essay, the ironically titled "Masters of History", Flanagan asks, "what if such centres no longer hold, and the most interesting things in the world have started to happen at its edges?"[14] Alluding to the novel he was writing at the time, Flanagan foreshadows his turn from history to fiction, and from realism to magical realism as an alternative vehicle for the "storyteller's" subaltern histories. Rushdie is again a benchmark author: "realism, as Salman Rushdie once pointed out, is often inadequate in its description of reality. In a magical land ... great things, both terrible and wonderful, remain possible".[15]

## Flanagan's Fictions

At the time of our writing this introduction, in July 2017, Richard Flanagan was the author of six novels: *Death of a River Guide* (1994), *The Sound of One Hand Clapping* (1997), *Gould's Book of Fish: A Novel in Twelve Fish* (2001), *The Unknown Terrorist* (2006), *Wanting*

---

11  Walter Benjamin, "Theses on the Philosophy of History", VI, cited in Richard Flanagan, "Return the People's Pedder!", in *The Rest of the World Is Watching*, ed. Cassandra Pybus and Richard Flanagan (Sydney: Pan Macmillan, 1990), 194.
12  Walter Benjamin, "The Storyteller: Reflections on the Works of Nikolai Leskov", in *Illuminations: Essays and Reflections*, trans. Harry Zohn, ed. Hannah Arendt (1968; New York: Schocken, 2007), 83–110.
13  Cassandra Pybus and Richard Flanagan, "Introduction", *The Rest of the World Is Watching*, 11.
14  Flanagan, "Masters of History", in *The Rest of the World Is Watching*, 132–3.
15  Flanagan, "Return the People's Pedder!", in *The Rest of the World is Watching*, 210.

(2008) and *The Narrow Road to the Deep North* (2013). His seventh novel, *First Person*, was published in October 2017.[16] In an interview with British journalist Alan Yentob for the television documentary *Richard Flanagan: Life After Death* (2015), Flanagan traces the origins of his mature fiction to a near-death experience as a young man when, in 1982, at the age of twenty-one, he was trapped beneath a kayak on the Franklin River. Inspired by that experience, *Death of a River Guide* is narrated by a drowning man, Aljaz Cosini, who in his dying moments is granted visions of the tangled histories of his family and his community, whose emotional impact he bears like a river in flood. This revelation of personal genesis and belonging also touches on the problem of artistic origins, the problem of how an authentic art or culture might emerge in a settler society beset by unresolved issues of migration, exile and illicit belonging.

The typewritten draft of *Death of a River Guide* reveals that it was originally to have been called "The Circle", with an epigraph from William Blake's *Jerusalem*: "I see the Past, Present, and Future existing all at once".[17] As a professionally trained historian attempting to write literary fiction, the problem Flanagan wrestled with during the early 1990s was how to realise in language and narrative form what he understood as the "circularity" of historical time. Such an aesthetic form would coincide with the circularity of lived experience in oral cultures, and might serve as an alternative to mainstream historical narratives, with their characteristically linear and teleological form:

> I knew exactly what it was going to be like. The struggle of '93 and '94 was to actually make it work ... I really didn't realize until I got into it how ambitious it was technically ... I wanted to write it in a circular structure, because I came to think that traditional forms of narrative were very European-based and very much a straight line. And it always interested me here that the people tell stories in a much more circular fashion. Essentially I come from a Tasmanian oral culture where stories are passed on from generation to generation. It wasn't a literary culture, it wasn't an intellectual culture – it wasn't a culture that had references in books or ideas. It only had references in stories and images – its own life and other lives – and they were all in the form of stories. I had grown up loving those stories. The more I thought about them the more incredibly circular they were in structure.[18]

Flanagan elaborates on these ideas in "Writing Landscape", a speech at the Melbourne Writers' Festival in October 1997. His theme was the artificiality of separating culture from nature by the idea of "landscape", which he associates with cultural elites detached from the lives of rural communities. This also leads to an insightful gloss on the recurring motif in his novels of the line and the circle – in this case as figures for merely travelling through a place rather than actually living in it:

> I never have written landscape ... because I don't find that as an idea it makes any sense either in life or writing ... The earth, the non-human natural world, of course figures prominently in what I write, because it has always figured prominently in my life. If my writing is about anything, it is about writing against landscape, against the pernicious

---

16  Richard Flanagan, *First Person* (Sydney: Knopf, 2017).
17  Richard Flanagan, edited typescript of "The Circle", dated June 1993, Flanagan Papers, NLA, Box 19.
18  Richard Flanagan, interview with Giles Hugo, undated typescript, Flanagan Papers, NLA, Box 19.

notion of there being a human world, and a non-human world that is always other than us. All I have tried to do in all my writing is remind people that all land is made up of stories, and to understand the land one must learn those stories and make up new ones. The land needs stories as much as it needs water and light, and we need stories in which the land figures as prominently as any human character.

My mother's family were north-west coast farming people and my mother gave to all her children a great abiding love for her land and its people. But it was a special and peculiar love, a love that was about being part of the earth rather than an observer of it. My mother and father couldn't pass a tree, a hillside, a patch of bush without filling that piece of country with a story – about ancestors, friends, or acquaintances and what they had done or had done to them here or there. Highways were their enemy, proposing as they did the vainglorious and foolish notion that the purpose of travel was to get from one point to the next as quickly as possible. My parents often seemed incapable of taking a straight line anywhere and instead we seemed to circle endlessly in our journeys, slowly going up this country road and down that lane, and all of them, unlike the highways, full of stories ...

Like a lot of the worst ideas, landscape is an idea of high European culture whose time really ought to be well and truly over. It seems to have arisen in the early throes of capitalism when a nascent bourgeoisie tried to deny the ongoing and total relationship we all have with the earth by presenting the natural world as outside of, and separate to our experience, a world emptied of politics and history, and as the centuries rolled by, increasingly and inevitably, of people themselves.[19]

The series of distinctions epitomised here by the imagery of the circle and the line derives in part from British historian Simon Schama's then recent and influential book *Landscape and Memory* (1995),[20] and foreshadows postcolonial and eco-critic Rob Nixon's later distinction between "vernacular" and "official" landscapes in *Slow Violence and the Environmentalism of the Poor* (2011):

A vernacular landscape is shaped by the affective, historically textured maps that communities have devised over generations ... By contrast, an official landscape ... is typically oblivious to such earlier maps; instead, it writes the land in a bureaucratic, externalizing, and extraction-driven manner that is often pitilessly instrumental.[21]

Like Tasmanian-born historian Henry Reynolds, Flanagan has indicated in recent interviews that he is likely to have had Aboriginal ancestors on his father's side of the family.[22] In 2008, he wrote an enthusiastic review of historian James Boyce's *Van Diemen's Land*.[23] Boyce's central thesis concerning the "indigenisation" of the settler population provides a more rigorously argued version of Flanagan's own fictionalised account of Tasmanian history in *Death of a River Guide*, while at the same time revising the

---

19  Richard Flanagan, "Writing Landscape", October 1997, Flanagan Papers, NLA, Box 5, Folder: "Speeches and Writings 1999".
20  Simon Schama, *Landscape and Memory* (London: HarperCollins, 1995).
21  Rob Nixon, *Slow Violence and the Environmentalism of the Poor* (Cambridge, MA: Harvard University Press, 2011), 17.
22  Richard Flanagan, interviewed in *Life after Death*.
23  James Boyce, *Van Diemen's Land* (Melbourne: Black Inc., 2008).

"monocultural nationalism" of the mid-twentieth-century histories. Boyce's story, Flanagan argues, is "a history of hope":

> It suggests that we are not dispossessed Europeans, but a muddy wash of peoples who were made anew in the merge of old pre-industrial, pre-modern European culture with an extraordinary natural world and a remarkable black culture. As much as a process of colonisation, Boyce's work suggests a history of indigenisation – a strange, uneven, frequently repressed, often violent process in which a white underclass took on much of the black ways of living.[24]

Cosini's death by drowning on the Franklin River in *Death of a River Guide* also alludes to the deaths of the Tasmanian wilderness photographers Olegas Truchanas, who drowned on the Gordon in 1972, and Peter Dombrovskis, who died while walking in the remote Western Arthurs in 1996. Truchanas and Dombrovskis are models for Flanagan both as artist-activist-adventurers and as *Tasmanian* artists who were regionally rather than nationally committed.[25] In the words of Harvard geographer Neil Brenner, Flanagan's work consistently engages at levels "above, below and around" the scale of nation while eschewing specifically – or narrowly – national identification.[26] "Though a nation", Flanagan believes, "Australia is not one country but many, and one of these is the country of Tasmania". Truchanas and Dombrovskis lived at that "edge": "They lived in Tasmania and made art about Tasmania, an island at once alien and marginal to Australia".[27]

In his public statements, Flanagan has often adopted an anti-national, anti-foundational stance that aims to disconnect his subject matter, which has often seemed canonically "Australian" and "historical", from the legend-making capacities of national history and the great Australian novel. As Geordie Williamson points out, Flanagan has spoken of his admiration for William Faulkner's "lifelong refusal to write an 'American' novel ... [and] we should also celebrate Flanagan's refusal to write an 'Australian' novel'".[28] Flanagan's references to other writers are more often to international modernist and magical realist authors than to an "Australian tradition", which he mocks in the opening pages of his first novel. In his acceptance speech after winning the Australian Literary Society's Gold Medal for *Gould's Book of Fish*, Flanagan spoke deliberately of his "small compass" and "limited aspirations" as a novelist, pushing back against the cultural-nationalist ethos of his host organisation, the Association for the Study of Australian Literature: "I am not arguing for some new nationalist literature ... My suspicion is that great novels are ever anti-national, rising beyond them, opposing fundamentally the nonsense of national pretensions".[29]

---

24   Richard Flanagan, "Van Diemen's Land", *Sydney Morning Herald*, 16 February 2008, reprinted in *And what do you do, Mr Gable? New and Collected Essays* (Sydney: Random House, 2015), 208.
25   Richard Flanagan, "It's Peter Dom", *Art & Australia* (Spring 2010), reprinted in *And what do you do, Mr Gable?*, 23–31.
26   Neil Brenner, *New State Spaces: Urban Governance and the Rescaling of Statehood* (New York: Oxford University Press, 2004), 68.
27   Flanagan, "It's Peter Dom", 28.
28   Williamson, "Literary Masterpieces from a Small Island", 17.
29   Richard Flanagan, "ALS Gold Medal Acceptance Speech", *JASAL: Journal of the Association for the Study of Australian Literature* 1 (2002): 117.

Flanagan's second novel, *The Sound of One Hand Clapping* (1997), was originally written as a screenplay and adapted as a novel only when he was unable to secure adequate finance for film production. After the critical success of the novel, however, a film version was released on 28 February 1998, produced by Rolf de Heer, directed by Flanagan, and starring Kerry Fox as Sonja Buloh. It is set in Tasmania during the hydro-industrial boom of the 1950s to the 1980s, drawing on the experiences of the postwar generation of European immigrants who had come to Tasmania to work on the dams. Its witness to intergenerational trauma also has a deeper personal resonance for Flanagan, as the story of the Buloh family is drawn from that of his wife, Majda Smolje, to whom the book is dedicated. Flanagan has said, "It struck me as very ironic that the people who were brought in to build these great dams were the Europeans who were seeking to flee exactly that Europe of Ruhr Valleys and all the horror that it had produced. People who were entirely shaped by history – the Poles, the Italians, the Yugoslavs".[30] In *Death of a River Guide* and *The Sound of One Hand Clapping*, Flanagan therefore constellates Tasmania's colonial and modern history not with that of mainland or continental Australia, but with Tasmania's antipodes, *Mitteleuropa*, especially the marginalised Eastern Europe of the Cold War era.

In his novels and public statements, Flanagan consciously exploits the longstanding ambiguity about Tasmania's relation to continental Australia in the popular spatial imaginary. As eighteenth- and early nineteenth-century maps of Van Diemen's Land indicate, Tasmania has long had an ambivalent status in representations of the Australian landmass and in relation to the idea of the continental nation. The existence of Bass Strait was not confirmed until George Bass and Matthew Flinders' circumnavigation of Van Diemen's Land in 1798–99. Thomas Kincade's *Map of New Holland*, published in 1790, shows the then-surveyed portions of New Holland and Van Diemen's Land in a solid line and the as yet unsurveyed portions in a broken line. Van Diemen's Land is connected uncertainly to the mainland with a solid line on the east and a broken line on the west. This uncertainty is sustained in the many contemporary maps of Australia that omit the island state altogether. As Tony Stagg and Philip Mead observe, citing the work of Elizabeth McMahon, "there is a well-recognised, and rhetorically complex, thematics of islandness that the literature of Tasmania contributes to", and "the back-story of this history haunts the literature of Tasmania in various ways".[31]

Flanagan's great-great-grandfather, Thomas Flanagan, was a convict who had been sent to Longford in 1851, and the penal history of Tasmania is again a thematic preoccupation of his third novel, *Gould's Book of Fish* (2001). It began with a simple inquiry at the State Library of Tasmania about whether there were any surviving images of the convicts from the Macquarie Harbour Penal Station on Sarah Island. Opened in 1822, its closure in 1833 is described in Book II of Marcus Clarke's classic novel of the convict system, *His Natural Life*.[32] Unable to locate any photographs from this period, the curator showed him instead the convict artist William Buelow Gould's watercolour paintings of fish, suggesting that they seemed to possess human faces. The origins of the novel also

---

30   Richard Flanagan, interviewed in *Life after Death*.
31   Tony Stagg and Philip Mead, "A Place of Stories: A Report on the Literature of Tasmania Subset of the AustLit Database", in *Resourceful Reading: The New Empiricism, eResearch and Australian Literary Culture*, ed. Katherine Bode and Robert Dixon (Sydney: Sydney University Press, 2009), 316–17.
32   Marcus Clarke, *His Natural Life*, ed. Lurline Stuart, Academy Editions of Australian Literature (1874; St Lucia: University of Queensland Press, 2001).

reveal Flanagan's growing ambitions as a writer, and his aspiration to locate his work within transnational contexts, albeit from an antipodean and island perspective.

The publishing proposal for *Gould's Book of Fish*, written for Nikki Christer at Pan Macmillan, captures Flanagan's synthesis of intensely local subject matter and point of view with his aspirations to model the form of the novel on world fiction:

> What I envisage is … a short novel … set in the remote Sarah Island on Tasmania's west coast in the 1820s, at which time the penal settlement there occupied in the popular imagination of the British Empire the morbid status that Devil's Island was to later acquire for the French … To be called *Gould's Book of Fish* … it is to take the form of a discovered ms written by a long-forgotten convict … (and here I am inspired by the unfinished biography of the 19th century peasant poet John Clare so recently and successfully aped in [Thomas] Pynchon's *Mason & Dixon*).

The narrator is William Buelow Gould, a convict forger sent to Sarah Island at the request of the surgeon to paint a series of natural history studies of the fish found around the island:

> The real-life Gould's pictures of the fish would form the organizing principle of the novel, something in the manner of Vargas Llosa's use of paintings in *In Praise of the Stepmother*. Each chapter would begin with a colour plate of one of Gould's studies of a fish, and be printed in a different coloured ink.[33]

Flanagan explained to Christer that his idea for the coloured type-faces was modelled on William Faulkner's plan for *The Sound and the Fury*.

Flanagan's elaborate framing apparatus uses the convention of the found manuscript. In the narrative present, Sid Hammet, a purveyor of fake antiques for the American tourist market, discovers a copy of the *Book of Fish*, a rare nineteenth-century book, in Hobart's Salamanca markets, but Professor Roman da Silva, an expert in colonial history, declares it to be a "pastiche".[34] When it disappears mysteriously from the bar of a Hobart pub, Hammet resolves to replicate the text from memory, though he is an unreliable narrator. While these postmodern devices undermine the authority of narrative history, as several postcolonial critics have noted,[35] they are in another sense a distraction from Flanagan's otherwise transparent political argument about a "colonial" or provincial art that is neither imperial nor national. As Jo Jones observes, "While reviewers have usually and adroitly discussed the novel … in the light of postmodern theory, they often seem to miss something at the heart of the novel, namely Flanagan's liberal or progressive politics".[36]

Hammet is acutely aware of the location from which he operates as a maker of fake antiques: he works in Hobart, not in Berlin or Buenos Aires or New York, which are also

---

33 Richard Flanagan to Nikki Christer, 11 November 1997. Flanagan Papers, NLA, Box 5, Folder, "Correspondence 2001".
34 Richard Flanagan, *Gould's Book of Fish* (London: Atlantic Books, 2001), 23.
35 Bill Ashcroft, "Reading Post-Colonial Australia", in *Postcolonial Issues in Australian Literature*, ed. Nathanael O'Reilly (Amherst, MA: Cambria, 2010), 15–40.
36 Jo Jones, "'Dancing the Old Enlightenment': *Gould's Book of Fish*, the Historical Novel and the Postmodern Sublime," in "The Colonial Present," special issue, *JASAL: Journal of the Association for the Study of Australian Literature* (2008): 114.

among the great cities of twentieth-century literary modernism. Realising that Americans will only ever buy one type of "story", "an American story", Hammet passes off his fakes as Shaker furniture brought to the colony on the transpacific gold-rush circuit in the 1850s.[37] When he discovers and then loses the *Book of Fish*, he transfers his energies from fake antiques to fake books, which have the same geopolitical relation to the global market. In the face of those critics who accuse Flanagan of belatedly recycling a style of magical realist fiction already popular elsewhere,[38] this framing device identifies a practice of provincial appropriation of canonical literary forms, including magical realism, that is self-reflexive about its own moment of intervention: its relation to national and global cultures is entirely contingent, opportunistic and defiantly unoriginal. Here, in anticipation, was the pre-text for Flanagan's response to winning the Man Booker Prize in London in 2014: "Literary culture is the vengeance of the edges on the centre".

In 2004, Flanagan became embroiled in a very public conflict with Paul Lennon, the Labor premier of Tasmania, over his government's support for a new $2 billion pulp mill to be built on the banks of the Tamar River near Launceston. The outcome was Flanagan's 2007 essay for the *Monthly*, "Out of Control: The Tragedy of Tasmania's Forests".[39] He told Alan Yentob, "I took six months to decide whether I'd do it or not because I was so fearful of what would happen to me and my family, and every day I worked on it I'd actually feel nauseated, because the more I researched it, the more I wrote, the more I realised what a shocking and terrible thing it really was". When businessman and environmental campaigner Geoff Cousins intervened in the debate as an opponent of the pulp mill, reprinting Flanagan's article for mass circulation, a media storm erupted that would see Flanagan vilified by local media and politicians. "I was shunned", he later recalled, "I was sort of cast out ... of my own community". At the height of the controversy, Lennon announced that "Richard Flanagan and his fiction is [sic] not welcome in the new Tasmania".[40]

Flanagan's next novel, *The Unknown Terrorist* (2006), had its origins in the crucible of this unwanted media storm: "I guess I also saw the way the media starts putting out an idea of you and people come to accept that idea rather than the truth of you, and that was really very much behind the whole idea of *The Unknown Terrorist*, because I thought if they can do that in the smallest place about a small thing, they can so easily destroy anyone". The novel is about a Sydney pole dancer, known professionally as the Doll, who is wrongly accused of being a pro-Islamist terrorist and persecuted to her death by the police and the national media. The other significant context was the moment of 9/11 with its supplementary inventions of "the Axis of Evil" and "the War on Terror":

> After September 2001 I felt I had become a stranger to my own time, the way I had of thinking about the world didn't seem to work anymore. What I found terrifying about the post-2001 world wasn't the terrorist attacks, terrible as they were, but in the elevation of them to this notion of a war. It laid the seeds for an entirely different society. Australia

---

37  Richard Flanagan, *Gould's Book of Fish* (London: Atlantic Books, 2001), 3.
38  Richard Flanagan, "Out of Control: The Tragedy of Tasmania's Forests", *The Monthly*, May 2007. https://bit.ly/2FrFCEI.
39  Richard Flanagan, "It's Peter Dom", *Art & Australia* (Spring 2010), in *And what do you do, Mr Gable?*, 23–31.
40  Citations from *Life after Death*.

had just passed some very draconian anti-terrorism laws. You could be arrested, taken away, tried by secret trial and imprisoned, and if a journalist reported on that, and thought there was an injustice to it, the reporter then could also be tried secretly and imprisoned secretly. This to me seemed an extraordinarily stupid law to pass.

As Theodore F. Sheckels argues in this volume, Flanagan began writing *The Unknown Terrorist* in despair at what seemed to be "a crisis of love in the world that expressed itself in these epidemics".[41]

Like *Gould's Book of Fish*, Flanagan's fifth novel, *Wanting* (2008), was inspired by a painting in a Tasmanian museum. Painted in 1842, when she was about seven years old, Thomas Bock's watercolour portrait of Mathinna, a little Aboriginal girl in a red Victorian dress, sparked Flanagan's interest when the curator of the museum lifted the frame to show him the girl's bare feet, which had been hidden beneath it. As Flanagan explains, the image of Mathinna resonated because it presented "this odd combination of the dress of the Age of Reason over an Aboriginal child at the end of what I knew had been this terrible war of extermination … it's the bare feet chopped off by the wooden frame".[42] In *Wanting*, Flanagan again probes the connections between the regional and global in his exploration of colonialism and its culture, and in the links between the historical figures of Mathinna, Sir John Franklin, the governor of Tasmania and Arctic explorer, his wife Jane, Lady Franklin, and the British world's most famous writer, Charles Dickens. As many reviewers have noted, however, the novel is neither a journey into the "historical exotic" nor even a simple case of the empire writing back to the centre, but rather a meditation on how the local and the centre are inextricably linked as each other's antipodes, as are reason and desire. As Giles Foden puts it, this was the nineteenth-century's "literary equivalent of globalisation".[43] Flanagan explains in his "Author's Note" to the novel that his concern is also to offer a corrective to the idea that Tasmanian Indigenous peoples did not survive colonisation, revealing instead how a pervasive Aboriginal presence continued in the "subsequent unfolding of Tasmanian history". His interest in the connection between Mathinna and Dickens plays out in his meditations on desire, its cost when it is denied, and the power it holds over humans at different transnational sites. For Flanagan, "That, and not history, is the true subject of *Wanting*".[44]

Flanagan's Man Booker Prize-winning novel *The Narrow Road to the Deep North* began life as a deeply motivated act of love for his father, Arch Flanagan, who had been a prisoner of the Japanese on the Thai–Burma Railway after the fall of Singapore in 1942. "I spent a lot of time with my father in his final years", he recalls, "often talking about very specific details. It was a way of being with each other". The book is dedicated to the memory of his father, prisoner *san byaku san jū go* (number 335), the Japanese number assigned to him in the camps as one of Dunlop's Thousand, "that now near-mythical group". Flanagan has said, "I am a child of the death railway".[45] His brother, the journalist and writer Martin Flanagan, co-wrote with their father a memoir that includes a short

---

41   Richard Flanagan, interviewed in *Life after Death*.
42   Richard Flanagan cited in Jason Steger, "A Journey Deep into His Soul", *Sydney Morning Herald*, 8 November 2008. http://bit.ly/2kdMtW1.
43   Giles Foden, "Review of *Wanting* by Richard Flanagan", 26 September 2009. http://bit.ly/2IDxJup.
44   Richard Flanagan, "Author's Note", *Wanting* (Sydney: Knopf, 2008), 256.
45   Richard Flanagan cited in Michael Williams, "Dinner with Richard Flanagan, a child of the death railway", *Guardian*, 26 September 2013. http://bit.ly/2IYaj6g.

history of Arch's childhood in rural Tasmania, a tribute written by Arch in memory of Dunlop, and the short story "My Brother's Keeper".[46] *The Narrow Road to the Deep North* had been gestating during the entire period that Flanagan was working on *The Unknown Terrorist* and *Wanting*: "[it] took me twelve years to write. I wrote it as five different novels, not just drafts, each novel was many drafts. I burned the manuscript of each one".[47] The novel takes as its subject intersecting stories of love and war which thread through the small towns of Tasmania, to other Australian states, and culminate in the global events of World War Two. Inspired in equal measure by the wartime accounts of the famous army surgeons and doctors Edward "Weary" Dunlop and Kevin Fagan, and by Arch Flanagan and his fellow prisoners of war on "the Line", the novel delivers a complex meditation on transnational experiences of war, totalitarianism, and, as Nicholas Birns suggests in this volume, the importance of love as the private event which links people in ways that war cannot.

The critical reception of the novel to date has centred on the question of its relation to nationalistic traditions of military history and storytelling, an issue that was only exacerbated by the controversial circumstances of its receiving the Australian Prime Minister's Literary Award for fiction in 2014.[48] Susan Lever, for example, argues that "his attitude remains conventionally patriotic": that the novel is "Flanagan's literary offering to history and national culture", and that "ultimately, it is a work of filial and national piety".[49] Robert Dixon has argued that "the reverse is true": that "the novel is anti-epic and antinationalistic; its point of view is vernacular and provincial"; that "it wrests the memory of the POWs back from the legend-making narratives of Australian history and Australian literature, reclaiming it instead for the people of a small island at the edge of the world, whose story it always was".[50]

Occluded Histories: The Circle and the Line

In the absence, to date, of a full-scale biography or critical survey of his fiction, *Richard Flanagan: Critical Essays* offers a snapshot of critical approaches to Flanagan's work by Australian, European and North American scholars written in the wake of his Man Booker win in 2014. The critical essays that make up this collection explore the key themes of Flanagan's writing and are loosely grouped here in categories that have emerged as recurring concerns.

A number of contributors note the imagery of the line and the circle in Flanagan's writing as shorthand for different kinds of writing, different understandings of history, and different forms of the knowable community. From his early historical writings to his emergence as a global writer of literary fiction, Flanagan's abiding interest in the occluded

---

46  Arch and Martin Flanagan, *The Line: A Man's Experience; A Son's Quest to Understand* (Camberwell East, Vic: One Day Hill, 2005).
47  Richard Flanagan, interviewed in *Life after Death*.
48  Bhakthi Puvanenthiran, "Richard Flanagan Shares PM's Literary Award", *Sydney Morning Herald*, 8 December 2014. http://bit.ly/2rXMcuz.
49  Susan Lever, "Heroes, Certainly", *Sydney Review of Books*, 26 November 2013. http://bit.ly/2rZ8qfM.
50  Robert Dixon, "Communications from Below: Scalar Transformations in Richard Flanagan's *The Narrow Road to the Deep North* (2013) and Steven Carroll's *A World of Other People* (2013)", *Antipodes* 31, no. 1 (June 2017): 199.

or subaltern histories of Tasmania has remained a constant in his reimagining of the past. This volume includes four essays focusing on this important theme. Robert Dixon's chapter, "Circles of Violence: Historical Constellations in *Death of a River Guide* and *The Sound of One Hand Clapping*", examines Flanagan's focus on the symbolically resonant image of the circle in place of the line, a narrative mode developed at the time of his vocational shift from history to fiction. Dixon argues that Flanagan's commitment to the circle affiliates his fiction with the oral histories embedded in the local and regional sites of Tasmania, which Flanagan believes have been suppressed in dominant versions of public memory. Dixon's central thesis is that Flanagan's concept of history was deeply influenced by the historical materialism of Walter Benjamin and Hannah Arendt. This not only finds expression in Flanagan's suspicion of linear narratives, represented in his novels through the image of the line, but also in his commitment to Arendt's concept of the "constellation", which aligns with the circular narratives of his works. Flanagan also turns to Benjamin's notion of historical materialism's "*weak* Messianic force" to rupture teleological narratives, offering alternative histories of the oppressed. Through Michael Rothberg's concept of "multidirectional memory", Dixon explores how Flanagan annexes these local histories to the global scale so that apparently disparate instances of traumatic remembrance intersect, illuminating each other in mutual recognition.

In his chapter, "Rewriting History: *Gould's Book of Fish*", Bill Ashcroft traces the legitimation of narrative history as it developed into a key discourse of modernity, becoming institutionalised in the nineteenth century as a "scientific discipline". This required an erasure of the subjective nature of historical interpretation, offering in its place singular narrative truths which obscured the marginalised histories of the colonised. What was lost is what Hayden White calls "rhetoric", the myriad ways in which "the chaos of forms" that constitutes the past may be configured. For Ashcroft, it is this element of rhetoric that Flanagan recovers in *Gould's Book of Fish*, albeit an unreliable swirling and circular rhetoric that undermines the possibility of any faithful record of the past. Unlike history, literature recovers not the "truth" of the past, but a *different* past. Invoking Augustine's conception of a "threefold present", which has affinities with Aboriginal cosmologies, Ashcroft acknowledges that literature can do what history cannot, imagining a different past and embedding it in the present in a way that bequeaths, in turn, an alternative future. Through its poetic truths and circular temporalities, literature offers the transformative potential of a different future in the present, attempting to balance and tolerate the very real contradictions of the past that official versions of history erase.

In "Contestations of Authority: Richard Flanagan's Australian Biofictions", Marc Delrez reads across the entire oeuvre of Flanagan's fiction, locating similar subversions of narrative history to those analysed by Dixon and Ashcroft. In his three main "biofictions", *Gould's Book of Fish*, *Wanting* and *The Narrow Road to the Deep North*, Flanagan undermines official accounts of the past, departing from the factuality of objective history to explore the fictional inner lives of his historical characters. Therein lies the liberating potential of unearthing fundamental truths otherwise excised from the historical records. Biofiction's acknowledged bi-temporality offers insights into how the present perpetuates the injustices of the colonial past while also offering other forms of knowing and understanding, along with the recovery of cross-cultural histories obscured by official history-making. However, where Ashcroft stresses the potentiality of utopian elements contained within fiction, its capacity to imagine a different world, Delrez argues that Flanagan's biofictions ultimately stage a series of "failed encounters" with the past, repeatedly foreclosing on the alternative pasts in which the reader is otherwise encouraged to invest through the sheer exuberance of Flanagan's stylistic invention. This points to the limitations of artistic representation when faced with the enormity of biofiction's challenge to official history in its repudiation of "received epistemologies".

Flanagan has described *Wanting* as a "meditation on desire", insisting that its true subject is "not history", but the determining force of desire in human affairs.[51] In her wide-ranging chapter, "The Genealogy of *Wanting*", Margaret Harris recognises that Flanagan's reconstruction of the past in that novel is "not in thrall" to history's truth claims, and she explores instead the "endless battle between ... reason and wanting" that is "the hinge" from which Flanagan's "meditation on desire" emerges. Situating the novel as neo-Victorian historical fiction, Harris argues that Flanagan invites his readers to imagine the relationship between the Victorian past and the contemporary present while refusing to posit a causal connection between them. The effect of the novel, in its privileging of the "meditation on desire", is another vision of history in which the present and the past are held in a constellation. For Harris, the novel's moral compass is set by its central character, the Aboriginal girl, Mathinna. Yet Flanagan's exploration of subaltern histories goes beyond a critique of the imperial self-delusions of its other historical protagonists – Charles Dickens, and Sir John and Lady Franklin – to an indictment of the entire colonial and Enlightenment project. Eschewing a linear narrative in favour of more circular narrative connections, Flanagan portrays the disparate manifestations of desire, linking Tasmania, the Arctic and the Antarctic, at the very edges of the British world, to the cosmopolitan centre of London in such a way that it effectively deconstructs the civil/savage binary. In this original contribution to the scholarship on *Wanting*, Harris explores how Flanagan's privileging of desire as the novel's subject also entails a refusal to valorise history as a master narrative, achieved through his use of the inventive freedoms of fiction. Along with the other contributors who address this key theme, Harris argues that what emerges in *Wanting* are alternative engagements with the past which open up "both multi-temporal and cross-cultural perspectives on historical understanding".

## Writing the Island: Antipodean Magical Realism, Affective Belonging and the Soundscapes of Flanagan's Tasmania

The thematics of islandness is another preoccupation that emerges in Flanagan's fiction, and is explored in three chapters in this volume. Tasmania's location as the margin and the edge from which he writes has offered Flanagan the narrative frame in which to crystallise his views on the importance of ecology, the environment, and a distinctive Indigenous and biocentric worldview, in opposition to the anthropocentric philosophy promulgated by Western culture and post-Enlightenment systems of knowledge. The island serves as the literary space in which to recover the suppressed cross-cultural encounters with both land and people denied and silenced by official historical accounts. It has also been in the distinctive and isolated island settings of Tasmania that Flanagan has realised his exuberant magical realist novels, *Death of a River Guide* and *Gould's Book of Fish*, which explore these key themes. Ben Holgate's chapter, "Greening a Narrative Mode: Antipodean Magical Realism and Ecocriticism in Richard Flanagan's Fiction", explores

---

51   Richard Flanagan, "Author's Note", *Wanting*, 256.

these preoccupations, arguing for a distinctive Australian, or even Tasmanian, species of magical realism which departs from the classic postcolonial formulation, in which a contest between two oppositional systems pits the magical realm of the colonised against the realist world of the coloniser. As Holgate points out, Flanagan blurs these categories by repositioning Tasmania's convicts and the white lower classes as both colonised and colonising. The cross-cultural links between black and white cultures in connection with the island space, once erased from official history and public memory, are reinstated through Flanagan's refusal of binary formulations. Importantly, Holgate argues that Flanagan's magical realist novels intertwine with biocentric and ecocritical worldviews endemic to island Tasmania, creating a third space in which "humankind is but one element of the universe" rather than its centre.

In her chapter, "Spatial Anxieties: Tourists, Settlers and Tasmania's Affective Economies of Belonging in *A Terrible Beauty*, *Death of a River Guide* and *Gould's Book of Fish*", Laura A.White explores Flanagan's recovery of Tasmanian historical circuits of affect silenced in official accounts of the past, tracing this retrieval from his early historical writing through to his later fiction. As White observes, while Flanagan traces the ways in which aspects of postcolonial tourism connect to earlier forms of imperialism, he insists on a deeper engagement with the past which recovers both Indigenous and early settler encounters that display a range of affective experiences of Tasmania. Flanagan excavates the suppressed history of intense human attachments to the island – for convicts, rural labourers and immigrants – thus providing a radical challenge to dominant historical narratives, which deny the affective elements of human belonging. Flanagan's sympathetic recovery of what affect theorist Sara Ahmed calls "affective economies" complicates the notion that all European settlers have been exploiters of the land, while also dispelling Tasmanian environmentalists' claims to be the first to express attachment to the Tasmanian wilderness in their perpetuation of the myth of the land as a primordial empty space of "terrible beauty". It is Flanagan's retrieval of historical circuits of affect as a revolutionary force of love, belonging and communal attachment that must be acknowledged in modern environmentalist efforts to stop the destruction of Tasmanian forests and rivers.

Joseph Cummins, in his chapter "'Smashing and singing and sobbing and howling': Sound and Richard Flanagan's Tasmania", explores how Flanagan utilises sound to register the living histories that haunt the island space. Flanagan's use of sound is a postcolonial departure from what Martin Jay calls "occularcentric" ways of knowing, an imperial impulse that controls and orders the world through sight. Cummins focuses on the three modalities of "the song, the scream and noise", revealing how Flanagan uses soundscapes to recover both the historical traumas of the past and their re-emergence in the present in a "transhistorical continuum". As concrete annotations of Indigenous presence, the sonorities of the island also foreground Indigenous traditions of understanding and feeling erased in the earlier colonial works of the Australian Gothic tradition. For Cummins, the Indigenous mapping of the island through sound offers a challenge to these earlier works, dispelling the "cult of forgetfulness on a national scale" that anthropologist W.E.H. Stanner called the Great Australian Silence.[52] Explored through Cummins' concept of "imagined sound", Flanagan's sounding of the island space is recreated as a world in itself, while also engaging the world beyond.

---

52   W.E.H. Stanner, *After the Dreaming: The 1968 Boyer Lectures*. (Sydney: Australian Broadcasting Commission, 1969).

## Of Others: Radicants, Terror and the City

Flanagan's focus on exile, on the trauma of migrant others, along with ways that fear is engendered and love forsaken at the great centres of imperial and national power, is explored in various ways in three essays in this collection. Salhia Ben-Messahel's chapter, "Richard Flanagan's 'Post-post' and the Mapping of the Altermodern", explores Flanagan's subversion of national discourse through his incorporation of migrants and racial others. Ben-Messahel reads Flanagan's characters as existing in a time-space that Nicolas Bourriaud terms "the altermodern", a space beyond the "post" of postcolonial Australia in which cultural identity coheres around concepts of nomadism, wanderings and successive enrootings, rather than in stable national constructs. Flanagan exposes how the idealism expressed in Australian nation-building fails to create a sense of belonging. Rather, as Ben-Messahel points out, the cast of broken, hurt and lost characters in *The Sound of One Hand Clapping*, *Death of a River Guide* and *The Narrow Road to the Deep North* all form identities of exile, which can claim no single affiliation to place or ancestry. She suggests that these characters have an affinity with the Deleuzian concept of "the radicant", an organism that exists in a state of precariousness and responds to the living conditions of a global environment. They also share a similarity with Victor Segalen's notion of "the exote", a figure of global dislocation. Through these postmodern formulations, Ben-Messahel argues that Flanagan's fiction reveals a nation that can never be completely integrated, disrupting the Australian myth of successful migrant assimilation into a single national identity. His characters carry with them traumas and histories of other cultures which belie the notion of a unified monocultural nation, their successive "enrootings" through shifting environments introducing his readers to "various elsewheres".

In 2006, Andrew McCann noted that Australian novelists rarely deal with contemporary political events, claiming that the publication in the same year of Flanagan's *The Unknown Terrorist*, Andrew McGahan's *Underground* and Linda Jaivin's *The Infernal Optimist* were evidence of "a perceptible shift … towards a much more direct and sometimes didactic engagement with a contemporary political climate".[53] In his chapter "Terror, Paranoia and Manipulation: The Politics of Fear in *The Unknown Terrorist*", Nathanael O'Reilly analyses Flanagan's turn to explorations of the media and government's role in engendering fear and white paranoia in their focus on the "War on Terror" in the aftermath of 9/11. In *The Unknown Terrorist*, Flanagan reveals how anti-terrorist surveillance increases government authoritarianism and, along with febrile media reportage, which creates viral media events, leads to the erosion of civil liberties. O'Reilly analyses the category of the other as the discursive object of fear, a shifting unstable construct of paranoid nationalism by which any citizen can be targeted through media and government rhetoric. He also explores the role and responsibilities of the writer in "a time of terror". As O'Reilly argues, in this novel Flanagan issues an urgent warning that still resonates in the current climate of recent terrorist events, where government rhetoric and the attendant media reportage reveal the need for community vigilance to protect the freedoms of democracy against "the politics and rhetoric of fear".

---

53  Andrew McCann, "Professing the Popular: Political Fiction Circa 2006", in "New Reckonings: Australian Literature Past, Present, Future," ed. Leigh Dale and Brigid Rooney, special issue, *Australian Literary Studies* 23, no. 2 (2007): 44.

While O'Reilly deals with the government and media's erosions of civil liberties through the rhetoric of fear, Theodore F. Sheckels, in his chapter, " Sydney, a City without Love: The Unknown Terrorist in *The Unknown Terrorist*", reverses the optic to concentrate on Flanagan's construction of the city of Sydney as the dominant "character" of the novel, a character that is depicted in negative and apocalyptic terms. Sensitive to Flanagan's acute engagement with contemporary popular culture, including both Australian and world cinema, Sheckels' reading provides an original perspective which suggests that Flanagan's much criticised departure in *The Unknown Terrorist* from his earlier style of literary fiction to what might be categorised as the "airport novel" or the "popular thriller" contains ethical and philosophical dimensions that are continuous with his concerns in both the earlier and later novels. For Sheckels, the city of Sydney is an urban centre that holds "a morally polluting force". His analysis suggests the unknown terrorist – the other, and the object of fear in the novel – may well be the "broader lack of love" that is a consequence of the city's moral degradation, and which appears throughout Flanagan's oeuvre as an abiding concern.

## Transnational Readings on Love and War: The Global Novel

Responding to Dixon's inquiry about the scale of the knowable community in Flanagan's fiction, two chapters in this volume focus on his global Man Booker win and his position as a transnational writer: Nicholas Birns' "'Fireless flame gone amorous': War amid Love in *The Narrow Road to the Deep North*" and Liliana Zavaglia's "'Out of the tear-drenched land': Transnational Sites of Memory in *The Narrow Road to the Deep North*". These chapters explore the two very different narratives that intertwine in the novel, revealing Flanagan's debts, as Birns suggests, to both Australian literature and the larger world canon relating to love and war.

Birns analyses the love theme of *The Narrow Road to the Deep North* not as a respite from the horrors of war, but rather as a fictional exploration that rightly embeds war within larger networks of memory, relationships and representation. Birns alters the lens through which the novel has predominantly been read – the public event of war – locating it instead within a counter-tradition of Australian war writing that includes the works of Kenneth Mackenzie and Kenneth Slessor, among others, poets who wrote of the "inwardness" of private life in wartime. As Flanagan's novel acknowledges, literature can neither fully represent nor redeem either love or war, but love remains the symbol of all that war cannot take. Beyond these debts to the Australian canon, Birns locates the transnational scale of Flanagan's work with links to Tolstoy and farther back to Homer, revealing its affinities with the long literary tradition of writers who have balanced stories of love and war to counterpoint each other. For Birns, what is most central to the novel is not the treatment of war as such, but its various iterations of love – encompassing not only the *eros* of the Amy Mulvaney plot, but also the expression of *philia* in the soldiers' intimate solidarity and postwar experiences. Flanagan's novel builds on a precedent located in both Australian and world literature that no longer situates love amid war, but rather war amid love.

Alternatively, Liliana Zavaglia explores the novel's war plot, relocating it from the national site at which it was initially read, to the transnational scale of global suffering and trauma with links to the literature of Holocaust witness. Taking up Dixon's argument about the multidirectional nature of memory in Flanagan's work, Zavaglia analyses *The Narrow*

*Road to the Deep North* as an exchange of memory between the sufferings of Australian soldiers on the Thai-Burma Railway and the trauma of the Auschwitz death camps. By tracing the novel's subtle intertextual connections with the works of Dante and Primo Levi, among other authors, Zavaglia locates its many sites of multidirectional memory, where events of seemingly individual or national historical significance are revised and reassessed through transnational comparison, relocating them at sites of collective violence and traumatic memory. Zavaglia suggests that this multidirectional matrix also raises one of Flanagan's key themes – the suppressed and occluded history of Indigenous suffering and trauma, which has been submerged in the militarisation of Australian history at least since the History Wars of the 1990s. Indeed, as Henry Reynolds argues in *Forgotten Wars* (2013), this is another form of forgetfulness on a national scale that is foundational to the Australian cult of Anzac.[54] For Zavaglia, what results is a text that transcends the national sites of canonical war literature, which reinforce myths of the Australian soldier-hero, to instead recover the subaltern history of Indigenous experience and trauma in its formation of a nexus with the Holocaust literature of Primo Levi.

This new collection of critical responses to Flanagan's writing, commissioned in the wake of his Man Booker win, offers a rich variety of theoretical and literary approaches, and new ways of understanding the importance of this determinedly regional writer's contribution to Tasmanian, Australian and world literature. Importantly, Flanagan's fictional worlds offer empathetic, often poignant, renderings of those whose voices have been lost beneath official accounts of history, stories from a small region that have made their mark on a global scale, and yet continue to be excluded in dominant imaginings of Australia. Flanagan's fiction offers a corrective to these exclusions and has a great deal to say about the losses, as well as the continuing potentialities of the past and its reimagining in the present. As such, Flanagan's literary contributions to the public conversation about history, politics, environmentalism, metaphysics and philosophy can be seen as a profound offering from the edge, to both the nation and the globe.

## References

Ashcroft, Bill. "Reading Post-Colonial Australia". In *Postcolonial Issues in Australian Literature*, edited by Nathanael O'Reilly. Amherst, MA: Cambria, 2010.
Benjamin, Walter. "The Storyteller: Reflections on the Works of Nikolai Leskov". In *Illuminations: Essays and Reflections*. (1968) Translated by Harry Zohn. Edited by Hannah Arendt. New York: Schocken, 2007.
Bixby, Patrick. "From the Postcolonial to Contemporary Reality of Globalization: Rushdie's Later Novels". In *Salman Rushdie's Midnight's Children*, edited by Reena Mitra. New Delhi: Atlantic, 2006, 119-29.
Boyce, James. *Van Diemen's Land*. Melbourne: Black Inc., 2008.
Brenner, Neil. *New State Spaces: Urban Governance and the Rescaling of Statehood*. New York: Oxford University Press, 2004.
Clarke, Marcus. *His Natural Life*. (1874) Edited by Lurline Stuart. St Lucia: University of Queensland Press, 2001.
Cocker, Jack, dir. *Richard Flanagan: Life after Death*. BBC Scotland, 2015. https://vimeo.com/135694839.
Craven, Peter. "Something Fishy Going On". *Age*, 10 November 2001, 9.

---

54   Henry Reynolds, *Forgotten Wars* (Sydney: NewSouth Publishing, 2013).

Direen, Rex. "Two Rhodes Scholars: Is Tasmania Ridiculous or Sublime?" Unpublished essay on Flanagan and Peter Conrad, Richard Flanagan Papers, NLA, Box 19.

Dixon, Robert. "Communications from Below: Scalar Transformations in Richard Flanagan's *The Narrow Road to the Deep North* (2013) and Steven Carroll's *A World of Other People* (2013)". *Antipodes* 31, no. 1 (June 2017): 184–205.

Flanagan, Arch and Martin Flanagan. *The Line: A Man's Experience; A Son's Quest to Understand*. Camberwell East, Vic: One Day Hill, 2005.

Flanagan, Richard. *First Person*. Sydney: Knopf, 2017.

———. (2011) *And what do you do Mr Gable? New and Collected Essays*. Sydney: Random House, 2015.

———. *Wanting*. Sydney: Knopf, 2008.

———. "Out of Control: The Tragedy of Tasmania's Forests". *The Monthly*. (May 2007). https://bit.ly/2FrFCEI.

———. "ALS Gold Medal Acceptance Speech". *JASAL: Journal of the Association for the Study of Australian Literature* 1 (2002): 116–18.

———. *Gould's Book of Fish*. London: Atlantic Books, 2001.

———. Letter to Nikki Christer, 11 November 1997. Flanagan Papers, NLA, Box 5, Folder, "Correspondence 2001".

———. "Writing Landscape", October 1997, Flanagan Papers, NLA, Box 5, Folder: "Speeches and Writings 1999".

———. *Death of a River Guide*. (1994). Ringwood, Vic: Penguin, 1996.

———. Edited typescript of "The Circle", dated June 1993, Flanagan Papers, NLA, Box 19.

———. *"Parish-Fed Bastards": A History of the Politics of the Unemployed in Britain, 1884–1939*. New York: Greenwood Press, 1991.

———. *A Terrible Beauty: History of the Gordon River Country*. Melbourne: Greenhouse Publications, 1985.

———. Interview with Giles Hugo, undated typescript, Flanagan Papers, NLA, Box 19.

Foden, Giles. Review of *Wanting* by Richard Flanagan. *Guardian Australia*, 26 September 2009. http://bit.ly/2IDxJup.

Jones, Jo. "'Dancing the Old Enlightenment': *Gould's Book of Fish*, the Historical Novel and the Postmodern Sublime," in "The Colonial Present," Special issue, *JASAL: Journal of the Association for the Study of Australian Literature* (2008): 114–29.

Lever, Susan. "Heroes, Certainly". *Sydney Review of Books*, 26 November 2013. http://bit.ly/2rZ8qfM.

MacFarlane, Robert. "Con Fishing". *Observer*, 26 May 2002. http://bit.ly/2x3Yoz4.

McCann, Andrew. "Professing the Popular: Political Fiction Circa 2006", in "New Reckonings: Australian Literature Past, Present, Future". Edited by Leigh Dale and Brigid Rooney. Special issue, *Australian Literary Studies* 23, no. 2 (2007): 43–57.

Nixon, Rob. *Slow Violence and the Environmentalism of the Poor*. Cambridge, MA: Harvard University Press, 2011.

Puvanenthiran, Bhakthi. "Richard Flanagan Shares PM's Literary Award". *Sydney Morning Herald*, 8 December 2014. http://bit.ly/2rXMcuz.

Pybus, Cassandra and Richard Flanagan, eds. *The Rest of the World Is Watching: Tasmania and the Greens*. Sydney: Pan Macmillan, 1990.

Reynolds, Henry. *Forgotten Wars*. Sydney: NewSouth Publishing, 2013.

Romei, Stephen. "Man Booker Winner Richard Flanagan's Triumph against Odds". *Australian*, 16 October 2014, 11.

Rushdie, Salman. "The Empire Writes Back with a Vengeance". *Times*, 3 July 1982, 8.

Schama, Simon. *Landscape and Memory*. London: HarperCollins, 1995.

Stagg, Tony and Philip Mead. "A Place of Stories: A Report on the Literature of Tasmania Subset of the AustLit Database". In *Resourceful Reading: The New-Empiricism, eResearch and Australian Literary Culture*, edited by Katherine Bode and Robert Dixon. Sydney: Sydney University Press, 2009. 315–24.

Stanner, W.E.H. *After the Dreaming: The 1968 Boyer Lectures*. Sydney: Australian Broadcasting Commission, 1969.
Steger, Jason. "A Journey Deep into His Soul". *Sydney Morning Herald*, 8 November 2008. http://bit.ly/2kdMtW1.
Williams, Michael. "Dinner with Richard Flanagan, a Child of the Death Railway". *Guardian*, 26 September 2013. http://bit.ly/2IYaj6g.
Williamson, Geordie. "Literary Masterpieces from a Small Island". *Weekend Australian*, 18–19 October 2014, 17.

# 1

# Circles of Violence: Historical Constellations in *Death of a River Guide* and *The Sound of One Hand Clapping*

*Robert Dixon*

Richard Flanagan is the author of six novels that with one exception, *The Unknown Terrorist* (2006), can be described as historical fictions. They exploit a series of stylistic registers: "antipodean magical realism" in *Death of a River Guide* (1994);[1] the trauma novel in *The Sound of One Hand Clapping* (1997); postmodern historiographic metafiction in *Gould's Book of Fish* (2001); neo-Victorian historical fiction in *Wanting* (2008); and what might be described as the global, Man Booker Prize-winning style of *The Narrow Road to the Deep North* (2013). Flanagan began his career in writing, after all, as a professional historian: he has an MA in history from the University of Oxford, where he was a Rhodes Scholar, and his first published books were works of non-fiction that are broadly indebted to the tradition of "history from below" represented by E.P. Thompson's *The Making of the English Working Class* (1963). In this chapter, I argue that the concept of history that emerges at the time of his first two novels, *Death of a River Guide* and *The Sound of One Hand Clapping*, is broadly historical materialist in the sense of that term associated with Walter Benjamin and Hannah Arendt. Flanagan's historical materialism has two interrelated strands: a suspicion of narratives of progress that finds expression in a *temporal* commitment to the constellation as an alternative to linear or teleological narrative forms; and a passion to recover the subaltern histories that such linear narratives suppress, which finds expression in a *spatial* and *scalar* commitment to local places at the margins of dominant social and political formations, including nation, empire and globe. These strands are expressed in the recurring symbols in Flanagan's novels of the circle and the line: the circle as a figure for oral histories embedded in the local experience of community and place; the line as a symbol of historicist narratives of nationalism, imperialism and totalitarianism.

Flanagan begins one of his earliest published essays with a quotation from Walter Benjamin's "Theses on the Philosophy of History": "To articulate the past historically ... means to seize hold of a memory as it flashes up at a moment of danger ... In every era the attempt must be made anew to wrest tradition away from a conformism that is about to overpower it".[2] In another essay, ironically titled "Masters of History", Flanagan asks, "what

---

1   Ben Holgate, "Greening a Narrative Mode: Antipodean Magical Realism and Ecocriticism in Richard Flanagan's Fiction", this volume.
2   Walter Benjamin cited in Richard Flanagan, "Return the People's Pedder!", in *The Rest of the World Is Watching: Tasmania and the Greens*, ed. Cassandra Pybus and Richard Flanagan (Sydney: Pan Macmillan, 1990), 194.

if ... centres no longer hold, and the most interesting things in the world have started to happen at its edges? ... Could it be possible ... that history was being made by ordinary people in ordinary places?"[3] Flanagan's philosophy of history is stated in embryo in these early essays, written in 1989 at the time of his turn from history to fiction, and it has largely remained unchanged in the novels that were to follow: there is the reverse optic of the edge looking back to the centre; the recovery of alternative stories marginalised by triumphalist national and imperial histories; and the rescaling of imagined communities from nation and empire to the province, the island, and the edge.

## Arendt and Benjamin

In comparing Flanagan's concept of history with those of Arendt and Benjamin, it needs to be said that none of them has any such thing as a systematic, fully resolved methodology or "philosophy of history". Arendt rarely engaged in methodological reflection, but in her various prefaces to *The Origins of Totalitarianism* (1951) she introduces the concepts of "apprehension" and "crystallization", opposing them, respectively, to the historicist concepts of "explanation" and "origins". In his review of *The Origins of Totalitarianism*, the political philosopher Eric Voegelin maintained that the book's argument was "roughly chronological", and that it was an attempt to trace the "origins" of contemporary phenomena back to the eighteenth century, from which "the essence of totalitarianism unfolded".[4] In reply, Arendt argued that her book does not deal with "origins", attempting instead a "historical account of the elements which [later] crystallized into totalitarianism".[5] In one of the earliest attempts to explicate Arendt's thinking, Seyla Benhabib established that Arendt had been influenced by her reading of the manuscript of Benjamin's "Theses on the Philosophy of History", which Benjamin entrusted to her before his death in 1940, and which she later edited for publication in *Illuminations* in 1968.[6] In Thesis XVIII, Benjamin writes:

> Historicism contents itself with establishing a causal connection between various moments in history. But no fact that is a cause is for that very reason historical. It became historical posthumously, as it were, through events that may be separated from it by thousands of years. A historian who takes this as his point of departure stops telling the sequence of events like the beads of a rosary. Instead, he grasps the constellation which his own era has formed with a definite earlier one.[7]

Arendt's concern to distance herself from historicist modes of explanation was motivated by a reluctance to make the Holocaust seem inevitable. To establish an "inevitable continuity" between the past and the present was to fall into the "trap of historical understanding", while

---

3   Richard Flanagan, "Masters of History", in *The Rest of the World Is Watching*, 132–3.
4   Eric Voegelin, review of "*The Origins of Totalitarianism*", *Review of Politics* 15, no. 1 (January 1953): 69.
5   Hannah Arendt, "[*The Origins of Totalitarianism*]: A Reply", *Review of Politics*, 15, no. 1 (January 1953): 78.
6   Seyla Benhabib, "Hannah Arendt and the Redemptive Power of Narrative", *Social Research* 57, no. 1 (Spring 1990): 189.
7   Walter Benjamin, "Theses on the Philosophy of History", in *Illuminations: Essays and Reflections*, ed. Hannah Arendt (New York: Schocken, 1968), 263.

Arendt's careful calibration of terms allowed her to maintain that "the future is radically underdetermined, and can never be foretold on the basis of the past"; that "the human capacity for action can always initiate the new and the unexpected".[8] This resistance to historical determinism was in sympathy with Benjamin's argument that each generation is "endowed with a *weak* Messianic power".[9] In contemplating each moment in the past not as if it were one in a "sequence of events like the beads of a rosary", but as an opening onto an alternative history, a history of what might have been, the historian redeems the past, saving it from the oblivion to which a teleological narrative would condemn it.

As a mode of understanding that is distinct from explanation and originary thinking, apprehension involves seeing the "elements" that have crystallised into the phenomena of the present through the lens of that crystallisation; it is also to experience the intellectual "shock" and "burden" of that insight while at the same time resisting its inevitability.[10] Crystallisation is the lens through which the elements of the constellation – "those currents of thought, political events and outlooks, incidents and institutions" – are understood to be meaningful, and it is "in retrospect and in retrospect alone" that they can be viewed as "harbingers" of the present.[11] For Arendt, the most powerful lens through which these "elements" could be apprehended was the concentration camp:

> As the crystalline structure through whose blinding foci the totalitarian form of domination is revealed, the camps show first that the belief in the juridical personality of humans had to be shattered; second that the moral personality in humans had to be destroyed; and finally that the individuality of the self had to be crushed.[12]

Arendt's methodology was therefore a perpetual struggle against historicism. In her reply to Voegelin, Arendt writes, "my first problem was how to write historically about something – totalitarianism – which I did not want to conserve but on the contrary felt engaged to destroy".[13] Her solution was to embrace Benjamin's notion of a fragmentary or materialist historiography, so as "to break the chain of narrative continuity, to shatter chronology as the natural structure of narrative, to stress fragmentariness, historical dead ends, failures and ruptures".[14] This places Arendt and Benjamin's notion of history at odds with that of Marx, which is oriented towards the future rather than the failures of the past. According to Ronald Beiner, "The task entrusted to historical materialism is not to make the future, but to save the past. Historical materialism is a way of comporting oneself, not toward the totality of the historical process, but toward certain instants of the historical past".[15]

Benjamin understands the conventional idea of progress as a projection into the future of a conception of time that is both "empty" and "homogeneous", a form of "temporal naturalism",[16] in which time is the neutral medium "in" which things simply

---

8   Benhabib, "Hannah Arendt", 171.
9   Benjamin, "Theses", 254.
10  Michael Rothberg, *Multidirectional Memory: Remembering the Holocaust in the Age of Decolonization* (Stanford: Stanford University Press, 2009), 42.
11  Benhabib, "Hannah Arendt", 172, 175.
12  Benhabib, "Hannah Arendt", 175.
13  Arendt, "Reply", 77.
14  Benhabib, "Hannah Arendt", 181–2.
15  Ronald Beiner, "Walter Benjamin's Philosophy of History", *Political Theory* 12, no. 3 (August 1984): 424.
16  "Walter Benjamin", *Stanford Encyclopedia of Philosophy*. https://stanford.io/2mkAnM2.

happen.[17] His understanding of an alternative method involves a form of historical intelligibility provoked by the construction of "dialectical images", culminating in quasi or "weak" Messianic moments in which apprehension interrupts history:

> Materialistic historiography … involves not only the flow of thoughts, but their arrest as well. Where thinking suddenly stops in a configuration pregnant with tensions, it gives that configuration a shock, by which it crystallizes into a monad. A historical materialist approaches a historical subject only where he encounters it as a monad. In this structure he recognizes the sign of a Messianic cessation of happening, or, put differently, a revolutionary chance in the fight for the oppressed past … blast[ing] a specific era out of the homogeneous course of history. (Thesis XVII)[18]

As a spatialised image of time, the metaphor of crystallisation indicates that through the dialectical image, the historian sees events from at least two facets or points of view – the present and the past – and momentarily stands outside the processual nature of progressive or stadial history.[19]

While one strand of Benjamin's thinking about crystallisation derives from the surrealist principle of montage, it also anticipates his thinking about photography, film and the cine camera. Benjamin wants history, especially the history of the oppressed, which is occluded by progressive narratives, to be made available to the historical materialist *now*, to flash up in *jetzeit* (now time):

> The true picture of the past flits by. The past can be seized only as an image which flashes up at the instant when it can be recognized and is never seen again … For every image of the past that is not recognized by the present as one of its own concerns threatens to disappear irretrievably. (Thesis V)[20]

In his earlier work on the Baroque *trauerspiel*, Benjamin speaks of the power of "settings" rather than narrative or sequential story.[21] These are moments of potential illumination, where the coming together of the perspectives of past and present – their formation as a crystal through which to look – can stop the triumphal progress of historical narrative. This moment of crystallisation is described in the famous passage about the angel of history:

> A Klee painting named "Angelus Novus" shows an angel looking as though he is about to move away from something he is fixedly contemplating. His eyes are staring, his mouth is open, his wings are spread. This is how one pictures the angel of history. His face is turned toward the past. Where we perceive a chain of events, he sees one single catastrophe which keeps piling wreckage upon wreckage and hurls it in front of his feet. The angel would like to stay, awaken the dead, and make whole what has been smashed. But a storm

---

17   Max Pensky, "Method and Time: Benjamin's Dialectical Images", in *The Cambridge Companion to Walter Benjamin*, ed. David S. Ferris (Cambridge: Cambridge University Press, 2004), 177–98.
18   Benjamin, "Theses", 262–3.
19   Peter Fenves, *The Messianic Reduction: Walter Benjamin and the Shape of Time* (Stanford: Stanford University Press, 2011).
20   Benjamin, "Theses", 255.
21   Judith Butler, "Benjamin and the Philosophy of History", European Graduate School Video Lectures, 2011. http://bit.ly/2L9YYO0.

is blowing from Paradise; it has got caught in his wings with such violence that the angel can no longer close them. This storm irresistibly propels him into the future to which his back is turned, while the pile of debris before him grows skyward. This storm is what we call progress. (Thesis IX)[22]

The storm is coming not from the future, but from the past. The angel would like to reverse the course of the catastrophe but what stops it is the sheer force – the *narrative* force – of progress, which offers no redemption. Benjamin asks, how can the debris of progressive history be re-read, how can it be crystallised into something that can flash up from the ruins of the past as significant for the present? To fight for the repressed past, the occluded history of the oppressed, is to blast it out of the continuum of homogeneous, empty time, the sequence of events Benjamin calls "happening", events as they are hegemonically understood, which forgets that other history, subjecting it to oblivion. Flanagan's papers in the National Library of Australia include a number of letters from the Tasmanian sculptor Gay Hawkes, written between 1991 and 1994, that are part of an ongoing correspondence discussing the philosophy of history and its relation to contemporary events, especially America's First Gulf War. On 9 December 1994, Hawkes enclosed a photograph of a wooden carving of a winged angel, her interpretation of the Angelus Novus, quoting, in German, from Benjamin's Thesis IX, "My wing is ready for flight".[23]

## Death of a River Guide (1994)

In Flanagan's first published novel, *Death of a River Guide* (1994), the complex ideas about historical apprehension condensed in Benjamin's famous image of the Angelus Novus are imaginatively translated into the plight of his first-person narrator, the river guide Aljaz (Ali) Cosini. Pinned underwater by the raging current of the Franklin River in flood with one arm pointing above the surface like a broken wing, Ali is granted a series of visions of his past life, the lives of his ancestors, and the history of Tasmania dating back to the near-destruction of its Aboriginal population in the Black War of the late 1820s and early 1830s. Ali experiences his visions as cinematic, a quality they share with Salman Rushdie's anti-nationalist, non-foundational reading of the modern Indian nation-state in *Midnight's Children* (1981). As Vijay Mishra argues, the techniques of filmmaking are integral to Rushdie's presentation of Saleem Sinai's narrative process, and to the "structural design" of *Midnight's Children* as a magical realistic text: by the late 1980s, those techniques were already part of "postmodernity's own brand of fragmented narrative".[24] Ali's visions begin unaccountably, like a cinematic projection: "breaking forth from a bizarre low angle, a ray of light shining up the gorge illuminating a world otherwise cast in darkness"; "like a spotlight in a theatre, the low ray of sunlight illuminates the arm".[25] Ali watches as if he were "simultaneously filmmaker, projectionist and audience" (53). As a symbol of time or

---

22  Benjamin, "Theses", 257–8.
23  Gay Hawkes to Richard Flanagan, 9 December 1994, Flanagan Papers, NLA, Box 13, Folder: Correspondence.
24  Vijay Mishra, "Rushdie and Bollywood Cinema" in *The Cambridge Companion to Salman Rushdie*, ed. Abdulrazak Gurnah (Cambridge: Cambridge University Press, 2007), 11, 19.
25  Richard Flanagan, *Death of a River Guide* (1994; Ringwood, Vic: Penguin, 1996), 14–15. All subsequent references are to this edition and appear in parentheses in the text.

history, the river offers up its images of the past, but it "cannot explain everything" (68): "my thoughts are overtaken by my vision" (30). This suggests Benjamin's fear of oblivion, the danger that the history of the oppressed will flash up but then be lost; it demands that the witness to the past feel the impact of intergenerational trauma like the water pounding and scouring Ali's flesh. The Franklin is a "river of visions" (169), a "river of events" (175); it is "the terrible soul history of his country" (152). In falling into the river, Ali has "entered the realm of the fabulous, of hallucination" (9); its waters are the "tide of the past" (264). The water is also the physical medium of crystallisation, a fluid prism that connects past and present: "I know I can't stop seeing what I am seeing, what took place back then" (79); it is a "river of tears" whose "rockpools of memory" (113) and "refracting waters" (106) constellate the past and present.

Ali's visions of his father Harry Lewis as a young boy coming to live at his Aunt Ellie's home in Strahan in the 1940s suggest Benjamin's utopian account of crystallisation in terms of the modern subject's immersion in the cinematic apparatus, and his hope that the cinema might be an aid to the apprehension of modern life. Benjamin associated the forensic capacity of cinema with his concept of the optical unconscious, which he announces in section XIII of "The Work of Art in the Age of Mechanical Reproduction" (1936). He begins with a reference to Freud's *Psychopathology of Everyday Life*, which he invokes to illustrate the enrichment of our perceptual world by the advent of film. Just as Freud's book had "isolated and made analyzable things which had heretofore floated along unnoticed in the broad stream of perception", so "film has brought about a similar deepening of apperception".[26] In *Death of a River Guide*, Ali's drowning conflates these reflections on the prosthetic vision of cinema with the *weak* Messianic power of historical materialism. Ali's fall into the river is his own "leap into the apparatus",[27] which allows him to see the past anew, as if through a prism, recovering moments in time lost to the "broad stream" of national and world history, and opening up registers of reality otherwise invisible to the human eye. As Howard Caygill observes, it is in Benjamin's thinking about film, in particular, that his concept of the optical unconscious assumes its most "overt political significance" by creating "the possibility of … an openness to the future".[28]

The Strahan sequence consists of a captioned series of slow-motion and freeze-frame visions – "Auntie Ellie, 1940"; "Auntie Ellie, 1941", "Auntie Ellie, 1946", "Harry, 1946" – in which Flanagan's cinematic narrative provides an alternative to historicism. Ali is increasingly aware of his own plunge into the apparatus: that is, the collapse between the image-space and the body-space of the spectator. The water, the medium in which the visions form, progressively engulfs his arm or wing: "I can feel that whereas my arm was formerly covered in water to a point a little beyond my elbow, now only my hand and wrist seem to feel the chill of the air" (186). Immersed in the apparatus of this cinematic counter-history, Ali's apprehension is facilitated by the variable speed of the camera, a form of prosthetic vision that discloses the advance and retreat of colonisation otherwise occluded by narrative history: "I watch the recent past of this place like some crazy speeded-up film; watch how European progress arrives with the mineral boom of the 1880s and 1890s

---

26    Walter Benjamin, "The Work of Art in the Age of Mechanical Reproduction" cited in Miriam Bratu Hansen, "Benjamin and Cinema: Not a One-Way Street", *Critical Inquiry* 25, no. 2 (Winter 1999): 341.
27    Sigrid Weigel cited in Hansen, "Benjamin and Cinema", 323.
28    Howard Caygill, *Walter Benjamin* cited in Hansen, "Benjamin and Cinema", 338.

## 1 Circles of Violence: *Death of a River Guide* and *The Sound of One Hand Clapping*

like a vast wave washing over the wilderness" (188). The effect is to de-naturalise history's explanation of time as progress, especially the narrative of Australia's nation-formation around the fulcrum point of Federation in 1901, as observed from the "edge" of that history at Strahan in Tasmania. Federation is the point in the stories of nation and family at which things "[begin] to turn bad" (193). The film speeds up, mimicking "European progress" around the boom years of the 1880s and 1890s, reaching a climax at Federation: "At the height of the great boom, in the year of federation, 1901, the mineral wealth of the west flows out through [Tasmania's] ports" (188). From this narrative and historical climax, "that year of self-congratulatory speech making", "[t]he film begins to slow further and further" (188), stopping altogether in 1940, 1941 and 1946, when Ali apprehends the home life of his Aboriginal ancestor, Auntie Ellie.

Flanagan's cinematic narrative applies the breaks to the history of nation, opening a window onto the otherwise forgotten details of the ordinary, everyday lives of the subaltern classes. Aunt Ellie is a descendant of the "convicts and blackfellas", an Aboriginal woman in a small, abandoned mining town in Tasmania in the 1940s. Like Benjamin's historian-as-collector, Ali's freeze-frame visions allow him to examine the ruined objects of her life, epitomes "blasted" out of history that reveal counter-narratives to the triumphal story of Nation. One such relic is her dead husband Reg's denture, touchingly on display in a glass on the dusty mantlepiece. It is evidence of a once "lucrative trade" in the healthy teeth of young, working-class Tasmanians that were extracted and sold to a firm in Pall Mall to make superior dentures for the wealthy. The young men of Strahan were motivated to sell their teeth for passage money to return to the mainland after the collapse of the mining industry. Sitting among the fading photographs and curling postcards on the mantelpiece, the dentures are "a small memorial to one man's sacrifice" (195).

The narrative of progress through homogeneous, empty time is slowed by the cinematic apparatus, providing, through its *weak* Messianic power, a way out of the teleology of narrative-driven national history. In the Strahan sequence of visions, Flanagan uses the steam train as one of his signature motifs to create a threefold crystallisation between the colonial past, the colonial present and a postcolonial, post-human future. Imported from Switzerland to serve the nineteenth-century mining boom, which has now receded, the train is later used for tourism and then abandoned altogether during the contemporary economic recession. Through a vertiginous use of prolepsis and the future anterior tense, Ali then witnesses a later vision of the Strahan railway overtaken by the return of nature:

> Not that the myrtles and manferns were yet sprouting in the main street of Strahan. Not that a railway carriage yet stood suspended in mid-air in the middle of the rainforest … no material relics of the once muscular railway yard and the once bustling town remained. Nothing. Save for a carriage that flew in the rainforest. (189)

The possibility of attaining a messianic point outside homogeneous empty time provides this post-human perspective, as the natural world grows back over the material fabric of the colonial past: "the rainforest … had already reclaimed the [ghost]towns of Pillinger and Crotty" (189). In this powerful and complex episode, Flanagan uses the magical realist device of literalising Ali's visions to create a temporal vortex, an eddy in the stream of time, in which Benjamin's *weak* Messianic power combines with the idea of the post-human to provide a vision that slows down and then derails the narrative machinery of progressive historiography, a vantage point in space and time outside its own seemingly relentless and all-encompassing command of representation.

Flanagan's stopping of time in Strahan in 1901 and 1946 allows the historian, in Benjamin's words, to "take cognizance" of time "in order to blast a specific era out of the homogeneous course of history".[29] The crystallisation of past and present stops the flow of narrative like "a historical time-lapse camera".[30] Such moments are "the sign of a Messianic cessation of happening … a revolutionary chance in the fight for the oppressed past". These are the moments of "departure", when the historian "stops telling the sequence of events like the beads on a rosary", establishing instead an alternative "conception of the present" that is "shot through with chips of Messianic time".[31] This also recalls Benjamin's discussion of the optical unconscious in the artwork essay: "Then came the film and burst this prison-world asunder by the dynamite of the tenth of a second". Again, "By close-ups of the things around us … by exploring the commonplace milieus under the ingenious guidance of the camera, the film … extends our comprehension of the necessities which rule our lives".[32] In this way, otherwise obscure lives are recovered from the triumphal history of Federation.

Ali's river of visions is also a device for representing the recurrence of transgenerational trauma, the multidirectional memories and embodied experiences of the oppressed. Among the novel's many constellations of violence is a series of beatings that are inflicted either as punishment for or denial of the racial or class identity of the victim. Because memory is constellated rather than linear, running contrary to the stream of narrative time, an apprehension of the past can begin at any point. For example, when Harry Lewis asks Auntie Ellie in 1946, "Is you an Abo[?]" (201), she beats him repeatedly to teach him not to speak of this again: it is "a methodical violence that Harry recognised did not come from her, but was learnt, as she wanted him to learn it" (201–2). Ned Quade, another of Ali's ancestors, is a convict on Sarah Island in Macquarie Harbour in 1832. It is "[t]he Devil's Island of the British Empire, the endpoint of the vast convict system, the remotest island of the remotest island of the remotest continent" (149) – that is to say, in Flanagan's terms, "the edge". Quade is called "the stone man" because of his capacity to take repeated punishment without apparent pain: "he will not betray his innocence with a single cry of suffering" (149). These beatings are echoed across the generations when Quade's granddaughter Rose is taunted by the cry "Convicts! Convicts! Convicts!" (54). They also anticipate the historically earlier beating and rape of Black Pearl by the sealer, who "slaps" into her the idea that only the white man is created in God's image (313), and again, closer to the narrative present, in Maria Magdelena Svevo's revelation to Ali that "This" – the image of his face in the mirror – "is an Abo" (250). Ali's own physical pain when he is pinned by the blast of history, witnessing the rape of his ancestor by the sealer, is an embodied echo of all these individual instances of violence in a constellation of transgenerational trauma. Pinned to the river of history, Ali takes the thrust of the river as Black Pearl does the blows and thrusts of the sealer: he is in this sense a *träger*, a bearer or carrier of history. Ali asks, "Why do I feel as if I am being destroyed by history?" (264). This trauma is manifest in the endemic trope of amputation: Ali's arm projecting above

---

29  Benjamin, "Theses", 263.
30  Benjamin, "Theses", 261.
31  Benjamin, "Theses", 262–3.
32  Walter Benjamin, "The Work of Art in the Age of Mechanical Reproduction", in *Illuminations: Essays and Reflections*, ed. Hannah Arendt (New York: Schocken, 1968), 236.

the water like a broken wing; Uncle Reg's extracted and commodified teeth; Harry Lewis' amputated thumb; the corpse of Ali and Couta Ho's dead baby, Jemma, "this missing limb": "I felt as if some substantial part of me … had been cut from my body" (264).

Ali's vision of the rape of Black Pearl is apparently the originary moment from which the "gale" of history blows: "I realise I am witness to the conception of Auntie Ellie's mother and to the genesis of all that I am … I realise I am entrapped, entombed in this all-encompassing water" (316). This moment suggests that the force of the stream of time "entraps" Ali in its linear flow, like historicism, revealing to him a "realist" narrative of origins or "genesis" that would make the traumatic events of history seem inevitable, leading to the telos of the present. But this is the "trap" of historicism that Arendt sought to avoid in her own account of the Holocaust, using the "*weak* Messianic power" of historical materialism to liberate the events of the past from the passage of time. Ali feels "entrapped" by the river, but his constellations of past and present hold out the promise of another mode of apprehension that would free him from the march of homogeneous empty time in the same way that Flanagan uses the resources of magical realism. This promise is expressed in the novel's alternative spatialisation of time as a circle rather than a line.

Ali's struggle in the final pages of the novel is to respatialise time from historicism's narrative of predetermined "genesis" to historical materialism's constellation, which is open to the future. Ali's dying visions take place as he is in the process of transforming from a person into the totemic sea eagle of his ancestors. Like Benjamin's angel, Ali is "unable to stay", sensing that his stream of visions is coming to a close. What has been a temporal sequence of images breaks up into a "bizarre series of fragments" (311), which then coagulate into a new spatial form. Near death, Ali beholds "an immensity of blue", in which there is "a fleck … at the centre of [a] vast emptiness" (322), and his vision of history is transposed from time to space, as this tiny fleck evolves and expands into vast galaxies and constellations, culminating in the image of historical time as a wheel-like structure rotating around Black Pearl. Even the "godforsaken water" in which he is "entrapped" (316) is transforming into new, circular shapes: "I feel the water swirling and whorling about me … and joining it is my head forming similar swirls and whorls … Celtic knots with the water, which is no longer destroying me but remaking me as something else" (321). This respatialisation of the line as a circle recasts Ali's family history not as a stemma leading from an origin through a "genesis" to the present, in which each event is determined by its place in a sequence as inevitable as Arendt feared the Holocaust to be, but as an eddy or constellation with Black Pearl "at the hub of them all, and everyone radiates out like spokes on a bicycle wheel from where she stands" (325). This alternative spatialisation of time and history corresponds with Ali's drowning, generating a final moment of apprehension.

In the final pages of the novel, Ali undergoes an apotheosis, as he is transformed into both the angel of history and the Indigenous totem of the sea eagle, and then elevated from the earth to the cosmos. His arm is transformed into a feathered wing, and the current of the Franklin becomes the "gale" (326) of history that lifts him out of one dimension into another, out of the line into the circle, out of a stream of water into whirling currents of air, where historical time is reconstituted as a constellation. This geometric representation of alternative forms of historical understanding is repeated in *The Narrow Road to the Deep North*, in which the Thai-Burma Railway, known to the allied POWs as "The Line", is a spatialisation of deterministic history – the history of nation and empire. As the Tasmanian war hero Dorrigo Evans understands it, "A line was something that proceeded from one point to another … A length without breadth, a life without meaning, the procession from life to death. A journey to hell". From his reading of Japanese poetry, however, Dorrigo experiences the multidirectional matrix of cross-cultural comparison that allows him to spatialise this Western image of time. In the haiku of the eighteenth-century poet Shisui, he discovers the form of the circle: "an endless mystery, lengthless breadth, the great wheel, eternal return: the circle – antithesis of the line".[33] In the final moments of *Death of a River Guide*, Ali finds himself released from the linear stream of time into the great wheel of his ancestors: "before Black Pearl has finished speaking he feels a warm updraught, and rising with it his body, wings out-stretched, feathers feeling every sensation of the crisscrossing air currents, rising in a spiral, a circle growing ever outwards" (326).

The typescript draft of *Death of a River Guide* in Flanagan's papers in the National Library of Australia indicates that it was originally to have been titled "The Circle", with a motto drawn from William Blake implying the structure of the constellation or dialectical image: "I see the Past, Present, and Future existing all at once".[34] This means that the technical and structural problems Flanagan referred to in an interview at this time – "the struggle of '93 and '94" – were about how to realise this overarching vision of the circularity of historical time, which coincides with the circularity of oral culture as an alternative to mainstream historical narrative in its linear form:

> I conceived of the structure and I wrote the beginning and the end very quickly … I knew exactly what it was going to be like. The struggle of '93 and '94 was to actually make it work. Because I really didn't realize until I got into it how ambitious it was technically … I wanted to write it in a circular structure, because I came to think that traditional forms of narrative were very European-based and very much a straight line. And it always interested me here that the people tell stories in a much more circular fashion.
>
> Essentially I come from a Tasmanian oral culture where stories are passed on from generation to generation. It wasn't a literary culture, it wasn't an intellectual culture – it wasn't a culture that had references in books or ideas. It only had references in stories and images – its own life and other lives – and they were all in the form of stories. I had grown up loving those stories. The more I thought about them the more incredibly circular they were in structure and they had very discursive elements within them but they always came in the end to a very tight point.[35]

Flanagan's alternative spatialisation of time as a circle or constellation is therefore connected with his scalar realignment of social space from nation to "edge", since it is always local histories – those of the remotest island of the remotest continent – that he constellates with equally local events in European history. Another of the novel's constellations therefore involves a realignment of social space that allows Flanagan to resist the narrative of Nation. He constellates Tasmanian history not with that of mainland or continental Australia, but with Tasmania's antipodes, especially the marginalised Eastern Europe of the Cold War era: Mitteleuropa and Tasmania; Trieste and Hobart (7, 147). This Tasmania/Slovenia axis has its biographical origins in Flanagan's marriage to Majda Smolej, the dedicatee of *Death of a River*

---

33   Richard Flanagan, *The Narrow Road to the Deep North* (Sydney: Random House, 2013), 27–8, 29.
34   Richard Flanagan, title page of an edited typescript of "The Circle", dated June 1993, Flanagan Papers, NLA, Box 19.
35   Richard Flanagan, "Interview with Giles Hugo", undated typescript, Flanagan Papers, NLA, Box 19.

*Guide*, but it is also an alignment that again allows him to "blast" Tasmania out of the logic of narrative history, with its telos of nation and empire.

The child of a Tasmanian father with Aboriginal heritage and a Slovenian woman who meet in Trieste after the war, Ali is delivered by the cigar-smoking midwife Maria Magdalena Svevo, whose real name is Ettie Schmitz (3, 5). As Marc Delrez points out, these allusions are to the modernist writer Aron Ettore Schmitz, whose pen name, Italo Svevo, alludes in turn to his own mixed Italo-German heritage, and whose major novel, *Zeno's Conscience* (1923), is the fictional memoir of the nicotine addict Zeno Cosini. The figure of the double-headed eagle on Maria's cigar box, which refers both to the crest of the Austro-Hungarian Empire and the Tasmanian sea eagle that is the totem of Cosini's Aboriginal ancestors, succinctly evokes his transnational identity. The proper name of Svevo therefore signifies "both the European pedigree which necessarily traverses a sense of Australian identity, and the fact that such Europeanness is always already the result of mixed ancestry and of a complex reconciliation of parts".[36] These references work to locate Flanagan's interests, in Neil Brenner's phrase, "above, below and around" the scale of the nation,[37] deftly avoiding any clear-cut association with "a sense of Australian identity". Like Svevo's Italo-German heritage, and like the city of Trieste, which is located at a liminal point between socio-political entities that were historically transient – the Austro-Hungarian Empire and the Third Reich – Ali Cosini's heritage is at once transnational and local, European and Tasmanian – though not necessarily "Australian".

Ali's death by drowning in the Franklin has a biographical source in Flanagan's own experiences kayaking as a young man.[38] It also alludes to the deaths of Tasmanian wilderness photographers Olegas Truchanas, who had been the first to kayak the upper Huon and Gordon Rivers and drowned on the Gordon in 1972, and Peter Dombrovskis, who died while walking in the remote Western Arthurs in 1996. Truchanas and Dombrovskis are models for Flanagan both as artist-activist-adventurers and as *Tasmanian* artists who were regionally rather than nationally committed.[39] That commitment was an important model for Flanagan's thinking about literature and scale. He has a historian's understanding of the way Federation nationalism and mid-twentieth-century cultural nationalism have distorted the story of Australian art. "Since Federation", Flanagan argues, "Australian art was seen to have a mission to make a single national culture in the image of either its great coastal cities or its mainland dry outback". He resists this "monocultural nationalism", re-invoking a pre-Federation spatial imaginary in which the colonies are themselves "nations".[40] This is close to the understanding of colonial nationalism as an overlapping mosaic of multiple scales described by contemporary historians like Alan Atkinson, in which the individual colonies "thought of themselves as nations".[41] "Though

---

36   Marc Delrez, "Nationalism, Reconciliation, and the Cultural Genealogy of Magic in Richard Flanagan's *Death of a River Guide*", *Journal of Commonwealth Literature* 42, no. 1 (2007): 123.
37   Neil Brenner, *New State Spaces: Urban Governance and the Rescaling of Statehood* (Oxford: Oxford University Press, 2004), 46.
38   Richard Flanagan, "Out of a Wild Sea", *Age*, 19 August 1995, in *And what do you do, Mr Gable? Short Pieces by Richard Flanagan* (Sydney: Random House, 2011), 1–9.
39   Richard Flanagan, "It's Peter Dom", *Art & Australia* (Spring 2010), in *And what do you do, Mr Gable?*, 23–31.
40   Flanagan, "It's Peter Dom", 28.
41   Alan Atkinson, *The Europeans in Australia, Vol. 3: Nation* (Sydney: University of New South Wales Press, 2014), xix.

a nation", Flanagan believes, "Australia is not one country but many, and one of these is the country of Tasmania".[42]

At the same time, Flanagan's identification with place at the local, pre- or sub-national scale is motivated by supra-national alignments and a transnational understanding of history: Strahan and Trieste; Slovenia and Van Diemen's Land. It is here that Flanagan's thinking about space and scale reconnects with the temporal figure of the constellation. Truchanas and Dombrovskis' experience of the great caesura of World War Two and the Holocaust led them to make that localised experience of place and time a lens through which to constellate other local points in time and space, while eschewing a "single national culture". Their attitudes to "the natural world of Tasmania", Flanagan believes, "can only be understood as a response to the immense human horror of World War II in Eastern Europe". "At the edge of the world", he argues, "where the contours of progress were more visible than at its centre, two photographers, refugees of the last great global conflict of nation and ideology against nation and ideology" understood "the conflict to come – of man against the natural world".[43] Out of this particular constellation would emerge the subject matter of Flanagan's second novel, *The Sound of One Hand Clapping*.

## The Sound of One Hand Clapping (1997)

Flanagan's disavowal of the framing power of national contexts is an enabling condition for apprehension. There are many such moments in his novels, and they are always multi-temporal and transnational, exemplifying the "dynamic transfers that take place between diverse places and times" that Michael Rothberg calls "multidirectional memory".[44] Building on Arendt and Benjamin's concept of crystallisation, Rothberg introduces the term "multidirectional matrix" to suggest the ways in which "remembrance both cuts across and binds together diverse spatial, temporal, and cultural sites".[45] This "additive" form of memory is offered as a counter to what he calls "competitive memory",[46] a zero sum game in which one event – pre-eminently the Holocaust – outranks or displaces others in public memory. As Flanagan says of the Soviet writer Vasily Grossman, "he didn't *compare* or *rank* the horrors of the Gulag and collectivisation and the Holocaust. Rather, and most chillingly, he *connected* them".[47]

The threads of such constellations of violence can be traced across Flanagan's body of work, and across the different times and places in which his novels are set. *The Sound of One Hand Clapping* is set partly in 1989, the year the Berlin Wall came down, and was published in 1997, the year after the Port Arthur massacre, about which Flanagan had written an essay on the theme of foundational violence and intergenerational trauma.[48] But for Maria Buloh, whose family were executed by the Nazis in Slovenia during the war, it is the camps set up by Tasmania's Hydro-Electric Commission for its immigrant workers that

---

42  Flanagan, "It's Peter Dom", 28.
43  Flanagan, "It's Peter Dom", 28, 30.
44  Rothberg, *Multidirectional Memory*, 3, 11.
45  Rothberg, *Multidirectional Memory*, 11, 34.
46  Rothberg, *Multidirectional Memory*, 3.
47  Richard Flanagan, "Soviet Man", *Age*, 18 September 2010, reprinted in *And what do you do, Mr Gable?*, 87 (my italics).
48  Richard Flanagan, "Port Arthur", *Age*, 29 April 1996, reprinted in *And what do you do, Mr Gable?*, 10–14.

bring back "all too painful memories of forced labour camps": "she knew it wasn't Stalin's USSR ... or Birkenau ... Knew it to be the snow-covered Hydro-Electric Commission construction camp called Butlers Gorge".[49] As in Arendt's work, it is the institution of the camp that most powerfully "break[s] the nation-state frame",[50] functioning as a "crystalline structure through whose blinding foci the totalitarian form of domination is revealed".[51] The connections apprehended by Flanagan's characters are the recurring "elements" of global modernity, linking totalitarianism, colonialism, imperialism, capitalism, genocide and environmental destruction. According to Rothberg:

> Multidirectional legacies of violence haunt the histories of indigenous peoples on a global scale and cut across the former Yugoslavia and other parts of the former Soviet bloc as well as Afghanistan, South Africa, Argentina, and other formerly colonized nations. Meanwhile, labor migrants and their descendants in Europe often find themselves confronted with the ghosts of the past at the same time that they experience the prejudices of the present.[52]

This suggests that Flanagan's novels might usefully be seen as belonging to a group of texts that Rothberg calls "multidirectional works": texts that connect instances of institutional violence and social injustice that are apparently separate in space and time. Rothberg's canon of multidirectional works dates from 1961, the year of the Eichmann trial in Jerusalem, and includes Michelle Cliff's *Abeng* (1984; connecting Nazi Germany and the Caribbean), Anita Desai's *Baumgartner's Bombay* (1989; the Holocaust and British India), Nancy Huston's *The Mark of the Angel* (1999; decolonisation in French Algeria and the Holocaust) and W.G. Sebald's *Austerlitz* (2001; the Holocaust and Belgian colonialism).[53] Such multidirectional works use the literary and historical imagination to "constitute the archive", grasping the "spiraling interactions" and "dynamic transfers that take place between diverse places and times during the act of remembrance",[54] and they do so in the interests of a redistributive justice that is appropriate to a globalising world defined by multidirectional legacies of violence and ecological devastation.

Flanagan's first two novels share a common structural principle of being divided into sections that are linked to specific places and times: in *Death of a River Guide*, they include Strahan in 1946, Macquarie Harbour in 1832, and Hobart in 1993; in *The Sound of One Hand Clapping*, it is Sarajevo in 1946, Butlers Gorge in 1954, and Hobart in 1967 and 1989. This principle of fragmentation is at once spatial and temporal, putting into practice the spatialisation of time as a prism or crystal rather than a linear sequence. It makes these novels "multidirectional" works in Rothberg's sense of being both transnational and multi-temporal switching points, or "spiraling interactions". In the opening section of *The Sound of One Hand Clapping*, captioned "Butlers Gorge, 1954", Maria Buloh steps out of the workers' camp to her death by hanging in the snow, repeating from the previous novel Flanagan's allusion to the angel of history. The alpine blizzard now serves a similar

---

49 Richard Flanagan, *The Sound of One Hand Clapping* (1997; Sydney: Vintage, 2012), 4. All subsequent references are to this edition and appear in parentheses in the text.
50 Rothberg, *Multidirectional Memory*, 19.
51 Benhabib, "Hannah Arendt", 175.
52 Rothberg, *Multidirectional Memory*, 28.
53 Rothberg, *Multidirectional Memory*, 27–8.
54 Rothberg, *Multidirectional Memory*, 11, 18.

purpose to the current of the Franklin River as symbol of historical time: "Some people say she was simply blown out of the town that night with the furious blizzard winds; that the tempestuous, billowing breath of the storm picked her up and that she rose with it like an angel" (1). This figure of the traumatised subject of modern history as an angel buffeted by its force echoes the figure of Aljaz Cosini pinned by the stream of time, though in the second novel, time is already respatialised as circles and eddies rather than the line, corresponding with the faceted, crystalline structure of the novel, which constellates different times and places: "the white flakes eddied and whirled in the air as if they were time passing not constantly but erratically ... the air was never still, but held endless circling complexities" (3).

It is this circling rather than linear structure, and specifically the prism of the camp, that allows Flanagan to constellate Butlers Gorge in 1954 with Sarajevo in 1946, and thereby the damage inflicted by Tasmania's postwar " dam-building boom" (5) on its people and its natural environment with the traumas of wartime Europe. As in *Death of a River Guide*, this is to invoke a transnational axis of comparison that "blasts" "Butlers Gorge 1954" out of the progressive history of the nation, reconnecting it instead with the "chronicles of centuries of recurring inhumanities" (4). This spatial and temporal realignment from nation to "multidirectional matrix" is facilitated by Tasmania's ambivalent status within the cartographic imaginary of nation, and of Butlers Gorge within that of modern Tasmania. The abandoned camp at Butlers Gorge, built in the 1950s by the state Hydro-Electric Commission to house workers building the Clark Dam, no longer exists, and the site is now subject to forest regrowth. As Tony Stagg and Philip Mead observe, Butlers Gorge is a "ghost town" that "only exists as a memory and as a place in a story".[55] It is one of many such "phantom" sites, including mining and logging camps, other Hydro-Electric construction villages, subsumed farms and submerged settlements, that now exist only in words. As eighteenth- and early nineteenth-century maps of Van Diemen's Land show, Tasmania has long had an ambivalent status in representations of the continental nation. This uncertainty is sustained in the many contemporary maps of Australia that omit the island state altogether: "There is a well-recognised, and rhetorically complex, thematics of islandness that the literature of Tasmania contributes to", and "the back-story of this history haunts the literature of Tasmania in various ways".[56]

The circularity of historical time corresponds with the temporal structure of traumatic memory. Bojan Buloh's repressed memories of his wife's rape and the execution of her father by the SS in Nazi-occupied Slovenia in 1943, her subsequent suicide at Butlers Gorge in 1954, and their daughter Sonja's own repressed memories of her mother's suicide, give to *The Sound of One Hand Clapping* the temporal structure of what Roger Luckhurst calls the trauma novel, a genre that flourished during the 1990s following the clinical definition of post-traumatic stress disorder in 1981.[57] When Sonja returns to Butlers Gorge from Sydney in 1989 in search of her parents' lost love and her lost childhood, time is

---

55 Tony Stagg and Philip Mead, "A Place of Stories: A Report on the Literature of Tasmania Subset of the AustLit Database", in *Resourceful Reading: The New Empiricism, eResearch and Australian Literary Culture*, ed. Katherine Bode and Robert Dixon (Sydney: Sydney University Press, 2009), 320–1.
56 Stagg and Mead, "A Place of Stories", 316–7. See also Elizabeth McMahon, "Wasted Memory and Generational History: Tasmania's Abandoned Places", in *Women Making Time: Contemporary Feminist Critique and Cultural Analysis*, ed. Elizabeth McMahon and Brigitta Olubas (Perth: University of Western Australia Press, 2006): 43–61.
57 Roger Luckhurst, *The Trauma Question* (London: Routledge, 2008).

experienced as circular: "In a growing gyre, she felt time circling her, at first slowly, as if waiting" (20). The circular temporality of Sonja's traumatic memory is layered on top of the other residues of historical violence that are now the signature themes in Flanagan's writing, especially the Black War and the convict system. As Sonja drives across the island from Hobart to the abandoned and overgrown site of Butlers Gorge, she moves backward through time, penetrating the surface map of modern Tasmania to the phantom maps of the past that lie beneath: "old convict towns now unravelling like used newspapers in the wind. Sonja Buloh drove through them and into the sheep country, in which occasional ancient gum trees stood as if brooding survivors of some terrible massacre, sharing their melancholia" (20).

The imagery of lines and circles is now the master-geometry of Flanagan's understanding of history. The colonial surveyors, with their "indian-inked maps", prefigure their successors, "the hydro-electricity engineers", who later, in their turn, impose "their straight lines … in the form of the wires" along which the electricity flows (21). The image condenses the linear shape of triumphal history as national progress in the literal form of "the wire", a deeply ambivalent word in Flanagan's lexicon because of its association with the camp. In this way, the engineering feats of colonialism and "turbo-capitalism" are expressed in the single master image of the line, with its echoes of the Black Line, the Strahan Railway, the Thai-Burma Railway and the wire of the camps that are the institutional prism through which all these moments in history are apprehended, constellated here in the increasingly dense and self-reflexive vocabulary of Flanagan's writing.

The landscape through which Sonja drives is inscribed by these histories while also being the site in which they are buried, like the structure of repressed memory: "The island busily, almost hysterically tried to bury its memory of a recent, often hideous past in a future of heavy industry" (21). This is what Rob Nixon calls the "slow violence" that occurs when "official landscapes" are forcibly imposed upon "vernacular landscapes":

> A vernacular landscape is shaped by the affective, historically textured maps that communities have devised over generations, maps replete with names and routes, maps alive to significant ecological and surface geological features … By contrast, an official landscape – whether governmental, NGO, corporate, or some combination of those – is typically oblivious to such earlier maps; instead, it writes the land in a bureaucratic, externalizing, and extraction-driven manner that is often pitilessly instrumental … More than material wealth is here at stake: imposed official landscapes typically discount spiritualized vernacular landscapes, severing webs of accumulated cultural meaning and treating the landscape as if it were uninhabited by the living, the unborn, and the animate deceased.[58]

As an example of such official landscapes, Nixon cites the building of megadams, which "displace and disperse those who had developed through their vernacular landscapes their own adaptable, if always imperfect and vulnerable, relation to riverine possibility".[59] When Sonja asks her father in 1989 how he felt about the rivers being dammed, he reminisces

---

58 Rob Nixon, *Slow Violence and the Environmentalism of the Poor* (Cambridge, MA: Harvard University Press, 2011), 17.
59 Nixon, *Slow Violence*, 18.

sadly about the riverine and rainforest landscapes buried by the waters of the dams (57-8). The Clark Dam, to which Sonja returns in 1989, is compared to the Berlin Wall, which also buries a vernacular landscape that is "immense, mysterious, [and] waiting" (25), and like which it is "ageing", its concrete fabric "decaying back into the natural world" (27).

Sonja's journey through remote Tasmania takes place in the same year as the fall of the Berlin Wall and the end of the Cold War era, which has so powerfully shaped the lives of her parents. In pulling these times and places into a constellation, Flanagan points to the way apprehension often requires the historian to connect places at "the edge" and in defiance of the "straight lines" of progress: for history is "unintelligible without comprehending its frontiers" (24). In his essay on the Port Arthur massacre, written during the siege in 1996, Flanagan writes "Tasmania was a society ... begat in great violence: against the Aborigines, the convicts and the land itself", and "the gunman's bullets ... connect a present and a past world of horrific violence".[60] The circularity of time, which allows the constellation of these different periods of history, also threatens the return of Sonja's repressed memories until "finally she felt sure of her time and place, sure that time had not bent back around and taken her once more into a past she wanted nothing of" (47).

Flanagan therefore uses the dam, whose waters cover the land near the site of Sonja's childhood home at Butlers Gorge, as both a monument to the triumphal beliefs of the modern nation and a symbol of the repressed traumatic memories upon which that nation is built: "this dam, which [Bojan] had with his sweat helped raise ... whose form with his soul had set like rock – this dam was meant to hold everything within" (345); "a gale ... which transformed time into a dam" (420). Flanagan evokes the nation-building rhetoric of postwar reconstruction by the inscription on its plaque: "FOR THE MEN OF ALL NATIONS WHO BY BUILDING THIS DAM HELPED HARNESS NATURE FOR THE BETTERMENT OF MANKIND 1955" (27). The ageing dam is a monument to the hubris of mid-twentieth-century Australian nationalism, now summoning "visions of another time, a distant time of triumphant belief and total confidence" (28). This is expressed officially by a local politician who, in his speech at Bojan's naturalisation ceremony in 1954, announces, "You ... are part of a new vision of a new Australia" (42). Flanagan's uncovering of intergenerational trauma blasts the immigrant experience out of this triumphant history of nation-building, realigning it instead with the trauma of wartime and Cold War Eastern Europe. The naturalisation ceremony is meant to be "a joyous, celebratory moment when the new Australians renounced their previous citizenship ... to become Australians" (42), but the axes of Flanagan's constellation will not allow this burial of past time.

The work of nationalistic representation is carried on by the film crew engaged by the Hydro-Electric Commission to record the building of the Butlers Gorge Power Station at Clark Dam on the Upper Derwent River.[61] The cameraman, Earl Kane, is a veteran of the newsreel era and continues to do this work in preference to going into the new TV studios, even though he knows it is only for propaganda purposes: "The Commission ... wanted it all recorded – on paper, on photographs, in film" (67). Kane's boss congratulates him on the images of Bojan Buloh breaking stone by hand with a hammer: "It's ... *heroic*, that's what it is, Earl, fucking heroic" (67). The state-sponsored documentary is part of the "official landscape" of twentieth-century Tasmania. Its antithesis is the forensic use of cinema that Benjamin had hoped for in the artwork essay, turning the camera against the

---

60  Flanagan, "Port Arthur", 11–12.
61  In reality, the opening took place on 21 November 1952.

ideologies of nationalism and capitalism. Flanagan undercuts the newsreel's heroic work by constellating the Clark Dam with another project elsewhere – "It could be some vast Soviet hydro scheme in Siberia" (67) – and true to Benjamin's utopian prediction, the camera, with its "dynamite of the tenth of a second", reveals another perspective within and against its ideological purpose. When Earl Kane watches the rushes of his film in the editing suite, he freezes the image of Bojan being dropped by crane into the steel reinforcing of the dam wall, which discloses another perspective on the heroic event: it looks "as if he is being imprisoned behind them bars forever" (69). Here, as in Ali's cinematic visions, Flanagan uses the techniques of cinema against the nation-building purposes to which it was applied, revealing that the triumphal story of postwar reconstruction is itself an act of representational violence.

It is the lens of the camp, in particular, that allows Flanagan to constellate the work of Tasmania's Hydro-Electric Commission and its slow violence against nature and the poor with the traumas of Eastern Europe. The camp at Butlers Gorge is built of demountable "cells" to house the immigrant workers, many of whom have personal experience of the concentration camps, including those of the Nazi and Soviet regimes. Butlers Gorge is not a unique instance, nor is it part of a *sui generis* "New World" history; as the very banality of its forms testifies, it is part of a transnational constellation of violence, one in a series of iterations of the camp across space and time: "Behind each door was a miserable cell of a room, identical to the one[s] … in which [Bojan] had lived for decades now, in various reincarnations at various hydro dam construction camps … no single one could ever be special" (52). Bojan's Polish workmate Pavel spent "[s]even years in the Gulag" after his family had been "thrown into a pit" by either the Germans or the Russians (107). Bojan has memories of his parents being persecuted by the Nazis and the Slovenian fascists for supporting partisans against the German occupation, and his wife Maria was raped at the age of twelve by an SS unit after being forced to witness her father's execution. Before coming to Tasmania, Maria and Bojan were detained in an Austrian refugee camp after fleeing from Slovenian border guards in the Julien Alps. On the night of Maria's suicide, the camp at Butlers Gorge is simply a part of this endless series:

> the whole black-and-white scene was lit up by the stark electric lights that ran up and down what passed for a street … on either side of the street were crude vertical-board huts with corrugated-iron roofs … to some who lived there it brought back all too painful memories of forced labour camps in the Urals or Siberia. But she knew it wasn't Stalin's USSR. Knew it wasn't Kolyma or Goli Otok or Birkenau. Knew it wasn't even Europe. Knew it to be a snow-covered Hydro-Electric Commission construction camp called Butlers Gorge that sat like a sore in a wilderness of rainforest. (4)

The Czech who discovers Maria's body hanging from a tree near the camp instinctively constellates the event with those in Eastern Europe: "the sight was one he had seen before in the Bohemian forests" (395). As a child, Bojan watched his world "break into pieces", and he has since "survived by camping in the fragments" (187). These pieces, now scattered across time and space, are apprehended through the lens of the camp in a future "attempt to make it all whole again" (187).

In his historical fictions, Flanagan therefore eschews the idea of history as a narrative of progress, seeking instead an apprehension of diverse elements from the past and present that can be held in a constellation, and seen through the critical prism that Arendt calls crystallisation and Benjamin the dialectical image. Flanagan is dedicated to the idea that public memory and the empathic imagination should work to recover from oblivion the histories of the oppressed, and to honour the alternative possibilities embedded in forgotten moments of the past. This resembles Benjamin's "*weak* Messianic power", in the sense that the past is not strongly determined by an inevitable progression towards the present and the future: rather, each moment recovered from the past is a small window onto an alternative history of what might have been. The elements in these constellations are "blasted" out of chronological history and exist in crystallisations that contain both synchronic and diachronic alignments: that is, they are both multi-temporal and cross-cultural or transnational, but never national or imperial. For this reason, Flanagan's writing can seem surprisingly a- and even anti-historical, wanting to show how the elements awaiting crystallisation recur across time and place. The recurring elements of these constellations are imperialism, colonialism, totalitarianism, genocide, capitalism and environmental destruction; their signature projects are gigantic engineering works, such as the invention and mass production of the steam locomotive, the automobile and the dam, and the institution known since Arendt as the camp, which secures the splitting of humanity into the human and the non-human. A historical materialist apprehension would seek, in Benjaminian terms, to liberate these elements from the grip of progressive narratives, including the narrative that Alan Atkinson, in the third volume of *The Europeans in Australia* (2014), calls *Nation*.

Flanagan's constellations of violence also have important scalar implications in the sense that he seeks to restore the ownership of stories and the agency in events from larger to smaller scales of the knowable community.[62] In Flanagan's novels and essays, Van Diemen's Land/Tasmania is associated with a set of thematic and historical concerns that make it an epitome of global modernity. These include the colonial or military occupation of sovereign territory, the theory and practice of genocide and penal servitude, the symbiotic relationship between turbo-capitalism and political corruption, and the consequences of climate change and environmental destruction. In Flanagan's social and historical imaginary, these phenomena operate transnationally, cross-culturally and trans-historically but they have local impacts. Flanagan has a recurring interest in carceral institutions as manifestations of a more general condition that he refers to, after Vasily Grossman, as "non-freedom".[63] This constellation repeats itself across time and space: in the nineteenth-century British penal colonies of New South Wales and Van Diemen's Land, in the Nazi Holocaust, the Soviet gulags and the Japanese prisoner-of-war camps of the twentieth century, and in twenty-first-century Australia's treatment of asylum seekers. He is interested in the recurrence throughout human history of the phenomenon of genocide – examples include the Nazi Holocaust, especially in Slovenia, and the Black War in Tasmania – and in comparative genocide studies as a mode of historical inquiry. Rothberg calls this the practice of " multidirectional memory", distinguishing it from the forms of Jewish and other exceptionalism he calls "competitive memory".[64]

---

[62] Robert Dixon, "'Communications from below': Scalar Transformations in Richard Flanagan's *The Narrow Road to the Deep North* (2013) and Steven Carroll's *A World of Other People* (2013)", *Antipodes* 31, no. 1 (June 2017): 184–205.
[63] Richard Flanagan, "Soviet Man", 92.
[64] Rothberg, *Multidirectional Memory*, 3.

## 1 Circles of Violence: *Death of a River Guide* and *The Sound of One Hand Clapping*

Flanagan's novels also have a pattern of temporal and thematic reiteration which they share with the international "trauma novel". Colonialism or the occupation of sovereign territory is represented in the novels through rape and other extreme forms of interpersonal violence: the rape of Black Pearl by a sealer in *Death of a River Guide*, the rape of Maria Buhlo and the execution of her father by Nazis in *The Sound of One Hand Clapping*, the torture of the unnamed machine breaker from Glasgow on the Cockchafer in *Gould's Book of Fish*, and the beating of Darky Gardiner in *The Narrow Road to the Deep North*. The camp appears in convict Port Arthur and the Aboriginal reserve on Flinders Island, but also in Nazi-occupied Slovenia, in the Soviet gulags, in the Japanese prisoner-of-war camps in South-East Asia, and in the detention centres of Australia's "Pacific Solution". The Tasmanian hydro-electric scheme, which brought war-ravaged Eastern European migrants to the remote regions of Tasmania during the era of postwar reconstruction, the clear felling of old-growth forests, and the Tasmanian government's long history of support for the woodchip industry, combine the themes of the camp, turbo-capitalism and "non-freedom" with environmental destruction. The capacity of these themes to recur across time and global space is epitomised by the classical Enlightenment projects of Bentham's prison and Stephenson's railway, which metastasise throughout Flanagan's novels as the convict railway on the Tasman Peninsula in *Death of a River Guide*, the Commandant's steam train in *Gould's Book of Fish*, and the Thai-Burma Railway, in both its British and Japanese incarnations, in *The Narrow Road to the Deep North*. In that novel, these themes annex Tasmania to the scales of nation and world via the subject matter of Australian prisoners of war working on the Thai-Burma Railway. Previous Booker winner Thomas Keneally commented that this was originally "an Australian story" that Flanagan's Man Booker win had now given to the world,[65] but the reality was quite otherwise: Flanagan had taken the story back from "Australia" for Tasmania, and then annexed Tasmania directly to the scale of the world.

In his historical fictions, Flanagan constructs an alternative genealogy for historical materialism that also aligns with current critical work on planetarity and environmentalism captured in Ian Baucom's concept of post-Anthropocene time as "History 4°".[66] Drawing on Dipesh Chakrabarty's profoundly influential essay, "The Climate of History: Four Theses",[67] and also returning to Benjamin's seventeenth and eighteenth theses on the philosophy of history, Baucom argues that Benjamin was presciently aware of the way in which the successive phases of human history are not only not "past", and layered synchronically in a heterogeneous present, but also that this larger history of "*homo sapiens*" is in turn embedded in the yet vaster history of what Benjamin called "organic life on earth":

> That ... is one of the keys to Benjamin's revolutionary historical method, to his determination to resist the narrative of historical progress by altering perspective, by looking back, over the shoulder of his "angel of history", at the shards of ruin and sedimented layers of history piling up at the angel's feet. Benjamin's messianic perspective ... thereby reveals itself as a perspective not toward the prophesied future ... but toward

---

65 Thomas Keneally cited in Stephen Romei, "Man Booker Prize Winner Richard Flanagan's Triumph Against the Odds", *Australian*, 16 October 2014, 11.
66 Ian Baucom, "'History 4°': Postcolonial Method and Anthropocene Time", *Cambridge Journal of Postcolonial Literary Inquiry* 1, no. 1 (March 2014): 123–42.
67 Dipesh Chakrabarty, "The Climate of History: Four Theses", *Critical Inquiry* 35, no. 2 (2009): 197–222.

the retroactive realization of a heretofore missed but still "revolutionary chance in the fight for [an] oppressed past": a past that is, in fact, neither "past" nor singular but multiply immanent in the present, as "civilizational" history; as the species history of *Homo sapiens*; as the history of organic life on earth; as the history of the universe; as the blended orders of biographical, nomological, biological, zoological, and geological time.[68]

It is this perception of the threshold between human and non-human history that Benjamin's eighteenth thesis and Baucom's "History 4°" share with Flanagan's rescaling of Tasmanian history, nested as it is within a series of ascending scales through the national and imperial to the planetary, and giving it profound ethical and even jurisprudential implications. As Baucom argues, "This new, planetary form of experience reorients the demands of justice from a desire for immunity from these [higher] orders and forces them toward a determination to refashion the biographical and nomological orders of our lives (our habits of dwelling, consuming, legislating) in relation to these other forces and forcings of planetary life – at this time and for times to come".[69]

## References

Arendt, Hannah. "[*The Origins of Totalitarianism*]: A Reply". *Review of Politics*, 15, no. 1 (January 1953): 76–84.
Atkinson, Alan. *The Europeans in Australia, Volume Three: Nation*. Sydney: University of New South Wales Press, 2014.
Baucom, Ian. "'Moving Centres': Climate Change, Critical Method, and the Historical Novel". *Modern Language Quarterly* 76, no. 2 (June 2015): 137–57.
——. "'History 4°': Postcolonial Method and Anthropocene Time". *Cambridge Journal of Postcolonial Literary Inquiry* 1, no. 1 (March 2014): 123–42.
Beiner, Ronald. "Walter Benjamin's Philosophy of History". *Political Theory* 12, no. 3 (August 1984): 423–34.
Benhabib, Seyla. "Hannah Arendt and the Redemptive Power of Narrative". *Social Research* 57, no. 1 (Spring 1990): 167–96.
Benjamin, Walter. *Illuminations: Essays and Reflections*. Edited by Hannah Arendt. New York: Schocken, 1968.
Brenner, Neil. *New State Spaces: Urban Governance and the Rescaling of Statehood*. Oxford: Oxford University Press, 2004.
Butler, Judith. "Benjamin and the Philosophy of History". European Graduate School Video Lectures, 2011. https://bit.ly/2Ls5lMU.
Chakrabarty, Dipesh. "The Climate of History: Four Theses". *Critical Inquiry* 35, no. 2 (2009): 197–222.
Delrez, Marc. "Nationalism, Reconciliation, and the Cultural Genealogy of Magic in Richard Flanagan's *Death of a River Guide*". *Journal of Commonwealth Literature* 42, no. 1 (2007): 117–29.
Dixon, Robert. "'Communications from below': Scalar Transformations in Richard Flanagan's *The Narrow Road to the Deep North* (2013) and Steven Carroll's *A World of Other People* (2013)". *Antipodes* 31, no. 1 (June 2017): 184–205.

---

68  Ian Baucom, "'Moving Centres': Climate Change, Critical Method, and the Historical Novel", *Modern Language Quarterly* 76, no. 2 (June 2015): 151.
69  Baucom, "Moving Centres", 156.

Fenves, Peter. *The Messianic Reduction: Walter Benjamin and the Shape of Time.* Stanford: Stanford University Press, 2011.
Flanagan, Richard. *The Narrow Road to the Deep North.* Sydney: Random House, 2013.
——. *The Sound of One Hand Clapping.* (1997). Sydney: Vintage, 2012.
——. *And what do you do, Mr Gable? Short pieces by Richard Flanagan.* Sydney: Random House, 2011.
——. *Death of a River Guide.* (1994) Ringwood, Vic: Penguin, 1996.
——. "Return the People's Pedder!", in *The Rest of the World Is Watching: Tasmania and the Greens*, edited by Cassandra Pybus and Richard Flanagan. Sydney: Pan Macmillan, 1990.
——. Edited typescript of "The Circle", dated June 1993, Flanagan Papers, NLA, Box 19.
——. Interview with Giles Hugo, undated typescript, Flanagan Papers, NLA, Box 19.
Hansen, Miriam Bratu. "Benjamin and Cinema: Not a One-Way Street". *Critical Inquiry* 25, no. 2 (Winter 1999): 306–43.
Holgate, Ben. "Greening a Narrative Mode: Antipodean Magical Realism and Ecocriticism in Richard Flanagan's Fiction", this volume.
Luckhurst, Roger. *The Trauma Question.* London: Routledge, 2008.
McMahon, Elizabeth. "Wasted Memory and Generational History: Tasmania's Abandoned Places". In *Women Making Time: Contemporary Feminist Critique and Cultural Analysis,* edited by Elizabeth McMahon and Brigitta Olubas. Perth: University of Western Australia Press, 2006.
Mishra, Vijay. "Rushdie and Bollywood Cinema". In *The Cambridge Companion to Salman Rushdie,* edited by Abdulrazak Gurnah. Cambridge: Cambridge University Press, 2007, 11–28.
Nixon, Rob. *Slow Violence and the Environmentalism of the Poor.* Cambridge, MA: Harvard University Press, 2011.
Pensky, Max. "Method and Time: Benjamin's Dialectical Images". In *The Cambridge Companion to Walter Benjamin,* edited by David S. Ferris. Cambridge: Cambridge University Press, 2004, 177–98.
Pybus, Cassandra and Richard Flanagan, eds. *The Rest of the World Is Watching: Tasmania and the Greens.* Sydney: Pan Macmillan, 1990.
Reynolds, Henry. *Forgotten Wars.* Sydney: NewSouth Publishing, 2013.
Romei, Stephen. "Man Booker Prize Winner Richard Flanagan's Triumph against the Odds". *Australian,* 16 October 2014, 11.
Rothberg, Michael. *Multidirectional Memory: Remembering the Holocaust in the Age of Decolonization.* Stanford: Stanford University Press, 2009.
Stagg, Tony and Philip Mead. "A Place of Stories: A Report on the Literature of Tasmania Subset of the AustLit Database". In *Resourceful Reading: The New-Empiricism, eResearch and Australian Literary Culture,* edited by Katherine Bode and Robert Dixon. Sydney: Sydney University Press, 2009, 315–24.
Voegelin, Eric. Review of "*The Origins of Totalitarianism*". *Review of Politics* 15, no. 1 (January 1953): 68–76.
"Walter Benjamin". *Stanford Encyclopedia of Philosophy.* https://stanford.io/2mkAnM2.

# 2

# Greening a Narrative Mode: Antipodean Magical Realism and Ecocriticism in Richard Flanagan's Fiction

Ben Holgate

"Maybe we have lost the ability, that sixth sense that allows us to see miracles and have visions and understand that we are something other, larger than what we have been told".[1]

Narrator Sid Hammet's opening remark in *Gould's Book of Fish* (2001) encapsulates a recurring theme of Richard Flanagan's fiction: the perception of human existence as something bigger than Western materialism and urban existence, of anthropic life as one element within a profound, mysterious cosmos. Flanagan conveys this transcendental awareness through a style of writing that frequently involves magical realist elements, and which is inextricably tied to a philosophy based on ecology and a connection to the Tasmanian landscape, a philosophy influenced by Indigenous Australians and their precolonial culture. In particular, Flanagan blends the magical and the ecological through his persistent leitmotif of wilderness, specifically Tasmania's unique and remote south-west wilderness.

Flanagan's work, therefore, provides an opportunity to examine the links between magical realism and environmental literature, a line of inquiry that has been lacking in literary scholarship. As Begoña Simal states, "little (if any) research has been devoted to exploring the precise interconnections between ecocritical writings and magical realist motifs".[2] Such an approach, however, is not unique to Flanagan. We see a mixture of magical realist and ecocritical writing, for example, in Indigenous Australian Alexis Wright's novel *Carpentaria* (2006), in which the Indigenous protagonist, Norm Phantom, has mystical powers, and Indigenous activists like Norm's son Will sabotage an iron-ore mine owned by a multinational corporation that wreaks havoc on the northern Australian environment.[3] Similarly, New Zealand Māori author Witi Ihimaera's novella *The Whale Rider* (1987), in which the young girl Māori protagonist is the incarnation of an ancient ancestral spirit, includes the slaughter of whales by commercial fishermen and the testing of nuclear bombs

---

1   Richard Flanagan, *Gould's Book of Fish* (2001; New York: Grove, 2002), 3. All subsequent references are to this edition and appear in parentheses in the text.
2   Begoña Simal, "Of a Magical Nature: The Environmental Unconscious", in *Uncertain Mirrors: Magical Realisms in US Ethnic Literatures*, ed. Jesús Benito, Ana Ma Manzanas and Begoña Simal (Amsterdam: Rodopi, 2009), 195.
3   Alexis Wright, *Carpentaria* (Artarmon, NSW: Giramondo, 2006).

in the Pacific Ocean by imperialist powers like the United States and France.[4] Yet what is unique to Flanagan is his portrayal of his home state's south-west wilderness as a fictional landscape of the human spirit as much as a geographic terrain, in which European notions of "civilisation" are made redundant and humankind's spiritual potential may be fully realised. In Flanagan's south-west, the wild illuminates the magical. He capitalises on the dual exoticism of Tasmania, in terms of its geography, as Australia's remote island state located south of the continental mainland with only the treacherous Southern Ocean separating it from Antarctica, and in terms of its brutal colonial history, as a penal colony for the British that involved the transportation and incarceration of minor felons and some political prisoners, and the attempted eradication of Tasmania's first inhabitants. My discussion in this chapter focuses predominantly on two of his best-known novels – his debut, *Death of a River Guide* (1994), and *Gould's Book of Fish* (2001) – both of which are mostly set in the south-west, in both its physical and metaphorical senses.

Magical realism, I contend, is often too narrowly conceptualised by literary scholars, largely because the generally accepted world canon of magical realist texts that is studied consists predominantly of works derived from a particular range of territories, namely Central and South America, North America, South and West Africa, the Caribbean, Europe and, to a lesser extent, India. Most critics, as Anne Hegerfeldt says, "have a certain group of core texts in mind when they speak of magic realism".[5] Hegerfeldt and Tamás Bényei, among others, recommend first examining a group of texts for which there is a degree of consensus about their being considered magical realist in order to formulate a definition of the narrative mode.[6] But if this group is ethnographically or regionally biased, the resultant definitions will be either flawed or incomplete. My argument is that magical realist fiction that emanates from other regions, such as Australasia and Asia, often challenges, modifies and expands our conception of what magical realism is, because different writers from different countries subject the narrative mode to differing intellectual and socio-cultural frameworks, and utilise it for diverse purposes. Flanagan is a prime example of this.

The definition of magical realism, of course, has been hotly debated since the term was first applied to fiction nine decades ago.[7] Many contemporary critics, such as Hegerfeldt, Jenni Adams and Wendy Faris, select groups of texts they consider to be magical realist and identify characteristics common to that particular group. The end result is quite often lists, such as Hegerfeldt's five "prototypical literary techniques",[8] Adams' "properties",[9] and Faris'

---

4   Witi Ihimaera, *The Whale Rider* (Auckland: Heinemann, 1987).
5   Anne Hegerfeldt, *Lies that Tell the Truth: Magic Realism Seen through Contemporary Fiction from Britain* (Amsterdam: Rodopi, 2005), 42.
6   Tamás Bényei, "Rereading 'Magic Realism'", *Hungarian Journal of English and American Studies* 3, no. 1 (1997): 149–79.
7   Although German art critic Franz Roh is generally credited as the first person to coin the term "magic realism" to identify a post-expressionist trend in European visual art in 1925, the Italian critic and writer Massimo Bontempelli was the first to apply the term "magical realism" (or *realismo magico*) to both visual art and literature in his bilingual (Italian and French) journal *900 (Novecento)* between 1926 and 1929. Bontempelli used the term to highlight "the sense of magic discovered in the everyday life of man and things". Seymour Menton, *Magic Realism Rediscovered, 1918–1981* (Philadelphia: Art Alliance Press, 1983), 52.
8   Hegerfeldt, *Lies that Tell the Truth*, 50–62.
9   Jenni Adams, *Magic Realism in Holocaust Literature: Troping the Traumatic Real* (Basingstoke, UK: Palgrave Macmillan, 2011), 4–5.

five primary characteristics and nine secondary characteristics.[10] The essential problem with this approach is that one critic's list is unlikely to match up to another critic's list. Also, the more peripheral the characteristic, the less likely it is that it will appear in other critics' lists. By contrast, I advocate a revised approach to the narrative mode that is both flexible and able to accommodate markedly different literatures from around the globe that are in a constant state of flux. My argument is that magical realism has constantly changing boundaries and is inherently unstable. Magical realism, like any form of writing that endures over the long term, itself remains in a state of flux. I take Alastair Fowler's point that any genre will undergo a continuous "metamorphosis" because each new work that enters a genre introduces a new element to that genre, which in turn changes the genre's nature. Like Fowler, I include within the term genre both the historical structured kinds as well as the "unstructured modes". A mode, as Fowler says, is "a selection or abstraction from kind" that has "few if any external rules, but evokes a historical kind through samples of its internal repertoire".[11] Magical realism, as most critics attest, is a narrative mode rather than a genre.

I propose that similarities, rather than characteristics, provide the building blocks that allow for a comparative analysis between different magical realist texts. In this respect I am drawing on the work of Adams and Hegerfeldt, who similarly adapt a family resemblance model for their respective studies on Holocaust and British magical realist fiction.[12] However, my approach differs from theirs in that I am not advocating a given list of similarities, but rather that the similarities among magical realist texts should remain open and changeable, resulting from a close reading of texts. The only factor that remains fixed is magical realism's solitary trait: the representation of the magical or supernatural in a quotidian manner that is embedded within literary realism. I am here building on Jacques Derrida's theory of "the law of the law of genre". Every genre, says Derrida, necessarily involves "a principle of contamination, a law of impurity", because no genre can exist in a pure form, in and of itself. In Derrida's view, any literary category (genre, mode, type or form) contains a "trait" that is common to all works within a particular category, by which readers recognise that category. The trait acts as a "code". Yet the trait means that a text "participates" in a genre, or more than one genre, without actually belonging to the genre(s): "Every text *participates* in one or several genres, there is no genreless text, there is always a genre and genres, yet such participation never amounts to belonging". The text cannot belong to a genre because the same trait that marks the text as participating in a genre does not in itself belong to that genre, or to any category for that matter: "In marking itself generically, a text unmarks itself". Derrida concludes that the "formless form" of literary categories points to "the possibility and the impossibility of taxonomy".[13] I propose a minimalist definition of magical realism that accords with Derrida's notion of a single, common trait for each genre. Without magical realism's solitary trait mentioned above, a text cannot be said to be magical realist.

---

10   Wendy B. Faris, "Scheherazade's Children: Magical Realism and Postmodern Fiction", in *Magical Realism: Theory, History, Community*, ed. Lois Parkinson Zamora and Wendy B. Faris (Durham, NC: Duke University Press, 1995), 163-90.
11   Alastair Fowler, *Kinds of Literature: An Introduction to the Theory of Genres and Modes* (Oxford: Clarendon Press, 1982), 23, 56.
12   Adams, *Magic Realism*, 5; Hegerfeldt, *Lies that Tell the Truth*, 44.
13   Jacques Derrida, "The Law of Genre," in *Acts of Literature*, ed. Derek Attridge, trans. Avital Ronell (London: Routledge, 1992), 227-31.

This minimalist definition allows a wide range of texts to participate in the category of magical realism without actually belonging to it. There is also an implied recognition that any magical realist text will participate in other generic kinds without belonging to any of them.

Flanagan typically constructs his novels within identifiable literary genres. *Death of a River Guide*, for instance, is a multigenerational family saga framed within memory flashbacks and visions by the protagonist, the river guide Aljaz Cosini, as he drowns under a flooded Franklin River. Nevertheless, the predominantly realist novel is imbued with magical or supernatural elements that are portrayed in a quotidian manner. Cosini believes that, during his protracted drowning, he has been "granted visions" that "I must share", otherwise "their magic will become as a burden".[14] Indeed, Aljaz thinks his own birth was somehow miraculous because he was born in his mother's caul (1). The narrator's visions include: native Tasmanian animals telling stories at a barbeque hosted by his late father, Harry, during which a Tasmanian tiger and a lobster recite past events of Cosini's family; the walls of a cathedral oozing blood during a funeral; and a bedspread stained with tears that won't wash off.[15] Similarly, *Gould's Book of Fish* is ostensibly a picaresque romp in the brutal, nineteenth-century, colonial Van Diemen's Land featuring the ongoing misfortunes of convicted forger and painter William Buelow Gould and framed within Gould's eponymous memoirs. Yet the book abounds with supernatural occurrences, such as the cover of Gould's notebook glowing with "a mass of pulsating purple spots" (13), the never-ending narrative of his notebook, and the metamorphosis of Gould into a weedy sea dragon that is the same fish into which Sid Hammet, in the fictional present two centuries later, had turned at the start of the novel. So while these two novels may participate in the family saga and picaresque, respectively, they do not belong to either genre, and, similarly, while they may participate in magical realism, they do not belong to that narrative mode.

What makes magical realism such an amorphous, shape-shifting narrative mode is the way authors utilise it for widely different purposes, often in order to portray issues relevant to their domestic setting or society. Magical realism's capacity to depict alternative belief systems that challenge dominant, orthodox systems of thought – usually, in the West, derived from a European, scientific rationalist view of the world – is what makes it such a formidable literary technique in this respect. Stephen Slemon, in his influential theory of magical realism as postcolonial discourse, argues that in a magical realist text "a battle between two oppositional systems takes place, each working toward the creation of a different kind of fictional world from the other". The two systems are "incompatible" and, as a result, "each remains suspended, locked in a continuous dialectic with the 'other'". In turn, magical realism's "characteristic" manoeuvre is that its "two separate narrative modes never manage to arrange themselves into any kind of hierarchy".[16] The two systems, or

---

14  Richard Flanagan, *Death of a River Guide* (1994; New York: Grove, 2002), 10. All subsequent references are to this edition and appear in parentheses in the text.
15  Marc Delrez argues that Flanagan draws on two different cultural and historical sources of the magical in *Death of a River Guide*: Indigenous Australian spirituality and European spirituality. Marc Delrez, "Nationalism, Reconciliation, and the Cultural Genealogy of Magic in Richard Flanagan's *Death of a River Guide*", *The Journal of Commonwealth Literature* 42, no. 1 (2007): 122.
16  Stephen Slemon, "Magic Realism as Postcolonial Discourse", in *Magical Realism: Theory, History, Community*, ed. Lois Parkinson Zamora and Wendy B. Faris (Durham, NC: Duke University Press, 1995), 409–10.

modes, are usually taken by critics in postcolonial contexts to mean the "magical" world of the colonised and the "real" world of the coloniser.

Flanagan's Tasmanian fiction, however, contains no such simple binary analysis of British colonisation. Rather, his novels introduce a complexity of the colonisation process by pointing out that the convicts were both colonisers and the colonised: colonisers because they participated in the annexation and exploitation of land from Indigenous Tasmanians; colonised because they themselves were oppressed by the British colonial military regime. Importantly, Flanagan's novels repeatedly portray ties between the white underclass and the dispossessed Indigenous people. In *Gould's Book of Fish*, for instance, William Buelow Gould, who initially regards the Indigenous population as "doomed savages" (216), eventually has an affair with the Indigenous woman Twopenny Sal. Yet their relationship is based on much more than sexual gratification: Gould learns her Indigenous language and beliefs (271) and, during a frenzied dance around a funeral pyre for one of her friends, the convict thinks "we shared something that transcended our bodies & our histories & our futures" (333). Although Gould achieves a nascent affinity with Tasmanian Aboriginal culture, he nevertheless recognises he does not, or perhaps cannot, understand it, professing: "I only sensed that I knew none of it" (333). In *Death of a River Guide*, the red-headed Aljaz Cosini comes to understand through his visions that he is, in fact, part Indigenous, and not merely the product of British (paternal) and Slovenian (maternal) genes. Cosini's Indigenous forebear Black Pearl was raped by a white sealer in 1828 on a Bass Strait island, off the coast of northern Tasmania. In other words, Flanagan's fiction depicts a commingling of the white underclass and the black dispossessed, by which the former learned from the latter during colonisation. In turn, this created a culture that was unique to Tasmania.[17] The author's alternative worldview, I suggest, is encapsulated in a passage that appears not in the two novels under consideration, but rather in his review of historian James Boyce's book *Van Diemen's Land* (2008). Boyce's book, he argues:

> suggests that we [Tasmanians] are not dispossessed Europeans, but a muddy wash of peoples who were made anew in the merge of an old pre-industrial, pre-modern European culture with an extraordinary natural world and a remarkable black culture. As much as a process of colonisation, Boyce's work suggests a history of indigenisation – a strange, uneven, frequently repressed, often violent process in which a white underclass took on much of the black ways of living. It suggests we have a connection with our land not solely based on ideas of commerce, and that there are continuities in our understanding of our land that extend back into pre-history. It is an argument, never more timely, that we are our own people, not a poor imitation of elsewhere.[18]

The key point is that Boyce confirms Flanagan's own philosophy that Tasmanians are not imitative Europeans, even though many of them are descendants of Europeans, but a people and a culture unique to their own landscape. Moreover, Tasmanians' ties to their

---

17 The black–white links are reinforced in Flanagan's other novels. In *Wanting* (2008), Van Diemen's Land governor Sir John Franklin and his wife, Lady Jane, adopt the Indigenous girl Mathinna in a misguided attempt to "civilise" her in Western culture. In *The Narrow Road to the Deep North* (2013), the protagonist, ex-POW Dorrigo Evans, belatedly realises the Indigenous Australian soldier murdered by their Japanese captors while under his command in Thailand was his nephew.
18 Richard Flanagan, "Van Diemen's Land", in *And what do you do, Mr Gable?: New and Collected Essays*, Richard Flanagan (Sydney: Vintage, 2011), 208.

local geography are influenced by Indigenous peoples' links to their land that extend back tens of thousands of years before European habitation.

Flanagan uses his fiction to reinstate this worldview in contemporary discourse. I say reinstate, because what was once taken as fact was subsequently erased from official history due to a collective wish to eradicate personal or familial associations with penal convicts and Indigenous people. In *Death of a River Guide*, this is referred to as the convict "taint" (65). Instead, "[c]hildren denied their parents and invented new lineages of respectable free settlers to replace the true genealogy of shame". In addition, "lies" were invented to hide the fact that convicts and Indigenous people "begat children to one another" (260). In *Gould's Book of Fish*, the same sentiment is encapsulated in the convict Gould's lament that Australia's population has "been trained to live a life of moral cowardice" and docility by making "accommodations with power". Tasmania, says Gould, has become "the island of forgetting, because anything is easier than remembering" (400–1).

My argument is that in order to overcome the lies, the social peer pressure to forget Tasmania's brutal past, Flanagan presents the Indigenous–non-Indigenous connections in a decidedly ecological context. By doing so, he not only presents this cross-cultural nexus in a fresh manner, but also focuses on the main common element between the two groups: that is, the land. Moreover, it is within this ecological framework that Flanagan uses magical realist elements, which reinforce his fiction's portrayal of an alternative worldview that challenges conventional perceptions of the present and the past. The transition from a precolonised landscape abundant in natural resources to a postcolonised landscape being progressively denuded of natural resources is summed up by Cosini thus:

> [M]y mind fills with a vision of when the English first arrived and the land was fat and full of trees and game. Had the loss begun at this time? ... From that time on, each succeeding generation found something new they could quarry to survive. First the emu disappeared, then the tigers, then the many different fishes and seals and whales and their rainbows became rare, then the rivers were stilled under dams, then the trees, and then the scallops and the abalone and the crayfish became few and were in consequence no longer the food of the poor but the waste of the rich. I wonder whether the memory of loss was carried with those who had originally peopled this land. Had it begun with them fighting for the land because, although they knew they belonged to the land, the English had an idea that a single man could own land for his own advancement? Had it begun with this idea of the land not as a source of knowledge but as a source of wealth? ... Or was it something the convicts and blackfellas shared, that divided them yet might one day bring them all together? (257–8)

The key themes here are: the loss of food and the destruction of the natural environment; the memory of that loss; and the shift in conceptual paradigms from the land as a public collective source of knowledge to a private individual's source of materialist riches. Cosini's comment describes what Alfred Crosby calls "ecological imperialism", the process by which European colonists conquered first the Americas, and subsequently Australia and New Zealand, by imposing not only foreign peoples and philosophies, but also animals, plants and ideas for exploiting the natural environment for commercial profit.[19] The "triumph"

---

19  Alfred W. Crosby, *Ecological Imperialism: The Biological Expansion of Europe, 900–1900* (Cambridge: Cambridge University Press, 1993).

of European colonists in these territories over their indigenous populations, as Graham Huggan and Helen Tiffin point out, was effected through environmental, and hence cultural, derangement premised on both ontological and epistemological differences about what it is to be human and animal: "The ultimate irony of this hegemonic triumph is that in the twenty-first century the West is increasingly attempting to re-think and re-capture practices generated through the very respect for animals and nature that the early settlers so righteously scorned".[20] Flanagan's fiction should be viewed as participating in this trend. Cosini's lament for a lost world above is shared by Gould in Flanagan's later novel, in which the convict forger expresses admiration for "patriot" Indigenous Tasmanians who were "free & noble" but who eventually gave up "their nation" in the expectation that they would be looked after by the government, which of course they were not (216, 219). I have written elsewhere of Gould's lament for a fading premodern society destroyed by the imperialist, rationalist culture to which Gould belongs.[21] Indeed, magical realism, as Michael Valdez Moses notes, often "expresses the nostalgia of global modernity for the traditional worlds it has vanquished and subsumed". The magical realist novel, he adds, is a "sentimental" fiction that encourages "readers to indulge in a nostalgic longing for and an imaginary return to a world that is past, or passing away".[22]

The "magical" elements in Flanagan's fiction, however, are much more than simply sentimental nostalgia, as they frequently contain an environmental ethic that highlights the connection to the land by both Indigenous Tasmanians and the white underclass, the combination of which creates the state's unique culture, in Flanagan's view. For this reason, his kind of magical realism is different to the type of magical realism we see in, say, Alexis Wright's *Carpentaria*, or Guatemalan Miguel Ángel Asturias' canonical magical realist work, *Men of Maize* (1949).[23] Both of these novels explore what happens to native peoples – Indigenous Australians and Guatemalans, respectively – when they lose their links to the land, community and ancestral customs. Wright's book is set in the Gulf Country of northern Australia in the fictitious town of Desperance, where the local Indigenous population battles racist white government officials, the judiciary and the police, as well as a multinational mining company that rides roughshod over Indigenous land rights. Asturias' novel is set among fields of maize and sugarcane tended by Guatemalan Indian farmers who battle the *Mestizos*, the descendants of the Spanish colonists. Critically, these two works focus on the Indigenous population. Flanagan's novels, by contrast, depict an interconnection between both the Indigenous and the oppressed colonial underclass, and their mutual bonds with the land. Vivian Smith is correct to identify a distinctly Australian strain of magical realism in *Death of a River Guide*, which is characterised by a conventional strand in white Australian writing that contains embellished, "amazing" or "tall" stories, or what is often called a yarn in the domestic vernacular.[24] Peter Carey's magical realist novel *Illywhacker* (1985) is another example of this. Yet the type of magical realism in Flanagan's fiction is additionally intertwined with a biocentric view of the world,

---

20   Graham Huggan and Helen Tiffin, *Postcolonial Ecocriticism: Literature, Animals, Environment* (London: Routledge, 2010), 11.
21   Ben Holgate, "'The impossibility of knowing': Developing Magical Realism's Irony in *Gould's Book of Fish*", *JASAL: Journal of the Association for the Study of Australian Literature* 14, no. 5 (2014). http://bit.ly/2wZryiK.
22   Michael Valdez Moses, "Magical Realism at World's End," *Literary Imagination* 3, no. 1 (2001): 105–6.
23   Miguel Ángel Asturias, *Men of Maize*, trans. Gerald Martin (London: Verso, 1988).
24   Vivian Smith, "Down the Franklin", *Times Literary Supplement*, 3 October 1997, 21.

in which humanity is but one element of the universe, and not the centre of it. It is this facet that sets his work apart from white, anthropocentric Australian fiction. His use of Tasmania's south-west wilderness as a setting for *Death of a River Guide* and *Gould's Book of Fish* is fundamental to this philosophy.

Like magical realism, the meaning of ecocriticism as a literary term has been subject to much debate. For a basic definition I shall borrow Cheryll Glotfelty's description: that is, "the study of the relationship between literature and the physical environment" that "takes an earth-centred approach to literary studies".[25] Ecocriticism's biocentric view of the world, in which humans are just one part of the entire ecosphere, contrasts with an anthropocentric view, in which humans are placed at the centre of the physical universe. The difference between the two reflects attempts by many historians and scientists over recent decades to recognise that humans, since the industrial age, have become a geological agent on the planet, prompting the idea to call this new geological age the Anthropocene era. As Dipesh Chakrabarty points out, the post-industrial effect of human-made global warming has led to "the collapse of the age-old humanist distinction between natural history and human history".[26] In other words, industrialised humans impact the environment such that the natural world constantly changes as a result; humans are no longer separate from the once stable (in relative terms) environment. Anthropocentrism, however, underpins much traditional literary criticism and fictional realism. More broadly, anthropocentrism provided a philosophical foundation for the rationalist, scientific ideals of the European Enlightenment, as well as the justification for the rapid expansion of European colonialism around the globe in the eighteenth and nineteenth centuries. In a postcolonial context, and therefore for much magical realist fiction, ecocriticism ought to play a vital role. As Huggan and Tiffin argue, the history of European conquest involved not only a massive environmental impact through the introduction of foreign peoples, plants and animals, but also often the treatment of the colonised peoples as being "part of nature", sometimes even as animals.[27] European colonialism's capitalistic structure and concomitant insatiable appetite for commercial profit resulted in significant environmental damage to colonised territories through changes to land use, in particular agriculture, mining and the general exploitation of natural resources.

While there is debate about the nature and primary purpose of environmental literary criticism, the approach I am advocating takes as its basic premise the connection between human culture and the physical world, and the reflexive relationship between the two; in other words, how humans affect the physical world and vice versa. Or, as Glotfelty says, ecocriticism at a theoretical level "negotiates between the human and the nonhuman".[28] Furthermore, ecocriticism is not so much a method, but more "an attitude, an angle of vision, and a mode of critique".[29] It is within this framework that I propose magical realism

---

25  Cheryll Glotfelty, "Introduction: Literary Studies in an Age of Environmental Crisis", in *The Ecocriticism Reader: Landmarks of Literary Ecology*, ed. Cheryll Glotfelty and Harold Fromm (Athens: University of Georgia Press, 1996), xviii.
26  Dipesh Chakrabarty, "The Climate of History: Four Theses," *Critical Inquiry* 35, no. 2 (Winter 2009): 201.
27  Huggan and Tiffin, *Postcolonial Ecocriticism*, 6.
28  Glotfelty, "Introduction", xix.
29  Henry Harrington and John Tallmadge, "Introduction", in *Reading Under the Sign of Nature: New Essays in Criticism*, ed. John Tallmadge and Henry Harrington (Salt Lake City: University of Utah Press, 2000), ix.

ought to be considered in terms of its relationship with environmental literary criticism. Magical realism, as Simal says, "concurs with environmentalism in its common disclosure of the interconnectedness of all ecosystems".[30] It follows, therefore, that the narrative mode offers writers a way in which to express this interconnectedness through imaginative forms. Magical realism's capacity for breaking down binaries, for creating a third space between the seemingly real and the unreal, enables a biocentric view of the world in which humans are presented as merely part of the biosphere and not at the heart of it.

Environmental destruction of the pristine wilderness as a result of colonisation and the rapacious appetite of Western capitalism for natural resources is foregrounded in both *Death of a River Guide* and *Gould's Book of Fish*. Cosini has visions in which his father, Harry, and Harry's workmates earn a living as "piners", harvesting by hand the giant Huon pine trees on the banks of the Gordon and Franklin rivers in the remote south-west, which even today is largely inaccessible by road. Interestingly, Flanagan does not depict the piners as wreaking havoc on the environment, given that they harvest selectively, cut trees by hand, and float the logs downriver without cargo boats. Piners as environmentalists is a thesis Flanagan laid out as a young writer, before publishing fiction, in his debut book, a historical work, titled *A Terrible Beauty: History of the Gordon River Country* (1985). In *Death of a River Guide*, Harry and his mates, in the mid-twentieth century:

> talked of how there was no money left in the game, of how they were the last pining gang on the rivers; talked of how it was all changing, of how not only the river people but the rivers themselves were doomed, to be damned forever under vast new hydroelectric schemes and already there was bush work to be had cutting exploration tracks for the Hydro-electric Commission's surveyors and geologists and hydrologists. (93)

The reference is to the Tasmanian government's controversial plan in the early 1980s to dam the Franklin River in order to generate hydro-electric power, which provoked a nationwide environmental public protest and which was only scuppered by the election in 1983 of a Labor federal government that prevented the project from proceeding.[31] The twentieth-century piners are the working descendants of the nineteenth-century convicts, who were forced to log the Huon pines while incarcerated on the penal settlement of Sarah Island in Macquarie Harbour. Cosini's forebear Ned Quade was one of those piner-convicts. Through this lineage Flanagan depicts the Tasmanian white underclass living in harmony with the natural environment. Critically, Harry's Aunt Ellie, who, despite her vehement and socially conscious denials that their family had Indigenous heritage (202), would nevertheless teach her nephew how to forage food from the bush and employ bush medicinal remedies. Above all, she instructs him, "they had to look after the land for the land was the spirit" (203). In other words, the Harry–Aunt Ellie relationship provides Cosini with a direct link to his family's convict and Indigenous pasts, both of which connect to the land.

---

30  Simal, "Of a Magical Nature", 213.
31  On the campaign to save the Franklin River, see two of Flanagan's essays in *And what do you do, Mr Gable?*: "It's Peter Dom" (23–31), about wilderness photographer Peter Dombrovskis, whose iconic images capture the Franklin's majestic beauty; and "Metamorphosis" (153–67), about the campaign figurehead and subsequent Greens politician Bob Brown.

Cosini has a natural affinity with the land, that emanates from his sporadic professional work as a guide for eco-tourists rafting down the Franklin River. Importantly, Cosini's perception of the south-west wilderness is a biocentric one, which contrasts with the anthropocentric views of the (mostly) urban tourists whose lives he is responsible for. Cosini recalls how, as a youth in the 1970s, when the river was largely "unknown", he saw "the strange and beautiful river" as "a whole, not as a collection of named sites that could be reduced to a series of photographs". Cosini feels that by "splitting the whole into little bits with silly names", the environmentalists and political activists had "stolen away" something of "the river's soul" (252). In other words, Cosini values the Franklin River for its intrinsic worth, or, as he puts it, "for its own sake", rather than as a natural feature that has been named, classified and effectively partitioned. Moreover, Cosini does not acquire an understanding of the river, geology, plants or animals through common or scientific names, but through "feelings", "intuitions" and the "spirit" of what these things are (121). By comparison, the tourist rafters are "frightened" and "terrified" by the river and the surrounding "vast unpeopled mountain ranges". Given that these urban dwellers' "only measure was man", they feel alienated from "this world in which the only measure was things that man had not made" (81). Moreover, the novel depicts humans as being anatomically part of the physical world, inseparable from it. Cosini recalls being born in fluid – the "translucent egg" within his mother's womb (1) – and dies underwater, in the torrential Franklin River, after falling and becoming wedged between submerged rocks. As Laura A. White says, by placing Cosini's immobilised body underwater, the novel allows him to see through new eyes, challenging received understandings of vision and exploring "a multiplicity of times and places through an interplay of body and mind".[32] In addition, Cosini is overwhelmed by the smell of the soil during heavy rains, "of earth eroding, of peat washing away" (14). Just as Cosini's fate is to merge physically with the natural world in death, so, too, is it the fate of his paternal grandfather, named Boy, who is a trapper in Tasmania's highlands. Harry finds his dead father caught under "a rotten myrtle limb" (71), his face, hands and arms partly eaten by Tasmanian devils (73). After burying his father under a stringybark, Harry returns weeks later to see the gumtree blooming "into massive lemon-coloured blossom", which he finds "miraculous" (74).

Flanagan takes this notion of humans being fused with the natural world a step further in *Gould's Book of Fish*, by breaking down the distinction between human and animal on multiple levels. This is most apparent in the metamorphosis of Gould into a weedy seadragon, the same fish into which Sid Hammet turns in the fictional present, two centuries later. In the opening narrative, Hammet stands by an aquarium in the Hobart home of his Vietnamese friend, Lau Phu Hung. "I was falling, tumbling, passing through glass and through water into that seadragon's eye while that seadragon was passing into me", says Hammet (38). Towards the end of the novel, Gould escapes execution by colonial soldiers by falling into the water at Macquarie Harbour and metamorphoses into a weedy seadragon. But he is a fish with miraculous longevity, as Gould the seadragon is eventually caught by Mr Hung for his aquarium, which is where Gould first sees Hammet. "Sid Hammet stares at me for too long", says Gould the fish. "I shall be you. I am ascending … passing through glass & air into his sad eyes" (402). The device is a typical

---

32  Laura A. White, "Submerging the Imperial Eye: Affective Narration as Environmentalist Intervention in Richard Flanagan's *Death of a River Guide*", *The Journal of Commonwealth Literature* 47, no. 2 (June 2012): 272.

magical realist conceit in that it disrupts conventional notions about time and place, and dismantles barriers, in this case between human and non-human. The novel's piscatorial theme is reinforced by Gould's various attempts to paint portraits of different human characters, which turn out to be portraits of different native fish (hence the book's title): for example, the Surgeon, who represents a corrupted version of the Enlightenment's scientific rationalism, becomes a porcupine fish (138); Sarah Island penal colony's Commandant, who is insane and possessed by extreme imperialist delusions of dictatorial grandeur, resembles a stargazer fish (173); and Gould's Indigenous lover, Twopenny Sal, appears as a striped cowfish (273).

By dissolving the boundaries between human and animal, *Gould's Book of Fish* dismantles what may be termed a "species boundary", in the sense of "a strict dividing line" between what is human and what is animal.[33] In this respect, the novel exhibits a quintessential aspect of magical realist fiction, in that it blurs the distinction between what is real and unreal and creates an intersection between the two, resulting in what critics commonly refer to as a "third space". This space is hybrid in nature because of "the purely natural way in which abnormal, experientially impossible (and empirically unverifiable) events take place", says Rawdon Wilson.[34] In addition, the novel transitions on this point from ecocriticism to zoocriticism, which is concerned with the rights and representation of animals.[35] Critically, Gould as a fish retains full consciousness and the ability to communicate with humans. Indeed, he is still in command of his rational faculties and is self-aware of his metamorphosis from human to animal, as well as the interrelationship between himself and his new fishy friends. "I live now in a perfect solitude", reveals Gould the fish. "We fish keep company it is true, but our thoughts are our own & utterly incommunicable. Our thoughts deepen & we understand each other with a complete profundity only those unburdened by speech & its complications could understand", he adds, reinforcing the notion that fish are sentient beings. "It is then untrue that we neither think nor feel. Indeed, apart from eating & swimming, it is all we have to occupy our minds" (397). The text here represents reality from a biocentric point of view – that is, from a fish's and not a human's perspective – thereby inverting the anthropocentric positioning of much literature on the eighteenth-century colonisation of Australia. Ultimately, the natural world attains a higher status in the hierarchy of existence than humans do. In this sense *Gould's Book of Fish*, as does *Death of a River Guide*, demonstrates an environmental orientation, because the non-human environment is used as a framing device and to suggest that human history is implicated in natural history. Furthermore, Flanagan's texts have an additional ethical orientation because they highlight that humans are accountable for the natural environment, which has just as legitimate an interest in existence as humans do.[36] A clue to this environmental philosophy appears when Gould finds a copy of Pliny the Elder's *Natural History* among the Surgeon's books. "In Pliny's observations I discovered that man, far from being central in this life, lived in a parlous world beyond his knowledge", reflects Gould (131). In other words, through the

---

33  Huggan and Tiffin, *Postcolonial Ecocriticism*, 139, footnote 2.
34  Rawdon Wilson, "Metamorphosis of Fictional Space," in *Magical Realism: Theory, History, Community*, ed. Lois Parkinson Zamora and Wendy B. Faris (Durham, NC: Duke University Press, 1995), 220.
35  Huggan and Tiffin, *Postcolonial Ecocriticism*, 18.
36  Lawrence Buell, *The Environmental Imagination: Thoreau, Nature Writing, and the Formation of American Culture* (Cambridge, MA: Belknap Press of Harvard University Press, 1995), 7.

ancient Roman naturalist's writings, Gould realises that humanity is not the centre of the universe – contrary to the dominant Enlightenment thinking of the day – but rather a confused element among all existing things. It is a realisation that eventually manifests in Gould metamorphosing from human to fish.

In a broader context, the fish in *Gould's Book of Fish* are a subset of the aquatic imagery that permeates not only this novel, but also *Death of a River Guide*, in which Cosini tells his life story while he slowly drowns underwater. By contrast, Gould is incarcerated for about eighteen months in a tidal cell carved into rock on Sarah Island, in which the water rises at high tide. He writes much of his notebook in cuttlefish ink and other aquatic materials that he can lay his hands on. The novel's central location, Sarah Island, is a tiny rock surrounded by water, initially the immense Macquarie Harbour at the edge of the southwest wilderness, and beyond that the Indian Ocean to the west and the vast Southern Ocean to the south. Similarly, the main location of *Death of a River Guide*, the Franklin River, also consists of water, becoming increasingly so as the narrative progresses and the river waters rise following days of torrential rain.

This maritime and aquatic imagery, I suggest, underscores the notion of Tasmania as an isolated island in these two Tasmanian-based novels. I say isolated because the island state is geographically remote, situated at the southern end of a continent positioned in the southern hemisphere, and remote from a nineteenth-century European viewpoint, given that convicts and free settlers travelled halfway across the world to arrive there. Tasmania as an island, however, also resonates as a literary device, for it is often within islands that unique ideas and cultures are allowed to emerge and percolate, protected from competing factors that might otherwise exist in more central, or continental, locations. "Islands have been useful to writers because their distinctive geographical formations have supplied narrative settings that isolate ideas," says Jean Arnold. This, of course, is the central theme I have tried to highlight in this chapter, in that Flanagan utilises magical realist techniques, infused with an environmental perspective, to portray a culture unique to Tasmania in which Indigenous and non-Indigenous peoples have strong ties to the land. As Arnold adds: "Because literary islands form settings for writers' imagined solutions to cultural or perceptual problems, these islands also have the power to reveal the unconscious concerns of the culture in which the writer lives and from which the literature arises".[37] Furthermore, the literary trope of the island has additional resonance in a colonial context, as Elizabeth McMahon says, because it is frequently presented as "a perfect object of control", in which such control is "often revealed as being unethical, solipsistic, even theomaniacal". Flanagan parodies this theme through the deranged, despotic Commandant in *Gould's Book of Fish*, who unsuccessfully attempts to transform the tiny Sarah Island convict gaol into a sovereign nation like Venice. Yet the novel also subverts the notion of control through the Commandant's eventual demise and the Europeans' thwarted attempts to tame – in an agricultural and industrial sense – Tasmania's wilderness. In addition, the literary island incorporates "a reflexive counter-image" in that the reader anticipates both this darker side of colonial-like control and "a site of escape and luxury." In other words, the notion of an island paradise is "matched by an equal measure of ugliness, evil and subjugation".[38] The

---

37  Jean Arnold, "Mapping Island Mindscapes: The Literary and Cultural Uses of a Geographical Formation", in *Reading Under the Sign of Nature*, ed. John Tallmadge and Henry Harrington (Salt Lake City: University of Utah Press, 2000), 24.
38  Elizabeth McMahon, *Islands, Identity and the Literary Imagination* (London: Anthem Press, 2016), 5, 6.

magical realism in Flanagan's fiction plays with this inherent counterpoint by examining the historical, social and racial hidden realities of Tasmania, and juxtaposing them against the idealised, or literally white-washed, "settler" views.

Flanagan's island of Tasmania takes on a special distinctiveness because much of its landmass consists of wilderness. And it is in this wilderness, in the south-west of the state, that the author locates *Death of a River Guide* and *Gould's Book of Fish*. The word wilderness is derived from the Anglo-Saxon "wilddeoren", in which the "deoren", or beasts, dwelt beyond the boundaries of cultivation.[39] Flanagan plays with this European concept of wilderness by portraying the south-west as an area that defies not only cultivation by the Europeans, but also habitation. By contrast, however, Indigenous Tasmanians both survive and thrive in the south-west, enjoying a nomadic lifestyle in harmony with the natural environment, despite its ruggedness. In other words, in European eyes, especially those of the nineteenth-century colonists, south-west Tasmania represents a remote wilderness within a remote island. This attitude of separateness reflects what Christopher Hitt identifies as the dominant traditional European element of the "sublime", the "humbling fear" induced by giant mountains, impenetrable forests, deep oceans and so on. Yet the European notion of the sublime, fuelled by Romanticism, is contradictory because it also involves an "ennobling validation" of nature. Instead, Hitt advocates a modified notion of an "ecological sublime", one that blends both humility and ennoblement, and which expresses a "universal" feeling of "human beings' encounters with a nonhuman world whose power ultimately exceeds theirs".[40] Flanagan's fiction similarly exhorts this concept of an ecological sublime. Moreover, as Greg Garrard says, the idea of wilderness is central to ecocriticism's challenge to the status quo of literary and cultural studies, because it does not share the mainly social concerns of the traditional humanities. Wilderness has "an almost sacramental value" that is "founded in an attitude of reverence and humility".[41] Indeed, Flanagan's fiction often seems to prioritise wilderness in the hierarchy of living things over humans.

In *Gould's Book of Fish*, Tasmania – or Van Diemen's Land as it was known during colonisation – is presented as "that island to which only the worst of all convicts were banished" (19), and Sarah Island as "the most dreaded place of punishment in the entire British Empire" between 1820 and 1832 (20). Moreover, the south-west wilderness which cuts off Sarah Island and the surrounding Macquarie Harbour from the cultivated farmlands of the northern, eastern and southern regions of Tasmania, is portrayed as "impenetrable wild lands" and "uncharted country" (19). When Gould escapes from the Sarah Island jail, he initially views the south-west with European eyes, thinking of it as a "crumpled labyrinth of cascades & rainforest & ravines & limestone tiers" that are beyond his comprehension. He does, however, follow his intuition, aiming to reach the mountain Frenchman's Cap, which he regards in symbolic terms as representing "the Frenchman's cap of liberty" (317). In other words, the south-west mountain is regarded in terms of liberty rather than bondage. Along the way, Gould meets up with his old convict friend Capois Death, who has also escaped, but Capois is unable to find sanctuary in the wilderness and meets his own death through being speared by two Indigenous men

---

39  Greg Garrard, *Ecocriticism* (London: Routledge, 2004), 60.
40  Christopher Hitt, "Toward an Ecological Sublime", *New Literary History* 30, no. 3 (Summer 1999), 606, 609–10.
41  Garrard, *Ecocriticism*, 59.

(321). Gould, on the other hand, ultimately does find a kind of spiritual redemption in the wilderness, which is depicted in a magical realist manner on two different levels. First, after dancing around the funeral pyre with Twopenny Sal, smeared with red ochre, thereby achieving a sort of transcendental awareness, Gould burns his notebook on the fire. While doing so, he realises that his notebook, which provides the metafictional framework for Flanagan's novel, does not end. Each time he thinks he has come to the last page, he finds there are "several more chapters". Importantly, upon throwing his notebook on the fire he sees on one page "a picture of a freshwater crayfish" (337). The act of burning his notebook, which contains his personalised record of life in the penal colony, results in an epiphany, as Gould comes to believe the literature of the past contains "lies", and that he is a kind of everyman, being both the hangman and the convict hanged, both the "flagellator" and the convict whipped, both the violent sealer and the Indigenous woman raped by the sealer (338). Gould's story, in other words, is representative of the underclass and the oppressed in colonial Tasmania. The second level of magical realist treatment occurs soon after the funeral pyre, when Gould stumbles across a freshwater crayfish while traipsing through the south-west. "It was shedding its carapace & emerging newer & larger, yet still the same", says Gould, in a phrase that reflects his own transition from European convict to indigenous resident: "I looked at the translucent shell the crayfish was abandoning & marvelled at its metamorphosis, at the magical power it had to appear one thing & become another, its ability to leave behind an image of itself that was no longer itself" (341). Gould's perception of the physical metamorphosis of the crayfish echoes his own spiritual metamorphosis in the wilderness and presages his own physical metamorphosis from human to fish at the end of the novel.

In *Death of a River Guide*, the urban tourist rafters view the Franklin River wilderness as a frightening threat, in contrast to Cosini's affinity with the natural environment. Just as Gould ultimately merges physically with the natural world, so too does Cosini. After successfully – albeit dangerously and recklessly – navigating a huge rapid which the tourists in his boat barely survive, Cosini is exultant. "He feels as if he is the rainforest and the river and the rapid" (299). Again, Flanagan uses the narrative technique of presaging the fate that is to befall his protagonist. After being wedged between submerged rocks and receiving the visions that enable him to understand not only his own life, but also that of his family and forebears, Cosini, on the point of death, feels himself merge with the natural world around him: "I am no longer sure if I am me, or me the river or the river me" (321). What both *Death of a River Guide* and *Gould's Book of Fish* illustrate in having their protagonists become one with the environment is how Flanagan's distinctive type of magical realism contains an ecocritical element that underpins his use of the narrative mode.

In conclusion, these two novels illustrate how Flanagan employs magical realist elements that are not only distinctively Australian – or even, arguably, Tasmanian – in their style, content and setting, but which also correlate with a long tradition of environmental writing in magical realist fiction. Magical realism, as I have shown, is notable for its capacity to depict a third space that exists at the intersection of the magical and the real, or the unreal and the real. It is within this third space that the intersection between humankind and the environment can also become apparent, shifting from an anthropocentric worldview, which is the traditional premise of European philosophy, to a biocentric one, which underpins an Indigenous Australian outlook. Flanagan's fiction portrays the link between magical realism and environmental literature largely through his use of Tasmania's south-west wilderness as a metaphorical and geographically literal site for spiritual redemption. William Buelow Gould flees into the wilderness to escape penal servitude and to discover a spiritual affinity with both the Indigenous population and the natural environment. Aljaz Cosini physically merges with the wilderness by drowning in the Franklin River and, in doing so, uncovers through magical visions his own personal lineage with Indigenous forebears. Flanagan's fiction not only highlights why scholarly conceptions of magical realism as a narrative mode may be modified and broadened by embracing literature from the antipodes and from beyond the orthodox world "canon"; his work is also instructive of how magical realism can have a high correlation with environmental literature. As the twenty-first century unfolds, bringing with it rising nationalist chauvinism and intolerance for views of the "other", as well as critical imbalances to the global environment, such literary explorations ought to gain in importance and value.

## References

Adams, Jenni. *Magic Realism in Holocaust Literature: Troping the Traumatic Real*. Basingstoke, UK: Palgrave Macmillan, 2011.
Arnold, Jean. "Mapping Island Mindscapes: The Literary and Cultural Uses of a Geographical Formation". In *Reading Under the Sign of Nature*, edited by John Tallmadge and Henry Harrington. Salt Lake City: University of Utah Press, 2000, 24–35.
Asturias, Miguel Ángel. *Men of Maize*. Translated by Gerald Martin. London: Verso, 1988.
Bényei, Tamás. "Rereading 'Magic Realism'". *Hungarian Journal of English and American Studies* 3, no. 1 (1997): 149–79.
Buell, Lawrence. *The Environmental Imagination: Thoreau, Nature Writing, and the Formation of American Culture*. Cambridge, MA: Belknap Press of Harvard University Press, 1995.
Chakrabarty, Dipesh. "The Climate of History: Four Theses." *Critical Inquiry* 35, no. 2 (Winter 2009): 197–222.
Crosby, Alfred W. *Ecological Imperialism: The Biological Expansion of Europe, 900–1900*. Cambridge: Cambridge University Press, 1993.
Delrez, Marc. "Nationalism, Reconciliation, and the Cultural Genealogy of Magic in Richard Flanagan's *Death of a River Guide*". *The Journal of Commonwealth Literature* 42, no. 1 (2007): 117–29.
Derrida, Jacques. "The Law of Genre". In *Acts of Literature*. Edited by Derek Attridge. Translated by Avital Ronell. London: Routledge, 1992, 227–31.
Faris, Wendy B. "Scheherazade's Children: Magical Realism and Postmodern Fiction". In *Magical Realism: Theory, History, Community*, edited by Lois Parkinson Zamora and Wendy B. Faris. Durham, NC: Duke University Press, 1995, 163–90.
Flanagan, Richard. *And what do you do, Mr Gable?* Sydney: Vintage, 2011.
——. *Gould's Book of Fish*. (2001) New York: Grove, 2002.
——. *The Sound of One Hand Clapping*. Sydney: Macmillan, 1997.
——. *Death of a River Guide*. (1994) New York: Grove, 2002.
Fowler, Alastair. *Kinds of Literature: An Introduction to the Theory of Genres and Modes*. Oxford: Clarendon Press, 1982.
Garrard, Greg. *Ecocriticism*. London: Routledge, 2004.
Glotfelty, Cheryll. "Introduction: Literary Studies in an Age of Environmental Crisis". In *The Ecocriticism Reader: Landmarks of Literary Ecology*, edited by Cheryll Glotfelty and Harold Fromm. Athens: University of Georgia Press, 1996, xv–xxxvii.
Harrington, Henry and John Tallmadge. "Introduction". In *Reading Under the Sign of Nature: New Essays in Criticism*, edited by John Tallmadge and Henry Harrington. Salt Lake City: University of Utah Press, 2000, ix–xv.

Hegerfeldt, Anne. *Lies that Tell the Truth: Magic Realism Seen through Contemporary Fiction from Britain*. Amsterdam: Rodopi, 2005.

Hitt, Christopher. "Toward an Ecological Sublime". *New Literary History* 30, no. 3 (Summer 1999): 603–23.

Holgate, Ben. "'The Impossibility of Knowing': Developing Magical Realism's Irony in *Gould's Book of Fish*". *JASAL: Journal of the Association for the Study of Australian Literature* 14, no. 5 (2014). http://bit.ly/2wZryiK.

Huggan, Graham and Helen Tiffin. *Postcolonial Ecocriticism: Literature, Animals, Environment*. London: Routledge, 2010.

Ihimaera, Witi. *The Whale Rider*. Auckland: Heinemann, 1987.

McMahon, Elizabeth. *Islands, Identity and the Literary Imagination*. London: Anthem Press, 2016.

Menton, Seymour. *Magic Realism Rediscovered, 1918–1981*. Philadelphia: Art Alliance Press, 1983.

Moses, Michael Valdez. "Magical Realism at World's End". *Literary Imagination* 3, no. 1 (2001): 105–33.

Simal, Begoña. "Of a Magical Nature: The Environmental Unconscious". In *Uncertain Mirrors: Magical Realisms in US Ethnic Literature*, edited by Jesús Benito, Ana Ma Manzanas and Begoña Simal. Amsterdam: Rodopi, 2009, 193–237.

Slemon, Stephen. "Magic Realism as Postcolonial Discourse". In *Magical Realism: Theory, History, Community*, edited by Lois Parkinson Zamora and Wendy B. Faris. Durham, NC: Duke University Press, 1995, 407–26.

Smith, Vivian. "Down the Franklin". *Times Literary Supplement*, 3 October 1997, 21.

White, Laura A. "Submerging the Imperial Eye: Affective Narration as Environmentalist Intervention in Richard Flanagan's *Death of a River Guide*". *The Journal of Commonwealth Literature* 47, no. 2 (June 2012): 265–79.

Wilson, Rawdon. "Metamorphosis of Fictional Space". In *Magical Realism: Theory, History, Community*, edited by Lois Parkinson Zamora and Wendy B. Faris. Durham, NC: Duke University Press, 1995, 209–33.

Wright, Alexis. *Carpentaria*. Artarmon, NSW: Giramondo, 2006.

# 3
# "Smashing and singing and sobbing and howling": Sound and Richard Flanagan's Tasmania

*Joseph Cummins*

Of Richard Flanagan's six novels, four are explicitly concerned with Tasmania and smaller surrounding islands. Beginning with *Death of a River Guide* (1994) and followed by *The Sound of One Hand Clapping* (1997), *Gould's Book of Fish: A Novel in Twelve Fish* (2001) and *Wanting* (2008), Flanagan could be called Australia's greatest author of Tasmania. These award-winning novels weave together concerns with Tasmania's rich and often violent histories of convictism, colonialism, global migration, and labour. Underpinning this is a depiction of island landscapes – colonial and urban Hobart, the Tasmanian wilderness, the Franklin and Pieman rivers, and Sarah and Flinders islands.

The title of this chapter is the opening line of a scene from early in Flanagan's second novel, *The Sound of One Hand Clapping*. This work traces the experiences of Sonja Buloh, her father Bojan, and her mother Maria, Slovenian migrants to Tasmania in the 1950s. Moving between the postwar years and the narrative present (the 1990s), the novel describes Bojan and Sonja's struggle to cope with the suicide of Maria, a young woman unable to overcome both the trauma of World War Two and the isolation of her new life in Tasmania. Bojan, working as a labourer on state infrastructure schemes in Tasmania's wilderness, and Sonja, who experiences abuse and abandonment, battle loneliness and self-degradation. The birth of Sonja's baby eventually brings father and daughter closer together.

The phrase "[s]mashing and singing and sobbing and howling"[1] signifies a group of sounds – a soundscape – heard by Sonja as she recalls her childhood, soon after the death of her mother. At the same time, these sounds are in the present of the novel, the sound of rain beating on the roof of a motel room in Tasmania. The sounds resonate across time, connecting the past and the present, operating in a similar way to T.S. Eliot's "objective correlative"[2] or Judith Wright's "outer equivalent for an inner reality".[3] Sound links Sonja's past and present emotional states with her memories, and reflects these in the surrounding natural environment. The sounds that Sonja hears, the "smashing and singing and sobbing and howling", are highly emotive, evocative of experiential extremes.

---

[1] Richard Flanagan, *The Sound of One Hand Clapping* (Sydney: Macmillan, 1997), 47. All subsequent references are to this edition and appear in parentheses in the text.
[2] T.S. Eliot, *The Sacred Wood: Essays on Poetry and Criticism* (London: Methuen, 1950), 93.
[3] Judith Wright, *Preoccupations in Australian Poetry* (Melbourne: Oxford University Press, 1965), xi.

The passage also features other sounds – "the noise of the chill wind" and "the sound of the rain that beat upon the motel room's aluminum window with a strange and insistent rhythm; sweeping, scratching, receding, as if hoping to gain entry, then despairing and leaving" (47). Flanagan's novelistic Tasmania has a sonorous texture: it is an island as much suffused with soundscapes of the natural world as it is with songs, screams and noise.

This chapter's contribution to the critical discourse surrounding Flanagan's Tasmanian novels is to examine the work of sound in creating the space of the island. This is not physical sound but what I call "imagined sound". Drawing from other work I have undertaken on sound in Australian literature and music, the concept of "imagined sound" is foundational to this chapter.[4] It is *imagined* sound because it is created by descriptive language, not through physical vibration. The idea, in part, emerges from Benedict Anderson's foundational study of nationalism, *Imagined Communities* (1983). Discussing the role of song in the formation of the nation, Anderson says, "[n]othing connects us all but imagined sound".[5] Imagined sound operates in two ways: it organises and interpolates the listener into the nation, and it bypasses the problems of both space and time, enabling listeners from across a vast space simultaneously to become one.[6] Imagined sound emphasises the importance of the imagination in the formation of spaces.

In contrast to thinking about sight, the focus on sound can offer new insights into how space and time are remapped and reconfigured in a different sensual harmony. Concentrating on sound is also a postcolonial move away from colonial and what Martin Jay calls "ocularcentric" ways of knowing and controlling the world through sight.[7] Through the concept of imagined sound, the island space-time of Flanagan's novels can be explored through the kinds of sounds that feature in his representations. How do various tonalities of sound – the song, the scream and noise – create the island in these novels? How does imagined sound link with the other thematic and conceptual forces at play in the novels, such as ideas relating to the Gothic, wilderness, and the non-linearity of the haunting?

The Western colonial and postcolonial "geoimaginary" of the island is defined by a collection of real and imagined paradoxes: past/future, local/global, origin/extinction, interior/exterior.[8] I use the term geoimaginary to describe the fusion of geographic fact and literary representation.[9] The central island described by Flanagan – the one on which

---

4   Joseph Cummins, "'I turn up the volume and walk towards home': Mapping the Soundscapes of *Loaded*, in "Critical Soundings," ed. Helen Groth and Joseph Cummins, special issue, *JASAL: Journal of the Association for the Study of Australian Literature* 15, no. 1 (2015): 1–11.
5   Benedict Anderson, *Imagined Communities: Reflections on the Origin and Spread of Nationalism* (1983; London: Verso, 1991), 145.
6   Anderson, *Imagined Communities*, 6.
7   Martin Jay, *Downcast Eyes: The Denigration of Vision in Twentieth-Century French Thought* (Berkeley: University of California Press, 1993). This imperative has been taken up by Paul Carter in *The Road to Botany Bay: An Essay in Spatial History* (London: Faber, 1987) and *The Sound in Between: Voice, Space, Performance* (Kensington: University of New South Wales Press, 1992).
8   John Gillis, *Islands of the Mind: How the Human Imagination Created the Atlantic World* (New York: Palgrave Macmillan, 2004); Godfrey Baldacchino, "Islands: Objects of Representation", *Geografiska Annaler: Series B, Human Geography* 87, no. 4 (2005): 248; Rod Edmond and Vanessa Smith, "Editors' Introduction", in *Islands in History and Representation*, ed. Rod Edmond and Vanessa Smith (London: Routledge, 2003): 5; Elizabeth McMahon, "Encapsulated Space: The Paradise-Prison of Australia's Island Imaginary", *Southerly* 65, no. 1 (2005): 20.
9   Elizabeth McMahon discusses the concept of geoimaginary in *Islands, Identity and the Literary Imagination* (London: Anthem Press, 2016).

he was born and continues to reside – was once called Van Diemen's Land; the name was changed to Tasmania in 1856. The fact that "Tasmania is the only state which systematically set about erasing its first half-century ... under a new name, [as if] it was determined to be born again" is another statement of island contradiction: the attempt to separate from the past sits uncomfortably beside the gravity of denied origins.[10]

For a number of Flanagan's characters, Tasmania/Van Diemen's Land, and the smaller islands that surround it, are an opportunity (whether voluntary or forced) to start again. Flanagan depicts all-powerful rulers, like the enigmatic Commandant; saviours, like the Protector George Augustus Robinson and Governor John and Lady Franklin; and great imaginers, like William Buelow Gould and Charles Dickens. As Gilles Deleuze states, "Dreaming of islands ... is dreaming of pulling away ... of being lost and alone ... of starting from scratch, recreating, beginning anew".[11] Flanagan also offers an explicit counterpoint to this worldview in *Wanting*: "Towterer ... lived not on an island, but in a cosmos where time and the world were infinite, and all things were revealed by sacred stories".[12] The Indigenous Australian perspective is integral to Flanagan's island geoimaginary.

Each "sounding" of Tasmania in Flanagan's four novels is slightly different, and each opens up the possibility of remapping the space of the island. I argue that, listened to together, these island soundscapes encompass both the historical traumas that lie hidden in the past, and their re-emergence in the present. In other words, through imagined sound, Flanagan's novels are a complex *sounding* of island contradiction, of the past and the present, of origin and extinction, of "roots and routes".[13] Violence, both Tasmanian and, in *The Sound of One Hand Clapping*, continental/European, is carried and expressed by all three tonalities of imagined sound, representing and linking both colonial and postcolonial temporalities. The three tonalities – the song, the scream, and noise – are the conceptual core of my method and argument, organising the analysis that follows. In this chapter, I discuss them in order of how they construct space: from the tight articulation created by the rhythmic structures of songs through to the disorientation and complexity signalled by noise.

Songs, featured prominently in *Death of a River Guide* but also present in the other novels, structure a relation between past and present, creating resonances between past memories and present experiences, what I have elsewhere called a "transhistorical continuum".[14] Songs also reference specific traditions of understanding and feeling, particularly when they are sung by Indigenous characters. The scream, which can be both situated within a song and uncoupled and free-floating, is a sound even more evocative of colonial violence and the return of that repressed. Flanagan's preoccupation with the sound of the human voice is underscored by both songs and screams, but voices are also often woven into a harmony featuring other sounds. Noise, central to *The Sound of One Hand Clapping*, particularly with Bojan's experience of the Tasmanian wilderness, is the tonality of sound that connotes

---

10   Jim Davidson, "Tasmanian Gothic", *Meanjin* 48, no. 2 (1989): 307.
11   Gilles Deleuze, *Desert Islands and Other Texts 1953–1974* (Cambridge, MA: MIT Press, 2002), 10.
12   Richard Flanagan, *Wanting* (North Sydney: Knopf, 2008), 58. All subsequent references are to this edition and appear in parentheses in the text.
13   Baldacchino, "Islands", 248.
14   Joseph Cummins, "Echoes Between Van Diemen's Land and Tasmania: Sound and the Space of the Island in Richard Flanagan's *Death of a River Guide* and Carmel Bird's *Cape Grimm*", *The Journal of Commonwealth Literature* 49, no. 2 (2014): 258.

extreme disorientation, where the past impinges on the present in catastrophic ways. Each tonality is also often hard to isolate. For example, a song could also be a scream – both are vocal utterances connected to colonial haunting. I have divided up the imagined sounds in accordance with their configuration of space, but this complexity and interconnectedness is simply another annotation on, or notation of, the "nervous duality" of the island.[15] These different sonic registers create cartographies; they *sound* the paradoxical foundations of the island as a geoimaginary of beginnings and endings.

Three theorisations of sound underpin these tonalities. The "soundscape" was first theorised by R. Murray Schafer.[16] I draw on Barry D. Truax's definition: a soundscape is "an environment of sound (sonic environment) with emphasis on the way it is perceived and understood by the individual, or by society. It thus depends on the relationship between the individual and any such environment".[17] Truax's focus on relation through sound – between the listener, or a society of listeners, and the surrounding sounds of a space – is the basis of the soundscape as a tool of close listening in literary works. In other words, how characters or narrators listen to their surroundings, how they listen to their island environment, creates a novelistic map of space, both for characters and readers. This sonic cartography creates connections across space and time. So while a soundscape maps a specific space-time, the mnemonic nature of certain sounds also means that the past is made present, like a sonic haunting. A soundscape can be comprised of a single sound element, or a number of sounds.

A general-purpose method for thinking about sound and space, the soundscape emphasises the connections created by sound. "The refrain", Gilles Deleuze and Félix Guattari's spatio-sonorous concept, offers a more specific theorisation of the rhythmic nature of sounds and the different spatiotemporalities that are created. Discussed in *A Thousand Plateaus* (1987), the refrain, "a prism, a crystal of space-time", is a repeating melody or rhythm that captures and organises territory.[18] There are three stages or types of refrain: the first – "A child in the dark, gripped with fear, comforts himself by singing under his breath" – describes the creation of a "centre in the heart of chaos". The second stage is the formation of a home space. "Sonorous or vocal components are very important: a wall of sound, or at least a wall with some sonic bricks in it". The final stage is the "line of flight" – in Deleuze and Guattari's language "a deterritorialisation" – the emergence from controlled and defined space. "One launches forth, hazards an improvisation … One ventures from home on the thread of a tune".[19] The refrains in Flanagan's novels often explicitly take the form of songs, "rhythmic, melodious patterns, small chants, ditties", and the spaces they create align with all three stages of the refrain.[20]

Opening out of the tightly structured spatio-sonorous work of the refrain and the sonic relation of the soundscape, noise is linked to the border space "between the abstract

---

15  Baldacchino, "Islands", 248.
16  Murray R. Schafer, *The Soundscape: Our Sonic Environment and the Tuning of the World* (Rochester, NY: Destiny Books, 1977).
17  Barry D. Truax, "Soundscape", in *Handbook for Acoustic Ecology* (Vancouver: A.R.C. Publications, 1978). http://bit.ly/2sqqtLx.
18  Gilles Deleuze and Félix Guattari, *A Thousand Plateaus: Capitalism and Schizophrenia*, trans. Brian Massumi (1980; London: Continuum, 1988), 358.
19  Deleuze and Guattari, *A Thousand Plateaus*, 343–4.
20  Elizabeth Grosz, *Chaos, Territory, Art: Deleuze and the Framing of the Earth* (New York: Columbia University Press, 2008), 54.

and empirical".[21] Noise also carries a negative valence linked to excess, distortion and disorientation. The discussions of noise that have emerged from cybernetic theory, where noise denotes non-signifying matter or meaninglessness, echo the *Oxford English Dictionary* definition: noise is "a sound, especially one that is loud or unpleasant or that causes disturbance".[22] A "vexatious fault line between nuisance and purpose, labour and rest, pleasure and pain",[23] noise is a sonic materiality resonating "outside understanding and beyond culture … [in] the nonsignifying province of value-free science and the primordial wilderness of raw nature".[24] With its utility as a sonic evocation of the border between civilisation and what lies beyond – the wilderness – noise is well suited to mapping the violence and trauma within the "nervous duality" of Flanagan's islands.

The spatio-temporal resonances of these three modes of sounding Flanagan's Tasmania also harmonise with the Australian Gothic, a representational tradition that has long contended with the ghosts of Tasmania's colonial past, particularly in the novelistic (and sonic) form.[25] Alongside Marcus Clarke's *For the Term of His Natural Life* (1874), one of the defining statements of the Australian Gothic is Clarke's *Preface to the Poems of Adam Lindsay Gordon* (1876). It is in this short but influential piece – where "savage winds shout among the rock clefts", with "cockatoos … shrieking like evil souls", and "the lonely horseman … hears strange noises in the primeval forest" – that the "weird melancholy" of the Australian Gothic landscape came to be one redolent with screams and noise.[26] Despite the impact it has had on the formation of literary (and other) sonic geoimaginaries, Clarke's weird melancholy soundscape maps a mythic non-place. As a recording of Australian sound, it is one that silences and obscures the presence of Indigenous Australians and the violence of the colonial period. Flanagan's island novels are just one of the ways this deafness, "the Great Australian Silence",[27] has been addressed.

Starting with *Death of a River Guide*, Flanagan's island novels are a testament to the continued resonance of stories about frontier violence and convict suffering. Weaving together these concerns within the confines of Tasmania and surrounding islands also emphasises the importance of the island geoimaginary as the location

---

21 Douglas Kahn, *Noise, Water, Meat: A History of Sound in the Arts* (Cambridge, MA: MIT Press, 1999), 25.
22 "Noise", *Oxford English Dictionary Online*. http://bit.ly/2sk7BOL.
The approach to noise within the frame of information transmission/interruption has been taken up most productively in relation to economics by Jacques Attali in *Noise: The Political Economy of Music* (Manchester: Manchester University Press, 1985), and to visual and sound art theory by Joseph Nechvatal, *Immersion into Noise* (Ann Arbor, MI.: Open Humanities Press, 2011).
23 Bruce Buchan and David Ellison, "Introduction: Speaking to the Eye", *Cultural Studies Review* 18, no. 3 (2012): 7.
24 George Revill, "Music and the Politics of Sound: Nationalism, Citizenship, and Auditory Space", *Environment and Planning D: Society and Space* 18, no. 5 (2000): 599.
25 Davidson, "Tasmanian Gothic"; Ken Gelder and Rachael Weaver, "The Colonial Australian Gothic", in *The Anthology of Colonial Australian Gothic Fiction*, ed. Ken Gelder and Rachael Weaver (Carlton, Vic: Melbourne University Press, 2007), 7; Ken Gelder, "Australian Gothic", in *The Routledge Companion to Gothic*, ed. Catherine Spooner and Emma McEvoy (London: Routledge, 2007), 121.
26 Marcus Clarke, "Preface", in *The Poetical Works of Adam Lindsay Gordon* (1876; University of Adelaide Library, http://bit.ly/2sqAAQT).
27 W.E.H. Stanner, *After the Dreaming: The 1968 Boyer Lectures*. (Sydney: Australian Broadcasting Commission, 1969); and Jane Belfrage, "The Great Australian Silence: Inside Acoustic Space" in *The Australian Sound Design Project* (Melbourne: University of Melbourne, http://bit.ly/2LFM8rS).

where such histories and stories are rooted, but also where they continue to be placed and retold from a postcolonial frame of reference. This temporal relation between past and present manifests as sound, particularly as a vocal energy in much of the imagined sound used by Flanagan. The connection between soundscapes and the events and spaces they narrate is a temporal link, through sound, between the postcolonial present and the colonial past of each novel.

The resonance of the past in the present – and, in *Death of a River Guide*, the present in the past – is at the core of how sound creates space in Flanagan's novels. Articulating colonial/postcolonial/island spatio-temporalities (and European continental traumas), violence and suffering cannot be buried in the past and forgotten. On Flanagan's island, the past is often *heard* in the present. Mapping the overlapping conceptual territory of sound, the island, and the Gothic, such sonic hauntings disrupt the experience of linear time.[28] In Flanagan's novels, the haunting also plays out on a formal level, constantly moving backwards and forwards between different times and spaces, both on the island and beyond it. Listening to Flanagan's islands means listening to the past, but also joining in the search for what is hidden – family origins, historically suppressed violence, or literal disappearance. So while Flanagan's island novels access some of the tropes of Gothic Tasmania/Van Diemen's Land, particularly the ghostly scream, his recognition of Indigenous histories and the engagement with the wider world of postwar migrant island histories means that these hauntings resonate in excess of the Gothic landscapes heard in Marcus Clarke's formulation.

The most detailed song soundscape in Flanagan's Tasmanian novels occurs in *Death of a River Guide*. Flanagan's first novel is structured around visions experienced by river guide Aljaz Cosini as he lies trapped under the flooding waters of the Franklin River: "I have been granted visions – grand, great, wild sweeping visions. My mind rattles with them as they are born to me. And I must share them, or their magic will become as a burden".[29] In Flanagan's trademark style, the narrative jumps back and forth across time and space as Aljaz witnesses his birth, the migration of his parents from Trieste to Tasmania, and more secret events in the lives of his ancestors. In this sense, *Death of a River Guide* is the most genealogically focused of Flanagan's works, tracing familial lines of connection and suppression alongside the forces of colonialism and frontier violence.

At the core of Aljaz's discovery of his family history – here ancestry is also colonial and postcolonial history – is a soundscape in a chapter titled "Black Pearl 1828". It is one of the last visions Aljaz has before drowning at the end of the novel, and offers a powerful alignment of island origin/extinction in its depiction of the rape of his Indigenous ancestor, Black Pearl, by an unnamed sealer:

> The woman being raped begins to sing a strange and forlorn song. Her song sounds the emptiness of the beach and the ocean, echoes the distant cry of the sea eagle, calls for the return screech of the black cockatoo. "Shut up, Black Pearl," warns the sealer as he thrusts in and out. "Shut up." But Black Pearl continues to sing to her brother the blue-tongued lizard, her mother the river, her father the rocks, her sister the crayfish that smells of woman … On and on the song goes, and after the sealer pukes and then falls asleep in a stupor, the two other women

---

28 Avery Gordon, "Some Thoughts on Haunting and Futurity", *Borderlands* 10, no. 2 (2011): 1–21.
29 Richard Flanagan, *Death of a River Guide* (Ringwood, Vic: McPhee Gribble, 1994), 10. All subsequent references are to this edition and appear in parentheses in the text.

come over and lie together with Black Pearl. They lie together on the land on which they once stood with pride. As they warm each other on the beach, they join in the low song that seems to cover all the sand. The song and the sound of the waves become one and on and on it goes, and though the women are now asleep the black cockatoo and the sea eagle sing. The wind in the boobiallas passes the song on to the wind in the gums, who teaches it to the wind in the myrtles and celery top pines, who then sings it to the river and to the rocks. (315–6)

In narrative terms this scene is one of revelation. Aljaz learns that Black Pearl is in fact the matriarch of one side of his family tree: "I realise I am witness to the conception of Auntie Ellie's mother and to the genesis of all that I am" (316).

The song of Black Pearl articulates a complex local natural environment. Although Black Pearl is being raped, the song she sings forms a web with her surroundings. She "sounds the emptiness" of her location while also performing a kind of call and response with birds and plants that appear to be of totemic importance. The blue-tongue lizard, the river, the rocks, the crayfish: each is directly addressed by the song. Through the connection and relation created by sound, Black Pearl is oriented within country, tied to family and totem. Black Pearl is also joined in her song by two other women, and their song "covers" the sand, "becomes one" with the sound of the waves. When the women sleep, this sonic connection and movement extends to the black cockatoo, the sea eagle, the wind, several species of tree, and finally the river and rocks. The movement of Black Pearl's song gestures towards the multilayered and all-encompassing nature of an Indigenous Australian worldview. While I have called it a song, the event that this soundscape emerges from, the violence of sealing (a commercial aspect of colonialism) that it marks and grieves, hints at the trauma of the scream.

Flanagan's representation of Indigenous song is also an important sonic feature in *Gould's Book of Fish* and *Wanting*. Along with *Death of a River Guide*, all three novels feature Indigenous songs of lament, often precipitated by acts of violence or death at the hands of colonists. In *Gould's Book of Fish*, Billy Gould relates how, following the death of Tracker Marks, the Indigenous woman Twopenny Sal "began singing, & the children joined her, the children singing together, & she singing an octave above them, forming a concord of such exactness, that I, though I understood none of the words, felt greatly moved". Later Gould also joins Twopenny Sal in a dance,[30] the cathartic release of which recalls the function of the song of the pub band in *Death of a River Guide*. In *Wanting*, the Protector sings a hymn, "his voice quavering and shrill", in an attempt to alleviate the suffering of one of his patients: "The black women seemed to be joining in – badly, it was true – but then he realised that they had merely altered their dirge-like keening to meld with his hymn" (15). These moments of sound in three of the four island novels are important to take into account because they are concrete annotations of Indigenous Australian *presence* – these are soundings of grief and remembrance, but also attempts to form links with non-Indigenous people. The songs are echoes of island isolation and death, at the same time as they create continuity and connection.

Songs in *The Sound of One Hand Clapping* also express profound sadness and loss. The point of difference is that the imagined refrains in this novel hint at folk songs or nursery rhymes with roots in the European continent. While the island imaginary is

---

30   Richard Flanagan, *Gould's Book of Fish: A Novel in Twelve Fish* (New York: Grove Press, 2001), 334, 339. All subsequent references are to this edition and appear in parentheses in the text.

"capable of representing a multitude of things",[31] from "colonial fantasies and extreme colonial realities",[32] this inflection casts Tasmania as an island of *routes* rather than *roots*, to draw on Baldacchino's formulation. Such a movement is also related to the confusion evoked by noise. Typical for the imagined sound of Flanagan's works, the human voices that take the form of song refrains are woven into a subtle harmony with sounds of the natural world. We encounter the following soundscape immediately after the departure of Maria Buloh:

> the gale rose and the wind began to cry such that it chilled even that wild wet earth.
> *Aja, aja*, it seemed to howl. *Aja, aja.*
> And the old, huge trees would be heard to crack and groan, and the new wires that scratched the vast night sky to whistle eerily, and none of the women who lay awake in the sagging beds that night were soothed by such sounds. (8)

The wind howls and cries, the trees groan, the wires whistle. This soundscape is a harmony of Gothic horror. In fact, while the wind seems to howl "*aja, aja*", the words of a lullaby that Maria sings to her infant Sonja, the soundscape does not pacify its listeners, having the opposite effect to the original intention of that type of song. If a lullaby is a song for children, this refrain is a deathly "line of flight", an escape for Maria, from motherhood and life.

Later in the novel we encounter another refrain of distress. This soundscape is even more closely aligned with the human voice. Here, imagined sound emphasises loss, suffering and death, mapping a space closer to the disturbing territory of the scream. After visiting her father, Sonja listens:

> But she could still hear him continuing to keen in his hut, each word a terrible lament, caught between a long single heaving sob. The whole an agonised prayer of loss that pursued her all that long drive back to Hobart.
> "*Madonna, Madonna, Madonna.*
> *Maria, Maria, Maria*". (257)

This song refrain is liturgical in its intensity, elevating Bojan beyond his mundane location into a higher realm of suffering. His words are both an entreaty to the divine Madonna, and a dirge for his own lost wife, Maria. At the same time, the emotion of this sound, "caught between a long single heaving sob", elongates Bojan's experience of loss. The scene could almost be open-ended in duration – we do not know how long Bojan has been or will continue crying. Each distinct word, repeated over and over, is a "terrible lament": there is a rhythm to this anguish. Such an accumulation of pain reaches all the way from Bojan's place of (island) isolation, in his hut, to Sonja, as she drives out of the wilderness and into Hobart.

---

31  Gillis, *Islands of the Mind*, 3.
32  Edmond and Smith, *Islands in History and Representation*, 6.

## "A memory of loss": The Scream

The extreme distress conveyed by these songs, and their predominantly vocal composition, lead us to the second tonality of imagined sound, the scream. Reflecting on the mistakes he has made in his life, Aljaz listens to a band play in a Hobart pub:

> When Aljaz heard the sound that then screeched forth from Shag's guitar he knew what Shag was playing upon that guitar, knew that fat old man wanted to make those strings scream: *If you leave you can never be free*. It was a dreadful noise, but there was something in it that even then I recognised. Now I know it was not a new song, but a song I had unknowingly carried within me for a long time. But what was it? Once more I hear the lead singer, shouting, screaming, joining Shag's guitar. Even back there in the bar Aljaz felt compelled to watch the singer's hands, outstretched as if he were being electrocuted, watch the fat of his face wobble and his forehead sweat and the few thin streaks of hairs that crossed it grow wet with exertion. He screamed it out until he looked worse than some animal in agony. He was no longer singing for the crowd or for the lousy money those behind the ringing till would give the band at the end of the night. Nobody in that bar knew, but I know it now. That he was not even singing for himself. That he was singing out of himself and out of his soul and out of a memory of loss so big and so deep and so hurting that it could not be seen or described but only screamed about. (257)

This soundscape encompasses the whole spectrum of sonic tonalities. Shag and the lead singer are performing a song refrain that also contains elements of noise, but this soundscape coheres around the scream. While the word "scream" has a strong presence in Flanagan's writing here, the core of this soundscape is concerned with drawing the past into the present, both Aljaz's recent history and the violence and shame experienced by his ancestors in Australia and overseas. Listening to the singer, Aljaz reflects that "he was singing out of himself and out of his soul and out of a memory of loss so big and so deep and so hurting that it could not be seen or described but only screamed about". Flanagan's use of polysyndeton – both "singing out of himself/his soul/his memory" and "so big/so deep/so hurting" – amplifies the historical depth of this loss. The past is funnelled into the present, arriving in a kind of affective vocal mass. The scream allows past island experiences of originary violence (also heard in the song of Black Pearl) to resonate within present movements towards extinction. Aljaz can make sense of the present using his newly acquired knowledge of the past, and sound is pivotal to how he makes this connection.

*Gould's Book of Fish* and *Wanting*, two novels firmly rooted in the nineteenth century, also feature screams that resonate with the island experience that haunts Flanagan's first novel. More specifically, Flanagan's description of the pub singer – "The singer's hands [were] outstretched as if he were being electrocuted … he looked worse than some animal in agony" (257) – recall the bodily abjection sounded by the screams issuing from the convict bodies in *Gould's Book of Fish*. Billy Gould describes the death of a weaver during corporal punishment: "His screeching dimmed to an odd gobby scream, as if he were trying to vomit all those steam spinning machines out of his mouth, & failing" (81). Such a violent demise prompts an act of pity from the evocatively named Capois Death, who "held the machine breaker tight & began to sing in a soft voice the songs he had learnt from his mother" (88). A scream is calmed by a refrain from "home". In *Wanting*, two screams evoke similar experiences of horror, both emerging from colonial iterations of the island. One scream issues from Governor Franklin as he dies while on a mission in search of the North Pole: "But then there erupted from him a sudden sound of infinite dread that rose and fell in the eerie dark beyond, then was lost forever" (177). Franklin, in search of a geographic ideal, is marooned and lost in the wilderness, his ship an island of death. A suppressed scream from Lady Franklin also reflects this colonial ideality. After the abject failure of her bid to adopt Mathinna, Lady Franklin views a portrait of the young Aboriginal girl: "'It really is a fine likeness of the child when she was at her most admirable', [the convict Bock] said as the wrapping paper fell to the floor. 'Predating her rather sorry decline'. Lady Jane wanted to scream" (197). Again, this scream sounds a colonial space mapped on an axis of suffering and death. While she does choke her reaction to the sight of the once healthy young girl, this scream reveals how Mathinna's misery haunts Lady Franklin.

## "There is only this": Noise

These screams and songs are sonic recordings of the suppressed violence and suffering that plague Flanagan's characters and the island they inhabit. Noise is the most intense realisation of the island as an isolated space haunted by the past. One of the central soundings of noise in *The Sound of One Hand Clapping* maps the island as a wilderness. In a brief soundscape early in the novel that echoes Clarke's weird melancholy, the narrator describes the landscape: "Above the soft noise of the rain were the desolate, harsh noises of Tasmanian rainforest, the wind up high in the forest canopy, the cries of black cockatoos and crows" (34). Once again, animal life is important in Flanagan's use of imagined sound, but it is the layering of "soft noise" and "desolate harsh noises" that sets up the island terrain of the novel.

With the exception of some brief descriptions of the grotesque noise of the giant pig Castlereagh in *Gould's Book of Fish*, in Flanagan's first two novels noise is anchored in the present (as opposed to an imagined colonial epoch), even if it is connected to past suffering. *The Sound of One Hand Clapping* features two noisescapes that correspond to the two central characters, Bojan and Sonja. Both of these scenes are pivotal moments for how the two characters cope with Maria's death. Bojan hears noise during his citizenship ceremony in 1954:

> There is only this, thought Bojan. Flesh and stretched bones and shit and wood that grows in trees that stretches flesh and flesh that flattens wood to make meaningless things such as this hut in which we are and this noise that means nothing. There was birth and there was love and there was death, and there were only these three stories in life and no others, but there was also this noise, this endless noise that confused people, making them forget that there was only birth and love and that each and everything died. (44)

This noisescape maps a complex spatio-temporal overlay. The "endless noise" is at once the meaningless droning voice of "the politician" as he delivers a speech of platitudes to the "new Australians" (42) assembled for their naturalisation ceremony. For Bojan, the hollow rhetoric of nation is a distraction from "birth", "love" and "death", the "three stories in life". Noise disturbs this essential signal, "making them forget that there was only birth and love and that each and everything died" (44). In other words, noise is in excess of an island experience defined by origin and extinction, isolation and connection. Bojan's island existence is one circumscribed by the place of Tasmania within the Australian nation, and his relocation from Europe to Australia adds to this disorientation. For Maria, as with Bojan, experiences on the European Continent during World War Two are not left behind; instead, they amplify the difficulty of life in the Tasmanian wilderness, contributing to Maria's suicide and precipitating Bojan's isolation. Noise encases and links these two spaces and times.

Sonja's noisescape is similarly intricate, recalling a moment from the same period of time that is depicted with Bojan above. Immediately after Maria's death, women from the workers' camp are taking care of Sonja:

> Sonja picked up the teapot, moved it past the tablecloth, and let the teapot fall to the ground where it smashed ... Though her face betrayed no such emotion she felt momentarily surprised that the sound of the smashing porcelain could not overwhelm the other sounds she carried within her. First the teapot, then the milk jug, then the saucers and the cups, all fell to the ground and broke into dozens of fragments. But no matter how many tea-set pieces fell to the ground the other noises always returned like a howling inside her head that would not leave: sounds of her father sobbing, of the blizzard wind that had beaten up their shack-home the night before, of her mother singing, of her mother singing. (46)

Sonja carries an internal trauma-scape marked by the terrible rhythm of her mother singing and her father crying. These screams are described as "noises" whose materiality overwhelms Sonja, the listener. The wind, a key sonic marker of isolation for Flanagan, binds these elements, placing characters and histories in the immediate present. The repetition of "her mother singing" creates a refrain, but one that haunts Sonja. The sound of porcelain smashing cannot override the power of a harmony of screams that map island existence. Even though it is a sad inversion of the playful soundscape normally associated with a children's tea party, for Sonja the noise of smashing porcelain is a memorial to both the death of Maria and the beginning of life without a mother.

Flanagan's island novels all feature imagined sounds – interconnected soundscapes composed of songs, screams and noise – that haunt pivotal narrative spaces, bringing the past into the present. Such haunted sonics refer us "to what's living and breathing in the place hidden from view: people, places, histories, knowledge, memories, ways of life, ideas".[33] Flanagan's island imaginary records buried colonial histories and their return in the postcolonial present with a symphonic range of imagined sound. From soundcapes of colonial violence, song refrains and screams of European trauma and the disorientation of noise, Baldacchino's aphorism – "[a]n Island *is* a World, yet an Island *engages* the World" – is played out through sound.[34] Flanagan's recognition of Indigenous presence, and its encasement within wider colonial soundscapes of violence and suffering, is significant. Listening to Flanagan's complex and unique use of imagined sound underscores the value of his contribution to the island literary imagination.

---

33   Gordon, "Some Thoughts", 3.
34   Baldacchino, "Islands", 248.

## References

Anderson, Benedict. *Imagined Communities: Reflections on the Origin and Spread of Nationalism*. (1983) London: Verso, 1991.
Attali, Jacques. *Noise: The Political Economy of Music*. Manchester: Manchester University Press, 1985.
Baldacchino, Godfrey. "Islands: Objects of Representation". *Geografiska Annaler: Series B, Human Geography* 87, no. 4 (2005): 247–51
Belfrage, Jane. "The Great Australian Silence: Inside Acoustic Space". The Australian Sound Design Project, the University of Melbourne, May 1994. http://bit.ly/2LFM8rS.
Buchan, Bruce and David Ellison. "Introduction: Speaking to the Eye". *Cultural Studies Review* 18, no. 3 (2012): 4–12.
Carter, Paul. *The Sound in Between: Voice, Space, Performance*. Kensington: University of New South Wales Press, 1992.
———. *The Road to Botany Bay: An Essay in Spatial History*. London: Faber, 1987.
Clarke, Marcus. Preface to *The Poetical Works of Adam Lindsay Gordon*. (1876) Adelaide: University of Adelaide Library, http://bit.ly/2sqAAQt.
Cummins, Joseph. "'I turn up the volume and walk towards home': Mapping the Soundscapes of *Loaded*". In "Critical Soundings". Edited by Helen Groth and Joseph Cummins. Special issue, *JASAL: Journal of the Association for the Study of Australian Literature* 15, no. 1 (2015): 1–11.
———. "Echoes Between Van Diemen's Land and Tasmania: Sound and the Space of the Island in Richard Flanagan's *Death of a River Guide* and Carmel Bird's *Cape Grimm*", *The Journal of Commonwealth Literature* 49, no. 2 (2014): 257–70.
Davidson, Jim. "Tasmanian Gothic", *Meanjin* 48, no. 2 (1989): 307–24.
Deleuze, Gilles and Félix Guattari. *A Thousand Plateaus: Capitalism and Schizophrenia*. (1980) Translated by Brian Massumi. London: Continuum, 1988.
Deleuze, Gilles. *Desert Islands and Other Texts 1953–1974*. Cambridge, MA: MIT Press, 2002.
Edmond, Rod and Vanessa Smith, eds. *Islands in History and Representation*. London: Routledge, 2003.
Eliot, T.S. *The Sacred Wood: Essays on Poetry and Criticism*. London: Methuen, 1950.
Flanagan, Richard. *Wanting*. North Sydney: Knopf, 2008.
———. *Death of a River Guide*. Ringwood, Vic: McPhee Gribble, 1994.
———. *Gould's Book of Fish*. New York: Grove Press, 2001.
Gelder, Ken. "Australian Gothic". In *The Routledge Companion to Gothic*, edited by Catherine Spooner and Emma McEvoy. London: Routledge, 2007, 115–24.
Gelder, Ken and Rachael Weaver, eds. *The Anthology of Colonial Australian Gothic Fiction*. Carlton, Vic: Melbourne University Press, 2007.
Gillis, John. *Islands of the Mind: How the Human Imagination Created the Atlantic World*. New York: Palgrave Macmillan, 2004.
Gordon, Avery. "Some Thoughts on Haunting and Futurity", *Borderlands* 10, no. 2 (2011): 1–21.
Grosz, Elizabeth. *Chaos, Territory, Art: Deleuze and the Framing of the Earth*. New York: Columbia University Press, 2008.
Jay, Martin. *Downcast Eyes: The Denigration of Vision in Twentieth-Century French Thought*. Berkeley: University of California Press, 1993.
Kahn, Douglas. *Noise, Water, Meat: A History of Sound in the Arts*. Cambridge, MA: MIT Press, 1999.
McMahon, Elizabeth. *Islands, Identity and the Literary Imagination*. London: Anthem Press, 2016.
———. "Encapsulated Space: The Paradise-Prison of Australia's Island Imaginary", *Southerly* 65, no. 1 (2005): 20–30.
Nechvatal, Joseph. *Immersion into Noise*. Ann Arbor, MI: Open Humanities Press, 2011.
Revill, George. "Music and the Politics of Sound: Nationalism, Citizenship, and Auditory Space", *Environment and Planning D: Society and Space* 18, no. 5 (2000): 597–613.
Schafer, Murray R. *The Soundscape: Our Sonic Environment and the Tuning of the World*. Rochester, NY: Destiny Books, 1977.

Stanner, W.E.H. *After the Dreaming: The 1968 Boyer Lectures.* Sydney: Australian Broadcasting Commission, 1969.
Truax, Barry D., ed. *Handbook for Acoustic Ecology.* Vancouver: A.R.C. Publications, 1978. http://bit.ly/2sqqtLx.
Wright, Judith. *Preoccupations in Australian Poetry.* Melbourne: Oxford University Press, 1965.

# 4

# Spatial Anxieties: Tourists, Settlers and Tasmania's Affective Economies of Belonging in *A Terrible Beauty*, *Death of a River Guide* and *Gould's Book of Fish*

Laura A. White

When the *Discover Tasmania* website promises that Port Arthur is "Australia's most ... evocative convict site and one of Australia's great tourist attractions",[1] it activates connections between tourism and imperialism that have increasingly become a subject of interest for tourism scholars. Recent work in postcolonial tourism studies encourages scrutinising specific contexts in which tourism both perpetuates and diverges from earlier forms of imperialism in order to refine general claims about tourism as a continuation of imperial circuits of travel and influence.[2] Richard Flanagan powerfully contributes to this project. Beginning in *A Terrible Beauty: History of the Gordon River Country* (1985), a historical study of Tasmania's Gordon River country that also delivers a reprimand to contemporary environmentalists, Flanagan argues that simply equating modern development – including tourism and commercial forestry – with settler colonialism contributes to the erasure of a range of affective encounters with the land. For instance, equating contemporary tourists with imperialists in regard to a detached position from which they survey and consume the land relies on a reductive notion of the imperial past which assumes that all settlers occupied a position of privilege from which they visually and economically consumed Tasmania. Flanagan forcefully rejects this formulation. He investigates ways that aspects of tourism do resemble and perpetuate imperialism, but he insists on a deeper engagement with the past that registers a variety of settler experiences. Flanagan models this approach in his historical scholarship, which explores how the myth of Tasmania as a terrible and empty land developed by universalising a single settler experience and how the repetition of this myth continues to silence histories of habitation that include a range of affective experiences: encounters of fear and awe, and love and hate, that enabled those who laboured on the land to feel a sense of belonging to it. In *Death of a River Guide* (1994) and *Gould's Book of Fish* (2001), Flanagan uses the novel form to map circuits of affect and reclaim suppressed histories of feeling for the land. Depicting tourists and juxtaposing them with historical and contemporary labourers,

---

1 "Port Arthur Historic Site", *Discover Tasmania*, http://bit.ly/2H6FoQj.
2 See for instance Anthony Carrigan, *Postcolonial Tourism: Literature, Culture and Environment* (New York: Routledge, 2010) and Colin Michael Hall and Hazel Tucker, *Tourism and Postcolonialism: Contested Discourses, Identities and Representations* (New York: Routledge, 2004).

Flanagan combats the narrative of continuous exploitation of the land that the equation of tourism with imperialism imposes.

Representations of tourists, settlers and environmentalists provoke questions about dynamics between individuals and groups, and Sara Ahmed's theorisation of affective economies offers a productive framework for analysing the attachment of individuals to collective bodies. Rather than understanding emotions as originating from and contained within individual bodies, Ahmed contends that emotions should be studied in terms of how they circulate across bodies and work to materialise collective identities. Specifically, Ahmed proposes that "in such affective economies, emotions *do things*, and they align individuals with communities – or bodily space with social space – through the very intensity of their attachments".[3] Feeling for the land, then, is not an innate quality that individuals have; it is created through circulations that include histories of production and consumption, some of which become suppressed. Removing emotion from containment within individual bodies and offering a model of economic circulation invites further attention to ways that power dynamics shape affective flows, an issue that is crucial to Flanagan's engagement with silenced histories of labour that haunt the figure of the settler. As Ahmed argues, "emotions may only seem like a form of residence as an effect of a certain history, a history that may operate by concealing its own traces".[4] Divya Tolia-Kelly takes this point further, suggesting that affect scholarship must do more to make traces of subsumed histories visible by attending to "geometries of power and historical memory that figure and drive affective flows and rhythms", and that distribute capacities to affect and be affected unequally.[5] This framework of affective economies enriches understanding of Flanagan's novels and their emphasis on emotions such as love by suggesting that emotions are not the private and limited experiences of individual characters; they are mobile historical forces that can bind individuals to one another and to the land. Connecting the novels to Flanagan's argument in *A Terrible Beauty*, I propose that Flanagan narrates the movement of affects in ways that complicate the equation of tourism with imperialism, helping to make historical power dynamics visible and enabling insight into a range of ways that people experience and express love for the land.

## Terrible Tasmania and the Power Geometries of Affect

In 1985, Flanagan published *A Terrible Beauty: History of the Gordon River Country*, a book that grew out of his training as a historian at the University of Tasmania, and his encounters with the land as a resident and avid canoeist.[6] This work predates Flanagan's novels, but introduces his enduring concern with the silenced histories of Tasmania and the importance of human connection with the land. It also demonstrates his consistent attention to affect and the ways that the circulation or suppression of affect participates in a range of power relations. In this study, Flanagan interrogates the myth of Tasmania as

---

3   Sara Ahmed, "Affective Economies", *Social Text* 22, no. 2 (2004): 119.
4   Ahmed, "Affective Economies", 119.
5   Divya P. Tolia-Kelly, "Affect – an ethnocentric encounter? Exploring the 'universalist' imperative of emotional/affectual geographies", *Area* 38, no. 2 (2006): 213–14.
6   Richard Flanagan, *A Terrible Beauty: History of the Gordon River Country* (Richmond, Vic: Greenhouse Publications, 1985), 63. All subsequent references are to this edition and appear in parentheses in the text.

an empty land and traces ways that the myth impoverishes understandings of the diversity of human attachments to the land. Turning to historical records of explorers and piners, Flanagan demonstrates how various vectors of power contribute to the force of the myth. First, he calls attention to the fact that only certain records of encounter with the land have been preserved and studied:

> The only records that exist of western exploration are those left by educated men such as Darke, Sharland, Calder and Gould. The uneducated and illiterate – the bulk of the explorers – the men who hacked the tracks out, who shouldered the heavy packs and grew rheumatic before their time in consequence, left virtually nothing. The words of a few men became, of necessity, accepted by all as the truth. (63)

Reliance on written records homogenises settler experience by neglecting specific positioning in relation to the land. Rejecting this approach, Flanagan reveals how aspects of class, literacy, and cultural context influence the range of signs that have been deployed to represent Tasmania. The adjectives "forbidding", "stern", "hideous" and "terrible" recur in the explorers' landscape descriptions because the features of Tasmania vary greatly from their frame of reference of "mundane meadows and daffodils of pastoral England" (66, 64). Lacking other vocabulary or conceptual reference points, negative descriptions echo one another to confirm Tasmania as the "terrible beauty" and silence a range of affective experiences. However, Flanagan contends that the application of negative adjectives by some explorers does not prove that other labourers did not have intense and varied feelings for the land, and his book works to reclaim some of these different circuits of emotion. By bringing working-class experience into dialogue with the myth, Flanagan recovers a plurality of settler experiences – of piners, convicts, and other labourers – that have been lost in the consolidation of the settler narrative and that can complicate representations that posit a continuous alienation from and exploitation of the land.

Flanagan's response to the myth of a terrible and empty land evidences his approach to affects as capable of creating effects: feelings of alienation and fear activated by this myth move through texts and time periods, connecting explorers' diaries to painting exhibitions to contemporary development discourse. As Ahmed explains, signs accumulate affect over time, and the more they move "the more affective they become, and the more they appear to 'contain' affect".[7] Signs appear to contain affects only by concealing how they are shaped by histories, and Flanagan insists on re-placing feeling in historical contexts. Then, when the signs that circulate affect emerge in the present in support of development or conservation discourse, Flanagan wants readers to recognise the histories they carry with them. As Flanagan identifies affective traces in the present day, he argues:

> The myth of the South-West as an awful land came to have great importance for both the modern developmental interests, who used it to justify their exploitation of the area, and by the conservationists, who used it to define their own vision of the area as a response unique in history. It is ironic that the conservationists should have used this myth in defining their movement; to do so was in fact detrimental to their cause as it denied the value and interest that the area had held for different people in the past. (2)

---

7   Ahmed, "Affective Economies", 120.

Flanagan explores how the affects evoked by the myth lend force to developers' depictions of a tradition of extracting resources from an otherwise empty waste land while also legitimising conservationists' claims to a unique love for this land and blocking a more complex narrative of belonging. He illustrates how accepting the representation of Tasmania as possessed of a terrible beauty requires ignoring experiences of Indigenous and working-class Australians, and he offers an alternative path. Disrupting the singular story of the settler by recovering diverse histories of habitation can extend affective results into the present, weakening historical justifications for destructive development, complicating understandings of similarities between tourism and imperialism, and offering a foundation for a more inclusive environmental coalition that values the varied ways that feelings attach individuals to Tasmania.

As a precursor to his fiction writing, Flanagan's historical study uncovers records of past encounters with the land that begin to counter the myth of the terrible, empty Tasmania, but his novels contribute in different ways by performing their own kind of affective work, imagining experiences that have only left traces in historical documents and creating avenues for readers to participate in the movement of emotions that can shape new collectivities. Speaking of his own practice, Flanagan describes how reading is an affective process in which emotions travel across bodies and signs: "I read incessantly, searching for the things that might move me … What is missed when people talk about books is the moment of grace when the reader creates the book, lends it the authority of their life and soul. The books I love are me, have become me".[8] While some critics have faulted him for trying to express such aims too directly within his novels,[9] his fiction both describes characters' transformations through affective encounters and offers such affective experiences – along with the potential for creation of meaning and coalition – to readers.

## The Figure of the Tourist and the Circulation of Affect

In the postcolonial landscape of tourism, financial and affective economies, imperial pasts and national futures intersect. The United Nations World Tourism Organization's 2015 *Annual Report* lauds the economic impacts of tourism, proclaiming it "a key driver of the global economic recovery, and a vital contributor to job creation".[10] Locally, the Tourism Tasmania corporate website acknowledges that the tourism industry manipulates affect to generate business: "Our role is to create demand for travel to the state by connecting people culturally and emotionally to Tasmania".[11] In the case of Tasmania, attempts to sell emotional connection have often involved marketing the island's convict past and its dramatic landscapes, and affects mobilised to encourage tourism thus also intersect with affects marshalled in environmental debates: as Flanagan chronicles in *A Terrible Beauty*, both development and conservation groups activate images of Tasmania that circulate affect and work to attach individuals to the group, and to its vision for Tasmania's

---

8   Richard Flanagan cited in Kate Kellaway, "Hook, Line and Thinker", *Guardian*, 9 June 2002. http://bit.ly/2LDNDqi
9   For instance see John Banville, "On the Fatal Shore", *New York Review of Books*, 26 September 2002, 77.
10  United Nations World Tourism Organization, *UNWTO Annual Report 2015* (Madrid: UNWTO, 2016). http://bit.ly/2Lb80KF.
11  Tourism Tasmania, 2016. http://www.tourismtasmania.com.au/.

future. Tourism and ecotourism are imbricated in these affective battles, as some envision tourism as an economic alternative to logging, which has sparked decades of protest, and others figure it as just another form of destructive development. For example, Tasmania's Premier Will Hodgman has encouraged ecotourist development projects, claiming, "We are looking after our precious natural areas but we're also going to use them to increase the number of tourists that come to this state, to grow our economy".[12] On the other hand, some Greens politicians and activists claim that building tourist infrastructure in forests supposed to be protected as National Parks and World Heritage Areas ignores long-term consequences for quick financial reward. Flanagan's depictions of tourism in his novels *Death of a River Guide* and *Gould's Book of Fish* engage with these distinctive financial and affective economies and provide opportunities to investigate how these forces shape the collective body of the tourist, align the tourist with the detached imperialist, and distinguish the tourist from the labourer.

In both novels, tourist bodies possess the power to move, but the economic power that enables physical mobility also influences the flows of affect. For instance, in the opening pages of *Gould's Book of Fish*, Sid Hammet is busily employed producing fake antiques to sell to American tourists. He buys old furniture that he further ages by battering it and urinating on it, forging commodities that tourists can purchase as "flotsam of the romantic past, rather than what they were, evidence of a rotten present".[13] Hammet and the job market of Hobart are struggling financially in "the rotten present", and the circulation of tourist capital is presented as a practical opportunity. However, Flanagan emphasises that economic and affective value do not reside in the forged chairs themselves. Tourists use the purchase of chairs to buy a version of the past that comforts them, and through this process, semiotic value generates material value; the stories that ostensibly authenticate the chairs by yoking them to a romanticised past perform the affective work of protecting the tourists in the present. Hammet reports: "The tourists had money and we needed it; they only asked in return to be lied to and deceived and told that single most important thing, that they were safe" (8–9). A feeling of safety does not reside in any single body or material object; it is created by the circulation of objects and signs. In this passage, the "we" – the local labourers – craft a product from a position of precarity and dependence on tourist dollars, while the tourists' position of economic power allows them to direct the flow of affect and insulate themselves from negative feelings that might be sparked by contact with histories of labour. The tourists don't want to have "to feel rotten that no-one could or would explain why the wealth of a few seemed so curiously dependent on the misery of the many", and they use the circulation of money to defer these questions (9). The movement of capital conditions the movement of affect and attaches individuals to the collective body of the tourist.

One effect produced through these parallel circulations of financial and affective capital is the silencing of stories – of convicts, labourers and immigrants – that linger around objects and would force tourists to confront their own role in human suffering. Hammet observes: "they were only after something that walled them off from the past and from people in general, not something that offered any connection that might prove painful or human. They wanted stories,

---

12  Will Hodgman cited in Michael Atkin, "Eco-tourism on Agenda in Tasmania as Government Accepts Proposals for Development in National Parks, World Heritage Areas", *ABC News*, 1 December 2014. https://ab.co/2L6Fx8y.

13  Richard Flanagan, *Gould's Book of Fish* (New York: Grove, 2001), 5. All subsequent references are to this edition and appear in parentheses in the text.

I came to realize, in which they were already imprisoned" (7). The language that Flanagan employs here illustrates the capacity of affect to move between bodies and signs "sideways" through associations with other figures and "backward" to reveal "the absent presence of historicity".[14] References to walls and prison evoke without naming the convict history of Tasmania, while positioning the financially privileged tourists as prisoners. Tourists redefine confinement in terms of security, revealing how their existence depends upon erecting a border that disclaims their implication in a history of capitalist exploitation; in their case, prison walls materialise a conceptual border that protects them from facing the suffering of labouring bodies in the current tourist economy or recognising their continuity with their counterparts in the convict past. Flanagan's language refuses to allow the tourists full control to separate themselves from these bodies or dictate the meanings that prisons circulate in the affective economy of Tasmania. He exposes how tourist identity depends on a continual struggle to control signs, yet he also leaves the collective body of the tourist in place as a sign, narrating a consolidation of identity rather than attempting to pluralise it as he does with the settler.

In *Death of a River Guide*, Flanagan also engages the figure of the tourist and uses similar language to describe the tourist's desire to remain protected; however, in this novel, the commodity is not an antique chair, but the land of Tasmania itself. Tourists want to consume the wilds of Tasmania, but only as controlled through familiar images and stories. As the narrator reveals, "despite their assertions that this is the most beautiful country, [the tourists] are already feeling a growing unease with this weird alien environment that seems so alike yet so dissimilar to the wilderness calendars that adorn their lounge-rooms and offices. It smells strongly of an acrid, fecund earth".[15] This depiction recalls the process Flanagan describes in *A Terrible Beauty* and allies the tourists with the explorers, who repeated one another's language to create the image of a terrible land. These tourists lack a vocabulary to describe their feelings when faced with a land that does not conform to their sense of beauty, and like those explorers, the rafters turn to available references, in this case photographs and wilderness calendars.

Elsewhere, Flanagan has devoted attention to ways that pictures of Tasmania carry affective meanings that have been mobilised by conservationists to support an idea of wilderness that is separate from the human, an imagining of uninhabited space that ignores both Tasmania's extensive history of human habitation and the simultaneous use of these images to encourage human presence through tourism. Flanagan's analysis of the photographs of Peter Dombrovskis and their reception helps illustrate concerns about the absence of humans in representations of Tasmania as wilderness. Some critics claim that Dombrovskis' images, such as the iconic photograph of the Franklin River at Rock Island Bend, are "determinedly false, refusing to acknowledge the human element of the natural world", while Flanagan argues that "his images are, finally, an idea of humanity" that was informed by Dombrovskis' embodied experience as part of the land: "He lived on one of the mountain's higher flanks, and for him the mountain showed that the natural world wasn't something separate from human beings but the essence of us".[16] The photographs

---

14  Ahmed, "Affective Economies", 120.
15  Richard Flanagan, *Death of a River Guide* (New York: Grove, 1994), 20. All subsequent references are to this edition and appear in parentheses in the text.
16  Richard Flanagan, "It's Peter Dom", *Art and Australia*, reprinted in *The Best Australian Essays of 2011*, ed. Ramona Koval (Collingwood, Vic: Black, Inc., 2011). Kindle edition. See also Cassandra Pybus and Richard Flanagan, eds. *The Rest of the World Is Watching: Tasmania and the Greens* (Melbourne: Pan Macmillan, 1990).

record Dombrovskis' lived connection with the Tasmanian land, but their circulation as part of a discourse of wilderness creates a dilemma for tourists who struggle to make sense of their own position within the landscape. In Flanagan's novel, when the tourists find that their location does not correspond with the available inventory of signs, the disjunction creates a feeling of fear which they attempt to control by insisting the land conform to familiar representations. They take photos in an effort to distance themselves and "reduce this land to its rightful role of decoration" (20). Ahmed's theorisation helps articulate the process through which the circulation of fear constructs tourist identity; she explains, "anxiety and fear create the very effect of borders, and the very effect of that which 'we are not', partly through how we turn away from the other, whom we imagine as the cause of our fear".[17] Taking photographs becomes a characteristic behaviour that attaches individuals to the collective identity of the tourist at the same time that it shows how fear materialises a border between the human body and the land, as tourists turn away from the land, which is imagined as the source of the fear.

Like the tourists in *Gould's Book of Fish*, these tourists seek to avoid feelings of unease about their human vulnerability, and they turn away from their embodied experience with the land to seek refuge in familiar signs. This characteristic turning away also depends on financial capital, which the tourists deploy in a furious and futile attempt to block the movement of negative affects and secure the illusion that they can view the world and live human life from a safe distance. Unlike the tourists in *Gould's Book of Fish*, who remain a collective body throughout, the tourists in *Death of a River Guide* are presented as individuals with distinct personalities: there is Sheena, whose arm has been withered by radiation, and Otis, who can't stomach the unfamiliar food served on the rafting trip (34, 133–4). Affects do not work to create attachments between these individuals and the land; rather, affects attach the tourists to one another, creating an exclusive human community that protects its borders, disclaiming the land as a threatening other and leaving Tasmania "as they had always conceived it in their ignorance, a grotesque Gothic horrorland" (132).

### The Labouring Body and the Work of Affect

Flanagan investigates connections between financial and affective economies through the figure of the tourist, and he further complicates these ties by juxtaposing tourists with a variety of bodies that relate to the land through labour: hunters, piners, convicts and contemporary canoeists, kayakers and rafters. While Flanagan highlights the incorporation of individuals into the collective body of the tourist, he simultaneously dismembers the body of the settler to reveal the multiplicity of identities and attachments it conceals. Flanagan makes a distinction between those who work on and relate to the land through their bodies, and those whose contact with the land remains indirect because of the mediating force of money. In *A Terrible Beauty*, he argues that environmentalist discourses often fail to make such distinctions between the methods and motives of commercial forestry companies and early piners who worked the land. To combat this oversimplification, Flanagan investigates the lives of piners and contends: "Long before the rivers of the South-West were household words, the piners knew and held deep feelings for the country through which they flowed. They loved and hated the rivers, but were

---

17   Ahmed, "Affective Economies", 132.

never indifferent to them" (77). While tourists are characterised by wilful ignorance, this statement introduces a link between knowledge and emotion that distinguishes piners' relations to the land. Their action of cutting trees might align them with forestry companies, but their affective orientation differentiates them. Flanagan analyses documents that illustrate how labour facilitates sensory contact with a land that lives in labourers' bodies and memories: one such diary entry reports, "there's something about that smell – it's not a bad smell – it's just a beautiful earthy smell and they are the sort of things that if I live to be ninety will still come back to me" (77). Further, he highlights a continuity between historical and contemporary sentiments by linking early piners' diaries to the statements of "river men" in the 1980s. Flanagan interviews Reg Morrison, a man who descends from a pining family, has operated a tourism business and supported protest against the proposed damming of the Gordon River. Morrison claims, "The Gordon and her tributaries are my life, financially and in every other way. If they dam her it would be like cutting off the blood to my body" (78).[18] Neither description uses the word love. Both, however, reveal an intense attachment to the land that dissolves boundaries as the land infiltrates the men's minds and bodies. Recovering these affective circuits, Flanagan demonstrates that love for the land does not exclude financial profit, but it involves ways of knowing the land that move alongside financial circuits, allowing piners and kayakers, unlike tourists and forestry companies, to cultivate an identity that derives from a sense of belonging to multiple human and non-human communities. In this text Flanagan emphasises "remarkable men" and chronicles masculine histories and identities, but he does expand beyond this gendered imagining in the novels (94); the novels include a range of women's experiences that contribute additional sources of knowledge. While analysing those stories is beyond the scope of the present study, it is important to acknowledge that the stories of male piners and convicts are not the only silenced stories of labouring on and loving the land, and the absence of all of these stories diminishes the possibility of a more inclusive understanding of relations with the land and a more diverse body of Tasmanian environmentalists.

In his novels, Flanagan is able to foreground stories of convicts, piners and river men in ways that counter their marginalisation in dominant narratives and show their potentialities for enriching understandings of human attachments to Tasmania. In *Death of a River Guide*, as the river guide Aljaz Cosini drowns, he has visions, and in one of these he watches his father, Harry, discover his own father who has been crushed to death by a falling tree branch. The narrator reports:

> It did not anger Harry that the carrion-eating devils had eaten half his father's face and parts of his hands and arms. That was how it was. It was the same law that allowed them to snare wallabies with the slag of blood about their mouths. But like he felt for the wallabies he felt for his father. He felt shock. The way that in death the pink bone of his father's skull looked so similar to the pink bone of the wallaby carcasses. (73)

Fear creates a border that separates the tourist body from the land, while shock creates an experience that links Harry with the land. Unlike the tourist, Harry does not seek to

---

18  For additional information about the contemporary debate and Morrison's role, see Lorena Allam, "Reg Morrison: The Man God Made Me", *Hindsight*, ABC Radio National, 27 July 2008. https://ab.co/2xpoTz3.

avoid confrontation with mortality and human vulnerability. He does not fail to experience emotion, even though the first report of emotion is a report of lack: he does not feel anger at the scavenging of his father's body. Harry accepts his father's death as part of a larger system of life and death because he has been immersed in it. His father and uncles taught Harry "to kill quickly and cleanly", and not to kill "things that didn't need killing" (69). These men instilled in Harry an awareness that they kill wallabies to support their own survival, and by providing daily examples of their respect for varied life forms – such as when they create paths for ants to leave the firewood before they burn it – they also convey to Harry a sense that even the smallest animals are fellow creatures that deserve respect. Flanagan acknowledges both difference and continuity with commercial hunting and harvesting, as Aljaz muses that as "each succeeding generation found something new they could quarry to survive … the emu disappeared, then the tigers, then the many different fishes and seals and whales" (258). Aljaz further posits that a colonising relation to land, including commercial hunting and harvesting, depends on an "idea of the land not as a source of knowledge but as a source of wealth" (258). For Harry, the land has been a source of knowledge – an affective knowledge that conditions his response to death. Every time Harry encounters the transformation of bodies through death, it generates a shock that impacts him, but even as he experiences intense physical, mental and emotional disruption at the death of his father, Harry refuses to separate and privilege human life. Harry's participation in circuits of affect complicates the narrative of the terrible, empty land by showing how emotional encounters operate to attach individuals to Tasmania. Flanagan's choice to narrate the boy's experience of shock diversifies the concept of love for the land by showing how this affective encounter with death actually functions to reconfirm Harry's sense of belonging to a community that connects human workers to non-human animals and the trees, rocks and soil of Tasmania.

Later in the novel, Flanagan expands upon the contrast between understanding the land as a source of knowledge and treating it as a source of wealth when he recounts Harry's work as a piner. Flanagan has argued in his journalistic writing that in contemporary Tasmania "logging is an industry driven solely by greed".[19] For Harry, though, his labour enriches his knowledge of the land. His way of knowing is not widely credited as knowledge, as the narrator reveals that the land which appeared "as an empty wilderness designated only as 'Little Known About This Country'" on maps was "well enough known to Harry and his workmates" (43). Belying cartographic emptiness, Harry encounters the land physically and emotionally through labour that Flanagan describes as driven by forces other than greed: Harry's body works through a "rhythmic ache" as he rows up the river, and he reports that "he liked looking up close at the big trees … huge majestic trees" (43). When he begins cutting, his "axe and saw will work in rhythm in the damp and the humid closeness and the heavy sweet smells of the peat-created wet earth, among the myrtles, craggy and towering and bearded with hanging festoons of lichens, cracked and scabbed with fluorescent orange fungi" (41). Contrary to tourists, Harry finds the forest familiar; he accepts his location "up close", and rather than turning away in fear, he stresses that his body operates in rhythm with the forest. He has access to a different vocabulary that allows him to express respect and wonder for distinct, interdependent life forms that constitute the collectivity of the forest. Recalling the excerpt of the piner's diary, Harry is attentive to the textures and smells that surround him, and he locates not only his body, but his sense of self, in relation to the

---

19   Richard Flanagan, "Paradise Lost – with Napalm", *Guardian*, 21 April 2004. http://bit.ly/2Jf8GBj.

interactions that connect distinct trees and lichen and fungi. While Harry depends on the trees for his financial livelihood and his actions destroy some of the "huge majestic trees", the trees provoke a circulation of joy and wonder that operate to attach him to the forest while the circulation of finances remains implicit. This fictional portrait of an individual piner reinforces Flanagan's argument in *A Terrible Beauty* that financial profit from the land does not invalidate the intimate contact between labourers and the land or disqualify the knowledge and sense of belonging created through it.

The labour of convicts, like the labour of piners, draws humans into connection with the land in ways that have been overlooked in dominant narratives, and Flanagan integrates this affective history of capital through the character of William Buelow Gould. In *Gould's Book of Fish*, Flanagan juxtaposes tourists who buy a version of the past that suppresses their complicity in present and past exploitations of the labour of others with the story of Gould. Gould's body does not share the physical mobility of the tourist, but as he participates in circuits of affect, he creates a movement across geographic and temporal borders that links convicts, slaves and animals as exploited resources. The convict Gould avoids physical labour by marketing his skill as a painter. Others dictate what he paints and collect the profits from his work, alienating him from his labour. Marx theorises that such labour leads to an estrangement from species: "in his human functions he no longer feels himself to be anything but an animal ... It changes for him the life of the species into a means of individual life ... in degrading spontaneous, free activity to a means, estranged labor makes man's species-life a means to his physical existence".[20] As convict, Gould becomes estranged from his humanity and from his connection with other humans, using his labour to secure his physical existence, but as painter, Gould uncovers a potential to redefine his humanity. Developing his own style of expression, Gould builds a sense of identity as convict-artist and calls attention to ways that dominant forms of representation collaborate to create the distance necessary for the imperialist/touristic gaze as well as the convict labour system.

Gould's liminal position as convict and artist, and as animal and human, leads him to devise a form of representation that refutes the landscape paintings that he claims "trash the truth as they reach ever upwards into the sky, as though we only know somewhere or somebody from a distance" (93). His paintings reject the divisions demanded by the systems of classificatory science, capitalism and imperialism that he is supposed to serve. Describing the work he does as painter, Gould confesses:

> I began taking liberties with that fish's face, so it was both the fish's knowing eye & the horror of the machine breaker's eye ... It was Capois Death's stare ... It was all that blood – of fish eyes & revolting slaves being torn apart & Maurepas' nailed shoulders haemorrhaging & the blood in the machine-breaker's eyes ... and it was my own fear at this cracked world in which I & they & everything was trapped. (90)

Gould identifies fear as his own response to confinement, but he also shows how fear circulates across signs and bodies, and across time and space to produce results. Fear allows him to reveal links between forms of oppression so that the eye of a dying fish echoes the eye of a dying convict, and the system of convict labour in Australia echoes the system of plantation slavery in

---

20 Karl Marx, *Economic and Philosophic Manuscripts of 1844*, trans. Martin Mulligan (New York: Prometheus Books, 1988), 74–5.

the Caribbean. The plurality expressed in the painting manifests ways that transportation and convict labour operated in material and ideological conjunction with other forced migrations, expanding the frame beyond the nation to expose global economic and affective circuits that have also been the subject of historical analysis by scholars such as Deirdre Coleman, Cassandra Pybus and Emma Christopher. Gould's artistic process enacts the dynamics these historians describe through which "a history of captivity, cruelty, torture, terror, and death … in turn created a history of resistance and, finally, emerging from the two, a history of cultural creativity".[21] Gould connects his own sensation of being trapped to other confined bodies that have been treated as disposable and erased from dominant histories, and he builds a form of representation capable of portraying a collective identity that links diverse bodies without collapsing their differences. Fear motivates this creation, and it compels Gould to turn towards rather than away from others. As opposed to the tourist, Gould can't use money to turn away from physical and psychological pain, and as he confronts suffering bodies in all their messiness, he finds a non-binary world in which affects interact with their opposites, not only in response to the circulation of finances. He realises that "At first, I tried, in spite of my artistick shortcomings, to create a record of this place, a history of its people & its stories … I just wanted to tell a story of love & it was about fish & it was about me & it was about everything" (384–5). Despite the movement of negative affects – of fear and horror that circulate through the violence and confinement that permeate his life – Gould finds that the story he would tell of Tasmania would express love and connection. A powerful effect, then, created by the retrieval of affective histories is a complication of the concept of love and belonging. Convicts and piners develop intense attachments to Tasmania in ways that are not always recognised as love and that complicate pictures of all settlers as detached exploiters of the land.

## The Recovery of Affect and the Revolutionary Force of Love

In a 2014 interview, Flanagan explained his belief not only in love, but in the work that love can do: "I do believe in evil, yeah. I believe in goodness and I believe in love. I think human beings and human history are the consequence of these hugely irrational forces. Much as we want to deny them and corral them, these are the things that propel us".[22] His novels demonstrate a similar conviction that human beings are "propelled" by affects and that love can actually provide a profound challenge to dominant historical narratives that try to "deny" and "corral" the irrational, affective elements of the human. In *Gould's Book of Fish*, Gould goes through an emotional journey to discover that love can radically disrupt existing systems of power. When Gould finds the notebook of legendary outlaw Matt Brady, he reads anxiously, searching for "any mention of a rebellion, plans for a revolution, or even something that might amount to an outline for an orchestrated uprising, a draft declaration of independence for the republic – anything that might fundamentally threaten the System" (350). Instead of political plans, Gould finds "nothing. Only page after page of more pathetick

---

21 Marcus Rediker, Cassandra Pybus and Emma Christopher, "Introduction", in *Many Middle Passages: Forced Migration and the Making of the Modern World*, ed. Emma Christopher, Cassandra Pybus and Marcus Rediker (Los Angeles: University of California Press, 2007), 2. See also Deirdre Coleman, *Romantic Colonization and British Anti-Slavery* (Cambridge: Cambridge University Press, 2005).
22 Richard Flanagan cited in Ramona Koval, interview with Richard Flanagan, *The Monthly Video*, 24 July 2014. http://bit.ly/2sqIfyd.

affirmations of love between a white man & a black woman" and he expresses his frustration and disappointment, "Love, love, love, thought I – is that all? Is that it?" (350). At this point, he does not recognise that love could be the force that he is seeking to "fundamentally threaten the System" because he reads it as a private connection that distracts from public action. His response serves to clarify that the love that holds animating, disruptive power is more than traditional romantic love whose institutional forms in marriage and the nuclear family provide material and semiotic support for nation and capitalism.

Through his paintings, Gould becomes aware of ways that love can circulate across bodies and across timeframes, creating communities that include human and non-human others. He also begins to realise that such movement holds transgressive power: "such things weren't what people wanted in paintings, they wanted their animals dead & their wives dead, they wanted something that helped them to classify & judge & keep the dead animals & dead wives & soon-to-die children in their place inside the prison of the frame" (386). Here, Gould acknowledges that works of art can provoke emotions, yet because these feelings reach across traditional borders of time and space, they also provoke discomfort in audiences, who, like the tourists, seek to preserve the prison of comfortable images and stories that secure the boundaries of their own identity. However, for Gould, as his body transforms, he finds "the sea was an infinite love that encompassed not only those I had loved, but those I had not … & they were all touching me & I them as Tracker Marks had a lifetime ago reached out & touched me" (396). Gould experiences love as a connection across time, place and bodies, and the word "touching" suggests a contact both physical and emotional. Romantic love in the form of an attachment to Twopenny Sal did not allow him to feel this kind of inclusive connection; however, the love he experiences as his body travels into fish form revises his understanding of love and helps to forge his understanding of himself in relation to multiple collective bodies – a national body of Australians as well as an international body of labourers and an inter-species body of exploited resources.

*Death of a River Guide* also concludes with Aljaz experiencing a love that confirms his identity by allowing him to take his place as part of the collective bodies of Tasmania. Similarly, what he defines as love encompasses more than a private, romantic pairing. A flashback to the relationship between Aljaz and Couta Ho shows how Couta Ho imagined their union before the death of their daughter, Jemma. Couta Ho tells Aljaz, "I thought maybe one day we could belong. Like people with families do, having their own time and their own place and growing old and crotchety and full of love in them. And other folks might even laugh at them just because they belonged there so powerfully" (111). Couta Ho recognises that love can create identity; by attaching individuals to one another, love can root a family in time and place and allow them to belong. However, love fails to generate this identity for Aljaz and Couta Ho, not only because they lose their daughter and their configuration as a nuclear family, but also because they do not yet understand the larger families to which love connects them. The rafting accident finally stops Aljaz from running from his loss. Once the river arrests the movement of his body, he becomes attuned to the movement of affect, and the novel ends with an encompassing sense of love, that like Gould's, works across borders of time and place and paradoxically confirms a sense of identity as the physical body dissolves and takes on new form. Aljaz's ancestors appear before him arranged in the shape of a wheel, and at the wheel's hub, Black Pearl, an Indigenous woman whose rape by a sealer Aljaz witnessed through his visions, holds his own daughter, Jemma. This visual display collapses temporal divides to reconfigure the body of the family, and it sparks in Aljaz a love that links feeling and knowing: "at last he knows the song and he knows. How much he loves them!" (326). Learning the history of his family has not been a purely intellectual exercise; it creates an affective knowledge through which he comes to locate himself and attach his sense of self to the collective bodies of Tasmania that include hunters and piners and kayakers and rivers. As in *Gould's Book of Fish*, love describes more than an exclusive, romantic connection: it activates a feeling of belonging to collective bodies that gains meaning by allowing for movement between past and present, presence and absence, human and non-human. However, the images of love that close both novels notably exclude the figure of the tourist, whose turning away from the land precludes this type of love.

Flanagan points directly to the work that this recovery of affect can accomplish. In the conclusion to *A Terrible Beauty*, Flanagan argues that Tasmanian environmentalists remain imprisoned by the myth of the terrible, empty land, and they must "examine and learn from those who lived and worked in the land they wish to preserve" (92). He identifies the scholarly work that volume performs as one part of retrieving the history of how "man has co-existed with the environment of the Gordon River country without destroying it" for over 20,000 years, and he urges that attention to these stories would nourish "a solidly based – both socially and ideologically – conservation movement" (92–3). Flanagan refutes the modern conservation movement's claim to be the first to express love for this terrible land, and in the process, challenges them not only to expand their historical awareness to include silenced stories, but also to rethink what it means to love the land, so that the movement of love can do the work of uniting a broader, more diverse collective body of Tasmanian environmentalists. While my chapter highlights the circuits of affects that shape tourists and male settlers, Flanagan's novels also operate more broadly to recover stories of settler women, Indigenous men and women, and Eastern European and Asian immigrant men and women, all of whom participate in circuits of affect that attach them in different ways to Tasmania. As Flanagan demonstrates, such a broad coalition is necessary to stop the destruction of Tasmania's forests and rivers. Using the increased publicity afforded by his 2014 Man Booker Prize win, Flanagan persists in advocating for Tasmania's environment, which faces ongoing threats from destructive development. During interviews that followed the award ceremony, Flanagan commented on the reopening of protected areas for logging due to the repeal of the forestry agreement that had brought an end to decades of debate between environmentalists and loggers, proclaiming: "I genuinely believe that people of Australia want to see these beautiful places, these sacred places, preserved, [but] the politics of the day is so foolishly going ahead and seeking to destroy them".[23] Flanagan continues to believe, thirty years after the publication of *A Terrible Beauty*, in the power of affect to create communities such as an inclusive Tasmanian conservation coalition: "In the end, the only answer we have to politics, to power, to horror, is the love we might know for each other".[24]

---

23　Richard Flanagan cited in Helen Davidson, "Richard Flanagan 'Ashamed to Be Australian' over Environmental Policies", *Guardian*, 14 October 2014. http://bit.ly/2H2SaPI.
24　Richard Flanagan cited in Marta Bausells, "Richard Flanagan on Love, Life and Writing", *Guardian*, 26 September 2015. http://bit.ly/2H1nuhC.

## References

Ahmed, Sara. "Affective Economies". *Social Text* 22, no. 2 (2004): 117–39.
Allam, Lorena. "Reg Morrison: The Man God Made Me". *Hindsight*, ABC Radio National, 27 July 2008. https://ab.co/2xpoTz3.
Atkin, Michael. "Eco-tourism on Agenda in Tasmania as Government Accepts Proposals for Development in National Parks, World Heritage Areas". *ABC News*, 1 December 2014. https://ab.co/2L6Fx8y.
Banville, John. "On the Fatal Shore". *New York Review of Books*, 26 September 2002, 77.
Bausells, Marta. "Richard Flanagan on Love, Life and Writing." *Guardian*, 26 September 2015. http://bit.ly/2H1nuhC.
Carrigan, Anthony. *Postcolonial Tourism: Literature, Culture and Environment*. New York: Routledge, 2010.
Coleman, Deirdre. *Romantic Colonization and British Anti-Slavery*. Cambridge: Cambridge University Press, 2005.
Davidson, Helen. "Richard Flanagan 'Ashamed to Be Australian' over Environmental Policies". *Guardian*, 14 October 2014. http://bit.ly/2H2SaPI.
Flanagan, Richard. "It's Peter Dom". In *The Best Australian Essays 2011,* edited by Ramona Koval, 272–7. Collingwood, Vic: Black, Inc., 2011.
———. "Paradise Lost – with Napalm". *Guardian*, 21 April 2004. http://bit.ly/2Jf8GBj.
———. *Gould's Book of Fish*. New York: Grove Press, 2001.
———. *Death of a River Guide*. New York: Grove Press, 1994.
———. *A Terrible Beauty: History of the Gordon River Country*. Richmond, Vic: Greenhouse Publications, 1985.
Hall, Colin Michael and Hazel Tucker. *Tourism and Postcolonialism: Contested Discourses, Identities and Representations*. New York: Routledge, 2004.
Kellaway, Kate. "Hook, Line and Thinker". *Guardian*, 9 June 2002. http://bit.ly/2LDNDqi.
Koval, Ramona. Interview with Richard Flanagan. *The Monthly Video*, 24 July 2014. http://bit.ly/2sqIfyd.
Marx, Karl. *Economic and Philosophic Manuscripts of 1844*. Translated by Martin Mulligan. New York: Prometheus Books, 1988.
Pybus, Cassandra and Richard Flanagan, eds. *The Rest of the World Is Watching: Tasmania and the Greens*. Melbourne: Pan Macmillan, 1990.
Rediker, Marcus, Cassandra Pybus and Emma Christopher, eds. *Many Middle Passages: Forced Migration and the Making of the Modern World*. Los Angeles: University of California Press, 2007.
Tolia-Kelly, Divya P. "Affect – an Ethnocentric Encounter? Exploring the 'Universalist' Imperative of Emotional/Affectual Geographies", *Area* 38, no. 2 (2006): 213–17.

# 5
# Rewriting History: *Gould's Book of Fish*

*Bill Ashcroft*

It is a truism that history is written by the victors, but less widely recognised that in any historical account History is the winner. This capitalised History is a relatively recent phenomenon. The question the human sciences had to face in the nineteenth century was, "What does it mean to have a history?" This question, Michel Foucault implies, signals a great mutation in the consciousness of Western society. It took an event, "certainly one of the most radical that ever occurred in Western culture, to bring about the dissolution of the positivity of Classical knowledge, and to constitute another positivity from which, even now, we have doubtless not entirely emerged".[1] That "event" that frames "our modernity" was the emergence of History.[2] Clearly, what it now means to have a history is the same as what it means to have a legitimate existence: history and legitimation go hand in hand. History legitimates "us" by defining "us".

Hayden White persuasively argues that history, seeking the title of "scientific discipline" in the nineteenth-century mould, needed to suppress the element of interpretation which had always given it its form, but which came to appear unstable and subjective.[3] The appeal to a moral or political authority underlying historical interpretation had to be sublimated by dissolving the authority to interpret into the interpretation itself. This, and the desire for the "scientific", generated a particular historiographic ideology: the demand for a single narrative truth, which was purely and "simply" the closest possible representation of events. The discipline of history emerged at a strategic moment of choice between possible discursive options, the apparently neutral narrative form succeeding by virtue of its resemblance to the purity of scientific disciplines. White asks the crucial question: what do we rule out when we constitute history in this rigorous scientific way and insist that any other procedure would reveal a want of discipline? His answer is *rhetoric*, which can be described as an awareness of the variety of ways of configuring a past which itself only exists as a chaos of forms. We can begin to understand Richard Flanagan's exuberant novel *Gould's Book of Fish* (2001) by seeing his reinstatement of rhetoric into historical discourse, albeit a form of rhetoric that is carnivalesque and excessive. The fact

---

1   Michel Foucault, *The Order of Things* (London: Tavistock, 1970), 219.
2   Foucault, *The Order of Things*, 220.
3   Hayden White, "The Politics of Historical Interpretation: Discipline and De-Sublimation", *Critical Inquiry* 9, no. 1 (1982): 120.

that Flanagan started out as a historian before he turned to fiction adds a certain gravitas to his boisterous undermining of historical method.

Australia, like the rest of the world, wants to enter History, because, as Ashis Nandy puts it, "Historical consciousness now owns the globe ... Though millions of people continue to stay outside history, millions have, since the days of Marx, dutifully migrated to the empire of history to become its loyal subjects".[4] When colonial societies are historicised they are brought into history, brought into the discourse of modernity as a function of imperial control – mapped, named, organised, legislated, inscribed. But at the same time they are kept at History's margins, implanting the joint sense of loss and desire. This is no less true of Australia than it is for Africa or India. Being inscribed into History is to be made modern because History and European modernity go hand in hand. History is that which keeps Australia locked into the embrace of empire with its promise of modernity and nationality. As Dipesh Chakrabarty says:

> So long as one operates within the discourse of "history" produced at the institutional site of the university, it is not possible simply to walk out of the deep collusion between "history" and the modernizing narrative(s) of citizenship, bourgeois public and private, and the nation-state.[5]

So the nation conspires with the imperial discourse of history in conferring the holy grail of modern being on postcolonial subjects. But as Franz Fanon suggests in *The Wretched of the Earth*, "Colonialism is not satisfied merely with holding a people in its grip and emptying the native's brain of all form and content"; it also "turns to the past of the oppressed people, and distorts, disfigures and destroys it".[6] This is certainly the case with Aboriginal pasts, but it applies to Australia as a whole, and particularly to Tasmania. Flanagan is always keen to insist that Tasmania, which people characterise as either a Gothic horror land or a Utopia, is not Australia. Consequently,

> they ought to try to come to terms with some of the tensions that make that mystery, to me, so interesting. I personally think it's a terrific place for a writer – there's an enormous well of subconscious experience that's accumulated over centuries.[7]

It is clear that Flanagan is deeply dubious about History. In an interview he says:

> it struck me on returning to Tasmania from Oxford how, for all its undoubted splendors, history was a very European and nineteenth century way of thinking; a railway line of thought, stopping at all forms of human progress on the way. But in Tasmania, this seemed an inadequate way of representing our lives there, our dreams and nightmares and jokes, of understanding that world, of understanding time, which came to me to seem the very essence of the consciousness of life, and which I suspected was perhaps

---

4   Ashis Nandy, "History's Forgotten Doubles", *History and Theory* 34, no. 2 (1995): 46.
5   Dipesh Chakrabarty, "Postcoloniality and the Artifice of History: Who Speaks for 'Indian' Pasts?" *Representations* 37 (Winter 1992): 19.
6   Franz Fanon, *The Wretched of the Earth* (New York: Grove, 1963), 209–10.
7   Richard Flanagan cited in Giles Hugo, "Richard Flanagan: The Making of a Tasmanian Best-Seller", *The Write Stuff* 1 (1995–6). http://bit.ly/2IVyLGl.

better understood as circular rather than linear. For this was the way it had always been explained to me in the stories I had heard, great circular tales that ended where they began, that digressed endlessly, whose meaning remained with you like a seed from a pharaoh's tomb, something that one day would grow into a wondrous tree bearing all manner of exotic fruit. It was the way Aborigines had once understood their cosmos and lived their understanding: camping in circles in circular or semicircular shelters; inscribing circles on their flesh and in stone; and it was the way I felt increasingly drawn to try and write.[8]

Flanagan is out to subvert History and although Tasmania is a good place for the circularity and digressions of a different story of the past, undermining History is no easy task, particularly as it undermines his own previous vocation. It is not a matter of offering a different history, for this alternative story would remain imprisoned in the discourse of History. The strategies Flanagan adopts, strategies that offer a flamboyant version of Hayden White's notion of rhetoric, meant that *Gould's Book of Fish* has annoyed reviewers and critics ever since.

One critic declared it "a monstrosity of a book",[9] suggesting its magnitude of "reference and style" results in little more than overladen pastiche. Alex Clark called it "one of the most fatiguingly inventive novels to have been published in recent years", presenting us with:

> a thoroughly confusing, wilfully convoluted and ultimately less than satisfying plot … a mixture of detailed portraits of fish and shaggy-dog stories, tales written frontwards, backwards and sideways, crammed with annotations and addenda, scraped together on loose leaves and dried fish skin and penned in numerous different coloured inks (as is this novel) … by page 38, when we are released into the story "proper", we already know that we can trust nothing we read from hereon in; that we are, possibly, in the hands of a madman.[10]

Even in positive responses, Flanagan's metafictional strategies are dismissed as a postmodern pastiche of other authors. There is no doubt about the numerous authors shanghaied into this enterprise: Whitman, Rabelais, Yeats, Sterne, Smollett, Joyce, Marquez, Ned Kelly, Borges, Faulkner, Flaubert, Blake, Voltaire, Cervantes and Melville – among others. Despite this, some critics still appear offended by the fact that Flanagan's Gould is a highly unreliable narrator, "the most untrustworthy guide you will ever trust, a man dead before his time".[11] The "real" William Buelow Gould was a forger and petty thief who was condemned to serve forty-nine years on Sarah Island off the coast of Van Diemen's Land. While imprisoned there, he made thirty-five paintings of different fish, which were gathered into a book now kept in the State Library of Tasmania: the paintings are accessible through its website. On the face of it, it seems that the persona of Gould

---

8 Richard Flanagan cited in Xavier Pons, "This Sad Pastiche: Texts and Contexts in Richard Flanagan's *Gould's Book of Fish*", *Commonwealth: Essays and Studies* 28, no.1 (Autumn 2005): 69.
9 Peter Craven, "Something Fishy Going On", *Age: Saturday Extra*, 10 November 2001, 9.
10 Alex Clark, "In the Hands of Madmen: *Gould's Book of Fish*", *Guardian Australia*, 1 June 2002. http://bit.ly/2H0TmDa.
11 Richard Flanagan, *Gould's Book of Fish* (Sydney: Picador, 2001), 61. All subsequent references are to this edition and appear in parentheses in the text.

allows Flanagan to expose the genocide of Tasmania's Indigenous people, the murderous legacy of Enlightenment rationalism, and the appalling conditions of the convict system.

But what is the value of this if we can't trust anything Gould says and if the story circulates into ever more bizarre situations? Might a "true" history be uncovered by the author's pen? "To be honest", says Sid Hammet, "I have come to the conclusion that there is not much in this life that one can be sure about ... I value truth ... where is truth to be found?" (4). History is like the stories tourists want, stories "in which they were already imprisoned, not stories in which they appeared along with the storyteller, accomplices in escaping" (9). Any national history such as Australia's cannot escape the civilising discourse bequeathed to it by Imperial History. This is a point of contradiction in the novel, because while Flanagan wants to subvert the "railway line" of history, the humanism of the book rages at the atrocities of colonial occupation that are obscured by Imperial History. This is a struggle over the truth and reality of the past that all decolonising discourse encounters.

"Truth and reality," says Hans Kellner, "are the primary authoritarian weapons of our time, an era characterised by nothing more than a debate over what is true of reality".[12] For this reason, if no other, they are difficult to ignore. Foucault, for instance, confirms the constructedness of these concepts time and again, yet "he will not dispense with them, but rather examines the way in which discourse creates reality as reality creates discourse. His own fictions, therefore, are true because they are based upon a certain reality; this reality is real, in part, because it has been figured by his fictions".[13] What strikes us in this is the fascinating intransigence of the dialectic of truth and fiction. The very act of piercing this dialectic to isolate the "thesis" – reality – is one which invokes the fictive, because constructive, strategies of our discourse. Aristotle's dictum that poetry is truer than history becomes ever more attractive the closer we examine historiographic texts.

The question of truth goes to the heart of the postcolonial response to Imperial History. There is no "true" history written by the colonised that might contest Imperial History; rather, the history of the margins offers a *different* story and in this difference lies its contestation. Because of their exclusion from the European institutions of History, colonised societies relied on their writers to conceive in literature a different history, very often a history that seemed to occupy a different space from official versions. It is this that identifies it rather than its presumed truth, and this is something Flanagan – historian turned novelist – seems to recognise implicitly. Although white settler culture was not as excluded from the institutions of history as black societies, it was caught, even before Federation, in the imperatives of a national history. Flanagan adopts a literary rhetoric of difference to oppose history, similar to that of other postcolonial writers, except that his swirling, layered and unreliable account is not only different but undermines any concept of the *possibility* of a faithful record.

This impossibility of fidelity to the past is the basis of Flanagan's subversion of history and once we see this, the layers, the "wilfully convoluted" transformations, deceptions and fabrications of the novel come to make perfect sense. Unreliability becomes the very medium of history and the first layer of this unreliability is seen in the layers of text through which the "past" comes to us. The novel uses a conventional framing device in

---

12  Hans Kellner, "Narrativity in History: Post-Structuralism and Since", *History and Theory* 26, no. 4 (December 1987): 6.
13  Kellner, "Narrativity", 6.

which Sid Hammet, a late twentieth-century character, discovers by chance a manuscript written by Billy Gould, which he reconstructs by memory once the original strangely disappears. The historical Gould's *Book of Fish* – a collection of thirty-five paintings of fish – is very different from Flanagan's *Gould's Book of Fish*, where Gould finds himself trapped in the narrative as both narrator and character. But there are not just two books, the historical Gould's and Flanagan's, but five: first, the novel itself; second, Gould's book of paintings in the State Library of Tasmania; third, the manuscript found by Sid, purportedly a second copy of Gould's book, in which the paintings are supplemented by an account of Gould's life and work; fourth, Sid's reconstruction of that writing after the unexplained disappearance of the manuscript; fifth, the strangest book of all – the one in which Gould finds himself in words written by himself, in a climax to the story of the continuing text of Flanagan's exuberant rejection of historical narrative.

To Professor Roman de Silva, to whom Sid Hammet takes Gould's book, History is truth and History has power: "History, Mr Hammet, is what you cannot see. History has power. But a fake has none" (22). But what Professor de Silva could not know is that History has power because it is a method rather than a truth (as the histories of nineteenth-century British historians amply reveal), an institutional formalisation of the stories we tell ourselves to make sense of our lives. The question of the truth or fiction of history may best be resolved in the concept of narrativity. The narrativity of contemporary history is its most salient and powerful discursive feature. One of the great illusions of narrativity is the assumption that the narrative doesn't simply tell a story but reflects the continuity of events. So great is the influence of narrativity that we assume that life itself is shaped like a story. It was this conflation of temporality and narrative sequence that underlay the nineteenth-century ideology of scientific method in historiography. The continuity of the stories written about history came to reflect the continuity of something transcendent called Human History: so transcendent in fact, that as Nandy says, everyone wants to enter its empire.

The pedantic Professor de Silva is committed to the link between truth and the historical record:

> "if we care to examine the historical records", continued the professor, but by then I knew he hated the *Book of Fish*, that he looked for truth in facts and not in stories, that history for him was no more than the pretext for a rueful fatalism about the present … On and on he blathered, taking refuge in the one thing he felt lent him superiority: words. (23–4)

So stories, indeed literature itself, provide an access to truth, the kind of truth Aristotle saw in poetry, but ironically, the narrative of history, the historical record, is alienated from truth by its very claim to provide a scientific record of the past. It just might be that Gould's *Book of Fish* could provide a truth unavailable to official history. The problem is that Gould's narrative of events is entirely at odds with his convict record:

> It sometimes seemed as if … Gould had been born with a memory but neither experience nor history to account for it, and had spent forever after seeking to invent what didn't exist in the curious belief that his imagination might become his experience, and thereby both explain and cure his problem of an inconsolable memory. (25–6)

It would seem indeed that Flanagan, in his determination to expose the deceptions and obfuscations of history, is trying as hard and as colourfully as he can to ensure that Billy Gould's story is beyond belief. The effect of Flanagan's method here is to raise the issue of the narrativity of history and to place it in the company of a story in which the fantastic is commonplace.

Narrativity is itself much deeper than the story. Hans Kellner, in his account of narrativity in history, analyses the work of Paul Ricoeur, F.R. Ankersmit and Hayden White, who all recognise in various ways that narrativity is a worldview, of which storytelling is a genre. The range of their positions reveals what a protean concept narrativity can be if separated from the story genre. For Ricoeur, narrativity authorises the historical enterprise in all its forms; regardless of the *forms* of representation, history rejects any disassociation of cause from effect. For Ankersmit, the narrative substance of history can never be simple translations of reality,[14] while for White, narrative was an option chosen in the nineteenth century at the birth of the discipline of history but which has restricted it ever since by excluding its rhetorical dimension.[15]

As Kellner explains it, in *Time and Narrative*, Ricoeur accepts the proposition that the "story" is elevated in historical writing, and that history is the comprehension of *plots*.[16] But this fails to explain how narrative remains the essence of history when history ceases to be about *events*. This is the key problem for all "narrativist" understandings of history, says Kellner. For an answer, Ricoeur turns to Augustine's treatise on time in the *Confessions*, which suggests that whereas time is experienced primarily as an absence, memory and expectation are also two key modalities of time, "so that one may speak of human time as a threefold present: a present of things past (memory), a present of present things, and a present of future things (expectation)".[17] For Ricoeur, Augustine solves the problem of the inevitable slippage of the present of the future into the present of the present and of the past by linking it to the *distentio animi*, "the stretching of the mind in different directions by the structure of temporal experience itself".[18] "I am no longer sure", says Hammet, "what is memory and what is revelation" (34). The *distentio animi* becomes a crucial aspect of Flanagan's depiction of the circularity of history.

The central and longest book is Gould's account of his imprisonment on the appalling Sarah Island. "This bellicose book, it was put to me, was the insignificant if somewhat curious product of a particularly deranged mind of long ago", says Hammet (19). This is because "while it is a matter of historical record that between 1820 and 1832 Sarah Island was the most dreaded place of punishment in the entire British Empire, almost nothing in the *Book of Fish* agrees with the known history of that island hell" (23). Gould survives on the island by making himself indispensable to the obese and pathetically ambitious prison surgeon, Tobias Lempriere, who speaks only IN CAPITALS and desperately wishes to be admitted to the Royal Academy of Science. He comes to believe that a taxonomic study of Tasmanian marine life will get him elected and commissions Gould to paint the

---

14   F.R. Ankersmit, *Narrative Logic: A Semantic Analysis of the Historian's Language* (The Hague: Martinus Nijhoff, 2013).
15   Kellner, "Narrativity", 14.
16   Paul Ricoeur, *Time and Narrative*, trans. Kathleen McLaughlin and David Pellauer (1983; Chicago: Chicago University Press, 1984), 174.
17   Kellner, "Narrativity", 15–16.
18   Ricoeur, *Time and Narrative*, 22; Kellner, "Narrativity", 16.

watercolours from which the plates for his study can be made. Gould paints the fish as avatars of the characters on the island:

> I could not then have known how much madness, this job of painting fish to further another man's reputation in another country, would come to overwhelm my life to such an extent that it would *become* my life – that I would, as I am now, be seeking to tell a story of fish using fish to tell it in every which way, even down to the sharkbone quill & the very sepia ink with which I write these words, made from a cuttlefish that squirted me only a few hours ago. (146)

Gould begins to discover the island's inhabitants in the fish he paints: Lempriere in a porcupine fish, the Commandant in a stargazer, Jorgen Jorgensen in a saw tooth shark. But he is dubious about his task. As he looks at each fish that must die to be painted he "began to wonder whether, as each fish died, the world was reduced in the amount of love that you might know for such a creature" (227). But it goes deeper than this, for Gould ponders on the consequences of the kind of taxonomic ordering in which he is engaged: "if we kept on taking & plundering & killing, if the world kept on becoming ever more impoverished of love & wonder & beauty in consequence, what, in the end, would be left?" (227–8). He imagines a world in which no more fish remained, where "Science knew absolutely every species & phylum & genus, but no-one knew love because it had disappeared along with the fish" (228). This is Gould's rebellion against all rigid lines of classification and such surrender to taxonomy is equivalent to the surrender to the "historical record". But Lempriere, the arch classifier, suffers a symbolic fate as the embodiment of nineteenth-century pseudo-science.

Lempriere is systematically defrauded by his mentor, Sir Cosmo Wheeler, who uses the surgeon's discoveries for his own benefit. Lempriere had been sending Aboriginal skulls to Wheeler as phrenological examples of the primitive character of the dark races. But when he ends up being eaten by his gigantic pet pig, Castlereagh, and is reduced to "the largest pig turd on the planet … [a] steaming obelisk of crap" (265), his own skull is disposed of in a barrel of skulls bound for Wheeler, and in a review of *Crania Tasmaniae*, his skull, MH-36, purportedly the skull of an Aboriginal, receives a long and enthusiastic account of its evidence of depravity, including the "*excessive animal passion of the sexual variety*" (338):

> one only has to look at the hideous depravity, the ovine set, and the generally regressive shape of skull MH-36 to understand why Crania Tasmaniae is one of the great scientifick achievements of our age … The marks of mental inferiority and racial degeneration are everywhere evident in the corrupted cranial features. (339)

This is not only a satire on phrenology, but also a critique of the narrative of history. The report on the skull is, like history, the confirmation of expectation. The final nails in Lempriere's coffin are two accompanying letters, one from the Royal Society awarding Sir Cosmo Wheeler a Commendation (for the marvellous discovery of the skull MH-36) and one from Wheeler to Lempriere informing him that his application for membership of the Society has been declined.

While Lempriere's obsession and his gory end are a testament to the absurdity of both phrenology and history as scientific narratives, the hub of this atrocious island is the delusional Commandant who embodies in extravagant fashion the deception and simulation on which history is based. Assuming the identity of a dead officer, the Commandant is clearly a deranged megalomaniac:

> he imagined – and we with him – himself being painted in a Roman toga, himself the subject of epic odes, himself founding a dynasty that would war in the name of his disputed memory, himself revered as Himself, & he saw no conflict between his despotick & dynastic desires, his official duties as an English officer in charge of an Imperial penal settlement & the high regard he held for Renaissance city-states such as Florence & Venice. (116)

The Commandant builds his own city-state: "When he spoke anything & everything became possible ... as long as he kept talking ... this offered us a purpose, a meaning, something which meant we weren't convicts ... Some alternate idea of ourselves, some steam machine by which we could remake ourselves & our world, for to escape being a convict, we had to escape who we were, escape our past & the future decreed by the Convict System" (117–18). In his delusion (exacerbated by the mercury he takes for syphilis) he builds a navy, most of whose ships enter the "growing trading fleet of the island" (113).

> "For what is a nation?" asked the Commandant of the Surgeon ... "but a people with a trading fleet? A language but a dialect with an army? A literature but words sold as provenance?" (175)

The absurdity of Sarah Island as a nation is a dismissal of nationalism itself. Flanagan is voluble about his identity as Tasmanian rather than Australian and his inspiration in the oral culture of the island.[19] But his suspicion of nationalism involves even a rejection of a national literature:

> I don't believe in national literature per se. I do believe in Australian writing ... But that's a different matter from a national literature. Nations and nationalisms may use literature, but writing of itself has nothing to do with national anythings. National traditions, national organisations, national prizes – all these and more are irrelevant.[20]

The Commandant's derangement has a lot to do with the fantasy of nationhood and he proceeds to embark on enterprises that salve his megalomania but also testify to the blizzard of simulation, deceit and dissembling that characterise the island and its history. At news from his purported sister (who turns out to be Thomas De Quincey) of the new railway phenomenon in England, he builds a railway.

When the Commandant decides to build this great railway system, which he somehow imagines will be linked with the outside world, both Gould and Capois Death are impressed into special service. Death is responsible for building the National Sarah Island Railway Station and connecting railway lines – all two hundred yards of them from the

---

19  Hugo, "Richard Flanagan".
20  Richard Flanagan, "Does Writing Matter?: Richard Flanagan Delivers the Inaugural Boisbouvier Lecture", *The Monthly*, October 2016. http://bit.ly/2xskR96.

station to the round house and back – and Gould is asked to paint a series of theatrical drop screens around the railroad tracks to give passengers the illusion they are actually going somewhere (167–83). Capois Death and Gould are then put to work on the Great Mah-Jong Hall, which fails to draw outside visitors as the Commandant had hoped (183–96). As the Commandant's health and sanity continue to deteriorate, the inmates begin to dream of rescue at the hands of the bushranger Matt Brady, a former Sarah Island inmate himself who became legendary after his escape.

Most significant is the Commandant's determination, in Big Brother fashion, to control history. As Professor de Silva pointed out, "history has power", and at the beginning of his rule the Commandant had given Jorgensen a critical responsibility: keeping all the records on the island, for "If I cannot control the past now … I will at least control it in the future" (276). This desire to control the future through the historical record is a neat personification of the function of Imperial History. The story that decides "what happened" is a story which determines "what is" and, as the Commandant realises, "what will be". For this reason history is of crucial importance in constructing a sense of identity.

In his *Lectures on Early English History*, Bishop Stubbs says:

> The knowledge of our own history is our memory, and so the recorded history of a nation is the memory of the nation: woe to the country and people that forget it; an infant people has no history, as a child has a short and transient memory: the strong man and the strong nation feel the pulsation of the past in the life of the present: their memory is vital, long and strong.[21]

Not only is history a narrative of who we are, but it is the thing which makes us "adult". Indeed, history has had a major role in producing a sense of being itself on a national level: "the national character has been formed by the national history quite as certainly as the national history has been developed by the working of the national character".[22] The history of empire is itself a narrative of a nation providing a memory – its own history – for those "infant" people, the colonised under its control. The historical record, even of critical histories, of the political and economic features of imperial control of India, for instance, miss entirely the ramifications of this transportation, the "expansion of nationality" as J.A. Hobson describes the imperial project.[23]

The historical record of Sarah Island therefore acts as a microcosm of Imperial History's need to provide a narrative of the civilising mission. In his fantasy of nation, the Commandant *must* have a record that confirms the rational and humane treatment of the convicts. This, as we already know from Gould's story, is laughably far from the case. The discovery of the complete fabrication of the historical record comes when Gould finds a crack in the roof of his cell through which he enters the Registry, full of books and most importantly the history of the penal colony. The Registry is administered by Jorgensen, who acts not only as librarian but also as the author of every fallacious record:

---

21 William Stubbs, *Lectures on Early English History*, ed. A. Hassall (1878; Oxford: Clarendon, 1990), 1.
22 William Stubbs, *The Constitutional History of England in Its Origin and Development* (1875; New York: Cambridge University Press, 2011), 1.
23 J.A. Hobson, *Imperialism: A Study*, ed. Philip Siegelman (1902; Ann Arbor: University of Michigan Press, 1965), 6.

> What I discovered between their clapboards was no chronicle of the penal colony I knew, the Commandant's nation of Nova Venezia. As I leafed through memorandum register after letter book after convict indent, I searched for records, drawings, mason's plans of the wonder of the Great Mah-Jong Hall.
>
> There were none. (316)

The astonishment Gould feels at the complete absence of any contact with reality is profound. As he makes his way through Jorgensen's writings, his feelings "passed from bewilderment to wonder as to why he might have written so much with so little foundation in life" (317). It was glaringly clear that the "old Dane" was selected by the Commandant to work upon the entire records of the settlement in a way that would accord with expectation and not reality. In fact the world described by Jorgensen was "at war with the reality in which we lived. The bad news was that reality was losing. It was unrecognisable. It was insufferable. It was, in the end, inhuman" (318). By speaking through Gould, the unreliable narrator, Flanagan is able to demonstrate how Imperial History hides "the truth" of its atrocious convict system, while at the same time refuting any possibility of a faithful record of the past.

According to Gould, the consequence of the fabricated history is to alienate us from time, within which our identity is situated. We are, so to speak, what we have become, and will become, but in these accounts time has become "something separate from us – so many equally weighted bricks that together made the wall of the present that denied any connection with the past, & thus any knowledge of our self" (319). This sealing off the past from the present gets to the crux of the way Flanagan presents the circularity of history, the intermixing of past and present: "Where waking and dreaming and nightmares under the Commandant had been one, with the old Dane's records they became hopelessly divided and opposed" (319). The division is one that is important to history because given time, and the accrued weight of history's narrative, our present comes to concur with the fabrication of the past. It is clear by the end of the novel that Flanagan thinks this is Australia's problem. The wall constructed by history between the present and the past prevents the country's knowledge of itself. But these fabrications are part and parcel of the very narrativity of history:

> by obeying the laws of pattern & succession, of cause & effect – which never characterise life but are necessary for words on paper – [Jorgensen] had created an image of the settlement that would persuade posterity of both the convicts' animality and the administrator's sagacity, a model of the power of unremitting, tempered discipline to transform pickpockets into cobblers & catamites into Christians. (320–1)

Even the life history of "Lieutenant Horace, latterly the Commandant", was down on paper "as implausible as the life of any saint" (321). Gould, who himself is the "most untrustworthy guide you will ever trust" (61), is compelled to toast, with a bottle of Schnapps, the brazenness of Jorgensen's lies and forgeries of smuggled convict letters attesting to the humane conditions.

As we saw, the tension in the novel comes from Flanagan's desire *both* to attest to the unreliability of history and to identify the cruelties that it obscures. This is a point at which the need for truth rubs up against the impossibility of any narrative providing it, the point where the need for an alternative story becomes a matter of justice. Flanagan resolves this by refusing to supply an alternative history, focusing rather on the ways in which history, particularly a national history, fabricates a story of civilisation and development. Gould feels a sickening horror and seems to see the faces of all those tortured convicts pleading for "something to appease their endless suffering that went unremembered & unrecounted" (325). His problem is that he is but a reader: "I had read & I had read & still the past went unavenged & unnoticed, & how was it possible for me to remake it as anything else?" (326). This is very ironic, given Gould's own story, but attests to the power of the historical text's claim on truth. What is never far from the surface in this account of Sarah Island is that its story is the story of the colony itself: "I toasted such a benign prison so marvellous you'd happily pay to leave England just to come & live here" (321).

This is the story both of colonial history and of the discourse of History. Ricoeur's central point about history and narrative is that "all change enters the field of human history as a quasi-event".[24] In effect, he reverses the hierarchy in Western historiography which privileges the long span of time over the particular event by showing how "any understanding of long time-spans must be saturated with forms of human understanding based upon human time as understood in particular by Augustine as a threefold present".[25] Particular events – and we must remember that "historical events" are those selected from a vast range of possibilities – are not the isolated occurrences of human experience, but they are themselves what Ricoeur calls "variables of the plot", the plot which "literally *comprehends*, 'grasps together' as an 'intelligible whole, circumstances, goals, interactions and unintended results'".[26] The analogical character of historical categories arises from the extension of the "threefold present" of human temporal understanding. It is the emplotment of the whole narrative, with its investment in human time, which gives the narrative its legitimacy, rather than any explicit referential function. "To follow a story", says Ricoeur,

> is to move forward in the midst of contingencies and peripeteia under the guidance of an expectation that finds its fulfilment in the 'conclusion' of the story … To understand the story is to understand how and why the successive episodes led to this conclusion, which, far from being foreseeable, must finally be acceptable, as congruent with the episodes brought together by the story.[27]

This is nowhere clearer than in the "story" of empire, in which the conclusion, the *telos*, is that which drives the story itself – the spread of civilisation to all mankind. History confirms, as much as any elaboration of the discourse of modernity, the supremacy of the modern, advanced, civilised West over the pre-modern, primitive, colonised societies. The narrative of events is one that cloaks, with the fiction of empiricism, the teleological and centripetal narrative of empire. Among the many things Gould admits to not knowing after his imprisonment, most telling is not knowing "why murdering the Pudding or Jorgensen is deemed a crime, while murdering a people is at best a question and at worst a scientifick imperative" (396). The story of the civilising effect of Sarah Island in the

---

24 Ricoeur, *Time and Narrative*, 109, 224.
25 Ricoeur cited in Kellner, "Narrativity", 16.
26 Ricoeur, *Time and Narrative*, 142; Kellner, "Narrativity", 17.
27 Ricoeur, *Time and Narrative*, 66–7.

Registry is symbolic of the duplicity of imperial history, obscuring not only the refined cruelties of the convict system, but worse, the genocide of a people.

Flanagan resists the dominance of the event, not only by interpolating a range of fantastic events but also more subtly by claiming that the change that history purports to record is a matter of transformation rather than a succession of events:

> Men's lives are not progressions, as conventionally rendered in history paintings, nor are they a series of facts that may be enumerated & in their proper order understood. Rather they are a series of transformations ... so complete & horrifying that at the end of his life a man may search his memory in vain for a moment of correspondence between himself in his dotage & him in his youth. (341–2)

It is not too far-fetched to suggest that Flanagan gains inspiration from the Aboriginal culture of Tasmania. If we compare this to the threefold present of Augustine's remembered past, present and anticipated future, we see that the privilege of memory within historical narrativity is replaced in Aboriginal cosmology with a luminous present to which the past and future do not appear through the *distentio animi*, the stretching of the mind in different directions, but are *embedded materially in the present*. The past is not so much an unknowable chaos as a constantly and wholly experienced present. This immense difference between the Dreaming and the Western narrative of history is embedded in the language itself. The Dreaming, for Aboriginal people, is the array of cosmogonic tales learnt as a child; it is the justification these tales provide for daily action; it is a name, totem, birth site, kin relationships, clan's land. It is a person's dance, song, skin painting. In short, it is the prolific and infinitely interpretable text of the Aborigine's world. That the Dreaming is all these things testifies to the pervasiveness of this incorporating ontology. It is clear how the Western strategy of narrative potentially confines and limits a non-Western cosmology in the name of the "superior" discourse of modernity.

But such a vision of the past and future circulating in the present is one that drives the Commandant's growing insanity. At the end of his crazed tyrannical rule of the island he becomes one for whom history as the story of the past collapses:

> In a growing delirium he spoke of how history, far from being past, was ever present. All those who had over the centuries deliberately or inadvertently discovered Van Diemen's Land, he now believed to be here, now, sailing into Twopenny Sal's bedroom. (272)

The Commandant has come full circle to realise that history is not an authoritative record of the past but that memory and expectation form a threefold present as Augustine suggests. Neither does history speak with a single authoritative voice. This is the point of the multiple voices of Flanagan's excessively layered, multi-voiced (and in the first publication variously coloured) text.

As Billy Gould says later, "reading had become for me the source only of disappointment & disillusionment" (386), so he decides to respond to his impotence as a reader and do something about the fabricated record of the island:

> Billy Gould attributed to the records a power only those immersed in paper too long can appreciate, if even then not fully comprehend. I worried that unless I did something, the lies I now dragged behind me would one day be all that remained of the settlement, &

posterity would seek to judge those who had gone before … through the machine of the Commandant's monstrous fictions! As though they were truth! As though history & the written word were friends, rather than adversaries! (346–7)

Gould finds himself in a powerful position with the entire history of the island at his mercy:

I intended first to paralyse the settlement by removing its basis of administration, the paper records of its invented history, the necessary fiction by which the reality of the prison-island was maintained. I had then determined that I would find Brady & deliver these records to him. (347)

The Registry confirms the observation of Professor de Silva that "History has power". But the words that are the "enemy" of history are friends to the transformation that characterises human life, as the bizarre transformations at the end of the novel confirm.

When Gould escapes from the prison after being accused of the murders of Lempriere and Jorgensen he is briefly reunited with Capois Death before Death is killed by natives (318–19), and later with Twopenny Sal, the black mistress of the Commandant as well as Gould, one of her children possibly being his. Sal and the other natives in her group use the Registry records to build a funeral pyre for her latest lover, Tracker Marks, while Gould sleeps. When he wakes and realises his precious records and even his *Book of Fish* are burning, he tries to stop their destruction, but halts only when he gets a glimpse inside the pages and realises the fire is described there, as well as events in the future. He sees "the book, where I then read what was now its beginning, a half-torn page, the first legible words of which were: 'for I am William Buelow Gould, sloe-souled, green-eyed, gap-toothed'" (372). These are words written by Gould himself earlier on in the story (105). It is astonishing enough, notes Xavier Pons,[28] that Gould should find his own story in print before he has finished writing it, and that the book should contain, "in perfect imitation of my style", Gould notes (374), the very pictures he painted. Even more extraordinary is the fact that the book pursues the story down to the narrative present, and into the future:

I then realised that the book was not near ended, that it contained several more chapters, & with mounting terror I read on the succeeding page of how – "I realised that the book was not near ended, that it contained several more chapters, & with mounting terror I read on the succeeding pages of how –" (374)

This book is not just a history of the settlement, but, as Gould recognises, a prophecy:

Billy Gould could not escape the growing suspicion that he had become entrapped in a book, a character whose future as much as his past was already written, determined, foretold, as unalterable as it was intolerable. What choice did he have but to destroy that book? (373–4).

---

28   Xavier Pons, "This Sad Pastiche: Texts and Contexts in Richard Flanagan's *Gould's Book of Fish*", *Commonwealth: Essays and Studies* 28, no.1 (Autumn 2005): 66.

The use of the third person throughout the novel occurs at various traumatic points, as when Gould discovers the enormous lie of the Registry. For Pons, "this suggests a split in a narrating subject who is not identical with himself, and who, splitting the narration still further, has himself become the creation of some unknown narrator who is both himself and more than himself".[29] This is more than a split; it is a multiplication, as Flanagan peppers his text with quotes from other writers, other voices who are also the voice of Billy Gould.

Flanagan himself, when interviewed, attests to life's circularity rather than linearity. This indeed is the assertion of Billy Gould, that narrative is incompatible with real life: "Stories as written are progressive, sentence must build upon sentence as brick upon brick, yet the beauty of this life in its endless mystery is circular. Sun & moon, spheres endlessly circling" (392). The fact that Gould should find his story in print before he had finished writing it is not simply a "fatiguingly inventive" ploy, nor merely *frolic* postmodernism,[30] nor a case of magic realism,[31] but a testament to the capacity of literature to do what History cannot, to encompass the circularity of life as the past and future circulate through the present. Where History is the narrative of events, Gould claims that life is a matter of transformation. His own metamorphosis at the end into a fish that had become his avatar in an apparently perfectly natural process confirms the transformative nature of life:

> There was for me no magick transformation, when hair fell out & skin slowly coarsened & divided into infinite scaling, when limbs seized & twitched & grew translucent & sharp-edged as fins, no dawning sense of wonder when I began to feel the propulsive power & fine control of the long tail sprouting out beyond my arse; no sense of panic as gills erupted behind my mouth & my need for water became something altogether more torturous & profound than can ever be described by the mere & derisive word thirst. (431–2)

Where he had thought there was something individually human about the fish, "the truth is that there is something irretrievably fishy about us all" (432). When Gould finally becomes a fish and enjoys the pleasures of the watery world, he and other fish now "understand each other with a complete profundity only those unburdened by speech & its complications could understand" (439). But more importantly, Gould's transformation has turned him into a prophet. When divers come searching for him:

> Sometimes I even want to tap with my long snout on those divers' goggles & say: You want to know what this country will become? Ask me – after all, if you can't trust a liar & a forger, a whore & an informer, a convicted murderer & a thief, you'll never understand this country … We've been trained to live a life of moral cowardice while all the time comforting ourselves that we are Nature's rebels. But in truth we've never got upset and excited about anything; we're like the sheep we shot the Aboriginals to make way for, docile until slaughter. (442–3)

---

29  Pons, "This Sad Pastiche", 66.
30  Robin Chen-Hsing Tsai, "(Post)Modernity in the Penal Colony: Richard Flanagan's *Gould's Book of Fish*", *Neohelicon* 38, no. 2 (2011): 381–93.
31  Ben Holgate, "The Impossibility of Knowing: Developing Magical Realism's Irony in *Gould's Book of Fish*", *JASAL: Journal of the Association for the Study of Australian Literature* 14, no. 5 (2014): 1–11.

To understand this country you can do no better than listen to one of its exemplars, "a liar & a forger, a whore & an informer, a convicted murderer & a thief". Gould has many identities and many voices but the strongest of these voices at the end of the story is clearly Flanagan's:

> Everything that's wrong with this country begins in my story: they've all been making the place up, ever since the Commandant tried to reinvent Sarah Island as a New Venice, as the island of forgetting, because anything is easier than remembering. They'll forget what happened here for a hundred years or more, then they'll reimagine it ... because any story will be better than the sorry truth that it wasn't the English who did this to us but ourselves, that convicts flogged convicts & pissed on blackfellas & spied on each other. (443)

In this way, Flanagan blocks off a favourite escape route for contemporary Australians – the idea that it wasn't us but the British who imported cruelty and wiped out the Aboriginal people. This is the source of that refusal to be sorry that marks the History Wars, the refusal to take responsibility, because we are not the criminals. To accept responsibility would be to plead guilty. And so we cling to History because any story is better than the true story. But this is the problem at the centre of the book. Where is that story to be found if History is a story of self-justification? In the end we are left with the poetic truth of literature.

Ultimately the novel, in all its outrageous exuberance, is a testament to the power of literature. For literature doesn't just give us a different story of the past; it has a utopian element, what Ernst Bloch calls its *vorschein* or "anticipatory illumination": the capacity not only to rail at the ugliness of the world, but to imagine a different world.[32] "I wanted to tell a story of love as I slowly killed those fish, & I told them how my paintings were not meant for Science or Art, but for people, to make people laugh, to make people think, to give people company & give them hope" (429). The power of literature is that it can do what history cannot – imagine a different future and thus transform the present, imagine the beauty of life to balance its ugliness. But literature unlike history can and must live with this contradiction:

> So there you have it: two things & I can't bring them together & they are wrenching me apart. These two feelings, this knowledge of a world so awful, this sense of a life so extraordinary – how am I to resolve them? (443)

The question is rhetorical because literature, by its nature, balances the contradictions of life just as it engages its transformative potentiality, its contingency, its constant circulation of past and future in the present. The beauty and wonder of the world are as limitless as its opposite, something that only imaginative writing can capture. We can take its truths from it and admit that our history is a fraud. But in the end it is the sense of possibility that literature illuminates, the sense that the world could be different, a sense that opens us up to a form of truth unavailable to History.

---

32 Ernst Bloch, *The Utopian Function of Art and Literature: Selected Essays*, trans. Jack Zipes and Frank Mecklenburg (Minneapolis: University of Minnesota Press, 1989), 111.

## References

Ankersmit, F.R. *Narrative Logic: A Semantic Analysis of the Historian's Language*. The Hague: Martinus Nijhoff, 2013.
Bloch, Ernst. *The Utopian Function of Art and Literature: Selected Essays*. Translated by Jack Zipes and Frank Mecklenburg. Minneapolis: University of Minnesota Press, 1989.
Chakrabarty, Dipesh. "Postcoloniality and the Artifice of History: Who Speaks for 'Indian' Pasts?", *Representations* 37 (Winter 1992): 1–26.
Chen-Hsing Tsai, Robin. "(Post)Modernity in the Penal Colony: Richard Flanagan's *Gould's Book of Fish*", *Neohelicon* 38, no. 2 (2011): 381–93.
Clark, Alex. "'In the hands of madmen': *Gould's Book of Fish*". *Guardian Australia*, 1 June 2002. http://bit.ly/2H0TmDa.
Craven, Peter. "Something Fishy Going On". *Age: Saturday Extra*, 10 November 2001, 9.
Fanon, Franz. *The Wretched of the Earth*. New York: Grove, 1963.
Flanagan, Richard. "Does Writing Matter?: Richard Flanagan Delivers the Inaugural Boisbouvier Lecture". *The Monthly*, October 2016. http://bit.ly/2xskR96.
——. *Gould's Book of Fish*. Sydney: Picador, 2001.
——. *The Sound of One Hand Clapping*. (1997) London: Picador, 1999.
Foucault, Michel. *The Order of Things*. London: Tavistock, 1970.
Hobson, J.A. *Imperialism: A Study*. (1902) Edited by Philip Siegelman. Ann Arbor: University of Michigan Press, 1965.
Holgate, Ben. "The Impossibility of Knowing: Developing Magical Realism's Irony in *Gould's Book of Fish*", *JASAL: Journal of the Association for the Study of Australian Literature* 14, no. 5 (2014): 1–11.
Hugo, Giles. "Richard Flanagan: The Making of a Tasmanian Best-Seller", *The Write Stuff* 1 (1995–6). http://bit.ly/2IVyLGl.
Kellner, Hans. "Narrativity in History: Post-Structuralism and Since", *History and Theory*, 26, no. 4 (December 1987): 1–29.
Nandy, Ashis. "History's Forgotten Doubles", *History and Theory* 34, no. 2 (1995): 44–66.
Pons, Xavier. "This Sad Pastiche: Texts and Contexts in Richard Flanagan's *Gould's Book of Fish*", *Commonwealth: Essays and Studies* 28, no.1 (Autumn 2005): 64–76.
Ricoeur, Paul. *Time and Narrative*. (1983) Translated by Kathleen McLaughlin and David Pellauer. Chicago: Chicago University Press, 1984.
Stubbs, William. *Lectures on Early English History*. (1878) Edited by A. Hassall. Oxford: Clarendon, 1990.
——. *The Constitutional History of England in Its Origin and Development*. (1875) New York: Cambridge University Press, 2011.
White, Hayden. "The Politics of Historical Interpretation: Discipline and De-Sublimation", *Critical Inquiry* 9, no. 1 (1982): 113–37.

# 6
# Richard Flanagan's "Post-post" and the Mapping of the Altermodern

Salhia Ben-Messahel

In Richard Flanagan's novel *The Sound of One Hand Clapping* (1997), one of the main characters, who is escaping from the harsh and desolate Tasmanian environment, claims that "to have a future [one] … must forget the past".[1] The weight of the past or (personal) history, a recurrent feature of Flanagan's writing, operates as part of the novelist's interrogation of the myth of a great southern land in the South Pacific. The deconstruction of national discourse and the incorporation of migrant others, meaning from a non-English background, into the multicultural framework, in three of Flanagan's novels, *Death of a River Guide* (1994), *The Sound of One Hand Clapping* and *The Narrow Road to the Deep North* (2013), seem to operate as a means to move beyond the post of the postcolonial nature of Australia and to design an alternative space where time is, to quote the critic and art historian Nicolas Bourriaud, "no longer the aftermath of a historical moment, but the infinite extension of the kaleidoscopic play of temporal loops in the service of a vision of history as a spiral which advances while turning back upon itself".[2] Thus, the examination of these three novels shows that as the main characters are respectively confronted by history (personal, social and political) they become agents of a time which Bourriaud terms the altermodern, implying a reconceptualisation of cultural identity around nomadism, wandering and, above all, successive enrootings. In these novels Flanagan retraces Australia's history through the livelihood of lost, hurt and broken characters and at the same time explores the impact of other nations on the development of character and identity. Migration, (his)stories and displacements interact with the ideal of the multicultural nation, subverting the Australian mainstream and reconfiguring reality. The use of the landscape as the place where natural and historical processes are manifested, and as the space for mindscape, the identity-creating projection that characters see in their surroundings, suggests that nation-building is never a process of belonging but rather an illusion, and that belonging implies redefining territory, as well as collective and individual identity.

The three novels depict characters whose identities are in constant motion and never the main foundation of existence. The stories design a set of dynamic connections within

---

1   Richard Flanagan, *The Sound of One Hand Clapping* (1997; London: Picador, 1999), 31. All subsequent references are to this edition and appear in parentheses in the text.
2   Nicolas Bourriaud, *The Radicant* (New York: Lukas & Stenberg, 2009), 186.

the space of world culture, and in so doing produce various itineraries and trajectories in the cultural landscape. The latent death of Aljaz Cosini in *Death of a River Guide* reactivates a past long gone but not dead along the banks of the Franklin River, so that the voyage back into the past and the memory of people and events become the privileged form of access to reality. History and personal story are embedded in the ebb and flow of the river currents, in the surrounding trees and rocks, and while Aljaz's personal story is part of the exploration of rivers, either in Tasmania or Western Australia, his recollections of his father's personal story delves into the historical development of the nation and sometimes into the national mythology, the stories of Old Bo, "the king of the piners",[3] and traumatised survivor of a Japanese war camp:

> Somewhere out in the middle of that sea, Old Bo began to tell stories, strange wonderful stories, and Smeggsy's eyes opened and as he listened he suddenly felt wide awake, so awake his mind left his body that rowed like a slow steam engine and entered the world of Old Bo's stories, a world where past, present and future seemed to collide and exist together. (230)

The interconnections of stories and history take place through the narrator's immersion into landscape and a territory, encapsulating a series of signs, markers and signatures, a semiotic system to interpret the past, the present (and the future), and providing access to specific time-spaces. Personal stories and histories subtly unravel through the system of the refrain defined by Gilles Deleuze and Félix Guattari in *A Thousand Plateaus*:

> The role of the refrain has often been emphasized: it is territorial, a territorial assemblage. Bird songs: the bird sings to mark its territory. The Greek modes and Hindu rhythms are themselves territorial, provincial, regional. The refrain may assume other functions, amorous, professional or social, liturgical or cosmic: it always carries earth with it; it has a land (sometimes a spiritual land) as its concomitant; it has an essential relation to a Natal, a Native. A musical "nome" is a little tune, a melodic formula that seeks recognition and remains the bedrock or ground of polyphony (*cantus firmus*). The *nomos* as customary, unwritten law is inseparable from a distribution of space, a distribution in space. By that token, it is *ethos*, but the ethos is also the Abode. Sometimes one goes from chaos to the threshold of a territorial assemblage: directional components, infra-assemblage. Sometimes one organizes the assemblage: dimensional components, intra-assemblage. Sometimes one leaves the territorial assemblage for other assemblages, or for somewhere else entirely: inter-assemblage, components of passage or even escape. And all three at once. Forces of chaos, terrestrial forces, cosmic forces: all of these confront each other and converge in the territorial refrain.[4]

In *Death of a River Guide*, Flanagan uses such a narrative technique and seems to make it his own signature. Indeed, as Sonja Buloh in *The Sound of One Hand Clapping* is putting her hand on the concrete surface of the hydro-electric dam, she feels the emanations of

---

3   Richard Flanagan, *Death of a River Guide* (1994; Sydney: Picador Pan Macmillan, 2004), 45. All subsequent references are to this edition and appear in parentheses in the text.
4   Gilles Deleuze and Félix Guattari, *A Thousand Plateaus: Capitalism and Schizophrenia*, trans. Brian Massumi (1980; London: Continuum, 2004), 334.

personal story and history (26–7), while Dorrigo Evans in *The Narrow Road to the Deep North* experiences the Thai-Burma Railway and urban Australia as projections of his own failures, his dark past and doomed present. Thus, the three novels operate through an achronological timeline that subverts the value of time and definition of history but that, in fact, constructs a psychogeography whereby individuals become dwellers, and identity is constructed through motion, through multiple enrootings.

None of Flanagan's characters can claim a single affiliation to place or ancestry; all of them remain eternal drifters, moving between cultures and spaces, temporary figures of a world in constant motion. The memory of the past, relived through different experiences and perspectives in the three novels, deconstructs official history in order to replace cultural others on the country's cultural map. Aljaz Cosini envisions historical events through family story and genealogy, and in so doing weaves a collective memory of place and people that subverts the nation's history. The Franklin River connects personal histories and embodies the affiliation of very diverse characters with place. Marc Delrez refers to Flanagan's association in the novel of the Australian uncanny with "a European spiritual tradition",[5] which he argues is visible through the story's intersection with other texts. Flanagan's second novel, *The Sound of One Hand Clapping*, shows an affiliation of genres and the use of palimpsest structures especially in the depiction of the migrant ordeal and social issues. The epigraph, a quote by Ivo Andric, the Yugoslav novelist, poet, short-story writer and Nobel Prize winner, focuses on military conflicts and their impact on young women's bodies and age, the poet wondering how young but old women can bear testimony for the casualties of war and history. Andric laments that these young women with grey hair may not live long enough to account for the cruelty of war, and argues that writing may at least retain the past and revive previous events for the sake of not forgetting. When he was awarded the Man Booker Prize in 2014 for *The Narrow Road to the Deep North*, Richard Flanagan declared: "Novels are not content. Nor are they a mirror to life or an explanation of life or a guide to life. Novels *are* life, or they are nothing".[6] Drawing on the novelist's claim that "novels *are* life", the three novels hold both the past and the present together but each is in a process of becoming, so that past and present are interchangeable and never rooted on a surface, both reminding the reader that the past is not past since it is not even past, and that the present is, in fact, a past, or the wraith of a constructed reality.

As a child, Sonja is left in the care of the Picottis and experiences a social space that is reminiscent of a Dickensian scene, especially in the way Umberto Picotti rakes in money and displays cruelty:

> But she [Sonja] could only watch in horrified fascination the way Picotti's gaudily ringed fingers felt each note, touched every coin with a slow sensuous pleasure, as if it were flesh and not cash he were fondling, and though they had not yet spoken so much as a word to each other she thought with the intensity and clarity that only children can think such things:
> How much I hate him. (122)

---

5 Marc Delrez, "Nationalism, Reconciliation, and the Cultural Genealogy of Magic in Richard Flanagan's *Death of a River Guide*", *The Journal of Commonwealth Literature* 42, no. 1 (2007): 122.
6 Richard Flanagan, Man Booker Prize acceptance speech, 14 October 2014. http://bit.ly/2sgNEZk.

The ambivalence of Picotti, a caricature of both the Mafioso and the Victorian figure of the ruthless landlord, is counterbalanced by the sense of egalitarianism that characterised the 1960s, embodied by the Heaneys, the antithesis to the Picottis:

> THE HEANEYS were that sort of family who were everywhere, that sort whose kids spread unavoidably like spilt gravy over the street – dirty and brown and everywhere and difficult to avoid and difficult to be rid of, that sort who stood by neighbours' fences asking them questions as to why they did this or that in the garden. (156)

The Heaneys are an Anglo-Australian family reminiscent of the working-class Pickleses in Tim Winton's celebrated novel *Cloudstreet* (1991); they embody the quintessential working-class family whose history is embedded in the geography of the country. Thus, Flanagan's stories design continuous connections and itineraries in the cultural, social and political landscape. Personal histories are bound to the environment so that history no longer confers a sense of reality but is only part of a given reality.

In *Death of a River Guide* and *The Sound of One Hand Clapping*, the references to the hydro-electric scheme and the construction of dams, which marked the social history of Tasmania in the mid-twentieth century and brought a significant number of migrant others into the existing local communities, subvert the common ideal of egalitarianism built on mateship, the fair go and the classless society. In *The Sound of One Hand Clapping*, the city of Hobart is depicted as an isolated geographic space on the margins of mainland Australia, the "arse end of everything", a rural place trying to be a city by shedding its colonial past and embracing industrialisation brought by more mechanisation and the automobile industry:

> in that month of April in the city of Hobart, nothing much looked like it could ever change around a town that had grown used to never being anything but the arse end of everything: mean, hard and dirty, where civic ambition meant buying up old colonial buildings and bulldozing them quick and covering the dust promptly with asphalt for cars most people were yet to own, where town pride meant tossing an unlucky derro found lying in the park into the can, and where a sense of community equated with calling anybody with skin darker than fair a boong bastard unless he wore snappy clothes in which case he was a filthy wog bastard. (119)

The ironic depiction of Hobart in 1959 as a city where social and cultural gaps are part of the daily reality, and where a latent segregation prevails, is iterated further on to show that, thirty years later, things have not changed. Sonja Buloh's return to Tasmania marks the confrontation of personal history and the history of the country, of the past and the present, so that reality is blurred, if not a fleeting moment in the spectrum of geographic space and time:

> You are not your past, Sonja counselled herself, can never be reduced or explained by the past. You are your dreams, which is why Sydney – that sly city of alluring promise – is the place for me … I am my dreams of tomorrow. The past is not your fate, and you make your chances like you drive a car, either slowly, risking nothing, gaining nothing, or fast, where all that matters is just what is in front of you at this moment, and everything that is behind you is totally irrelevant. (23)

## 6 Richard Flanagan's "Post-post" and the Mapping of the Altermodern

In this passage the past encapsulates a doomed reality, Sonja's personal history and enrooting in the Tasmanian environment, the world and story of working-class migrants whose future depended on the hydro-electric scheme, but as Sonja reflects, the past is just a momentary phase that can no longer direct the future. As an expatriated Tasmanian in Sydney, Sonja encountered different forms of subjectivities and adapted to an environment that is an antithesis to her past in Tasmania. She integrated into Sydney as a radicant, an organism that separates from its primary roots, the past and family history, and adapts through a new enrooting in another story and place, thus taking precedence over reality. Sonja's thought echoes Prospero's belief, in *The Tempest*, that "we are such stuff as dreams are made on",[7] and stems from Sonja's childhood fantasy when she found comfort in the unreal world of American television as a means to escape from her present and create the illusion of a reality. Yet it is by returning to the point of origin, the space of childhood and the dramatic departure from the home of her mother, when she was a very young child, that Sonja is able to confront her past and assemble the missing parts of her personal story.

In his novels, Flanagan therefore designs characters that never entirely belong, despite their being in place. Such characters, despite the fact that some may surface as marginal figures, tend to fit in with Nicolas Bourriaud's definition of the radicant. In his critical book of that name, Bourriaud draws on the Deleuzian concept of the rhizome to introduce the concept of "the radicant" as an organism that advances in all directions and then can adapt to various contexts through enrootings. Bourriaud argues that the radicant is part of a universe made of spatial precariousness, and that as such responds to the living conditions of a global environment. Referring to Victor Segalen and to the idea that the individual is an *exote*, someone who travels between cultures, Bourriaud argues that the "figure of the exote helps us better appreciate today's art, which is haunted by figures of travel, expedition, and global dislocation".[8]

In Flanagan's writing there seems to be a similar approach to otherness and multiculturalism, so that characters often appear to move within cultures and adapt to every single part of the geography they come to traverse. This, in fact, implies that no one or nothing can ever be completely assimilated to someone or something else; that complete fusion can never be achieved. One can then only assimilate or blend in to a certain extent as there will always be a trace or part of one of the cultures that will prevail and resurface in due course. In *Death of a River Guide*, for instance, Aljaz Cosini is trapped within the ebb and flow of the Franklin River, and as he is hanging between life and death becomes the object of an animated landscape, of a geographic space that encompasses past, present and future events. His memory of the river is annihilated by the very natural forces of the river itself; his own self becomes part of the geography, an element of place, "of the gorge and the mountains and the cliffs and the maelstrom" (289). The river is a central protagonist, subverting the artificial made-up world of industrialised society, but it also interacts with the character's life and fate. The role of the river echoes Flanagan's own statement that the river not only informs his personal life but also shapes it:

> I came to realise that most contemporary culture, including its literature, is made by people for whom the measure of the world is what is man-made. But the Franklin taught

---

7   William Shakespeare, *The Tempest* (London: Routledge/Arden, 1992), IV. I, 104.
8   Bourriaud, *The Radicant*, 20.

me this: that the measure of this world are [sic] all the things not made by man. And it was this sense that has come to inform me and all I have written since.[9]

Aljaz's psychological displacements through time and place retrace the pathways of his personal history as well as those of his ancestors, and in so doing deconstruct the very ideal of the multicultural nation, just as Sonja Buloh does when she is travelling back to her childhood place to confront her past and her father. Both novels depict the wretchedness of an Australia marred with violence and racism, a land of historical emptiness, economic greed and social disparities. The past in Europe, Slovenia, and the new beginning in Australia – which has become a past to be forgotten – have had an impact on the way Sonja and her father embrace the notion of "space": that is, the Tasmanian environment and the political space of nation. Sonja recalls the abuse from her father but also their fishing experience and the way she saw the town of Hobart, a place with no fixity, belonging to all times and part of a never-ending system or space: "It could have been the 1840s or the 1940s. It could have been Eastern Europe. But it was, as she had written across her schoolgirl's folder, Hobart, Tasmania, Australia, Southern Hemisphere, the World, the Solar System, the Universe. It was 1967" (12).

Tasmania presents not a landscape of hope, but one of historical and personal trauma: a colony and space of migration, the embodiment not of freedom but of enclosure. It is "a land at once alien and familiar" (20), given "strange new names" and cut into "neat counties with quaint reassuring English names such as Cumberland and Bothwell" (21). It surfaces as a prison camp for migrant others in search of an El Dorado, "Australia's Ruhr Valley" (21), hoping to be part of the Australian Dream, as one of the officials asserts during the naturalisation ceremony:

> "The path to the new Australia is lit not only by the electricity that will come forth from your labours here at Butlers Gorge, but by your conviction that the new world can be better than the old …
>
> "You bring your hope and determination", continues the politician, "and in return receive the great gift of English civilisation, the English language and our belief in justice and fair play" (42, 44).

This poignant and subversive scene embodies the complexity of postwar migration to Tasmania, depicting the hopeful view of the authorities seeking capital gains through cheap labour and demographic expansion, and reflecting both the misery and hope of men and women in search of social opportunities in the antipodean place. The Eurocentric references to a new Australia, meaning an Australia rid of its colonial past through technological advances and economics, are ironic considering that the hard labour of post-World War Two migrants translated into the latter's sense of hopelessness and discarding from the mainstream. Indeed, Bojan Buloh's experience and development encompass the solitude of the migrant, of the individual caught in a multicultural wasteland. He compares himself to an old tree "full of canker and parasitic insects" (341), reflects on his shabby existence, caught in the inferno of migrant labour and alcoholism, and compares his own self with the fissures of the dam:

---

9   Richard Flanagan, *And what do you do, Mr Gable? New and Collected Essays* (2011; North Sydney: Random House, 2015), 329–31.

for Bojan Buloh found that he had turned into concrete. But behind him a huge wild river was pressing and he was breaking, so slowly and inexorably breaking, and what he had held back for so many years was no longer able to be contained.

The fissures were opening into thread-thin fractures, and the penned-up water was pushing hard, infiltrating – countless tons of water pushing the dam face ever outwards. The fractures were expanding into cracks and the cracks growing ever larger and the water like some caged animal that had recognised its time now pushed the pieces, at first pebbles then boulders of concrete outwards with the force of missiles. (345–6)

Bojan Buloh experiences the vitality and force of the natural body of water from the river not in a spiritual but rather in a psychological manner. Thus, he neither fits in Anglo-Australia nor can he relate to his country of birth. The only way that he can relate to Australia is through the birth of his grandchild, symbolically a girl, during an event that comes as an epiphany. Speaking on the title of the novel, Flanagan insists that his characters are neither here nor there, that redemption can only be achieved through love, which is, in fact, what happens with the birth of Sonja's child:

these characters, as Dante wrote, were not living, nor yet were they dead; and … their lives are utterly bereft until they managed to manifest the love that they have for one another, and redeem themselves through that love. Until that time, each character knows the sound of one hand clapping, which I take to be an infinite nothingness.[10]

In the same interview, Flanagan refers to his interest in migrant experiences and how migrant stories are not only part of the history of the land and people, but also carry with them the histories of other places:

I grew up in a small mining town in a remote part of Tasmania, full of immigrants. And from a very young age, I remember their most extraordinary stories. It never ceased to astonish me how they imprinted upon one's soul in such a remote place. You might have written the great epic movement of history of the last 100 years – fascism, nationalism, communism, the disappearance of nations, languages – and all that would exist in one person's own story.[11]

Flanagan's interest in personal experiences in hostile environments and the way history distorts reality forms part of his 2013 novel *The Narrow Road to the Deep North*, which explores Australia's past in the context of its Asian-Pacific environment. Drawing on his father Arch Flanagan's real experience as a prisoner of war during World War Two, Flanagan explores world conflicts and the involvement of Australia as a mature nation through the story of Alwyn "Dorrigo" Evans, shifting from Australian to Asian settings. In an essay titled "Lest We Forget", Flanagan refers to the atrocities and consequences of conflicts and war on individuals, referring to the feeling of oblivion that seems to take precedence over the cult of remembrance:

---

10  Chat Books. "A Chat with Richard Flanagan about *The Sound of One Hand Clapping*". CNN.com, 4 April 2000. https://cnn.it/2xpBzWV.
11  Chat Books, "A Chat with Richard Flanagan".

We say we remember the fallen, and if we do that at best sporadically and inadequately, we hardly give thought to the many, many more who did not fall, but who returned home maimed, sometimes not only in body but also in mind and soul.

We forget the great truth of the ages: that war, even if it is sometimes necessary, is always evil. And we forget that the essence of its evil is that it inevitably demands of some soldiers that they do terrible things that would horrify and repulse them in any other situation …

We forget that the horror of an atrocity is not just that visited on its victims, but also on the people who commit those atrocities. Not necessarily bad people or psychopathic people, but ordinary human beings who must live with the horror of their actions for the rest of their lives.

And we forget these ordinary human beings are young men who have friends and families, that the horror within them comes to affect many and passes like a shot through the decades and sometimes generations.[12]

*The Narrow Road to the Deep North* raises such issues through the evolution of Dorrigo Evans from his younger days to his old age, as he experiences conflicts of different natures both at home and abroad. The examination of human darkness and experience relies on Giorgio Agamben's definition of the camp as the *nomos* of modernity, "the space that is opened when the state of exception becomes a rule",[13] a dislocating localisation in Siam,[14] run by Japanese and Korean soldiers, and where the main character and Australian prisoner of war, Dorrigo Evans, has ironically and tragically become a commanding officer among his fellow prisoners, being committed to their "well-being" as a means to maintain them alive as long as possible. The narration of war experience and life on the Thai-Burma Railway harks back to tales of Australian courage in the face of adversity at Gallipoli, along with the sense of mateship and nationhood. Speaking about the Thai-Burma Railway, Dorrigo likens the spatial organisation and appropriation of geographic space through the railway lines to a perpetually redesigned space, which is (re)conceived by a number of contingent forces, structure and/or powers:

> For the line was broken, as all lines finally are; it was all for nothing, and of it nothing remained. People kept on longing for meaning and hope, but the annals of the past are a muddy story of chaos only.
>
> And of that colossal ruin, boundless and buried, the lone and level jungle stretched far away. Of imperial dreams and dead men, all that remained was long grass.[15]

This passage seems to encapsulate the post-structuralist concepts and the geophilosophy of Gilles Deleuze and Félix Guattari, a system that advocates space, a constantly redesigned space which is structured by various and contingent power structures; a system that

---

12   Richard Flanagan, "Lest We Forget", in *And what do you do, Mr Gable ? New and Collected Essays* (2011; North Sydney: Random House, 2015), 245.
13   Giorgio Agamben, *Homo Sacer: Sovereign Power and Bare Life*, trans. D. Heller-Roazen (1995; Stanford: Stanford University Press, 1998), 168–9.
14   The name of Siam was officially changed to Thailand after the war on 20 July 1948.
15   Richard Flanagan, *The Narrow Road to the Deep North* (Sydney: Random House, 2013), 316. All subsequent references are to this edition and appear in parentheses in the text.

clearly dismisses verticality, transcendence and, above all, binarism; a system that relies on subsequent deterritorialisations and reterritorialisations:

> Multiplicities are defined by the outside: by the abstract line, the line of flight or deterritorialization according to which they change in nature and connect with other multiplicities. The plane of consistency (grid) is the outside of all multiplicities. The line of flight marks: the reality of a finite number of dimensions that the multiplicity effectively fills; the impossibility of a supplementary dimension, unless the multiplicity is transformed by the line of flight; the possibility and necessity of flattening all of the multiplicities on a single plane of consistency or exteriority, regardless of their number of dimensions.[16]

The depiction of the POW camp, reminiscent of the Nazi death camps, focuses on human cruelty at its worst and on human degradation, Dorrigo being the anti-hero who adapts to camp life and its rules. The camp is a modern-day manifestation of Dante's inferno[17] that functions as a heterotopia, a space of otherness characterised by overcrowding, very poor health conditions, very basic shelter, and filth, which reflects and triggers the most irrational and violent basic instincts of human existence. Dorrigo Evans' memory implies that his mind has become like the prison camp, an oxymoric space ("this reality of dreams and nightmares", 118), and that the past is an object of enclosure: "There was around him an exhausted emptiness ... forever unravelling and refurling a limitless dream or an unceasing nightmare, it was hard to know – from which he would never escape" (413). Such a feeling of confinement in a specific space and place is also consistent with his married life with Ella, when he realises that he gave up his freedom, his real love story with his uncle's wife, Amy Mulvaney.

Dorrigo is trapped in a modernised and peaceful commercial world of pretence marked by "boundaries and surveillance, where everything was known and nothing needed to be experienced" (79). He, in fact, burrows into the middle-class Australian dream of Melburnian society, hoping to forget his flaws. Yet, as he recalls the horror of the camp years later, and when he is in his seventies, Dorrigo concedes that reality hinges on different worlds: "This world and a hidden world that was a real world of wild, flying particles spinning, shimmering, randomly bouncing off each other, and new worlds coming into being in consequence" (466). The character's statement implies that many worlds form individual experience and that it is their "bouncing off each other" that designs the space that Bourriaud calls "the altermodern", where reality is a conglomeration of transitory surfaces and forms that become mobile. Altermodernity thus designates "a construction plan that would allow new intercultural connections, the construction of a space of negotiation going beyond postmodern multiculturalism, which is attached to the origin of discourses and forms rather than to their dynamics".[18] In the story, Dorrigo avoids going home right after his release from the POW camp but when he eventually does, he is caught in the older cultural spaces that are less mobile, being held up by a marital life he chose out of reason, a prisoner of his failures and a prisoner of his past in the camp. Yet,

---

16  Deleuze and Guattari, *A Thousand Plateaus*, 9–10.
17  See Liliana Zavaglia, "'Out of the tear-drenched land': Transnational Sites of Memory in *The Narrow Road to the Deep North*", this volume.
18  Bourriaud, *The Radicant*, 40.

rather than providing a Manichean tale, Flanagan manages to establish a link between the Australian and the Japanese characters, soldiers and persecutors alike, and in giving them all a voice constructs an intercultural space between Asia and Australia.

*The Narrow Road to the Deep North*, like most stories by Flanagan, relies on constant shifts between different times and places. Dorrigo Evans, for instance, highlights the dual nature of memory and reality, and conveys the idea that history is not only fake but above all a malleable instrument, ironically referring to the "order and discipline that is the very lifeblood of the Empire" (48), and to Rudyard Kipling's thoughts on remembrance, justice and the temporary nature of things (253–4). The story's initial aim at rewriting the personal story of Flanagan's father and in the process the story of his fellow prisoners and the camp rulers, for example the story of Nakamura, commander of the POW camp, interrogates the relations between Australia and Asia not only throughout the war but also in the postwar era, at a time when the country's political space is reconfigured in the Asia-Pacific region.

Some critics hailed Flanagan's work as an epic, reminiscent of canonical works such as Joseph Conrad's *Heart of Darkness* for its symbolic imageries and references, its examination of human struggle between civilisation and barbarity, and the effects of colonialism.[19] Yet the novel also refers from the very beginning to the haiku (29, 131), celebrating the evanescence of things, and referring to the natural environment, the Burmese jungle, and the daily performing of crimes against humanity (269), juxtaposing the horror of war and geopolitics with individual choices made for the sake of respectability or personal ambition. The development of Dorrigo Evans, a character modelled on the real Australian surgeon and war hero, Ernest Edward "Weary" Dunlop, evolves from a youth marked by self-doubt and uncertainty to an old age marred by doubt and regrets. The episodes dealing with camp life and the daily facing of an impending death are thus told with a detached tone that marks the main character's inability to confront the heart of the experienced darkness that cost the lives of Asian (Burmese, Malayans, Thais, Javanese, Tamils) and Australian prisoners. Moreover, there are several occasions in the novel when the narrator refers to the main character's inability to express things, since "words – all the words that did not say things directly – were for him the most truthful" (11) and since "all life is only allegory and the real story is not here" (5).

The interweaving of stories between the past, present and future not only shows that history is neither static nor legitimate but that geography and settings respectively encapsulate a succession of stories that are enrooted in diverse and changing locations and never cease to trigger successive forms of belonging, so that Asia, just like Australia, surfaces as a space of conflicts and cultural diversity. The novel relies on digressions and a chronology that is never linear, conveying a sense of time made of fleeting moments or fragments of individual experience, with its shifting narrators and perceptions – providing different viewpoints and conveying a Rashomon effect, so that contested interpretations of events or disagreements and evidence for them, subjectivity or objectivity, memory and perception, are dealt with in the rewriting of historical events.[20] In this novel, which can be

---

19   Peter Conrad, "Tim Winton's *Eyrie* and Richard Flanagan's *The Narrow Road to the Deep North*", *The Monthly*, October 2013. http://bit.ly/2xskR96.
20   Robert Anderson, "What Is the Rashomon Effect?", in *Rashomon Effects: Kurosawa, Rashomon and Their Legacies*, ed. Blair Davis, Robert Anderson and Jan Wallis (Abingdon: Routledge, 2016), 66–85.

read as a tribute to his father but also to all the other Australian POWs, Flanagan does not forget the silenced others, meaning here the POWs from non-English backgrounds who fought and received little recognition, and who also died on the Death Railway:

> There are no names of the hundreds of thousands who died ... on the Death Railway. The Allied POWS were but a fraction – some 60,000 men – of those who slaved on that Pharaonic project. Alongside them were a quarter of a million Tamils, Chinese, Javanese, Malayans, Thais and Burmese. Or more. Some historians say 50,000 of these slave labourers died, some say 100,000, some say 200,000. No one knows.
> And no one will ever know. Their names are already forgotten. There is no book for their lost souls. Let them have this fragment. (26)

Such a fragment clearly incorporates the novel's references to the haiku, the poetic style that surfaces at times in the book, along with its symbolic title, deriving from the 1669 Matsuo Basho classic. When interviewed about the writing of the novel, Flanagan underlined the difficulty of writing about the horror of the war without affecting culture:

> I felt, in a way, that spoke to the challenge I faced, which was to try to write about this great evil that the Japanese people were responsible for, but honouring all that is great and truly beautiful about their culture, and their literature truly is. And so that's why I called the book, "The Narrow Road to the Deep North", which is of course the title of one of the most famous works of Japanese literature: A *haibun* by Bashō, the great haiku poet.[21]

Flanagan not only attempts to provide an account of his father's war experience but rewrites history using a deconstructionist approach, playing with language and references:

> And throughout it, there's a lot of very famous haikus reversed. So things like: "blow after blow, on the monster's face, a monster's mask", which is Basho's famous haiku: "Day after day / On the monkey's face / A monkey's mask". There are many, many inversions of haikus, which those who know Japanese literature will see very clearly what's being done there.[22]

It is even ironic that on several occasions Dorrigo Evans is rebuked for speaking in literary quotes: "Do you ever use your own words?" (21, 88). Moreover, iterations in specific dramatic instances that "The world is. It just is" (215, 217) convey an existential and fatalistic statement, often with Faulknerian undertones, about the reality of the world over time:

> Rock to gravel to dust to mud to rock and so the world goes, as his mother used to say when he [Dorrigo] demanded reasons or explanation as to how the world got to be this way or that. The world is, she would say. It just *is*, boy. (3)

---

21 Ramona Koval, interview with Richard Flanagan. *The Monthly Video*, 24 July 2014. http://bit.ly/2sqIfyd.
22 Koval, interview with Richard Flanagan.

The association of disparate elements and "the substitution of one language for another, the new one contenting itself with subtitling the old one, without ever getting started on the process of translation that would establish a possible dialogue between past and present, the universal and the world of differences",[23] through the scope of postcolonial deconstruction seems to generate a space for altermodernity, past the post of postcolonial Australia. In fact, Flanagan's novel associates heterogeneous elements to make connections "in the infinite text of world culture. In a word, to produce itineraries in the landscape of signs by taking on the role of *semionauts*, inventors of pathways within the cultural landscape, nomadic sign gatherers".[24]

Dorrigo Evans' various experiences and encounters become the sum of a fragmented world that does not confer negativity but rather sustains the diversity of cultures and human relations within national and global environments. The character, just like Flanagan the novelist, fits in with Sneja Gunew's coining and definition of the term "globaletic writers":

> [writers who] facilitate new relations between national cultures and the global … The very elements that have been traditionally associated with their constitutive oppression, the belief that they are at home nowhere or in more than one place, … that they can navigate the structures of belonging in multiple ways, not least by challenging the complacent assumptions or self-evident universalisms that undergird many forms of both nationalism and globalisation.[25]

Gunew's definition and argument also apply to Flanagan's other novels, including *The Sound of One Hand Clapping*, which delves into the irony of multiculturalism and questions its validity by depicting characters who interact and operate within national and global cultures/environments. The novel's central idea concerns the barbarism of an old world left behind, set in Europe, and the harshness of the new host country, Australia:

> They were drinking not to enjoy the present, but for the more urgent reason of wanting to forget the past and to deny the future. Their destination was not pleasure but oblivion, and they wished to arrive as quickly as possible. (264–5)

Bojan Buloh's confinement reflects the flaws of migrancy and multiculturalism, along with the artificial nature of postcolonial Australia: "He did not believe in words like Nation. Like History. Working Class. Management. Efficiency. National Interest. Creeping Socialism. Or even words like Technology. Economics. Wilderness. Lifestyle. Or Future" (182). Bojan Buloh (like any other character in Flanagan's fiction) bears testimony that Australia's postcolonial nature is an ambiguous if not a hollow concept, considering that it invariably reflects the colonial past and erases any cultural singularity under the guise of the politics of multiculturalism, which is, after all, an Anglo-centred concept. A third-person narrator

---

23  Bourriaud, *The Radicant*, 14–15.
24  Bourriaud, *The Radicant*, 39.
25  Sneja Gunew, "'A Multilingual Life': The Cosmopolitan and Globalectic Dimensions of Shirley Geok-lin Lim's Writings", *Asiatic: IIUM Journal of English Language & Literature* 8, no. 1 (June 2014): 12.

exposes the existing frontier spaces within the Australian landscape by commenting on Bojan Buloh's grief and sense of loss:

> OBSERVE BOJAN BULOH this night of remorse.
> Watch how through the frontierland of Australian suburbia he in his FJ searches for escape once more, how he travels past houses new and raw as a gutted roo, their bloody viscera carved out of the bush only an instant ago, along roads that merge into deep muddy drains, heading into this land of no footpaths, no concrete edging. (281)

The exterior narrative voice adopts the style of Victorian novels, surfacing like a character out of time to provide statements on the characters, the ongoing events and reality. And yet it is in this "land of no footpaths" that the Buloh family inscribes its own story, meandering along the darkest depths of the past and struggling to connect. Flanagan, in fact, suggests that the Buloh family transcends the idea of history owing to their personal story and experience through a scarred social and geographical environment:

> There's a line somewhere in the book that talks about how, in the end, people do stand somewhere beyond history, because history cannot take into account the great irrational forces of hate and of love.
> At the end of a century, of the greatest horrors committed in the name of historical forces – nationalism, industrialism, fascism and communism – I was intrigued as to how two characters might seek to somehow speak of their own humanity in a way that was an act of defiance against these historical forces, against history. It seemed to me that the only way they could do that, and the most profound, subversive and moving way they could do it, would be in the love they would show each other.[26]

The novel inscribes the family story in landscape as part of the many stories that compose the cultural map of the nation, not as a multicultural canvas marked by genealogy and history but rather as a radicant space, the place of successive enrooting. Sonja considers she is neither made of "lace", like her mother, nor of "wood", like her father (383). She only identifies with Maria, her estranged mother, through the wild and snowy Tasmanian landscape, which she calls "My Maria" (280, 424), and with her father through the stone and concrete structure of the river dam. Sonja is able to reconnect with him through a cathartic moment brought about by Bojan's making of the Huon pine cradle for his future (and fatherless) granddaughter. The reconnection between Sonja and Bojan can only take place through the coming to life of the child since they both remain apart, "in a world that has since perished into peat, in a forgotten winter on an island of which few have ever heard", in "the whispering land. At that precise moment, around which time was to cusp" (425).

In *The Narrow Road to the Deep North*, Dorrigo Evans remembers his experience as a medical student at the University of Melbourne and how some Australians could relate to their ancestors from the origin of the nation to their British ancestry, which then fascinated him, and he realises that those family stories placed within the scope of history were in fact "fiction greater than anything Trollope ever attempted" (12). In saying so, Dorrigo conveys a message that forms the backbone of Flanagan's fiction, which is that there is no

---

26   Chat Books, "A Chat with Richard Flanagan".

such thing as "otherness" since "being other" would imply an "I" referent against whom the other would be assessed and viewed. In a discussion of Australian fiction and Australian culture, Sneja Gunew mentions those other "countries" that form the continent, Australia, referring to Indigenous countries but also to "those wispy filaments attached to those who once came from a place other than England or Ireland".[27] Gunew insists that those "other countries" and diasporic filaments subvert the multicultural framework of the nation:

> In addition, what might "Australia" look like when these other motherlands are acknowledged as spaces of origin? Australia is the mother who is not mother, the uncanny place that will never give birth: the stillborn. For white Australians, the country is the dead centre, the mother who ingests life. Life, rather, exists in the cities, on the edge where the land is covered over, pressed under, and where the subject is lost in the automatic, automaniac maze: life in death, death in life. The maternal space is always elsewhere, though repressed; in other cultures, though disavowed.[28]

Gunew's points can clearly be applied to the examination of the story, especially as Dorrigo Evans is experiencing Australia's pains at extricating itself from the British past and advancing in the twentieth century and the thriving sixties and seventies. As the epigraph from Issa Kobayashi's haiku suggests, Dorrigo comes to the realisation that "In this world we walk on the roof of hell gazing at flowers" (391). The botanical reference is all the more interesting in that it ties in with Nicolas Bourriaud's concept of the radicant. Indeed, Flanagan's novel, like all other stories, introduces readers to various elsewheres, all of them radicant spaces and part of an altermodernity that presupposes that there are no origins, no endings, no clear hierarchy, but rather multiple combinations in a universe where disparate elements can function together, and where cultures advance like ivy, through successive enrootings in shifting environments.

## References

Agamben, Giorgio. *Homo Sacer: Sovereign Power and Bare Life* (1995). Translated by D. Heller-Roazen. Stanford: Stanford University Press, 1998.
Anderson, Robert. "What Is the Rashomon Effect?" In *Rashomon Effects: Kurosawa, Rashomon and Their Legacies,* edited by Blair Davis, Robert Anderson and Jan Wallis. Abingdon: Routledge, 2016.
Bourriaud, Nicolas. *The Radicant*. New York: Lukas & Stenberg, 2009.
Chat Books. "A Chat with Richard Flanagan about *The Sound of One Hand Clapping*". CNN.com, 4 April 2000. https://cnn.it/2xpBzWV.
Conrad, Peter. "Tim Winton's *Eyrie* and Richard Flanagan's *The Narrow Road to the Deep North*". *The Monthly*, October 2013. http://bit.ly/2xskR96.
Deleuze, Gilles and Félix Guattari. *A Thousand Plateaus: Capitalism and Schizophrenia*. (1980) Translated by Brian Massumi. London: Continuum, 2004.
Delrez, Marc. "Nationalism, Reconciliation, and the Cultural Genealogy of Magic in Richard Flanagan's *Death of a River Guide*", *The Journal of Commonwealth Literature* 42, no. 1 (2007): 117–29.

---

27  Sneja Gunew, "Stammering 'Country' Pedagogies: Sickness for and of the Home", *Journal of Australian Studies* 29, no. 86 (2005): 73.
28  Gunew, "Stammering 'Country' Pedagogies", 76.

Flanagan, Richard. *And what do you do, Mr Gable? New and Collected Essays*. (2011). North Sydney: Random House, 2015.
Flanagan, Richard. Man Booker Prize acceptance speech, 14 October 2014. http://bit.ly/2sgNEZk.
——. *The Narrow Road to the Deep North*. Sydney: Random House, 2013.
——. *Death of a River Guide*. (1994) Sydney: Picador, 2004.
Gunew, Sneja. "'A multilingual life': The Cosmopolitan and Globalectic Dimensions of Shirley Geok-lin Lim's Writings". *Asiatic: IIUM Journal of English Language & Literature* 8, no. 1 (June 2014): 12–24.
——. "Stammering 'Country' Pedagogies: Sickness for and of the Home". *Journal of Australian Studies* 29, no. 86 (2005): 71–82.
Koval, Ramona. Interview with Richard Flanagan. *The Monthly Video*, 24 July 2014. http://bit.ly/2sqIfyd.
Shakespeare, William. *The Tempest*. (1611) London: Routledge/Arden, 1992.

# 7
# Contestations of Authority: Richard Flanagan's Australian Biofictions

*Marc Delrez*

In the introduction to *Biographical Fiction: A Reader*, Michael Lackey notes that the genre of "biofiction" has now "become so dominant with well-respected authors that it is no longer possible to dismiss it as an inferior, misguided, illegitimate, or irrelevant form".[1] Lackey further contends that this emerging generic respectability places a twofold onus on the critic, who must chart for biographical fiction a narrative space "uniquely its own"[2] – quite distinct from those of the historical novel or of life writing in its various guises – while identifying the major defining features of the object thus created. In his view, biographical fiction differs from the classical historical novel (as memorably defined by the Hungarian Marxist philosopher Georg Lukács)[3] because its intense focus on the individual subject's psychological interiority cannot be reconciled with "the objective proportions of history".[4] On the other hand, it should also be distinguished from the art of autobiography, as the latter does not normally claim the right to invent, establishing with the reader a tacit or explicit pact which prohibits "a purposeful or strategic alteration of fact".[5] By contrast, it is part of the conventions governing biographical fiction that it may deliberately flout factuality in its gesturing towards "a more substantive truth" which is inseparable from our specific standpoint on the past and therefore contains a form of anachronism meant to seem heuristic rather than fallacious. In other words, Lackey suggests that, over and beyond the predictable distinction between the free creative writer and the fact-obsessed historian (or biographer), what tends to characterise biographical fiction is the novelist's determination to approach the past dialectically, not only as a document that throws light on the present but also as one that proves open to interrogation from the angle of our inherited contemporary perspective(s). In this sense, the insights provided by the genre will prove "consciously and strategically bi-temporal".[6]

Clearly, this sort of conceptualisation accommodates the speculations about the constructed nature of all truth – including historical truth – fostered by postmodern,

---

1 Michael Lackey, ed., *Biographical Fiction: A Reader* (New York: Bloomsbury, 2017), 12.
2 Lackey, *Biographical Fiction*, 3.
3 Georg Lukács, *The Historical Novel* (1937; Lincoln: University of Nebraska Press, 1987).
4 Lackey, *Biographical Fiction*, 1.
5 Lackey, *Biographical Fiction*, 9.
6 Lackey, *Biographical Fiction*, 10.

post-structural and postcolonial scholarship in the latter part of the twentieth century. Indeed, Lackey's critical descriptions display great sensitivity to the political intentions often encoded within the aesthetic calibrations of "biofiction", for example in historiographic metafictions of the sort described by Linda Hutcheon.[7] However, it is remarkable that his groundbreaking anthology somehow fails to circumscribe any identifiable postcolonial, let alone Australian contribution to the genre, with the exception of a brief reference to David Malouf, whose name is included on the strength of the Afterword to *An Imaginary Life* (1978), which states that what the author here "wanted to write was neither historical novel nor biography, but a fiction with its roots in possible event"[sic].[8] There is no doubt that Malouf's novella, which addresses the later life of the Latin poet Ovid after he was banished by the emperor Augustus and largely slipped from the historical record, meets all of the genre's defining criteria. Yet it may be argued that *An Imaginary Life* is hardly representative of a distinctive tradition of biographical fiction as it developed in Australia, not on account of any felt polemical quality characterising Malouf's views about the past,[9] but rather because it fails to focus on any reputable agent of Australian history. It can be shown that, by contrast, most practitioners of "biofiction" in this country manifest a nationalist bias, predisposing them to invest in and imaginatively investigate, by preference, a brand of character ostensibly descending in more or less a direct line from an embattled national past.

Simultaneously, a lot of the comments offered in *Biographical Fiction* by way of vindication of the fictional biographer's right to invent, together with the claim that the novelist may access a level of truth denied to the historian, will seem astonishingly consonant with many of the ideas mooted in the context of Australia's History Wars,[10] and also during the public debate which surrounded the publication of Kate Grenville's *The Secret River* (2005). As we know, even the more "literary" (and progressive) of historians, such as Inga Clendinnen and Mark McKenna, attempted at the time to reassert a sense of the "fundamental difference between history and fiction",[11] insisting that "all writers and critics have an obligation to remember to distinguish between the two".[12] This, in turn, prompted a response by creative writers who emphasised the significance of their own contribution to the historical project under construction in contemporary Australia.[13] In consequence, there may well be, in this country, a tradition of enlightenment (or self-consciousness) about the complexity of the relationship that may be forged between a historical novel and the "real" past, which is bound to inflect the reception of Lackey's

---

7   See Linda Hutcheon, *A Poetics of Postmodernism: History, Theory, Fiction* (New York: Routledge, 1988).
8   David Malouf, *An Imaginary Life* (London: Chatto & Windus, 1978), 153.
9   As Peter Pierce reminds us, "David Malouf richly imagines key moments in Australian history" in his later work, which is not to say that he necessarily borrows the codes of "biofiction". See Peter Pierce, "Problematic History, Problems of Form: David Malouf's *Remembering Babylon*", in *Provisional Maps: Critical Essays on David Malouf*, ed. Amanda Nettelbeck (Nedlands, WA: Centre for Studies in Australian Literature, 1994), 183.
10  See Stuart Macintyre and Anna Clark, *The History Wars* (2003; Melbourne: Melbourne University Press, 2004).
11  Sarah Pinto, "History, Fiction, and *The Secret River*", in *Lighting Dark Places: Essays on Kate Grenville*, ed. Sue Kossew (Amsterdam: Rodopi, 2010; Cross/Cultures 131), 189.
12  Mark McKenna, "Writing the Past", *Australian Financial Review* (16 December 2005), Review, 1.
13  See for instance Kate Grenville, "The Question of History: Response", *Quarterly Essay* 25 (February 2007): 66–72.

elaborations about biographical fiction. In other words, in this particular case, like elsewhere, the fashion for "biofiction" has pre-existed the critical recognition of the genre, while it may also be the case that, in this country, a great deal of the relevant material turns out to be implicated in a longstanding postcolonising historiographic project conducted collectively. As Gail Jones puts it, there is more to this than a mere doffing of the cap to "the principle of engaged history-writing (such as we see practised by Inga Clendinnen, Henry Reynolds and Anna Haebich, to mention a few)", in that the peculiar role devolving on the creative artists must be recognised also, possibly in terms of a necessary struggle with "the inclusion of time in one's imagining of other people's sufferings".[14]

It is not too difficult to show that the creative engagement with iconic figures of the nation's past has long exercised the imagination of canonical Australian writers, so that here, too, the genre of "biofiction" has acquired prominence at the hands of "well-respected authors": witness the classic status achieved by Patrick White's *Voss* (1957), which ponders the fate of the Prussian explorer Ludwig Leichhardt, or by James McAuley's verse epic on another explorer, the Portuguese *Captain Quiros* (1964). White again revisits history, as well as the historical novel, with his rewriting of the Eliza Fraser myth in *A Fringe of Leaves* (1976). Further, what appears as a "long lineage of fictional histories"[15] dealing with the national past reached a peak of discursive intensity in the years of Reconciliation, at a time when the narrative of the country's foundation became increasingly contested.[16] Notable biographical novels produced in this fraught context include Robert Drewe's and Peter Carey's respective renditions of the experience of the bushranger Ned Kelly, *Our Sunshine* (1991) and *True History of the Kelly Gang* (2000); Kate Grenville's *The Secret River*, which fictionalises the life of her own great-great-great-grandfather, Solomon Wiseman, as an attempt to recreate a sense of the socio-economic and psycho-political conditions which informed (and facilitated) frontier violence at the time of settlement in New South Wales; or Grenville's romanticised portrait of the colonial administrator William Dawes in *The Lieutenant* (2007). These two would become part of *The Secret River* trilogy with the publication of *Sarah Thornhill* in 2011.[17]

Richard Flanagan's interest in the figure of George Augustus Robinson, as manifest in both *Gould's Book of Fish* (2001) and *Wanting* (2008), can then be seen to rehearse the comparable project of historical correction earlier initiated by Robert Drewe in *The Savage Crows* (1976) or Mudrooroo in *Doctor Wooreddy's Prescription for Enduring the Ending of the World* (1983), and testifies to a similar determination to subordinate fictional writing to a revisionary examination of the ideological conditions prevailing at the nation's origins.

---

14  Gail Jones, "Speaking Shadows: Justice and the Poetic", in *Just Words? Australian Authors Writing for Justice*, ed. Bernadette Brennan (St Lucia: University of Queensland Press, 2008), 79–80.
15  Pinto, "History, Fiction, and *The Secret River*", 186.
16  In 1991, the federal government passed the Aboriginal Reconciliation Act, which established the Council for Aboriginal Reconciliation. The stated goal of the latter was to assist in producing a united Australia built around mutual recognition and respect between Indigenous and non-Indigenous Australians. Thus, Reconciliation was instituted as an official strategy, largely dependent on an ambitious pedagogical program, by which all Australians, be they dispossessed Aborigines or empowered settlers, might feel that they properly belong in the nation. To achieve this aim, the Council initially set itself the symbolic deadline of 2001 for the completion of its activities, so that the last decade of the twentieth century tends to be especially associated with reconsiderations of the national past, fictional or otherwise.
17  On the literature of "Concern", see Nicholas Birns, *Contemporary Australian Literature: A World Not Yet Dead* (Sydney: Sydney University Press, 2015).

While these two novels by Flanagan contain quite an impressive gallery of additional historical figures made to cross paths with the most fantastic of fictional characters, it is also noteworthy that *The Narrow Road to the Deep North* (2013), which seeks to rehearse the war traumas endured by the author's father, sets out to do so through an evocation of the figure of Edward "Weary" Dunlop, a much-admired army officer renowned for his inspired leadership of Australian POWs active in the construction of the Thai-Burma Railway in 1943. Thus this novel, too, documents the author's propensity for imaginatively approaching the national past from the assumed vantage-point of carefully selected historical personages – even though, in this case, the mythic figure of national fame appears under the fictional name of Alwyn "Dorrigo" Evans. It is of course relevant that Flanagan, formerly a Rhodes Scholar in history at the University of Oxford, was formally trained as a *bona fide* historian. It may then be argued that his motivations and methods as a writer can usefully be construed in terms of a strategic wish to dislodge factuality by means of aestheticism. In my view, this should not be understood as a petulant rejection of evidence-based protocols of knowledge in favour of a counterfeit, solipsistic apprehension of reality, but rather as a serious imaginative descent into sensed correspondences between art and science, fiction and history, invention and truth. Thus, if imagination itself may have seemed to be on trial all through the History Wars, Flanagan's response seems to lie in his development of an art of "biofiction" meant to probe the homogeneous imperatives informing contemporary perspectives on the past, and to excavate contrasting spaces of experience not obliterated by any subjective subjugation to the ostensible authority of fact.

My contention is therefore that Flanagan's consistent questioning of authority, an aspect of his imagination that has inflected his work ever since the publication of *Death of a River Guide* (1994), contains a philosophical dimension which parallels his unmistakable political preoccupations.[18] The political intentions of his conception seem most perceptible in some of his less obviously historical novels, like *The Unknown Terrorist* (2006), which is set wholly in present-day Sydney. This is a text which, from the outset, reflexively draws attention to the fact that its characters inhabit a world "of today", where "the past" only persists as a category of obsolescence: "The past was a garbage bin of outdated appliances … an embarrassment of distressing colours and styles about which to laugh".[19] Accordingly, it has been remarked that an aesthetic "shift"[20] had taken place from earlier "magic realist" material to this rather sober, arch-realist narrative where the great metropolis appears to be strictly observed, despite certain dystopian overtones that make it seem "depraved and debased".[21] Thus Flanagan here purposefully diminishes the scope of representation, anchoring the narrative in a flat contemporaneous epoch dominated by commercial and dehumanising cultural fashions. This grounding in the prevalent zeitgeist

---

18  Laura A. White, for example, addresses Flanagan's first novel as a critique of colonialist epistemologies in her "Submerging the Imperial Eye: Affective Narration as Environmentalist Intervention in Richard Flanagan's *Death of a River Guide*", *Journal of Commonwealth Literature* 47, no. 2 (2012): 265–79.

19  Richard Flanagan, *The Unknown Terrorist* (Sydney: Picador, 2006), 7. All subsequent references are to this edition and appear in parentheses in the text.

20  See Andrew McCann, "Professing the Popular: Political Fiction circa 2006", *Australian Literary Studies* 23, no. 2 (2007): 44.

21  Jen Webb, "Distant Context, Local Colour: Australian 'Post September 11' Fiction", in "Common Readers and Cultural Critics," ed. Russell Smith and Monique Rooney, special issue, *JASAL: Journal of the Association for the Study of Australian Literature* (2010): 7.

is ironically acknowledged in the author's sarcastic "Notes on Sources" for this book, again identified as consubstantial with the present moment: "I took this novel from everywhere – ads, headlines, gossip, bar talk, along with the grabs of politicians and the sermons of shock jocks – no-one, after all, was doing contemporary fiction better" (325). A form of paradoxical humour may then be encoded in this fiction of negative resources, modelled on escapist media, while it is of course relevant to the book's imitative mode of conceptualisation that the main protagonist, an unprepossessing young woman aptly known as the Doll, is conformist and materialist and "entirely in line with contemporary social values".[22] The lethal effects of this addiction to the epistemic consensus become apparent when the Doll, whose physical appearance deceptively suggests an "exotic" background (6), falls victim to just the sort of unthinking xenophobia that she herself embodies. The fact that she learns in consequence, and comes to intuit the dangerous vacuity of her own existential choices, only enhances the effectiveness of the formal experimentation conducted in the book. Indeed, Flanagan here devises a fiction of depleted reality meant to jolt the reader into an awareness of loss, inevitable when historical insight is sacrificed in favour of *hic et nunc* perceptions considered as absolute.

This insistence on what may be called, after Žižek, the "desert of the real",[23] implies that *The Unknown Terrorist* might even include itself – its own self-conscious realism and popular idiom – in the onslaught against seductive codes of expression masquerading as sovereign truth. In this sense, while it is of course incontestable that the novel, which is dedicated to David Hicks,[24] seeks to expose the manipulative "use of terrorism by governments and the media to exert, maintain, and increase power",[25] one should not underestimate the irony implicit in Flanagan's decision to embrace and thus underwrite this level of discourse in his very attempt to oppose it. Andrew McCann sees this as a matter of the novel being "obviously conflicted about its popular affiliations".[26] Arguably, this sort of recognition may serve to mitigate critical perceptions of the novel's flaws, sometimes identified as a tendency to flaunt its ideology, "making a political point at the expense of the characters and the plot".[27] There is indeed another dimension to Flanagan's indictment, evident in the contrapuntal modulations of the novel's frustrating close, which invite the antithesis of political resignation even as the text underlines closure with its comment that "Everything ... [resumes] its accustomed course even when life is at its most terrible" (319). A dispiriting paradox is involved here: while it may seem as if

---

22  Webb, "Distant Context, Local Colour", 7.
23  See Slavoj Žižek, *Welcome to the Desert of the Real! Five Essays on September 11 and Related Dates* (London: Verso, 2002).
24  David Matthew Hicks (b. 1975), one of the first people to have been convicted under the US Military Commissions Act, is an Australian citizen who was detained by the United States in Guantanamo Bay detention centre from 2001 to 2007, on a charge of providing material support for international terrorism. After a long controversy his conviction was eventually overturned by the US Court of Military Commission Review in February 2015.
25  Nathanael O'Reilly, "Government, Media and Power: Terrorism in the Australian Novel since 9/11", in *From Solidarity to Schisms: 9/11 and After in Fiction and Film from Outside the US*, ed. Cara Cilano (Amsterdam: Rodopi, 2009), 296. See also Nathanael O'Reilly, "Terror, Paranoia and Manipulation: The Politics of Fear in Richard Flanagan's *The Unknown Terrorist* (2006)", this volume.
26  McCann, "Professing the Popular", 50.
27  Magdalena Ball, "Book Review: *Wanting* by Richard Flanagan", *Blogcritics Books*, 23 December 2008; cited in Webb, "Distant Context, Local Colour", 2.

recent catastrophic events – including the relentless repetition of actual terrorist attacks worldwide – has given the lie to the novelist's claim that no real threat justified an escalation in security legislation in Australia or elsewhere, so that the "War on Terror" really depended on "myths or imaginings",[28] it remains true that the urge to drive security into institutions, allying it with the forces of establishment, only serves to consolidate the primacy of the current world order, together with the attendant repression of subversive energies. In this sense, the novel also reads as a cautionary tale, with its reminder that the cornerstone of realism is the occultation of ontological alternatives, and an "embrace of disappointment" (9) bound to engender violence and fear.

It is consistent with this diffidence towards the dangers of tautological representation that Flanagan's more experimental (magic realist) novels conduct an attack directed against any sense of predictable reality.[29] Laura A. White, for one, similarly considers that the author problematises his own realism as a medium "enabling recognition of the neglected persistence of imperial ontology in narrative strategies, even within postcolonial … writing".[30] Clearly, his historical "biofictions", too, operate within this logic, not only by tracing those legacies of conquest whereby our inherited, oppressively real present tends to perpetuate former injustices, but also by probing into fossilised dimensions of change potentially lodged within the narrative of the national past. Thus *Gould's Book of Fish*, which takes the form of a fictionalised biography of William Buelow Gould (1801–1853), sets out to question the formal premises on which this Van Diemonian convict painter based his still-life artworks, as illustrated notably in his *Sketchbook of Fishes in Macquarie Harbour*, today kept in the State Library of Tasmania. It is indeed significant that, in the novel, Gould comes to relinquish his initial realistic manner, learnt from Jean-Babeuf Audubon's illustrated natural history of the birds of America and based on "a bruised talent for nothing more than reproduction",[31] in favour of a more distorting medium born of his own growing identification with his objects of study. Tellingly, when asked by the Sarah Island authorities to assist in the taxonomic project of classifying local species of fish, his protracted scrutiny of the latter induces in him a form of sympathetic unsettlement whereby he feels bound "to fight back as the blackfellas had" (214). Such instinctive resistance notwithstanding, he progressively succumbs to this curious form of inverse conquest, down to the moment when he finally becomes a fish, "breathing water, falling, rising, my weight as nothing compared to what I had once known" (395). While the book's concluding scene can only depict, in any realistic reading of the plot, the protagonist's death by drowning in the harbour, the novel resolutely presents this, in magic realist mode, as a shattering of historical ego through which another narrative can begin to emerge. Flanagan's espousal of the biofictional genre thus allows him to deviate creatively from the script of official history – the "real" Gould differed in many key respects, as he spent only three years at Macquarie Harbour Penal Station, after which he was granted his Certificate of Freedom – and, in the process, to construe empiricist history-writing as a form of authoritarian censorship.

---

28 Bruce Bennett, "Of Spies and Terrorists: Australian Fiction after 9/11", *Asiatic: IIUM Journal of English Language and Literature* 2, no. 1 (June 2008): 14.
29 See Ben Holgate, "Greening a Narrative Mode: Antipodean Magical Realism and Ecocritism in Richard Flanagan's Fiction", this volume.
30 White, "Submerging the Imperial Eye", 276.
31 Richard Flanagan, *Gould's Book of Fish: A Novel in Twelve Fish* (2001; London: Atlantic Books, 2003), 92. All subsequent references are to this edition and appear in parentheses in the text.

Compared to the ambivalences of *The Secret River*, for example,[32] Flanagan's adjudication upon the narrative of settlement entirely eschews self-righteousness, as *Gould's Book of Fish* acknowledges the foundational "complicities and moral compromises of colonial times",[33] suggesting also that these only found endorsement through the callous partialities of institutionalised history – so that "the postcolonial present is defined by its colonial past".[34] This is why, in the economy of Flanagan's fiction of epistemological redress, no return to "normality" is envisaged for the protagonist, and his liberation from his carceral plight can only take the form of a dissolving of his historical identity, a cancellation of mind and body experienced as "an immeasurable pain of penance" (394). As suggested by those commentators who have approached the novel as a critique of the Enlightenment project,[35] all this implies a rejection of teleological objectives and a disavowal of Darwinian progress as well as of any linear conception of time.[36] Flanagan resists the modern notion that history works like an ever-growing storehouse of facts, or like an expanding archive accruing to potentially infinite accumulations of experience. To the contrary, he privileges a "complex and abstract" approach to the past seen as "a space of irretrievable loss",[37] while the passage of time induces a relentless whittling away of possibility sharpened with the advent of every new, intransigent historical fact. The mutation of historical biases sketched in his work consequently responds in part to the prospect of some intuited metaphysical recovery of eclipsed forms of knowing. It is revealing that, within such a scheme, Gould's ontological and epistemological demise, the requisite for an imaginative return to some original root of experience, is found to be inextricable from an immersion into the Aboriginal body, since his dying dive into the inland sea of Macquarie Harbour is registered in terms of envelopment in the briny scent of the sex of his native mistress. Thus a strange genesis attends upon the staged attrition of Gould's historical character, culminating as it does in a suspended moment when he finds himself to be:

> subsisting on nothing more than the smell of woman & then I was … riding her scent & she mine & then I was her scent & we were beyond her scent, & we were making our revolt our own way, & I thought … *How will I die knowing this?* – all this that is beyond us, all this that goes on & on, ever outwards, world without end. (397)

This then provides resolution for the narrative of a sort that seems all the more decisive since, in the course of this ecstatic mutual exploration of submerged alterities, "she … [tells

---

32   See Eleanor Collins, "Poison in the Flour", *Meanjin* 65, no. 1 (March 2006): 38–47.
33   Jo Jones, "'Dancing the old Enlightenment': *Gould's Book of Fish*, the Historical Novel, and the Postmodern Sublime", in "The Colonial Present," ed. Gillian Whitlock and Victoria Kuttainen, special issue, *JASAL: Journal of the Association for the Study of Australian Literature* (2008): 125.
34   Ben Holgate, "The Impossibility of Knowing: Developing Magical Realism's Irony in *Gould's Book of Fish*", *JASAL: Journal of the Association for the Study of Australian Literature* 14, no. 5 (2014): 4.
35   See Jo Jones, "'Dancing the old Enlightenment'"; Paul Stasi, "'Nothing was reconciled, everything was beautiful': *Gould's Book of Fish* and the Critique of Colonial Modernity", *La Habana Elegante: Segunda Época* 47 (Spring–Summer, 2010), http://bit.ly/2Jd01iH; and Doro Wiese, "Resisting Biopolitics through 'Diaphanous Wonder': Richard Flanagan's *Gould's Book of Fish* (2003)", *Rupkatha Journal on Interdisciplinary Studies in Humanities* 6, no. 3 (2014): 142–53.
36   See also Jesse Shipway, "Wishing for Modernity: Temporality and Desire in *Gould's Book of Fish*", *Australian Literary Studies* 21, no. 1 (2003): 43–53.
37   Jo Jones, "'Dancing the old Enlightenment'", 116.

him] her true name" (396), in an important correction of his earlier guilty ignorance, even as he was buying her favours, of his sex-mate's actual "Aboriginal name" (327).

The novel's climactic close, together with this symbolic disclosure, then serves to vindicate Flanagan's unexpected declaration in an interview that *Gould's Book of Fish* narrates essentially "a love story about a poor white convict and a black woman, and as such ... is a novel that speaks to the heart of contemporary Australia".[38] Arguably, this approach to the book as "a love story" requires that the reader should recognise the prominence of "the Aboriginal natives ... in the book's architecture", despite their being "barely seen" in the narrative,[39] indeed in accordance with the transformative reach of a text where "we are something other, larger than what we have been told" (3). Prior to such evolution, it seems noteworthy that Gould, being "one of a procession", hardly expected to be known, let alone remembered postcoitally, by somebody lured to undress by "promises of tobacco & pisco" (273-4); while he himself, as we have seen, never bothered to find out the real name of a woman variously designated by her exploiters as The Mulatto, Cleopatra or Twopenny Sal, and realised too late that his "knowing so little" amounts to "a vague but real sin, terrible & unspeakable" (327). The book's conclusion consequently gestures towards an "absolution of love" (274) freeing the narrative from the centripetal impulses on which it had been founded up to this point, and retrospectively launches it on a theme of infinity. In other words, the counter-evolutionary drift of Flanagan's biographical fiction can be seen to aim at an unravelling of aggregated racial prepossessions, whereby the ingrained engrossments of exotic lust are allowed to mutate, albeit programmatically, into a form of love raised to cross-cultural proportions.[40] In this respect, it is worth remarking on the structural resemblance with *The Narrow Road to the Deep North*, which similarly rehearses, from the strategic position of the historical victim, the traditionally polarised narrative of Australian–Japanese relations in the wake of World War Two. In this case also, the clash of cultures is encoded as battling versions of "the idea of the whole world under one roof",[41] though the book, significantly titled after a famous *haibun* by the seventeenth-century Japanese poet Matsuo Bashō, attempts to consume its own biases through the frequent reference to classic Japanese poetry, so that verse insertions sporadically disrupt the otherwise cursive linearity of the prose text. Flanagan himself has described the novel as a cross-cultural object, an Australian odyssey "composed of linked haiku"[42] and modelled on Ryūnosuke Akutagawa's *Rashōmon*, whose form therefore strives to escape engulfment within the obsessions of a culture – or in the traumas of the past. It is in keeping that an important aspect of the novelist's research when writing this book has consisted of breaking the temporal frame, seeking to "meet with the Japanese people as

---

38   Richard Flanagan cited in Stasi, "'Nothing was reconciled'".
39   Stasi, "'Nothing was reconciled'".
40   Flanagan is quite explicit about this issue of racial intermixture in his essays, as in his review of James Boyce's *Van Diemen's Land* (2008), a book about frontier violence in Tasmania which confirms the novelist's belief that there are grounds for considering the first colonisers of the island less as "dispossessed Europeans" than as "a muddy wash of peoples made anew in the merge of a pre-industrial, pre-modern European culture with an extraordinary natural world and a remarkable black culture". See Richard Flanagan, "A Terrible, Beautiful History of Hope", *Sydney Morning Herald*, 16 February 2008. http://bit.ly/2JhWNuu.
41   Richard Flanagan, *The Narrow Road to the Deep North* (2013; London: Chatto & Windus, 2014), 125.
42   Richard Flanagan, "Freeing My Father", *Sydney Morning Herald*, 21 September 2013. http://bit.ly/2sqCh04.

they are now".[43] Crucially, these have included real-life protagonists of his novel (as it were), notably some of the former Japanese commanders and Korean guards entrusted with the construction of the Death Railway, and therefore guilty of persecutions against "Dunlop's Thousand" (and also, as we have seen, against his own father). The tension between *personae* and world-historical characters, evident in the discovery that evil has today deserted the scene of encounter, constitutes an interpellating footnote to history and justifies Flanagan's conviction that this book, too, had to comprise a love story to make up for its exploration of cross-cultural shallows.[44]

Thus it appears that Flanagan's ethical project is adequately served by his espousal of biographical fiction, a genre that, as Lackey points out, encourages a "focus on the psychological subject's interiority",[45] ideal to document that inner ground of conquest which is susceptible to transformation within a fiction of self-reversible *personae*. It is worth insisting that the overturning of collective personality tentatively sketched in the work implies a repudiation of easy forms of polarised identification in terms of perpetrators or victims. Arguably, the overcoming of resentment pursued with *The Narrow Road to the Deep North* gains in credence from the fact that the book deals with a chapter of their national history in which Australians were very much sinned against, so that any initiative towards forgiveness issuing from these quarters will seem acceptable. By contrast, as frequently emphasised by commentators, attempts to obtain exoneration from collective guilt over the manner of the nation's foundation have tended to be marred by the unabashedly domineering position from which the hand of friendship – the kiss of love – was extended to the Aboriginal peoples. In this respect, a veritable naked descent into the psychic configurations of responsibility, inherited or otherwise, may still be pending, and will be hampered as long as Australians "continue to identify with the position of Other – outsider, victim or underdog" – even as they benefit from the material consequences of colonisation. In this context, Jo Jones usefully highlights Flanagan's questioning in *Gould's Book of Fish* of white Australia's complacent "connection to the disenfranchised Other, such as the convict, bushranger or pioneer of our national folklore".[46] It is relevant that Gould's anguish, expressed in a rhetorical question apparently aimed at Twopenny Sal – "Do you think I was only gaoled?" (260) – is followed by a riddling passage of introspection in which he views himself as variously gaoled and gaoler, hunted and hunter, saint and sinner, in a never-ending quest for identity projecting him as ultimately "untranslatable and unknowable even to … [himself]" (261).

This self-proclaimed undecidability needs to be further pondered in the light of the novel's Afterword, which takes the form of a historical archive and provides a final shift in perspective with the revelation – a "last gasp admission that all the novel's central characters are emanations of the same cracked, aquatic psyche"[47] – that Gould has all along ventriloquised the voices of colonial authority, including those of Jorgen Jorgensen (the colony's appointed chronicler) and of the Commandant (the tyrannical ruler of Sarah Island). The suggestion is clearly that, for all his dedication to "Love & Liberty" (404), Gould

---

43   Flanagan, "Freeing My Father".
44   Flanagan, "Freeing My Father". See also Nicholas Birns, "'Fireless flame gone amorous': War Amid Love in *The Narrow Road to the Deep North*", this volume.
45   Lackey, *Biographical Fiction*, 1.
46   Jones, "'Dancing the old Enlightenment'", 125.
47   Shipway, "Wishing for Modernity", 49.

has ultimately been unable to escape the authoritative "master-narrative" of the nation's view of itself, or to shoulder as a whole the burden of confrontation with unpleasant beginnings. In this sense, Flanagan's biofiction stages its own frustrated impulses, finally yielding to a species of resignation in the light of which the search for community is curbed and the effect of consent becomes barbarous. This ending had in fact been anticipated through some delirious passages in the narrative where the protagonist had felt unhinged and composed of "the many strange forms of ... [his] dream" (353), including imaginings by the mad Surgeon and Commandant. The list of Gould's fictional "aliases" in the "*Colonial Secretary's correspondence file*" (404) then testifies to the narrator's final epistemic alignment with the sort of "card sharping in history" (286) conducted by Jorgensen in the island's Registry as the latter, when entrusted with the task of chronicling life in the penal colony, had tampered with "the entire records of the settlement, in a way that would accord with expectation & not reality". It is of course ironic that the resulting "extraordinary conceit of an alternative world" (284) should in time form the template for the narrative of reason and progress that would find its way into the history books, in spite of being not a history of the convict but "one of the colonizer, a history specially tailored to satisfy the egos of those already in charge".[48] The further irony, however, lies in the fact that the strategic rehearsal of fictional perspectives conducted in *Gould's Book of Fish*, by dint of paradoxically culminating in the finalities of the official archive, somehow points to the novel's continuing entrapment in historical conventions about factual truth. It may then be sensed that the spirit presiding over the book's ending is that of parody: Flanagan constructs above all a mimicry of historiography's reliance on complacent stories, one that is immensely inventive and entertaining but ultimately incapable of displacing any sense of "rueful fatalism about the present" (20).

This being said, it is still remarkable that, among the avatars underlying Gould's biofictional identity, there is one which differs from the others in view of the exceptional liberties taken in the treatment of a "real" historical figure. Indeed, the character of Capois Death retains in the novel an affiliation with his origin in fact, the historical François Capois (1766–1806), known as Capois-la-Mort, a hero of the slave insurgency in Saint-Domingue which led to the independence of Haiti in 1804. By introducing such a character into his fictional revision of Tasmania's past, Flanagan devises an aesthetic of historical conflation, the effects of which are several. First, he is ostensibly invoking the virtuality of a rebellion by the convict-slaves of Van Diemen's Land of the sort that François Capois waged with success in the realm of actuality, thus releasing a dormant seed of insurrection within a novel otherwise characterised by a nearly unanimous acceptance of the tyranny of rule. It is indeed significant that, when moved to Sarah Island, even Capois Death himself has no other option, to ensure survival, than to connive with the forces of establishment, and with the Commandant in particular. Concurrently, because of his complexion he becomes a token of fated affinities with the local Aborigines, signalling the desirability of a political alliance that equally fails to materialise since, in the fictional economy of the book, he suffers an ignominious and pointless death in a swift skirmish on the outskirts of the Black War. The implicit potential for subversion encoded in Capois Death is then displaced onto another "biofictional" character, the no less historical bushranger Matthew Brady (1799–1826) who becomes a symbolic receptacle and representative for all the revolutionary velleities in the colony:

---

48 Ashley Rose Whitmore, "Reconfigurations of History and Embodying Books in *Gould's Book of Fish*", *Postcolonial Text* 7, no. 2 (2012): 11.

Some said he was tall & swarthy with a Maori-like tattoo down one cheek; others that he was half-Samoan & and that this explained his war-like propensity; others yet that he was short, freckled & wore his red hair in two long ponytails. For the Scots he was William Wallace, for the Irish he was Cú Cucalain; for all, a hero. (312)

Arguably, such diverse attractiveness allows the "lustrous legend" (196) woven around Brady to magnetise and dispel the discontent brooding in the colony in a way that ultimately serves an ideal of political quiescence. It is apt, then, that the "real" bushranger achieved posterity under the moniker of "Gentleman Brady", earned as an effect of his good breeding when robbing his victims – which further alludes to the respectability that may be gained through the myth-making process. By contrast, however, the novel points to the existence of another, more real Brady than this historical one, indeed "one who might avenge History" (312) through his ability to expose the mendacity of "official records", supplanting it with "a truthful account" that may be more faithful in its rendering of "the horror of the settlement" (313). The bushranger's attested lawlessness is thus rewritten, quite literally, as a propensity towards iconoclasm of the historiographic sort.

It is then this alternative hero that Gould quixotically seeks out in the book's final chapters, when he roams the dense rainforests of southwestern Van Diemen's Land in the hope of finding the one who will relieve him of the heavy tomes of archives stolen from the colonial Registry. Unsurprisingly given his prepossessions, as dictated to him by the figments of his historical imagination, he will fail both to connect with this beacon of true protest and to recognise the exact nature of his seditious power. Indeed, Gould's fugitive quest reaches an end point in a deserted Aboriginal village where, among some dilapidated huts, he chances upon evidence of a massacre: "mounds of bones & a host of human skulls" (342) piled up on an old fireplace. His response to this remains strangely muted as he seems to keep his indignation for Matt Brady's journal, a small nondescript volume bound in wallaby hide and written in kangaroo blood, discovered on the site, which precipitates his despair. It turns out that Brady, far from fomenting any revolution – the book issues no "orders for a jacquerie, [nor] any mention of a rebellion" (350) – had been living peacefully with the now dispersed community, nursing thoughts about "love between a white man & a black woman", and about "building a white man, black woman home, the whole something other than either in the merge" (350). Despite his own involvement with Twopenny Sal, Gould dismisses the sentiment as futile and ultimately "incomprehensible" (349), revealing his inability to take his orders from this type of leader even though the experience of reading the journal has importantly destabilised his temporal awareness: "Time ... well, what did I care about *time* now? Perhaps it halted or started or danced or fell asleep or went to the pub for several Larrikin Soups" (348). Thus Flanagan's convict artist remains immured within his own cognitive carapace, preferring to stick to the security of a known script which his own abortive mutiny only confirms, rather than facing the perils of discovery limned in Brady's cryptic aphorism: "'To love is not safe'" (350).

*Gould's Book of Fish* then proves repetitive in its insistence that the cross-cultural encounter constitutes a glaring absence, perhaps the main missed opportunity, at the heart of Australian history, whilst also making it clear that the agents of such history were in no position to "fully comprehend"[49] the extent of the loss incurred. It may not be the least irony that, in the counter-history of a penal colony provided in the

---

49 Holgate, "'The Impossibility of Knowing'", 10.

novel, the convicts are shown to be shackled also to their own limited conception of community, which prevents them from abandoning the conventional stance of history to move beyond stases of protest or self-pity. The form of biographical fiction therefore becomes, in Flanagan's hands, a type of inverse documentary report about the past which, for all its exuberant inventiveness, and no matter how much the factual dimension is augmented by means of fiction, somehow forecloses the very avenue of investigation which the reader is invited to imagine. A similar contrapuntal aesthetics is explored in *Wanting*, the very title of which encapsulates the notion that a crucial phenomenal deficit is encompassed within any factual outline of the past. It is possibly relevant that, as he returns with this novel to contemplating traumatic contact histories in Tasmania, Flanagan adopts a more sober, realistic tone as well as a line of stricter historical accuracy. Importantly, this does not soften the asperities of his evocation; perhaps the contrary is true, as is for example apparent in the Conradian accents of his incidental picture of Edward Curr (1798-1850), a manager of the Van Diemen's Land Company in the 1830s and early 1840s, represented in the book as one of "a party of London investors that owned the northwestern quarter of the island".[50] Under a façade of admiration for this figure's "muscularity of character and purpose" (178) as well as for his "honesty" (180) and capacity for "profound judgements", the narrator smuggles the portrait of a Kurtz in disguise,[51] albeit one who remains "unafraid of the horror he has discovered in himself" (181). Indeed, this "strange hero of the Black War", whose gift of eloquence ranks him among "the emissaries of God, science, justice", believes above all else in the cautionary value of having "several staked heads" (180) erected on the ridge of his hut. In a few swift strokes Flanagan therefore summons a sense of the abominations of local history, one that is seen as another "heart of darkness", while maintaining his narrative focus at all times on characters who remain temperamentally and chronologically incapable of sharing that insight.

Other than the dismal Curr/Kerr and an assortment of richly framed though minor colonial officials, the novel's cast of historical characters notably comprises "the Chief Protector of Aborigines, George Augustus Robinson; Charles Dickens; the explorer and former governor of Tasmania, Sir John Franklin; and his wife, Lady Jane".[52] Such a profusion of biographical material raises the question of where the novel is supposed to be weighted, especially since, as the above list fails to mention, it also includes a sketch of the life of Mathinna (1835–1852), an Aboriginal girl who was adopted by the Franklins and kept at Government House, Hobart, during Sir John's period of office as Lieutenant-Governor of the island (1837–43). As the text makes clear, Mathinna was also the daughter of Towterer, a Port Davey chieftain and king "of the great mountains and wild rivers" (56), which makes her an extension of Twopenny Sal, the protagonist's mistress in *Gould's Book of Fish*. The later novel then testifies to Flanagan's abiding interest in this figure, a point of fugue within the work to which he returns in a sort of heuristic infinite rehearsal of material, ranging from the fictional to the pseudo-historical. In view of the "sparse

---

50   Richard Flanagan, *Wanting* (North Sydney: Random House, 2008), 178. All subsequent references are to this edition and appear in parentheses in the text.
51   The company manager's surname is spelled "Kerr" in the book, probably as a further indication of his felt proximity to Conrad's Kurtz.
52   Brian Daniel Deyo, "Rewriting History/Animality in J.M. Coetzee's *Dusklands* and Richard Flanagan's *Wanting*", *ARIEL: A Review of International English Literature* 44, no. 4 (October 2013): 101.

archival fragments"[53] extant about Mathinna, the novelist indeed had no other choice than to exercise his imagination within the scope allowed by the genre of biographical fiction. Arguably, this character, who turns up more than once, in more or less fictionalised form, in Flanagan's novels, also constitutes a touchstone of his aesthetic intentions, so that it seems imperative to form an adequate judgement of the structural role she plays in the "deft muscular montage"[54] central to *Wanting*, a novel which has been seen to be disparate at the level of plot and which consequently relies on "imaginative assembly in narration".[55]

It is indeed noteworthy that, so far, all criticism of *Wanting* has tended to tackle it in parts, whether as a speculative rewriting of the life-experience of George Augustus Robinson,[56] of Charles Dickens,[57] or of Lady Jane and her Aboriginal "charge".[58] It can be felt that, taken separately, these narrative strands "gesture less to imaginative postcolonial critique than to histories of extinction discourse", evident in the proleptic elegy surrounding the demise of Mathinna, "the poster girl of Indigenous dispossession".[59] However, this would amount to ignoring the estranging effects achieved through Flanagan's orchestrated collision of historical perspectives, as when the holocaust affecting Tasmania's Aborigines in the dishonourable material circumstances of Flinders Island is pitted against more traditional landmarks of European history: "It was 1839. The first photograph of a man was taken, Abd al-Qadir declared a jihad against the French, and Charles Dickens was rising to greater fame with a novel called *Oliver Twist*" (3). It is of course significant that, within the concatenated structure of *Wanting*, the abuse of Mathinna somehow flies in the face of Dickens himself, whose pretensions to civilised superiority depend on his view of the savage as "someone who succumbs to his passions" (83). In this sense, Sir John Franklin's represented ignominy, beyond the obvious debunking of colonial authority that it encodes, also points to a larger questioning of our historiographic inheritance and of the transparency of time on a global scale. A quantum leap in historical consciousness is then sketched with Flanagan's reminder, in the Author's Note to the novel, that some 16,000 Tasmanians today "identify as Aborigines", so that the "terrible anguish" (256) about their forthcoming extinction, as mirrored in the book, has proved deceptive, indeed like an evolutionary red herring.

In the last analysis, with his apparently gratuitous interest in Dickens, the author allows his art of biographical fiction to outgrow the nationalist parameters often associated with the genre in Australia, and elsewhere in his own oeuvre. By dint of the structure of *Wanting*, he contrives an essential articulation of the national tradition of history with a globalised historical perspective, resulting in the delineation of a continuous and homogeneous spatio-temporality presented as oppressive and subject to a revisionary focus. What emerges is a veritable philosophy of history, characterised by a feeling of

---

53  Penny Russell, "Girl in a Red Dress: Inventions of Mathinna", *Australian Historical Studies* 43, no. 3 (2012): 342.
54  Amanda Johnson, "Making an Expedition of Herself: Lady Jane Franklin as Queen of the Tasmanian Extinction Narrative", *JASAL: Journal of the Association for the Study of Australian Literature* 14, no. 5 (2014): 14.
55  Johnson, "Making an Expedition of Herself", 8.
56  See Deyo, "Rewriting History/Animality", 100–15.
57  See Catherine Lanone, "Revisiting *Great Expectations*: The Postcolonial Persistence of Dickens", *Études Anglaises* 65, no. 1 (2012): 19–29.
58  See Johnson, "Making an Expedition of Herself", 1–21.
59  Johnson, "Making an Expedition of Herself", 4, 9.

metaphysical entrapment within all achieved/archived knowledge and accompanied by the conviction that the artist has a responsibility to oppose sanctioned narratives felt to enshrine a progressive depletion of cultural resources. Indeed, all of Flanagan's novels considered in this chapter, just like the early *Death of a River Guide*, share a preoccupation with abortions of cross-cultural sensibility repeatedly suffered in the course of Australian (and specifically Tasmanian) history. Taken together, these cohere into a void which the novels attempt to respond to in a sort of contained, subversive dialogue. It is remarkable that this latent dialogue consistently steers clear of any fashionable native temptation, of the sort which posits an Aboriginal cognitive position as a vicarious identity role model beckoning to Australian settlers eager to legitimate their continuing occupation of the continent. Instead of a mystical absorption into the body or spirit of place, and for all his ecological respect for Tasmanian landscapes, Flanagan represents instead a succession of historical failed encounters with the white man's cultural and racial "other", which return like a haunting and the expression of an unshakeable bad conscience. Ultimately, his manifold experiments with realism, just like his addiction to history and to biographical fiction, operate less as a celebration of creativity than as an index of artistic limitation, and therefore point to the enormity of the challenge implicit in any repudiation of received epistemologies. In this context, even the comparatively greater exuberance of the magic realism at work in *Gould's Book of Fish* finally reads like an admission of imaginative defeat in the face an implacable historical record, though it is also suffused with a unique cross-cultural emotion that gives poignant direction to an edge of new possibility. This hermeneutic opening, tentative as it is, depends on a reined-in recognition, perceptible in spite of the successive novels' relentless circumscription of fact, of the need to go on searching for remedial foundations lodged within the interstices of documented time.

## References

Bennett, Bruce. "Of Spies and Terrorists: Australian Fiction after 9/11", *Asiatic: IIUM Journal of English Language and Literature* 2, no. 1 (June 2008): 10–20.
Birns, Nicholas. *Contemporary Australian Literature: A World Not Yet Dead*. Sydney: Sydney University Press, 2015.
Collins, Eleanor. "Poison in the Flour", *Meanjin* 65, no. 1 (March 2006): 38–47.
Deyo, Brian Daniel, "Rewriting History/Animality in J.M. Coetzee's *Dusklands* and Richard Flanagan's *Wanting*", *ARIEL: A Review of International English Literature* 44, no. 4 (October 2013): 89–116.
Flanagan, Richard. *The Narrow Road to the Deep North*. (2013) London: Chatto & Windus, 2014.
———. "Freeing My Father". *Sydney Morning Herald*, 21 September 2013. http://bit.ly/2sqCh04.
———. "A Terrible, Beautiful History of Hope". *Sydney Morning Herald*, 16 February 2008. http://bit.ly/2JhWNuu.
———. *Wanting*. North Sydney: Random House, 2008
———. *The Unknown Terrorist*. Sydney: Picador, 2006.
———. *Gould's Book of Fish*. (2001) London: Atlantic Books, 2003.
Grenville, Kate. "The Question of History: Response", *Quarterly Essay* 25 (February 2007): 66–72.
Holgate, Ben. "'The Impossibility of Knowing': Developing Magical Realism's Irony in *Gould's Book of Fish*", *JASAL: Journal of the Association for the Study of Australian Literature* 14, no. 5 (2014): 1–11.
Hutcheon, Linda. *A Poetics of Postmodernism: History, Theory, Fiction*. New York: Routledge, 1988.
Johnson, Amanda. "Making an Expedition of Herself: Lady Jane Franklin as Queen of the Tasmanian Extinction Narrative", *JASAL: Journal of the Association for the Study of Australian Literature* 14, no. 5 (2014): 1–21.

Jones, Gail. "Speaking Shadows: Justice and the Poetic". In *Just Words? Australian Authors Writing for Justice*, edited by Bernadette Brennan. St Lucia: University of Queensland Press, 2008, 76–86.

Jones, Jo. "'Dancing the Old Enlightenment': *Gould's Book of Fish*, the Historical Novel, and the Postmodern Sublime", in "The Colonial Present," ed. Gillian Whitlock and Victoria Kuttainen, special issue, *JASAL: Journal of the Association for the Study of Australian Literature* 2008: 114–29.

Lackey, Michael, ed. *Biographical Fiction: A Reader*. New York: Bloomsbury, 2017.

Lanone, Catherine. "Revisiting *Great Expectations*: The Postcolonial Persistence of Dickens", *Études Anglaises* 65, no. 1 (2012): 19–29.

Lukács, Georg. *The Historical Novel*. (1937) Lincoln: University of Nebraska Press, 1987.

Macintyre, Stuart and Anna Clark. *The History Wars*. (2003) Carlton, Vic: Melbourne University Press, 2004.

Malouf, David. *An Imaginary Life*. London: Chatto & Windus, 1978.

McCann, Andrew. "Professing the Popular: Political Fiction circa 2006", *Australian Literary Studies* 23, no. 2 (2007): 43–57.

McKenna, Mark. "Writing the Past". *Australian Financial Review*, 16 December 2005, 'Review' 1–2.

O'Reilly, Nathanael. "Government, Media and Power: Terrorism in the Australian Novel since 9/11". In *From Solidarity to Schisms: 9/11 and After in Fiction and Film from Outside the US*, edited by Cara Cilano. Amsterdam: Rodopi, 2009, 295–315.

Pierce, Peter. "Problematic History, Problems of Form: David Malouf's *Remembering Babylon*". In *Provisional Maps: Critical Essays on David Malouf*, edited by Amanda Nettelbeck. Nedlands, WA: Centre for Studies in Australian Literature, University of Western Australia. (1994) 183–96.

Pinto, Sarah. "History, Fiction, and *The Secret River*". In *Lighting Dark Places: Essays on Kate Grenville*, edited by Sue Kossew. Amsterdam: Rodopi, 2010, 179–97.

Russell, Penny. "Girl in a Red Dress: Inventions of Mathinna", *Australian Historical Studies* 43, no. 3 (2012): 341–62.

Shipway, Jesse. "Wishing for Modernity: Temporality and Desire in *Gould's Book of Fish*", *Australian Literary Studies* 21, no. 1 (2003): 43–53.

Stasi, Paul. "'Nothing was reconciled, everything was beautiful': *Gould's Book of Fish* and the Critique of Colonial Modernity", *La Habana Elegante: Segunda Época* 47 (Spring–Summer, 2010). http://bit.ly/2Jd01iH.

Webb, Jen. "Distant Context, Local Colour: Australian 'post September 11' Fiction", in "Common Readers and Cultural Critics," Special issue, *JASAL: Journal of the Association for the Study of Australian Literature* 2010: 1–14.

White, Laura A. "Submerging the Imperial Eye: Affective Narration as Environmentalist Intervention in Richard Flanagan's *Death of a River Guide*", *Journal of Commonwealth Literature* 47, no. 2 (2012): 265–79.

Whitmore, Ashley Rose. "Reconfigurations of History and Embodying Books in *Gould's Book of Fish*", *Postcolonial Text* 7, no. 2 (2012): 1–16.

Wiese, Doro. "Resisting Biopolitics through 'Diaphanous Wonder': Richard Flanagan's *Gould's Book of Fish* (2003)", *Rupkatha Journal on Interdisciplinary Studies in Humanities* 6, no. 3 (2014): 142–53.

Žižek, Slavoj. *Welcome to the Desert of the Real! Five Essays on September 11 and Related Dates*. London: Verso, 2002.

# 8
# The Genealogy of *Wanting*
Margaret Harris

*Wanting*, Richard Flanagan's fifth novel, published in 2008, returns to the terrain of the Tasmanian wilderness traversed in his debut novel, *Death of a River Guide* (1994), and to some of the same history presented in his third, *Gould's Book of Fish* (2001). Flanagan insists in his Author's Note that *Wanting* "is not a history, nor should it be read as one".[1] He is nonetheless explicit about "certain characters and events in the past" whose histories he has invoked: Sir John Franklin (1786–1847), Arctic explorer and governor of Van Diemen's Land from 1837 to 1843; Jane, Lady Franklin (1792–1875), notable for her initiatives and interventions both as wife and widow; the Aboriginal girl Mathinna (ca 1835–1852), taken into the Franklin household but abandoned when they left Tasmania; and Charles Dickens (1812–1870), author, editor and public figure, at a turning point in his life.

Flanagan's Author's Note also alludes to his choice of title:

> The stories of Mathinna and Dickens, with their odd but undeniable connection, suggested to me a meditation on desire – the cost of its denial, the centrality and force of its power in human affairs. That, and not history, is the true subject of *Wanting*. (256)

My interest in this chapter is in the mix from which Flanagan's "meditation on desire" emerges, and his discerning and delineating the "odd but undeniable connection" that is the hinge of *Wanting*. Flanagan's fascination with "this endless battle between desire and disciplining desire and reason and wanting"[2] is spelled out frequently in the novel. Consider Dickens' reflections as he leaves his meeting with Lady Franklin in chapter 4, threatened by what he experiences as the monstrous blackness of London after their talk of cannibalism. In this passage there are evident echoes of the famous opening of *Bleak House*: thus "he faced the morning gloom, thick flakes of soot eddied around him like

---

1  Richard Flanagan, *Wanting* (Sydney: Knopf, 2008), 255. All subsequent references are to this edition, and appear in parentheses in the text. The Author's Note (256) directs readers' attention to www.richardflanaganwanting.com.au (retrievable from http://bit.ly/2suhGrX), where in "Postscript" Flanagan provides a list of his principal sources, and a few paragraphs on each of the historical figures who appear as characters in the novel. The Vintage Books edition (2009 and subsequently reprinted) does not include this two-page afterword.
2  Flanagan, interview with Ramona Koval, "Wanting: Richard Flanagan". *The Book Show*, ABC Radio National, 12 November 2008. https://ab.co/2LHmbYK.

black snow, and nothing seemed bright" (31) picks up Dickens' reference to "soft black drizzle, with flakes of soot in it as big as full-grown snow-flakes – gone into mourning, one might imagine, for the death of the sun"[3] as part of the whole evocation of a city that has reverted to the primeval. These reflections go deeper, as Dickens seizes on the imperative for civilised men to keep in check the passions generally, and sexual drives particularly, in order to maintain their distinction from the savages. He dreads "becoming, finally, the savage he feared himself to be" (44). The reiterated phrase, "undisciplined heart" (43), is from *David Copperfield*, a novel with a clear autobiographical component in which Copperfield as narrator asks whether he will be the hero of his own life. Notwithstanding Flanagan's disavowal of "literary ambition", the quotation of "undisciplined heart" is one of the many literary references that are tactically enlisted to serve in the "endless battle".[4]

Most reviewers and commentators have accepted Flanagan's claim that he conceived *Wanting* as a moral reflection rather than a historical record. The import of his claim warrants consideration. In the obvious sense, *Wanting* is a historical novel, but not of the ilk concerned with fidelity to costume and furnishings as a means of recreating the past. *Wanting* can appropriately be described as a neo-Victorian novel, and I concur with Kate Mitchell in seeing the neo-Victorian as a sub-genre of historical fiction.[5] *Wanting* "enable[s] us, as readers, to conceptualise the *relationship* between the Victorian past and our present", though not as Mitchell implies, citing Mieke Bal, as an act of memory "in which the past is continuously modified and redescribed even as it continues to shape the future".[6] The construction of the Victorian past in *Wanting* is not in thrall to history's claim to truth, and in places Flanagan's fictional account deviates in detail from the historical record.[7] More to the point, the novel resists positing a causal connection between that past and our present. The effect is both to privilege the "meditation on desire" and to propose an idea of history that in Robert Dixon's words offers "an apprehension of diverse elements from the past and present that can be held in a constellation".[8]

---

3   Charles Dickens, *Bleak House* (1852–3; London: Oxford University Press, 1948), 1. An early example of Flanagan's acknowledged occasional "free use of sentences and phrases from Dickens's own work" (Author's Note, 256), this passage in its turn is echoed in Conrad's *Heart of Darkness* (1899) where the narrator Marlow muses that London was once among "the dark places of the earth", following an emotive reflection on English seafarers, including Sir John Franklin and his vessels *Erebus* and *Terror* sailing "on the ebb of [the Thames] into the mystery of an unknown earth" (Joseph Conrad, *Youth, Heart of Darkness, The End of the Tether: Three Stories* (1902; London: J.M. Dent, Collected Edition, 1946, 47–8).
4   Flanagan, interview with Ramona Koval, "Wanting". *Wanting* is suffused with literary references – an example among many is Lady Jane's reference to Wordsworth, with whom "she agreed … , after all, that the sublime was ever to be found in the solitary" (50). It may not be drawing too long a bow to observe that in Jonathan Swift's *Gulliver's Travels*, Book 4 (1726), the land inhabited by the hyper-rational, horse-like Houyhnhnms and the debased, human-like Yahoos, falls in western Tasmania.
5   Kate Mitchell, *History and Cultural Memory in Neo-Victorian Fiction: Victorian Afterimages* (Basingstoke, UK: Palgrave Macmillan, 2010), 13.
6   Mitchell, *History and Cultural Memory*, 13.
7   Flanagan demonstrably referred to more historical accounts than he lists in his "Postscript" (cf. n. 1). While I will identify some of these, my primary concern is not to produce a comprehensive list of his sources, though I am concerned to examine his treatment of sources. His training as a historian is pertinent, and theories of history that underpin his thinking are discussed elsewhere in this volume by Delrez and Dixon.
8   Robert Dixon, "Circles of Violence: Historical Constellations in *Death of a River Guide* and *The Sound of One Hand Clapping*", this volume.

Granted that history is not the subject of *Wanting*, the moral drama is played out in a particular set of historical contexts, deploying the inventive freedom of fiction to offer an alternative version of received histories. Flanagan's choice of historical personages and events – the stories of Dickens and Ellen Ternan, and of the Franklins and Mathinna – and the imaginative connections he makes among them, are fundamental to his novel. Further, the moral compass that is set by the Aboriginal girl Mathinna goes beyond rebuke of the wilful self-delusions of the Franklins and Dickens, to condemnation of paternalistic European colonialism and misguided Enlightenment aspirations.[9] Chronologically, the novel runs from 1839 through events in Tasmania in the early 1840s, to England in 1857 and events centring on the performances of Dickens' play *The Frozen Deep* in Manchester. The novel does not proceed along this chronological arc, however. Flanagan uses quick cross-cutting shifts in time and place to bring home the disparate manifestations of wanting that circulate around his fictionalised historical figures. This cinematic method has the effect of establishing affinities and contrasts that converge into constellations that limn another set of moral reflections around "the catastrophe of colonisation" (Author's Note, 256).

The key dynamic of *Wanting* is set in train by the counterpointing of the Franklins' story with Dickens', worked through a range of motifs including frozen Arctic wastes, and Leda and the swan. The particular contrast depends on the celebrity of both Sir John and Dickens, each in his way an epitome of British imperial values: on the one hand abroad, as heroic explorer, and on the other as the eulogist of the family and home. Much of the "wanting" is parental. Flanagan shows Dickens' love for Ellen Ternan to be inflected both by the death of his youngest child Dora (presented in chapter 2), and by his character Little Nell: "Everyone calls me Nell … On account of your *Old Curiosity Shop*, sir. Little Nell" (206–7). The death of Dora resonates through Dickens' repudiation of his wife Catherine and his emerging relationship with Nelly, young enough to be his daughter and treated like one in his will.[10] In contrast and in parallel, Mathinna is the adopted, abused and abandoned child of the Franklins. She is the catalyst for Lady Franklin's maternal longing, and the victim of Sir John's quasi-paternal desire. I will have more to say about the elements of Flanagan's interpretation and invention in *Wanting*, but for now, I offer the proposition that the novel's pervasive stress on the destructive force of desire is comprehensively over-determined.

To begin with the title. The *Oxford English Dictionary* offers definitions of "wanting" both as noun and adjective. The nuances of these definitions are projected in the ambiguities and ambivalences that suffuse the novel. Thus as a noun "The fact or action

---

9   Mathinna focalises the clash of cultures, and hence the Black War of white settlers on Aboriginals during the early decades of the colonisation of Van Diemen's Land. Flanagan's "very small post made up of only a few books" he drew on for "historical truth" lists George Augustus Robinson's diaries and James Boyce's *Van Diemen's Land*: see Richard Flanagan, "Postscript". In "Rewriting History/Animality in J.M. Coetzee's *Dusklands* and Richard Flanagan's *Wanting*", *Ariel: A Review of International English Literature* 44, no. 4 (October 2013): 89–116 (101), Brian Daniel Deyo lists the historical personages depicted in *Wanting*, explaining that he will focus on Robinson "with passing reference" to Mathinna and the Franklins "[s]ince the episodes on the English author fall outside the scope of my reading". I adopt this somewhat disingenuous position in respect of the Black War.
10  Both Michael Slater, in *Charles Dickens* (New Haven, CT: Yale University Press, 2009), 616–18, and Claire Tomalin, in *The Invisible Woman: The Story of Nelly Ternan and Charles Dickens* (1990; rev. ed., London: Penguin, 1991), 188–90, bring out that Dickens' testamentary provision for Nell approximated that made for his unmarried daughter Mamie.

of desiring; an instance of this; (a) desire, longing, or craving"; and as an adjective "not present or forthcoming; absent, lacking; missing". The entries for the adjective reference Daniel 5:27 as an allusion that plays subliminally into Flanagan's novel: "Thou art weighed in the balances, and art found wanting" (*King James Bible*). This verse forms part of Daniel's ominous interpretation of the writing of the mysterious moving finger at Belshazzar's feast. In relation to *Wanting*, a particular usage is relevant: "having or showing (sexual) desire or longing; passionate; ardent".[11] All of the central characters in Flanagan's novel experience intense longing in some form, often inarticulate; and in the case of Dickens and Franklin, definitely sexual, however refracted.

Flanagan provides further prompts to his readers in his choice of two epigraphs that flag a leading idea of the text to follow in their allusion to the equivocal nature of "wanting". In combination, they propose that human existence is marked by absence and incompleteness, that worldly success is meaningless, and that reason is powerless to constrain the excesses of desire. One of the epigraphs comes from Dostoevsky's *Notes from Underground* (1864), and the other from the Old Testament book of Ecclesiastes. Here is the Dostoevsky quotation:

> You see, reason, gentlemen, is a fine thing, that is unquestionable, but reason is only reason and satisfies only man's reasoning capacity, while wanting is a manifestation of the whole of life.[12]

There are connotations in circulation beyond the literal meaning. *Notes from Underground*, as Bakhtin points out, is a confession, and dialogic – a markedly intertextual work,[13] as is *Wanting*. Another noted critic of Dostoevsky, Joseph Frank, locates the speaker, the underground man, in "a social-cultural context very clearly delimited in time", proposing that he becomes "a parody of the attitudes of the 1840s" in Russia, when many intellectuals espoused utopian ideals in adapting to Western culture.[14] The invocation of *Notes from Underground* locates the tension of desire and reason in the broad context of post-Enlightenment thinking that pervades *Wanting*'s obsession with civilisation and savagery.

The Biblical quotation "That which is wanting cannot be numbered" is from a much-cited passage in Ecclesiastes 1: 15 (King James Version). The preceding verse contextualises: "I have seen all the works that are done under the sun; and, behold, all is vanity and vexation of spirit".

Here, then, is a dense set of resonances, homing in on the particular circumstances of Van Diemen's Land in the late 1830s into the 1840s.

---

11  "Wanting", *Oxford English Dictionary Online*. http://bit.ly/2JfVH29.
12  The attribution of the quotation in the text is simply "Fyodor Dostoevsky". Flanagan quotes from the Vintage Classics edition of *Notes from Underground*, translated and annotated by Richard Pevear and Larissa Volokhonsky (London: 1993), 28. Other translations, like that of Michael R. Katz, Norton Critical Edition (New York: 1989) use "desire" rather than "wanting".
13  M.M. Bakhtin, *Problems of Dostoevsky's Poetics*, trans. Caryl Emerson (1984), in *Notes from Underground*, translated and edited Michael R. Katz, Norton Critical Edition (New York: 1980), 146–8.
14  Joseph Frank, *Dostoevsky: The Stir of Liberation, 1860-1865* (1986), reprinted in the Norton Critical Edition, 222–5. Flanagan's website "Postscript" includes a section on "Jerrold, Dostoevsky and the Crystal Palace", that brings together Dickens' friend Douglas Jerrold's coinage of the description, the Crystal Palace, with Dostoevsky's terrified reaction when he visited it in 1862 and his satirising the Russian socialist N.G. Chernyshevsky's view of it as symbolic of a new world order in *Notes from Underground* (see e.g. Vintage edition, 24–5).

## The Franklins in History and Fiction

The history of Tasmania as recounted in English from the nineteenth century is frequently a tale of imperial dominion. In *Wanting*, the focus is specifically on Sir John Franklin's term as governor of Van Diemen's Land (the name "Tasmania" became official only in 1856, though Lady Franklin was an early adopter, using it already during her residence there).[15] Since the later twentieth century, the ugly history of the dispossession of the Indigenous inhabitants by white invaders sent to the end of the earth to set up a penal settlement has been in dialogue with Enlightenment narratives of exploration and natural history. It is just such a dialogue about "the catastrophe of colonialisation" (Author's Note, 256) into which *Wanting* intervenes.

Sir John and Lady Franklin figure large only in certain histories of Tasmania. While Lloyd Robson's magisterial *A History of Tasmania* of 1983 devoted a seventy-page chapter of traditional narrative history to "Franklin and Problems of Government",[16] a short version of that *History* gave him just two pages, concluding:

> Franklin seldom satisfied the mandarins of Downing Street ... and became the victim of terrorism by rumour, his own bluff incompetence, the malevolence of men who respected strength and authority rather than flexibility and liberalism, and the ill-advised intervention of the governor's wife in official transactions. The Franklins, admirable and cultivated, were the wrong people in the wrong place at the wrong time.[17]

In large measure this represents what remains the generally accepted version of Franklin's gubernatorial career and his wife's role in it, although there are dissenting voices.[18] A

---

15  Further on nomenclature, it is inaccurate to call Sir John's wife "Lady Jane", as Flanagan does. The woman born Jane Griffin was accorded the courtesy title of "Lady Franklin" when Sir John was knighted in 1829. Alison Alexander, her most recent biographer, is emphatic: "her husband was only a knight, and she was not the daughter of a peer": see *The Ambitions of Jane Franklin Victorian Lady Adventurer* (Sydney: Allen & Unwin, 2013), 30. For convenience I follow Flanagan in using "Lady Jane" to refer to the character, otherwise "Lady Franklin".

16  Lloyd Robson, *A History of Tasmania, Vol. 1: Van Diemen's Land from the Earliest Times to 1885* (Melbourne: Oxford University Press, 1983), Chapter 15.

17  Lloyd Robson, *A Short History of Tasmania* (1985; Melbourne: Oxford University Press; second edition revised by Michael Roe, 1997), 21.

18  There is a copious literature on Sir John, ranging from contemporary nineteenth-century accounts through late nineteenth-century biographies down to naval historian Andrew Lambert's *The Gates of Hell: Sir John Franklin's Tragic Quest for the North West Passage* (New Haven, CT: Yale University Press, 2009), which revisits the accounts of Franklin's Arctic voyages, concentrating on the scientific significance of his journeys. Francis Spufford, *I May Be Some Time: Ice and the English Imagination* (1997; New York: Picador, 1999), is an influential cultural history of polar exploration, while Adriana Craciun further contextualises Franklin's reputation in *Writing Arctic Disaster: Authorship and Exploration* (Cambridge: Cambridge University Press, 2016). Flanagan mentions two books by Ken McGoogan as "useful": *Fatal Passage: The Untold Story of John Rae, the Arctic Adventurer Who Discovered the Fate of Franklin* (Toronto: HarperCollins, 2001) and *Lady Franklin's Revenge: A True Story of Ambition, Obsession, and the Remaking of Arctic History* (Toronto: HarperCollins, 2005). Extended attention to Lady Franklin is relatively recent: Alison Alexander's *The Ambitions of Jane Franklin* makes a positive case for her achievements, and an important suite of articles by Penny Russell develops a revisionist reading of Lady Franklin in contexts that include feminist and postcolonial theory, e.g. "Wife Stories: Narrating Marriage and Self in the Life of Jane Franklin", *Victorian Studies* 48, no. 1 (2005): 33–57. McGoogan and Alexander acknowledge and revise earlier

different tradition of writing history is represented by Henry Reynolds' *A History of Tasmania* (2012). Reynolds chose to begin with the arrival of European maritime expeditions between 1772 and 1802, emphasising the significance of Tasmania's geographical position, the Indigenous people, and Enlightenment aspirations, without explicit concern for minutiae of local political history. Franklin is mentioned by name a couple of times only. While Flanagan necessarily has recourse to the narratives of Tasmanian social and political history, it is with the broader intellectual tradition that he is aligned.

*Wanting* touches on all the aspects of the Franklins' time in Tasmania enumerated by Robson, with some variations of historical fact, and without such explicit value judgements. Flanagan's version emphasises that both Franklins were well-meaning but wrong-headed, their reason betrayed by desire. Sir John is rather bumbling, his consort unwomanly in her interventions into political activity, her independent explorations, and her apparent repression of maternal feeling. They are shown to resent their feelings of fondness towards the Indigenous inhabitants, purporting to treat them – especially Mathinna – as subjects of experiment, while exposing their own weakness and self-delusion. In this respect they are like the Protector George Augustus Robinson, presented in the early chapters as being confident in his mission of "raising his sable charges to the level of English civilisation" (2), but dying a confused and disappointed man towards the end of the novel. Flanagan's reading of the diaries of this "London builder of strong religious beliefs"[19] informs his characterisation, but Robinson is not the narrator as has been suggested.[20] Rather, as the epithet "sable charges" indicates, Flanagan is using – to good effect – a kind of free indirect discourse that plays several points of view against each other in an economical setting of the scene in Van Diemen's Land in the context of other events of 1839, enumerated in the closing paragraph of chapter 1: "the first photograph of a man was taken, Abd al-Qadir declared a jihad against the French, and Charles Dickens was rising to greater fame with a novel called *Oliver Twist*" (3). The sentence casts a wide net, twining together a major technological advance, reference to a Muslim uprising against French colonial power in North Africa, and mention of the early career of a major player in the novel. Such unexpected conjunctions occur elsewhere in *Wanting*, destabilising historical assumptions – all "inexplicable" for Robinson, working on a lecture on pneumatics and committed to facts.

Franklin's celebrity as Arctic explorer is another story entirely. He enlisted in the Royal Navy as a boy under the patronage of his cousin by marriage, the navigator and cartographer Captain Matthew Flinders. By the 1820s he was leading expeditions to the Arctic in search of a navigable sea route between the Atlantic and Pacific oceans. His expedition of 1826–7 produced significant scientific data (geographical, geological and metereological), so that in 1829 he was knighted for his exploits and these contributions

---

works including Kathleen Fitzpatrick, *Sir John Franklin in Tasmania 1837–1848* (Melbourne: Melbourne University Press, 1949), in which Franklin is "a man who had become a legend in his own lifetime, both for courage and sheer beauty of character" (374), and Frances Woodward, *Portrait of Jane: A Life of Lady Franklin* (London: Hodder and Stoughton, 1951). Such judgements are reiterated in both *Australian Dictionary of Biography* entries (for Sir John, by Fitzpatrick 1966, and for Lady Franklin, by Woodward, also 1966), and Oxford *Dictionary of National Biography* entries (respectively B.A. Riffenburgh and Dorothy Middleton, both 2004).

19   Flanagan, "Postscript".
20   Salhia Ben-Messahel, "Colonial Desire and the Renaming of History in Richard Flanagan's *Wanting*", *Commonwealth: Essays and Studies* 36, no.1 (Autumn 2013): 23.

to knowledge. Ironically, since by then the Admiralty was no longer investing in Arctic journeys, he defaulted to a career in civil service, being appointed governor of Van Diemen's Land in 1836. Though many of his aspirations as governor were thwarted by local interests, he did achieve better treatment of convicts and supported some enduring educational and scientific initiatives.

Sir John was recalled to London in 1843. In 1844, with Arctic exploration once again in favour, he was able to organise a new expedition in quest for the Northwest Passage, setting off in 1845 in command of the *Erebus* and *Terror*, vessels which had visited Hobart in 1840–41, in the course of the first British Antarctic Expedition sent to ascertain the location of the South Pole. A critical sequence of *Wanting* is set during a farewell ball on board these ships in chapter 7, hosted by the expedition in return for the hospitality extended to them in Hobart. In 1847, after *Erebus* and *Terror* failed to return, a search expedition was despatched, the first of many, with Lady Franklin being the prime mover in a good proportion of them. Dr John Rae reported in 1854 that he had obtained from the Inuit items belonging to Franklin's expedition, and also had from these "Esquimaux" (sic) accounts of discoveries of bodies and evidence that the last survivors had eaten human flesh: "From the mutilated state of many of the corpses and the contents of the kettles, it is evident that our wretched countrymen had been driven to the last resource – cannibalism – as a means of prolonging existence".[21] It was this report that led Lady Franklin to seek a meeting with Dickens.

*Wanting* refers to but does not depict Sir John's expeditions. There is only a glimpse of him in the field when he is dying at the beginning of chapter 7, though from the beginning he is shown as doomed. chapter 2 ends with a riff on the year 1851, parallel to that on 1839 that closes chapter 1, suggestively drawing together the death of Dickens' small daughter with Lady Franklin's farewelling "the second of what were to be numerous failed expeditions in search of a fable that had once been her husband", the publication of *Moby-Dick* ("a novel about finding a fabled white whale") and "London's Great Exhibition [that] celebrated the triumph of reason" along with British technological superiority (8). Franklin's fame from his 1820s exploits is a given, as the fate of his 1845 expedition and the accusations of cannibalism motivate Lady Franklin's approach to Dickens for support in 1854. Her lobbying of Dickens is central to establishing the counterpoint of the antipodean Franklin story with aspects of the life of the English novelist.

Lady Franklin's motivation has been a matter for debate, though commentators, whether partisan or otherwise, concur that she was a capable strategist who exercised her ability to persuade and pressure in the interests of redeeming her husband's reputation, and establishing for herself the reputation of a perfect Victorian wife and widow. Like Sir John, Lady Franklin had a life that extended beyond her sojourn in Tasmania. She travelled extensively, in the Mediterranean in the late 1820s and early 1830s, subsequently in Tasmania and on the Australian mainland, and later in Europe and the Americas. In Tasmania, she was responsible for significant educational and cultural initiatives, including the construction of a Greek classical temple originally intended to serve as a sculpture museum (in *Wanting*, mocked for the presumption that "the island needs its own Ancients and Mythology", 103), a short-lived Anglican school, and the Hobart regatta.

---

21   Report dated 29 July 1854, in the *Times*, 23 October 1854, 7. This passage, quoted by Charles Dickens in "The Lost Arctic Voyagers", *Household Words* 10, no. 245 (2 December 1854), 361, appears in *Wanting* (26) with the substitution of *alternative* for *resource*.

As well as historical accounts of the Franklins' time in the colony, there have been a number of fictional treatments that tend to focus more on Lady Franklin than on Sir John.[22] A notable recent instance is Jennifer Livett's *Wild Island* (2016), where the Franklins are part of an extended canvas of historical and imaginary characters. *Wild Island* resonates curiously with *Wanting* not only because it depicts the Franklins, but also because it makes play with the work of another Victorian novelist. Charlotte Brontë's *Jane Eyre* (1847) has frequently stimulated neo-Victorian fictions, of which Jean Rhys' *Wide Sargasso Sea* (1966) is the best known. In addition, Francis Spufford connects Jane Eyre's reading of *Bewick's History of British Birds* with the history and mythology of the Arctic, in which Coleridge's *The Rime of the Ancient Mariner* and Mary Shelley's *Frankenstein* also figure.[23] The imagery of birds in *Wanting* distantly alludes to these sources.

Livett's variation on *Jane Eyre* is that Rochester's marriage to Bertha was void since she was already married to his older brother. With Jane Eyre, Edward Rochester travels to Van Diemen's Land in search of his brother, and much else follows, although that strand of the plot melts into the background of a narrative that comes to life with the fortunes of a fictitious character whose story resonates with Jane Eyre's and who for a time is well placed to observe the Franklin household, including the care extended to Mathinna by Sir John's daughter by his first marriage, Eleanor (who does not figure in *Wanting*).[24]

## The Depiction of Mathinna

*Wild Island* approaches the Franklin narrative through the Aboriginal girl Mathinna, who is central also to *Wanting*. The scant historical record, well summarised by Alison Alexander, has been astutely analysed by Penny Russell, who declares that she is not undertaking "another fruitless quest to discover the truth of Mathinna's history". Rather, Russell brings out that Mathinna is essentially a textual construct (pictorial, verbal). Her article traces "the process by which certain fictions have become fixtures in her story, while

---

22  Amanda Johnson has provided an account of some of these in "Making an Exhibition of Herself: Lady Jane Franklin as Queen of the Tasmanian Extinction Narrative", *JASAL: Journal of the Association for the Study of Australian Literature*, 14, no. 5 (2014): 1–21. In an unpublished paper, "The Myths of Lady Franklin" (c. 2008), provoked by *Wanting*, Penny Russell brings the historian's perspective honed in her decades of research on Lady Franklin to bear on fictional treatments: "Often, as in Flanagan's novel, it is not as herself that she appears, but as a legendary figure who is fast assuming proportions of Gothic horror in the limited literary imagination of the twenty-first century, Lady Jane Franklin". Russell takes issue with Flanagan's portrayal of Lady Jane as "an inescapable self-improver in whose mind Van Diemen's Land and her own ambitions had become one" (103).
23  Spufford, *I May Be Some Time*, 11–15.
24  Jennifer Livett, *Wild Island* (Sydney: Allen & Unwin, 2016). Flanagan refers to the tradition of fictional portrayal of the Franklins on his website – for instance Sten Nadolny's *The Discovery of Slowness* (1983; trans. from the German by Ralph Freedman, 1987; Edinburgh: Canongate, 2003), also mentioned in his interview with Ramona Koval. In this novel Sir John falls in love with Lady Franklin's niece and companion Sophia Cracroft, but admits as much "only to himself, not to her" (282); Mathinna does not feature. Maria Teresa Chialant identifies "some affinities" between *Wanting* and Matthew Kneale's novel *English Passengers* (2000) in terms of "the setting (Tasmania), the time (the nineteenth century), a double plot, with both English and Aboriginal characters, and a strong ethical approach to the issue of British colonialism", in "Dickens, the Antipodes and the Neo-Victorian Novel: Richard Flanagan's *Wanting*" in *Reflections in/of Dickens*, ed. Ewa Kujawska-Lis and Anne Krawczyk-Laskarzewska (Newcastle upon Tyne: Cambridge Scholars Press, 2014), 208–21 (211).

others have been quietly abandoned".[25] Russell proceeds to offer "a detailed reading of the cultural production of two of the earliest, and most enduring, images of Mathinna":[26] Thomas Bock's portrait of Mathinna, and a memoir of 1869 in the Hobart *Mercury* that in turn drew on an item published on 20 February 1857.[27] She also gives some attention to a version of the memoir, James Bonwick's *The Last of the Tasmanians: or, the Black War of Van Diemen's Land* (1870), mentioned by Flanagan as "[t]he earliest account of Mathinna's life in book form".[28]

In *Wanting*, Flanagan picks up the theme of adoption and abandonment developed by "Old Boomer" in his story of Mathinna, attributing an unacknowledged maternal longing to Jane Franklin, and suggesting that Mathinna was left behind at the Queen's Orphan School when the Franklins returned to England in 1843 on the advice of their medical practitioner that the child might not survive transplanting from Van Diemen's Land. She ended up in the Aboriginal community at Oyster Cove near Hobart when the surviving residents at Wybalenna on Flinders Island were sent there in 1847, only to descend into drink and depravity. Russell teases out the additions made by "Old Boomer" to the 1857 *Mercury* report, which include the claim that she was the daughter of a powerful Aboriginal leader; that George Robinson, the Protector, was involved in her going to live at Government House; and her role as a favourite there – implying that she was approaching womanhood when she left. Russell's search of records suggests she was "more like eight years old", having lived with the Franklins for about two or three years. Russell establishes that Mathinna had "a much more varied life history" than "Old Boomer" relates (including her two periods of residence on Flinders Island), and that "Old Boomer's" account of Mathinna's death lacks any documentary substantiation.[29] Flanagan supplies detail, adding her rape, garrotting with "the filthy red scarf from her hair" (247), and drowning by another Aboriginal person. The effect is to intensify awareness of the cost to the victim of the educational experiment to which she has been subjected.

While Flanagan largely follows "Old Boomer", the influence of the Bock portrait in his imagining is more pervasive and insidious. He gives an account of its impact on him:

> I was about twenty when I saw this painting of Mathinna as a seven-year-old child in a beautiful Regency red dress. When I was shown the painting and the person who showed me told me the story, he lifted the wooden frame off the painting, it was framed in a little oval frame, and beneath that oval frame were two bare feet. I realised that they'd used the frame to cut off that complete assertion of who she was. Like at the end of the day they'd dressed her up in the dress of reason, but there she was asserting her blackness, her Aboriginality, and they'd denied her that with a wooden frame. And I thought how all their lives really are a war that never ends between wooden frames and bare feet.[30]

---

25   Alexander, *The Ambitions of Jane Franklin*, 130–8; Penny Russell, "Girl in a Red Dress: Inventions of Mathinna", *Australian Historical Studies* 43, no. 3 (2012): 342.
26   Russell, "Girl in a Red Dress", 343.
27   "Something of the Past, by 'Old Boomer'", 7 June 1869, cited in Russell, "Girl in a Red Dress", passim.
28   Flanagan, "Postscript".
29   Russell, "Girl in a Red Dress", 351.
30   Flanagan, interview with Ramona Koval, "Wanting". Later in the interview, Flanagan expands his account of the origin of *Wanting* in the portrait of Mathinna by talking about other contributory elements: his experience with Bunuba men and their boots, the "two types of mythologies" of "the European world and the Indigenous world", and Dickens' *Household Words* articles.

Mathinna enters running, barefoot, in chapter 3: not quite the beginning of the novel as Flanagan describes it in the Koval interview. The passage is echoed as she dies, returning her to childhood innocence and pleasure (3 and 247). Tammy Ho Lai-Ming notes that Flanagan "refers to Mathinna's feet regularly, even obsessively", pointing out the synecdoche of the part standing for her whole body.[31] In the course of the novel, Mathinna resists shoes, the intolerable badge of assimilation into European customs. Returned to her kin, she sets shoes aside completely. The cluster of images around feet and shoes comes full circle at the end of the novel. Mathinna, the Aboriginal child no longer fleet of foot, now deprived of life by co-option and coercion into European ways, is lifted onto his sled by the kindly character Garney Walch, who had conveyed her on the last stage of her journey from Wybalenna to Government House in chapter 7 (112–13). Even a good father like Garney Walch (an invention of Flanagan) can minister only in death. Garney estimates the girl – who reminds him of his long-dead daughter – to be just seventeen years old as he leads her out of sight, "her dirty feet jolting over the sled's back as the ox took up its burden, their light-coloured soles disappearing into the longest night" (252). As Rohan Wilson observes, "Only when Mathinna is dead and the landscape is left empty, quiet, and 'darkening' (252) can the novel find a satisfactory resolution".[32]

Flanagan's modification of the historical record in relation to the portrait is telling. In the novel, Sir John commissions the portrait as a gift for his wife, and presents it to her "in an act that was composed equally of contrition and cunning" (197) as they are sailing away from Van Diemen's Land. His contrition is for his rape of the child, figuratively recounted at the end of chapter 7; his cunning is an effort to assuage any guilt Lady Jane may feel about leaving Mathinna and to remind her of their aspirations to scientific study of the natives. She is forced to concede "that her great experiment was the most ignominious failure" (195), having boasted "Wisely … we removed her from the pernicious influence of the dying elements of her race, then introduced her to the most modern education an Englishwoman can receive" (121). But Lady Jane rejects the gift, throwing it overboard, and giving rein to her emotions in the admission "I loved her" that closes chapter 9 (198).

In fact, it was Lady Franklin who commissioned the watercolour, now in the Tasmanian Museum and Art Gallery (another version is in private hands), for scientific purposes. Lady Franklin explained that Mathinna's portrait was "extremely like", revealing

> the influence of some degree of civilisation upon a child of as pure a race as they, and who in spite of every endeavour … retains much of the unconquerable nature of the savage; extreme uncertainty of will and temper, great want of perseverance and attention, little if any, self controle, and great acuteness of the senses and facility of imitation.[33]

She sent Bock's careful representation of the Aboriginal child back to England along with her collection of Aboriginal skulls, one of which Lady Jane displays to Dickens in chapter 4 (30).[34] Flanagan makes Lady Jane's jettisoning the portrait a crucial marker of her denial

---

31  Tammy Ho Lai-Ming, "Cannibalised Girlhood in Richard Flanagan's *Wanting*", *Neo-Victorian Studies* 5, no. 1 (2012): 17, 32. Ho provides detailed references.
32  Rohan Wilson, "Extinction Discourse in *Wanting* and *Doctor Wooreddy's Prescription for Enduring the Ending of the World*", *Antipodes* 29, no. 1 (June 2015): 13.
33  Lady Franklin cited in Alexander, *The Ambitions of Jane Franklin*, 132–3.
34  Alexander, *The Ambitions of Jane Franklin*, 129–34.

of love for the child, and her destructive suppression of maternal feelings. Her reactions are aligned with world events of 1844 that resonate with the earlier comments on 1839 and 1851 in a lapidary conjunction of extinction of species, nihilism and the will to power, and technological revolution: "The last pair of great auks in the world had just been killed, Friedrich Nietzsche born, and Samuel Morse sent the first electrical communication in history. It was a telegram that read: *What God hath wrought*" (198).

Tammy Ho Lai-Ming comments "[t]hat Flanagan does not make Mathinna the first-person narrator and instead mediates her subjectivity through the omniscient third person might seem an unfortunate choice for an author attempting to give voice to a marginalised figure".[35] So it might, were it not that Flanagan, in dramatising Mathinna's reponses to unfamiliar sights and experiences, shows both her imperfect understanding of the English language, especially written, and her familiarity with it when she chooses, in a way that depicts the nature of her intelligence. Her undelivered letter to her father (121) follows closely one dictated by Mathinna to Sir John's daughter by his first marriage, Eleanor, who was largely responsible for the child.[36] This material on her education in the central chapter 7 is recalled near the end, where she loses facility with English through disuse and disinclination.

Mathinna's Aboriginality is declared in her self-expression through dance, and her affinity with the animal world, cumulatively presented. Among the various species with whom she is associated, the black swan becomes particularly significant (a native to Australia, and another denial that white is the norm). Ho discusses in detail the dense fabric of imagery Flanagan weaves, drawing on the Greek myth of Leda and the swan in which the god Zeus in the guise of a swan rapes the maiden Leda. Roast black cygnets are consumed at Robinson's grand dinner for the Franklins, where Lady Jane announces her wish "to adopt a native child, as though it were the final item to be ordered off a long menu" (69), an ironic conflation of ideas of civilised and barbaric behaviour including cannibalism, and proleptic of Sir John's ravishing Mathinna costumed as a black swan for the bestiary-themed fancy dress ball. Mathinna epitomises the Tasmanian Aboriginal population both animal and human, both seemingly doomed to extinction – "a terrible anguish which I have tried to mirror in my novel", Flanagan says in his Author's Note, adding in respect of the people "They did not [die out]. Nor were they absent from the subsequent unfolding of Tasmanian history" (256). Such a perspective on the narrative of history, where twenty-first-century hindsight shows that what many in the nineteenth century saw as inevitable did not in fact come to pass, is inherent in Flanagan's text.

### Charles Dickens, *The Frozen Deep*, and Ellen Ternan

In the mid-1850s, Dickens was generally restless, unhappy in his marriage though successful in his career. He was at the peak of his powers, entering what biographers and critics call his "dark" period, and taken up by his activities as editor and contributor to his journals, *Household Words* (1850–59) and *All the Year Round* (1859–70), as well as by his fiction. With *Bleak House* (1852–3) and *Hard Times* (1854) behind him, in 1856 Dickens was working on *Little Dorrit* (serialised December 1855–June 1857), with its mordant

---

35  Ho, "Cannibalised Girlhood", 22.
36  Alexander, *The Ambitions of Jane Franklin*, 131.

commentary on bureaucracy. In *Wanting*, Flanagan complicates his version of Dickens, the apostle of hearth and home, by signalling also his credentials as a social critic, writing of *Little Dorrit*, the work in progress, as "a new novel raging against government men and government absurdity, the heart-killing world of government regulations and government offices" (72). *A Tale of Two Cities* (1859), *Great Expectations* (1859–60), *Our Mutual Friend* (1864–5) and *The Mystery of Edwin Drood* (1870) were to come. One thread through Dickens' fiction from *Little Dorrit* on – though explicit also in *David Copperfield* (1849–50) – has to do with heroes and heroism, a Victorian concern heralded in Thomas Carlyle's *On Heroes, Hero-Worship and the Heroic in History* (1841). In *Little Dorrit*, and in his play *The Frozen Deep*, Dickens experimented with characters whose heroism is manifested by inner conflicts through which they remain faithful to a personal ideal of conduct. *The Frozen Deep*, jointly written with Wilkie Collins, novelist and contributor to *Household Words*, was first performed in January 1857, based on what Dickens claimed as "a mighty original notion".[37] In respect of the play, which figures so large in *Wanting*, biographer Michael Slater points out:

> Both the concept of courageous men destined to go on a long and hazardous journey, like the Arctic explorers, and the concept of a flawed hero who has to fight against dark passions in himself (very unlike the kind of heroes Dickens had so far created), were ... personally very important and significant for Dickens at this time.[38]

What then did the famous novelist have to do with the famous explorer? Just how does the conjunction of the two male celebrities play out?

The explicit link between the Franklins and Charles Dickens is made in chapter 4 of *Wanting*, in an episode dramatising Dickens' waiting upon Lady Franklin at her house on Pall Mall on 19 November 1854. In the novel, Lady Jane inveighs against the reprint of Rae's report, originally published in the *Times*, then embellished with engravings for its appearance in the *Illustrated London News* of 28 October (25). As it happened, the allegations of cannibalism were convincingly proven in 1857 by Leopold McClintock's expedition – organised by Lady Franklin – which also found evidence that Franklin had died on 11 June 1847, well before the last survivors perished, so that he was absolved of the unthinkable sin of cannibalism. Flanagan dramatises Lady Franklin's conversion of Dickens to her cause. He succumbs partly because exploration and the Arctic provide an ideal of heroism that polarises the civilised and its dark shadow, savagery, in a way directly related to his current state of mind.

Dickens' train of thought as depicted in the novel is utterly consistent with the position developed in his two *Household Word* articles, from which *Wanting* includes quotations.[39] Flanagan takes us in and out of his characters' minds, so that we see how Dickens and Lady Jane appear to each other: a nice touch is Dickens' observation that "Rather than

---

37  The phrase is from a letter of Dickens to W.H. Wills: *The Letters of Charles Dickens, Vol. 8*, ed. Graham Storey and Kathleen Tillotson (Oxford: Clarendon Press, 1995), 81, and transposed into conversation in *Wanting* (78).
38  Slater, *Charles Dickens*, 406.
39  Dickens's article "The Lost Arctic Voyagers" was divided over two issues, and was the lead in both: *Household Words* 10, no. 245, 2 December 1854, 361–5 and *Household Words* 10, no. 246, 9 December 1854, 385–93. The italicised passages in *Wanting*, 41–2, are almost verbatim from the first *Household Words* piece, 362; those on 46–7 are from 364 (first instalment) and 392 (second).

the black of a widow's weeds, she wore a green and purple dress" (24), though Flanagan later has her don "black mourning" (71).[40] Their thoughts go to their vulnerabilities: Lady Franklin thinks of Mathinna, Dickens of ice and the association of Arctic wastes with manly friendship and heroism as he works himself to a rhetorical pitch, in an attack on the Esquimaux and savages more generally that now reads as out-and-out racism. The chapter is only one-third through when Dickens takes his leave from her, his reflections turning to the misery of his marriage before some joking with his literary friends Wilkie Collins and Douglas Jerrold, with a neat conversion to dialogue of part of a letter to his assistant W.H. Wills when he declares, "I am rather strong on voyages and cannibalism" (38).[41] He sets to work on his article, with accompanying thoughts of his early love Maria Beadnell, merging into recriminations against his wife. Flanagan here anticipates by a few months the reappearance in Dickens' life of Maria Beadnell, now Mrs Winter, in early 1855. Dickens' meditation takes place while in the public sphere the Crimean War is being fought to safeguard British imperial interests, generating new talk of heroism and manliness.

In the course of composition, Dickens takes Franklin's book *Journey to the Polar Sea* from the shelf,[42] and feels Franklin write himself into being, as Dickens too creates himself through words and performance. Flanagan has Dickens find evidence of Franklin as epitome of English manly uprightness in his text, and jocularly manifests his satisfaction: "Rather than countenance the thought of cannibalism, Sir John had eaten his own boots. Dickens felt cheered. That was an Englishman. Stout heart, stewed boots, decency dressed up as diet" (46). Dickens works himself up by his rhetoric, connecting women with his surrenders to passion. Ironic distance is not steadily sustained as the chapter ends with the florid declaration that "he would pay the cost, immense and crippling, of his ultimate failure to discipline his own great undisciplined heart. It would be the price of his soul" (48).

The presence of Dickens in *Wanting* goes well beyond this literal connection with Lady Franklin and her crusade. Dickens never went in person to Australia, though he actively considered making the journey on two occasions in the 1860s (Flanagan has him contemplate it: "He resolved to move to Australia" – 73). He famously sent some of his characters there, as well as his son Plorn. And Dickens has been himself transported in the fiction of others, for example in Peter Carey's *Jack Maggs* (1997), which Kylie Mirmohamadi and Susan K. Martin describe as "a complex re-imagining of Dickens and

---

40  Frances Woodward notes that when the Admiralty removed the names of Franklin and his crew from the books early in 1854, because of the length of time they had been gone, Lady Franklin refused to claim her widow's pension and according to her step-daughter Eleanor "changed her deep mourning … for bright colours of green & pink" (*Portrait of Jane*, 285). Spufford repeats this detail, observing that "though she had mourned his *absence* readily, she declined to mourn his *death* until evidence of it was forthcoming" (*I May Be Some Time*, 119). Spufford's analysis of the important association of ice and morality in accounts of polar exploration is illuminating for Flanagan's novel, as in his comment on Mary Shelley's "anatomising the attractions of emptiness to a particular male sensibility, Romantic, self-driven, and ever willing to exceed the limits of the human body" (62).
41  *The Letters of Charles Dickens, Vol. 7*, ed. Graham Storey, Kathleen Tillotson and Angus Easson (Oxford: Clarendon Press, 1993), 470.
42  Probably the 1824 one-volume reprint of *Journey to the Polar Sea (Narrative of a Journey to the Shores of the Polar Sea in the Years 1819-20-21-22)* (London: John Murray, 2 vols., 1823). *The Letters of Charles Dickens, Vol. 7*, 470 n5, gives detail about other of Dickens' sources.

his role in cultural configurations of empire and colony".[43] But Dickens existed in the cultural imaginary of colonial Australia in more insidious ways, as Mirmohamadi and Martin argue. They explore "the cult of Charles Dickens – the constant producing and re-producing, reading and re-reading, memorising, discussion, performance, and circulation of his words – in the cultural life of colonial Australia"; and further consider "the ways in which Australians across all the colonies not only read Dickens's work, but read the world, and the local societies around them, through Dickens".[44] This influence is another of the subliminal currents in *Wanting* and the invocation of an iconic Dickens in this way one of its most original features.

Lady Franklin's approach stimulated and reinforced Dickens' fascination with the Arctic, apparent in a number of articles in *Household Words* through to 1857, and most fully realised in *The Frozen Deep*.[45] Since his childhood, Dickens had engaged in amateur theatricals. From 1851 when he purchased Tavistock House in London, he organised private theatricals ostensibly for his children, performed at Twelfth Night (6 January). It was readily apparent and freely acknowledged that the loss of Franklin's last expedition coloured *The Frozen Deep*, the production of which in January 1857 was far more elaborate than any of Dickens' previous theatrical ventures, though acted by family and friends, with Dickens himself playing the villain-hero, Richard Wardour. The success of *The Frozen Deep* in private performances in London, including one attended by Queen Victoria, led to further performances being planned to take place in the vast Manchester Free Trade Hall as benefits for the family of Dickens' friend Douglas Jerrold, who had died suddenly on 8 June. Robert Brannan makes the important point that the text of *The Frozen Deep* was "little more than the skeleton" requiring to be fleshed out in performance: Dickens' own role was crucial, praised by professional critics in the Tavistock House performances, and lauded to the skies in Manchester.[46] Wilkie Collins wrote that "Dickens surpassed himself … He literally electrified the audience",[47] his encomium assimilated into *Wanting*: "it was

---

43   Kylie Mirmohamadi and Susan K. Martin, *Colonial Dickens: What Australians Made of the World's Favourite Writer* (Melbourne: Australian Scholarly Press, 2012), 136. There is now a considerable body of discussion on Dickens in such terms: e.g. Jennifer Gribble, "Portable Property: Postcolonial Appropriations of *Great Expectations*", in *Victorian Turns, NeoVictorian Returns: Essays on Fiction and Culture*, ed. Penny Gay, Judith Johnston, and Catherine Waters (Newcastle upon Tyne: Cambridge Scholars Press, 2008), 182–92; and with reference to *Wanting* specifically, Maria Teresa Chialant, "Dickens, the Antipodes and the Neo-Victorian Novel: Richard Flanagan's *Wanting*". Larissa McLean Davies gives a skewed reading in "Magwitch Madness: Archive Fever and the Teaching of Australian Literature in Subject English", in *Teaching Australian Literature: From Classroom Conversations to National Imaginings*, ed. Brenton Doecke, Larissa McLean Davies and Philip Mead (Adelaide: Wakefield, 2011), 129–52. She proposes that *Wanting* is "a neo-colonial hybrid canonical text" (138) that seeks canonical validation through affiliation with *Great Expectations* – one of Dickens' novels not prominent in Flanagan's. Moreover, she fails to take the point of the imbrication in *Wanting* of blackness and savagery with reasoned civilisation both in the imperial centre and the colonial periphery.
44   Mirmohamadi and Martin, *Colonial Dickens*, 4–5.
45   The *Household Words* contributions and subsequent contact of Dickens and Lady Franklin are conveniently documented in Robert Louis Brannan, *Under the Management of Mr Charles Dickens: His Production of "The Frozen Deep"* (Ithaca, NY: Cornell University Press, 1966), 12. Brannan gives a detailed discussion of the genesis, staging and reception of the play.
46   Brannan, *Under the Management*, 4–5.
47   *The Letters of Charles Dickens, Vol. 8*, 421 n5.

the greatest performance of the play that I could have imagined … You literally electified the audience" (210).

The plot of *The Frozen Deep* is thoroughly melodramatic. The first act has a group of women in a country house in Devon awaiting the return from an Arctic expedition of their menfolk: a husband, a father, a brother, and a "husband that is to be" (Clara Burnham's fiancé, Frank Aldersley).[48] Richard Wardour had been a childhood friend of Clara, but before he can declare his suit she has promised herself to Aldersley. Both men set off on Arctic voyages, and they are brought together in the second act when the crews of their respective vessels, stranded in ice, join forces to send a group of able-bodied men to find help. The vengeful Wardour volunteers to go when one of the group is injured, Aldersley already being of the party. In the third act, the women have gone to Newfoundland with a search party: Wardour staggers in carrying Aldersley, delivers him to Clara and dies.

It was in connection with the Manchester performances of the play that Dickens came to know Ellen Ternan. For these public performances, he considered it inappropriate for female members of his family and household to take the stage given the infamy of actresses as a group. Fortunately and fatefully, reputable and respectable talent was available in the Ternan family, mother and three daughters. Claire Tomalin's groundbreaking research established the lasting relationship of Dickens with Ellen, bringing out the difference in their ages (in 1857 Ellen was eighteen and Dickens forty-five). Tomalin also stresses the paradox if not hypocrisy of Dickens as strict father, extolling the values of family life while maintaining a household with a mistress.[49] In a virtuoso passage, Flanagan associates the idea of family in the mid-nineteenth century with the technological and commercial power of the railways:

> [T]here were opportunities to be had in family, and just as there were railway speculators, there were family speculators. Few had gambled so boldly and profited so handsomely as Lady Jane, the exemplary devoted wife, or Dickens, the very bard of family. But celebrating family was one thing. Practising it, Dickens had discovered, was something else again. (32)

The railways convey Dickens' troupe from London to Manchester, a very different venue from London. For a start, the city is the new face of industrial civilisation, as has been made apparent early in *Wanting* in George Robinson's pride in his Manchester-like buildings fit for "a great modern town" (11). Yet there is culture, in the form of the Manchester Art Treasures Exhibition. Here, the party pauses "by an old master's painting of Leda and the Swan, hung, as were all the salacious old masters, on the highest row" (165–6). The allusions to the Leda legend so strongly invoked earlier in the novel are revived, with Dickens' friend and first biographer John Forster insisting enigmatically that "Harmony and discord is what it means" (166). Ellen Ternan's reaction – "I could eat those babies" (167) – associates women with cannibalism, and brings to Dickens' mind his dead daughter Dora. Desire can take over when characters are in costume and playing a part. Sir John's violation of Mathinna was carried out under the disguise of a black swan; the virtual consummation of the attraction of Dickens and Nelly Ternan is to be during a theatrical performance.

---

48  Brannan, *Under the Management*, 102.
49  Tomalin, *The Invisible Woman*, 87.

Tomalin is circumspect and necessarily proceeds by deduction in accounting for the attraction of Dickens and Ellen, and reconstructing events. Flanagan is free to dramatise – and does so. The Manchester sequence of *Wanting* (chapters 10 and 12) incorporates Flanagan's major changes to the historical record. He makes three main modifications of fact, of which the visit to the exhibition is the first, in order to bring his meditation on desire to a climax.

The second is to have Maria Ternan fall ill so that Ellen plays Clara Burnham for one extraordinary performance and weeps over Dickens as Wardour.[50] Their developing attraction has been shown in chapters 8 and 10, which include London rehearsals, and discussions between Dickens and Ellen in their Manchester hotel, one in which she gives him pointers about his acting technique (in fact she sometimes coached him for his public readings), and another that includes the suggestive scene of their eating cherries. As the play reaches its climax in chapter 12, there are parallel epiphanies for Dickens and for Lady Jane.

In the climactic recognition scene on stage, Flanagan has Ellen and Dickens depart from the script. He appropriates reactions of Maria Ternan, profoundly moved by acting with Dickens, sobbing "Oh, it is so sad, it is so dreadfully sad. Oh, don't die! Give me a little time! Don't take leave of me in this terrible way – pray, pray, pray!"[51] The account is Dickens' own, in which he quotes himself as saying to the actress "My dear child, it will be over in two minutes – there is nothing the matter – don't be so distressed!"[52] Michael Slater points out that the speech attributed to Maria is not in the text of *The Frozen Deep*, and further conjectures that since whispers between the actors would have held up the action, "Could it possibly be that Dickens was writing most of this speech for her retrospectively?"[53]

The third modification is to bring Lady Franklin to Manchester. Fact is complemented by Flanagan's imagination as Lady Jane travels there, to see *The Frozen Deep* at Dickens' invitation. The sequence is formally symmetrical with their meeting in Pall Mall in chapter

---

50  In the Manchester performances of *The Frozen Deep*, Maria Ternan took the role of Clara and Ellen took the smaller part of her friend Lucy Crayford. In the farce, John Baldwin Buckstone's *Uncle John: A Petite Comedy in Two Acts* (1833), Dickens' role was that of an old man in love with a young girl he has educated, the girl's part played by Ellen. See Brannan, *Under the Management*, 69; also *The Letters of Charles Dickens, Vol. 8*, 412 n1.

51  *The Letters of Charles Dickens*, Pilgrim edn, vol. 8, Dickens' letter to Lavinia Watson 487–9, esp 488 (7 December 1857), and the remarkably similar passage in one to Angela Burdett-Coutts, vol. 8, 432–4 (433) (5 September 1857), each drawn on by Flanagan for the intense scenes between Dickens and Ellen on stage. Peter Ackroyd quotes extensively from these letters in a biography acknowledged by Flanagan as particularly useful in his reading on Dickens ("Postscript"). He offers the interpretation that Ellen speaking her own lines as Lucy seemed like "*the one thing missing in his life*" so that caught up in the drama Dickens "saw himself as Ellen's actual love": see Peter Ackroyd, *Dickens* (London: Sinclair-Stevenson, 1990), 791. Ackroyd has Dickens declaim from a speech of Wardour in *The Frozen Deep* on one of his twenty-mile nocturnal walks during the rehearsal period: "Young, with a fair sad face, with kind tender eyes, with a soft clear voice. Young and loving and merciful. I keep her face in my mind, though I can keep nothing else. I must wander, wander, wander – restless, sleepless, homeless – till I find her!" (773), a passage verbatim from the play (Brannan, *Under the Management*, 156–7, and see the slightly modified version in *Wanting*, spoken by Dickens as Wardour – 236). Examples of near-quotation from the play in Flanagan's novel could be multiplied.

52  *The Letters of Charles Dickens, Vol. 8*, 433.

53  Slater, *Charles Dickens*, 433.

4. Driving from the railway station, she experiences unseasonable heat: "like a spectator on a volcano, she was enjoying these marvellous sensations of a most modern city when her landau carriage, taking a side road to avoid the flyblown corpse of a horse, became caught up in a funeral cortege" (233–4) – a child's funeral, ceremonious as the service for Dora Dickens would assuredly have been, and as Mathinna's obsequies, despite Garney Walch, are not. Lady Jane's sense of fulfilment in "[h]er life, as a studied melancholy" (234) is disturbed, and Dickens' electrifying performance disturbs her even more, evoking Mathinna as she last saw her. As Dickens casts aside his scripted speech in favour of one that "was – improbably, inexorably, inescapably – describing his soul" (237), she panics and rushes from the theatre. Dickens' epiphany, of the cost of saying "no to love" (239), is an epiphany also for her, but for him there is a future with Ellen, sketched later (241). In the melodramatic mode of *The Frozen Deep*, Flanagan pulls out all stops, again as in chapter 4 associating a city with malign natural events and devolution, while obliquely referring to a Dickens novel (here to *Hard Times*). The point of having Lady Jane witness a performance of *The Frozen Deep* (as it happens, the last, and the one in which Ellen plays Clara) is to bring home to her the extent to which she is wanting (lacking), as Dickens comes to the realisation that "he could no longer deny wanting" (241).

This consideration of some aspects of the narrative complexity of *Wanting* has dwelt on the relation of Flanagan's fiction to other discourses – history, mythology, literary texts. In accepting his assertion that the "meditation on desire" is "the true subject of *Wanting*" (256), the resonance of the term "meditation" should be reckoned with. I am not proposing that any particular form of meditation is in question: rather, it is a matter of taking on board qualities common to meditative practices, to do with immersion in reflection enabling fuller knowledge and developing compassion. The dialogue in *Wanting* between a twenty-first-century present and a Victorian past is not an either/or debate as in those neo-Victorian novels and historiographic metafictions that implicitly valorise and interrogate history as the master narrative. It opens new multi-temporal and cross-cultural perspectives on historical understanding through the constellations it constructs.

## References

Alexander, Alison. *The Ambitions of Jane Franklin Victorian Lady Adventurer*. Sydney: Allen and Unwin, 2013

Bakhtin, M.M. "Problems of Dostoevsky's Poetics". (1984) Translated by Caryl Emerson. In Fyodor Dostoevsky, *Notes from Underground* (1864). Translated by Michael R. Katz. New York: Norton, 1989.

Ben-Messahel, Salhia. "Colonial Desire and the Renaming of History in Richard Flanagan's *Wanting*", *Commonwealth: Essays and Studies* 36, no.1 (Autumn 2013): 21–32.

Brannan, Robert Louis. *Under the Management of Mr Charles Dickens: His Production of "The Frozen Deep"*. Ithaca, NY: Cornell University Press, 1966.

Carciun, Adriana. *Writing Arctic Disaster: Authorship and Exploration*. Cambridge: Cambridge University Press, 2016.

Chialant, Maria Teresa. "Dickens, the Antipodes and the Neo-Victorian Novel: Richard Flanagan's *Wanting*". In *Reflections in/of Dickens*, edited by Ewa Kujawska-Lis and Anne Krawczyk-Laskarzewska, 208–21. Newcastle upon Tyne: Cambridge Scholars Press, 2014.

Conrad, Joseph. *Youth, Heart of Darkness, The End of the Tether: Three Stories*. (1902) London: J.M. Dent, Collected Edition, 1946.

Davies, Larissa McLean. "Magwitch Madness: Archive Fever and the Teaching of Australian Literature in Subject English". In *Teaching Australian Literature: From Classroom Conversations to National Imaginings*, edited by Brenton Doecke, Larissa McLean Davies and Philip Mead, 129–52. Adelaide: Wakefield, 2011.

Deyo, Brian Daniel. "Rewriting History/Animality in J.M. Coetzee's *Dusklands* and Richard Flanagan's *Wanting*", *Ariel: A Review of International English Literature* 44, no. 4 (October 2013): 89–116.

Dickens, Charles. *Bleak House*. (1852–3) London: Oxford University Press, 1948.

———. "The Lost Arctic Voyagers", *Household Words* 10, no. 245 (2 December 1854).

Dostoevsky, Fyodor. *Notes from Underground*. (1864) Translated by Michael R. Katz. New York: Norton, 1989.

Fitzpatrick, Kathleen. "Sir John Franklin". (1966) In *The Australian Dictionary of Biography*. Melbourne: Melbourne University Press, 1994.

Fitzpatrick, Kathleen. *Sir John Franklin in Tasmania 1837–1848*. Melbourne: Melbourne University Press, 1949.

Flanagan, Richard. *Wanting*. Sydney: Knopf, 2008.

———. "Postscript". [2008] http://bit.ly/2suhGrX.

Frank, Joseph. "Dostoevsky: The Stir of Liberation, 1860–1865". (1986). In Fyodor Dostoevsky, *Notes from Underground* (1864). Translated by Michael R. Katz. New York: Norton, 1989.

Franklin, John. *Journey to the Polar Sea* (*Narrative of a Journey to the Shores of the Polar Sea in the Years 1819-20-21-22*. London: John Murray, 1823.

Gribble, Jennifer. "Portable Property: Postcolonial Appropriations of *Great Expectations*". In *Victorian Turns, NeoVictorian Returns: Essays on Fiction and Culture*, edited by Penny Gay, Judith Johnston, and Catherine Waters. Newcastle upon Tyne: Cambridge Scholars Press, 2008, 182–92.

Ho Lai-Ming, Tammy. "Cannibalised Girlhood in Richard Flanagan's *Wanting*", *Neo-Victorian Studies* 5, no. 1 (2012), 14–37.

Johnson, Amanda. "Making an Exhibition of Herself: Lady Jane Franklin as Queen of the Tasmanian Extinction Narrative", *Journal of the Association for the Study of Australian Literature (JASAL)* 14, no. 5 (2014): 1–21.

Koval, Ramona. Interview with Richard Flanagan. *The Monthly Video*, 24 July 2014. http://bit.ly/2sqIfyd.

———. "Wanting: Richard Flanagan". *The Book Show*, ABC Radio National, 12 November 2008. https://ab.co/2LHmbYK.

Lambert, Andrew. *The Gates of Hell: Sir John Franklin's Tragic Quest for the North West Passage*. New Haven, CT: Yale University Press, 2009.

Livett, Jennifer. *Wild Island*. Sydney: Allen and Unwin, 2016.

McGoogan, Ken. *Lady Franklin's Revenge: A True Story of Ambition, Obsession, and the Remaking of Arctic History*. Toronto: HarperCollins, 2005.

———. *Fatal Passage: The Untold Story of John Rae, the Arctic Adventurer Who Discovered the Fate of Franklin*. Toronto: HarperCollins, 2001.

Mirmohamadi, Kylie and Susan K. Martin. *Colonial Dickens: What Australians Made of the World's Favourite Writer*. Melbourne: Australian Scholarly Press, 2012.

Mitchell, Kate. *History and Cultural Memory in Neo-Victorian Fiction: Victorian Afterimages*. Basingstoke, UK: Palgrave Macmillan, 2010.

Nadolny, Sten. *The Discovery of Slowness*. (1983) Translated by Ralph Freedman, 1987. Edinburgh: Canongate, 2003.

Riffenburgh, B.A. "Sir John Franklin". (1966) *The Oxford Dictionary of National Biography*. Oxford: Oxford University Press, 1994.

Robson, Lloyd. *A Short History of Tasmania*. (1985) Second edition revised by Michael Roe. Melbourne: Oxford University Press, 1997.

———. *A History of Tasmania, Vol. 1, Van Diemen's Land from the Earliest Times to 1885*. Melbourne: Oxford University Press, 1983.

Russell, Penny. "Girl in a Red Dress: Inventions of Mathinna", *Australian Historical Studies* 43, no. 3 (2012), 341–62.
——. "Wife Stories: Narrating Marriage and Self in the Life of Jane Franklin", *Victorian Studies* 48, no. 1 (2005): 33–57.
Slater, Michael. *Charles Dickens*. New Haven, CT: Yale University Press, 2009.
Spufford, Francis. *I May Be Some Time: Ice and the English Imagination*. (1997) New York: Picador, 1999.
Storey, Graham and Kathleen Tillotson, eds. *The Letters of Charles Dickens, Vol. 8*. Oxford: Clarendon Press, 1995.
Storey, Graham, Kathleen Tillotson and Angus Easson, eds. *The Letters of Charles Dickens, Vol. 7*. Oxford: Clarendon Press, 1993.
Tomalin, Claire. *The Invisible Woman: The Story of Nelly Ternan and Charles Dickens*. (1990) Revised edition. London: Penguin, 1991.
Wilson, Rohan. "Extinction Discourse in *Wanting* and *Doctor Wooreddy's Prescription for Enduring the Ending of the World*", *Antipodes* 29, no. 1 (June 2015): 5–17.
Woodward, Frances. *Portrait of Jane: A Life of Lady Franklin*. London: Hodder and Stoughton, 1951.

# 9
# Terror, Paranoia and Manipulation: The Politics of Fear in *The Unknown Terrorist*

Nathanael O'Reilly

Richard Flanagan's fourth novel, *The Unknown Terrorist* (2006), was published during the height of the War on Terror, just five years after the September 11 attacks on the United States. The novel is undoubtedly a product of its time, written and published during the Howard era when fears of terrorist attacks dominated Australian society as a result of the attacks in the United States on 11 September 2001, the Bali bombings in 2002, and the terrorist attacks in Madrid in 2004 and London in 2005. Citizens' fears of a terrorist attack in Australia were manipulated and heightened by both the media and the federal government. *The Unknown Terrorist* was one of three Australian novels focused on terrorism published in 2006: the others are Andrew McGahan's *Underground* and Linda Jaivin's *The Infernal Optimist*.[1] Despite the passing of over a decade since the publication of *The Unknown Terrorist*, during which time the international network known as ISIS and ISIL has come into existence and become the most dangerous contemporary terrorist organisation, the novel remains remarkably prescient and relevant, especially its criticisms of the media and government's use of the politics and rhetoric of fear. Indeed, with the recent Brexit vote and passage of the Investigatory Powers Act in the United Kingdom, and the victory in the United States presidential election of Donald Trump, who won largely due to his successful use of the politics of fear, in particular the demonisation of immigrants, Muslims and any group who could be depicted as "Other" to white America, the politics and rhetoric of fear clearly remain a dominant weapon in the contemporary "post-truth" Western media and political environments. This chapter focuses on Flanagan's critique of the Australian media and government's use of the politics and rhetoric of fear during the post-September 11 Howard era.

Although fear, anxiety and paranoia reached new levels in Australian society in the years between the September 11 attacks, the Bali bombings and the publication of *The Unknown Terrorist*, fear (and related topics such as terror, paranoia, anxiety and xenophobia) has been a central concern of Australian literature since early in the colonial era. Australian history, including the histories of the British colonies that later became Australian states, is full of fears and anxieties, many of which are exhibited in numerous forms of cultural production from the past two centuries, including folk songs, ballads,

---

1   Andrew McGahan, *Underground* (Crows Nest, NSW: Allen & Unwin, 2006); Linda Jaivin, *The Infernal Optimist* (Sydney: Fourth Estate, 2006).

poetry, drama, fiction, visual art, and film. The centrality of fear in Australian culture has been noted by academics from a variety of disciplines, including history, politics, cultural studies and anthropology, as well as public intellectuals, journalists and politicians.[2]

The particular focus of cultural productions addressing fear has often shifted in response to national and international events, and thus the object of fear may be the Indigenous peoples, the physical environment, immigration, invasion by Asian nations, multiculturalism, communism, the Cold War and nuclear proliferation, refugees or Islamic fundamentalists, and other threats (real and imagined), depending on the particular cultural and historical moment during which the work of art is produced. Furthermore, the degree of fear, terror, paranoia and anxiety present within Australian society varies in response to local, national and international events, as well as the degree to which the media and the government manipulate societal fears, and thus may be depicted as arriving in waves. From a contemporary vantage point, the years between 2001 and 2006 may be perceived as an era in which fears of a possible terrorist attack within Australia reached their zenith. Indeed, Jean-François Vernay and I argued in 2009 that fear as a subject matter for Australian literature became more pervasive after the September 11 attacks,[3] and thus Flanagan's *The Unknown Terrorist* should be read as a novel that captured the zeitgeist, and engaged in urgent national and international debates regarding the threat of terrorism and Islamic fundamentalism, the role of the media in provoking citizens' fears, the measures that governments should take to maintain security, and the difficulty of maintaining free, democratic societies while fighting both internal and external threats.

Frank Moorhouse was one of the first Australian writers to expose the changes taking place within Australian society in the aftermath of the 9/11 attacks. In his seminal essay, "The Writer in a Time of Terror", Moorhouse addresses the issue of anti-terrorist legislation and demonstrates that although Big Brother-type surveillance and intelligence-gathering has been common practice in Australia since the creation of the Australian Security Intelligence Organisation (ASIO) in 1949, there has been an increased and somewhat irrational concern with national security since 2001, which has resulted in an "authoritarian mind-set" impinging on individual and civic liberties.[4] In two books published in the five years before the appearance of Flanagan's *The Unknown Terrorist*, Ghassan Hage argued that Australian society is plagued by fears. In *White Nation* (2000), Hage contends that many contemporary Australians are beset by worry, and that worrying is for many people "the last available strategy for staying in control of social processes over which they no longer have much control".[5] Hage expands his thesis in *Against Paranoid Nationalism* (2003), describing contemporary Australian society as a "paranoid nationalist culture"; he claims that Australian society is "defensive", "suffers from a scarcity of hope", and creates paranoid citizens "who see threats everywhere".[6] Hage is particularly critical of the Howard government, claiming that Howard's administration took a previously

---

2   Nathanael O'Reilly and Jean-François Vernay, "Terra Australis Incognita? An Introduction to Fear in Australian Literature and Film", in "Fear in Australian Literature and Film," ed. Nathanael O'Reilly and Jean-François Vernay, special issue, *Antipodes* 23, no. 1 (June 2009): 5–9.
3   O'Reilly and Vernay, "Terra Australis Incognita?", 5.
4   Frank Moorhouse, "The Writer in a Time of Terror", *Griffith Review* 14 (Summer 2006/7): 58.
5   Ghassan Hage, *White Nation: Fantasies of White Supremacy in a Multicultural Society* (1998; New York/Annandale, NSW: Routledge/Pluto, 2000), 10.
6   Ghassan Hage, *Against Paranoid Nationalism: Searching for Hope in a Shrinking Society* (Annandale, NSW: Pluto, 2003), xii, 3.

existing yet marginalised "subculture of colonial White paranoia" and moved it to the centre of Australian culture. The members of contemporary Australian society Hage dubs the "newly marginalized" include "urban dwellers … stuck in insecure jobs", farmers, and small-business owners; Hage argues that such people are self-centred, "jealous of anyone perceived to be 'advancing'", and that they project their fear "onto everything classified as alien", generating a "paranoid form of nationalism".[7]

In Carmen Lawrence's *Fear and Politics*, published during the same year as Flanagan's novel, she bluntly states, "Fear sells – and it gets governments elected".[8] Commenting on contemporary Australian society during the first decade of the twenty-first century, the period Flanagan uses as the setting for *The Unknown Terrorist*, Lawrence argues:

> It seems that now, more than ever before, we are invited to feel insecure; we are worried about becoming victims of crime or disease, afraid of weapons of mass destruction, of terrorist attacks, and invasion by hordes of greedy strangers. Those who raise these fears hope that, by concocting and exaggerating threats to our survival, by pushing the panic button, they can control us.[9]

Just two years later, in 2008, highly respected Australian political correspondent Michelle Grattan wrote that Australia is "a community that now has the fear of terrorists in its DNA".[10] The fearful, paranoid, suspicious, xenophobic and irrational Australian society Flanagan depicts in *The Unknown Terrorist* is closely based on reality. Writing from an American perspective, Richard Carr zooms out from the national to the global, noting that

> [although] terrorists have claimed a role on the world stage at least since the late 1950s … the fall of the Twin Towers in New York City on September 11, the story behind the destruction, and the resulting casualties pushed … terrorism to the center of public consciousness. Airports large and small adopted strict security measures; governments suspended individual rights as a means of aborting terrorist plots; national security alerts cautioned citizens against ignoring the potential threat lurking behind the apparently ordinary.[11]

Carr then zooms back in to narrow his focus again on the national, arguing that "half a world away from the fallen Towers", Australia "vigorously took up the war on terror. The terrorist was no longer the remote figure featured briefly in a news broadcast; he *might* be the bloke next door";[12] or, in Flanagan's narrative, the young aspirational working-class woman working as a pole dancer in a Kings Cross strip club.

In 2007, Rachael Weaver argued that contemporary Australian novelists rarely "produce fiction that explicitly and self-consciously deals with the current political climate", and that the publication within the same year of Flanagan's *The Unknown Terrorist*

---

7   Hage, *Against Paranoid Nationalism*, 4, 20–1.
8   Carmen Lawrence, *Fear and Politics* (Carlton North, Vic: Scribe, 2006), 126.
9   Lawrence, *Fear and Politics*, 126.
10  Michelle Grattan, "A Dangerous Web", *Age*, 26 December 2008. http://bit.ly/2H5z6jU.
11  Richard Carr, "A World of … Risk, Passion, Intensity and Tragedy: The Post-9/11 Australian Novel", in "Fear in Australian Literature and Film," ed. Nathanael O'Reilly and Jean-François Vernay, special issue, *Antipodes* 23, no.1 (June 2009): 63.
12  Carr, "The Post-9/11 Australian Novel", 63.

and Andrew McGahan's *Underground* was therefore an unusual and significant event.[13] In the same year, Andrew McCann argued that "Never before, it seems, has political writing critical of the government, its policies and a prevailing sense of neoconservative status quo appeared to be so attractive".[14] McCann claimed that the publication in the same year of Jaivin's *The Infernal Optimist*, McGahan's *Underground* and Flanagan's *The Unknown Terrorist* "all point to a perceptible shift in the field of Australian literary production … towards a much more direct and sometimes didactic engagement with a contemporary political climate defined by neoconservative, neo-imperialist and narrowly nationalist approaches to both foreign policy and domestic issues". McCann goes on to argue that the novels by Flanagan, McGahan and Jaivin "all unfold in ways that are clearly sensitive to issues of audience and accessibility. This gives them the sense of intervening into a public debate, and of trying to motivate critique".[15] McCann identifies the primary subject of Flanagan's critique in *The Unknown Terrorist* as "the ways in which the government and the media administer popular consciousness in the interests of a xenophobic, anti-democratic agenda".[16] To put it another way, McCann contends that Flanagan critiques the media and government's manipulation of Australian society through the politics and rhetoric of fear, creating terror and paranoia in the service of their agenda.

Although *The Unknown Terrorist* was not as successful in terms of winning awards and being shortlisted for prizes as Flanagan's other novels, especially *The Narrow Road to the Deep North, Wanting* and *Gould's Book of Fish*, it was longlisted for both the Miles Franklin and the International IMPAC Dublin Literary Awards, and reviewed widely in such publications as the *New York Times*, the *Observer*, the *Independent*, the *Washington Post*, the *Times Literary Supplement*, the *New York Times Book Review*, *Australian Book Review* and the *Sydney Morning Herald*. In his review for *Eureka Street*, Michael Ashby declares Flanagan "has come up with a veritable novel 'for our times'", arguing that Flanagan succeeds to such an extent "that real recent events, that are more current affairs than history, have walk-on roles or close contextual significance", and the result is "a gripping tale of … Sydney … in the midst of a terror campaign".[17] McCann argues that part of Flanagan's novel's "claim on our attention" is "the idea that a prize-winning author has been forced by political realities into a more populist genre".[18] Indeed, *The Unknown Terrorist* is unique in Flanagan's body of fiction in that it could most accurately be classified as a thriller and a work of popular fiction, whereas his previous books of fiction were experimental, literary, historical novels. One may posit that Flanagan decided that the urgency of his subject matter required that it be delivered via a more immediate and accessible genre, one that in some ways reflects the sensationalism, fast pace and high drama of contemporary media productions.

However, this is not to suggest that *The Unknown Terrorist* is in any way a shallow or frivolous "airport novel". On the contrary, Flanagan's subject matter is serious, urgent and thoroughly examined. Furthermore, it must be noted that Flanagan creates a hybrid of the

---

13   Rachael Weaver, "Histories of the Present", *Overland* 187 (Winter 2007): 81.
14   Andrew McCann, "Professing the Popular: Political Fiction Circa 2006", in "New Reckonings: Australian Literature Past, Present, Future," ed. Leigh Dale and Brigid Rooney, special issue, *Australian Literary Studies* 23, no. 2 (2007): 44.
15   McCann, "Professing the Popular", 46.
16   McCann, "Professing the Popular", 50.
17   Michael Ashby, review of *The Unknown Terrorist*, *Eureka Street* 16, no. 15 (17 Oct. 2006): 23.
18   McCann, "Professing the Popular", 50.

thriller and literary novel genres. As Jen Webb argues in writing about the conflation of the literary and thriller genres in post-September 11 novels by Flanagan and McGahan, the novels' political focus "changes them from the sort of novel that is designed primarily to pass the time, to the sort of novel that is designed as something to think with, something explicitly involved with public life and public critique".[19] Webb describes Flanagan's *The Unknown Terrorist* and McGahan's *Underground* as "extraordinary archives of a period of Australian, and global, history … infused with … rage, and outrage".[20] Flanagan uses *The Unknown Terrorist*, Webb contends, to "hold society to account for what has happened" to Australian culture.[21] In a 2006 interview with Kerry O'Brien, Flanagan declared, "We [Australians] are more frightened, we are more frightening, we are less free, we are more unjust, we are more callous",[22] and *The Unknown Terrorist* unflinchingly depicts such a society.

*The Unknown Terrorist* is set in Sydney circa 2006 and focuses on two main characters: Gina Davies, a twenty-six-year-old pole dancer who uses the stage names Krystal, the Black Widow, the Russian Doll, and, most often, the Doll; and Richard Cody, a middle-aged nationally known television journalist. The action takes place over just four days, creating a fast-paced plot-driven narrative which borrows heavily from the thriller genre. The plot is triggered by the discovery of three unexploded bombs at Sydney's Homebush Olympic Stadium. Flanagan introduces the news of the bombs into the narrative through the media when the Doll hears it on the radio while sunbathing at Bondi. The news of the unexploded bombs has no immediate negative effect on the Doll; on the contrary, Flanagan's narrator depicts the radio as running

> the same news it always seemed to run and its repetition of distant horror and local mundanity was calmly reassuring. More bombings in Baghdad, more water restrictions and more bushfires; another threat to attack Sydney on another al-Qa'ida website … a late unconfirmed report that three unexploded bombs had been discovered at Sydney's Homebush Olympic stadium … while here at the beach, waves rolled in, crashed, and rolled out again, taking all this irrelevant noise with them, as they always had, as they always would.[23]

Flanagan creates a stark, ironic contrast between the news disseminated by the media and the Doll's mental state: "There was nothing on earth she wanted at that moment, nothing she felt denied her that she wished to have, no ambition she felt unfulfilled" (12). Thus, at the beginning of the novel, the Doll is unaffected by the media and government's use of the politics and rhetoric of fear, free from terror and paranoia, blissfully ignorant of the role she is soon to play as public enemy number one in a drama created in collusion by the media and government in order to manipulate the fears of her fellow citizens. Rather, she enjoys a hedonistic, materialistic, thoughtlessly superficial life that may be seen as representative of the excesses of Western culture during late capitalism.

---

19  Jen Webb, "Distant Context, Local Colour: Australian 'Post September 11' Fiction", in "Common Readers and Cultural Critics," ed. Russell Smith and Monique Rooney, special issue, *JASAL: Journal of the Association for the Study of Australian Literature* (2010): 6.
20  Webb, "Distant Context", 6.
21  Webb, "Distant Context", 8.
22  Richard Flanagan cited in Webb, "Distant Context", 8.
23  Richard Flanagan, *The Unknown Terrorist* (New York: Grove Press, 2006), 12. All subsequent references are to this edition and appear in parentheses in the text.

The passage quoted above is just one of numerous instances in *The Unknown Terrorist* in which Flanagan depicts the media disseminating information intended to create, perpetuate and exacerbate fear amongst the populace, whether the object of the fear be terrorist attacks, natural disasters, Muslims, immigrants or refugees. Indeed, the media is a ubiquitous presence in Flanagan's novel, continually influencing the characters' lives through its various manifestations, including television, radio, newspapers, magazines, the internet and electronic billboards. Bruce Bennett argues that Flanagan's "principal target" in *The Unknown Terrorist* "is the Australian media, whose journalists and their employers fall too readily for government propaganda and make their ratings-based reputations on vastly exaggerated projections of violent threats to people and property".[24] The relationship that Bennett identifies between the government and the media in the novel is of crucial importance, and in many instances Flanagan depicts the government as deliberately using the media as a tool with which to manipulate Australian citizens, many of whom seem incapable of thinking for themselves and resisting propaganda and fabricated, sensationalised narratives.

When Richard Cody, Flanagan's primary representation of the media, is first introduced into the narrative, he is entering the Chairman's Lounge, the strip club where the Doll works, after reporting on the unexploded bombs at the Olympic Stadium. Cody's initial assessment of the story is that it is "repetitive" and "pointless: three bombs had been found, each in a kid's backpack. The crowd was evacuated, the area sealed off. Nothing else would happen now" (21). Flanagan's narrator depicts the television media's presentation of the story as repetitive, vacuous, and thoroughly contrived:

> He [Cody] had continued saying the same thing over and over ... while a string of so-called experts – mostly consultants wanting a job as an expert in security, terror, politics – commented on each other's remarks, which in turn repeated and elaborated the few brief comments made by the police and government spinners, all pretending that in this vortex of nonsense might be found some sign predicting what might next occur. (21)

During a private conversation between Cody and Jerry Mendes, his boss at the television network, held outside a mansion during a lunch party, Mendes describes people who care about the truth in journalism as "fuckwits", declaring, "They think the truth has power, that it will carry everything before it. But it's crap. People don't want the truth" (26). Mendes goes on to argue that "People want an exalting illusion ... Find that sort of story, ginger it up with a few dashes of fear and nastiness, and you've hit gold" (26–7). Mendes makes it clear that from the point of view of a television executive the rhetoric of fear is necessary to create a successful story, and Cody soon takes Mendes' message to heart and begins to employ the rhetoric of fear in order to further his own career.

After the private conversation, Cody and Mendes return inside to the lunch table, where Cody inserts fear into his conversation with the wealthy and influential guests, "inflating several stories he had heard of 'dangerous Islamic types' who had been allowed into the country", and soon the guests begin to "come round to Richard Cody's views" (28). Determined to impress his companions, Cody talks "with passion of the atrocities committed in London, at Beslan, in Madrid and Bali … He felt himself more and more

---

24 Bruce Bennett, "Of Spies and Terrorists: Australian Fiction After 9/11", *Asiatic: IIUM Journal of English Language and Literature* 2, no. 1 (2008): 13.

moved by his own unexpected emotion, found himself speaking about the end of innocence and the shocking destruction of the ordinary lives of good people" (30). Sensing the power of his rhetoric of fear, Cody declares, "Our civilization is under attack" (31), then proceeds to argue "for the necessity of torture, properly managed" (31), tells his fellow guests "dark tales of terrible plots foiled, of the mass poisonings and bombings and gassings planned and, through vigilance, averted, offering vivid descriptions of how Australians might otherwise have died en masse in the very heart of Sydney" (32). While creating his fear-based narrative, Cody feels "the fear take hold" of his audience and senses "the pull of a story, the power of its telling", as his audience listens in silence, "their imaginings now hot-wired to his images of conspiracy, fanaticism, horror" (32). Here Flanagan provides some of the motivations for Cody's subsequent concoction of the narrative about the Doll being "The Unknown Terrorist" and critiques the media more broadly for their use of fear and terror, and their manipulation of the truth in the service of creating content that will deliver high ratings and revenue.

After leaving the lunch party, Cody determines to create "a story that no one would forget" (33). Just a few hours later, Cody visits the Chairman's Lounge, where the Doll dances naked for him. The Doll and Cody leave the club within minutes of each other; recognising the Doll on the street, Cody offers to pay her for oral sex. When the Doll declines, Cody interprets her rejection of his offer as a personal insult. The next evening, after recognising the Doll in the security camera footage being constantly replayed on television, Cody begins working on a story about her, partly motivated by her refusal to prostitute herself to him, partly by his recent demotion, and partly by the success of his storytelling and conversation at the lunch party:

> Richard Cody wandered his Vaucluse home with his phone, piecing together not so much the truth of Gina Davies' life as rehearsing the story he would present about it. He remembered with pride how he had held the table at Katie Moretti's with his tales of the three bombs and terrorists and evil. He wanted to do the same again, but this time mesmerising not a dozen people, but millions. (106)

As Cody dwells on his story, he begins to convince himself that it makes sense, despite the lack of evidence. The Doll had been recorded by a security camera entering an apartment building with Tariq, a man of Middle Eastern appearance with whom she had sex. Tariq becomes a suspect in the investigation of the alleged attempted bombing of Homebush Olympic Stadium, and thus the Doll becomes a suspected accomplice according to the contorted "logic" of the media, the government and the security forces. From Cody's point of view,

> the more he thought about it, the more it all made sense, and what at first seemed ludicrous – a pole dancer an Islamic terrorist! – now seemed insidious and disturbing. What better cover? … It was obvious what was going on, and it was up to him, Richard Cody, to expose what was happening. And what a story it would be! What ratings they would get! It had everything – sex, politics, even bombs! (107)

Cody makes numerous phone calls to contacts in the government, intelligence community and police force while researching the story, but is unable to ascertain a motive and learns that not only is Gina Davies not a Muslim, there is "no evidence that Gina Davies knew anything about Islam" and she is not known to have ever "received any terrorist training" (112). However, Cody does not perceive the lack of motive or evidence of involvement with the alleged terrorist cell to be proof of the Doll's innocence; on the contrary, he views them as "merely problems to be overcome. His instinct was to create a story in which he more and more believed, in order to allow him to further create that story" (112). Throughout the novel, Flanagan critiques the manufacture, distortion and exaggeration of narratives by the media and governments to suit their own agendas, while simultaneously engaging in a metafictional commentary on the process of the construction of any kind of narrative.[25] The more time Cody spends on the story about the Doll, the more he becomes convinced of the truth of his own fiction; moreover, Cody develops a degree of fear, even terror, in response to his own story: "as he talked to others on his phone, as he heard from the ASIO spook Siv Harmsen of the capacity of terrorist suicide bombers 'to kill many hundreds of people at, say, a major sporting event', he was rightly horrified" (112). In response to Cody's description of the possibility of a terrorist attack on a sporting event as "horrifying", Siv Harmsen, the ASIO officer heavily invested in creating a terror-filled population, proclaims, "It is horrifying … and we need stories that remind people of what horrifying things might just happen" (112). Through the character of Harmsen, Flanagan repeatedly critiques the role that the intelligence community (and the government more broadly) plays in creating, disseminating and perpetuating fear, terror and paranoia, in addition to eroding civil liberties and diminishing the power of citizens within democratic societies.

Although the television personality Cody plays a central role in Flanagan's narrative, television is not the only branch of the media used to disseminate and heighten fear, terror and paranoia. The morning after the Doll's encounter with Tariq, she sits in a coffee shop near Tariq's apartment building as the police conduct a raid. While the Doll and the other customers wait for permission to leave the premises, she flicks through a newspaper, finding it full of stories containing information that seems designed to produce terror and paranoia: "She skipped past the front pages linking the bombs at Homebush with an al-Qa'ida website threat to bomb Sydney, ignored a story on a gruesome child murder, [and] a feature about another attempt to bomb the Australian embassy in Jakarta" (88). Newsreaders on the radio report deaths caused by a suicide bombing in Baghdad and then follow that report by stating that police are "seeking the companion of the suspected Middle Eastern terrorist who was photographed by a security camera entering his apartment two nights earlier, before eluding a police raid" (120). The back-to-back reports of the Baghdad bombing and the police search for the Doll serve to conflate the two separate events in the minds of listeners, thus simultaneously exacerbating the degree of fear amongst the populace and seemingly lending credibility to the suggestion that the Doll is complicit in the attempted attack on the Olympic Stadium. Radio is used by the government as a medium through which to advance its agenda and produce terror. At one point in the narrative, the Doll and her friend Wilder listen to a politician declare on the radio that "'terrorists are subhuman filth'", and "'The government needs to be doing more to ensure they are hunted down and eliminated'" (121). The radio goes on to report that "unnamed security sources" have "linked the family of the male terrorist to Islamic fundamentalist groups in the Middle East"; in response, "Wilder, for the first time that the Doll had ever known, looked frightened" (121). As the plot progresses, the Doll and

---

25  In this respect, *The Unknown Terrorist* shares concerns with Flanagan's brilliant metafictional, postmodern, postcolonial novel *Gould's Book of Fish* (2001).

## 9 Terror, Paranoia and Manipulation: The Politics of Fear in *The Unknown Terrorist*

Wilder both become increasingly fearful as a result of the continuous media coverage, and soon the Doll comes to believe that there is no way out of her predicament: "The police, if she turned herself in, were not going to believe her ... the media, if she approached them, would set her up ... killing herself seemed attractive but painful and difficult" (141).

Throughout the novel, Flanagan emphasises the ubiquity of the media in all its forms. While the Doll browses in a central Sydney shopping centre, she notices

> a large rear projection screen set up outside an electronics store showing crowds leaving the Homebush Olympic stadium after the previous day's bomb scare. That image gave way to a close-up of a kid's backpack being unzipped to reveal a bomb. But only when it cut to armed police taking up positions around Tariq's apartment block did the Doll give it her undivided attention. (91)

The news report proceeds to show "a blurry photograph of a bearded man in Arabic dress ... beneath which ran a banner saying, again and again: 'SUSPECTED TERRORIST ELUDES POLICE DRAGNET'" (92). During this scene, the Doll does not yet know that she is a suspect and fails to make the connection between the footage of Tariq's apartment building and the Olympic Stadium bomb scare. As she leaves the shopping centre, a woman in a black burka accidentally bumps into the Doll; due to the relentless negative depiction of Muslims by the media, the Doll thinks of the woman in the burkah "as something terrifying and unknown, an evil spectre she had seen so often in films, a short, stubby Darth Vader" (93). The Doll reacts angrily to the collision with the burka-clad woman, yelling, "'Fuck off! ... Just fuck off back to wherever you're from'" (93). Flanagan uses this scene to suggest that the constant creation and dissemination of fear, terror and paranoia by the media and the government have led to xenophobia and racism being widespread throughout society. Moreover, the Doll ironically possesses the very attitudes and prejudices that soon lead to the vilification of her by the media, government and society in general.

Several hours after the Doll's encounter with the woman in the burka, the Doll watches TV at home, observing "the screen filled with armed police taking up position[s] around Tariq's apartment block" (95). The newsreader describes "'a failed police stakeout of a notorious Islamic terrorist'" and states that police have released footage from a security camera "'showing the terrorist suspect entering an apartment building ... with a female accomplice' ... The grainy images showed a couple hugging each other as they entered a building ... The Doll felt her mouth go dry. The man was Tariq. The woman was her" (95). Thus, the Doll becomes the object of fear via the media's use of images and the rhetoric of fear. The Doll is depicted as guilty by the media and the government based solely on the circumstantial "evidence" captured on the CCTV footage of her with Tariq in the lobby of his apartment building. The Doll's mere association with Tariq is enough for her to be depicted as guilty of involvement in terrorism, despite the fact that neither she nor Tariq was actually involved in any terrorist activity. As Silvia Albertazzi notes, the Doll "is guilty only of being caught with the wrong man in the wrong place by a surveillance camera", and thus becomes a "convenient scapegoat for a world of globalized terror".[26] Tariq is now described as a "notorious Islamic terrorist", rather than a suspect,

---

26 Silvia Albertazzi, "'And then I smiled': Recent Postcolonial Fiction and the War on Terror", *Le Simplegadi* 15 (April 2016): 20–1.

and the Doll as an "accomplice" (95). Here Flanagan highlights the power of rhetoric to alter the public's perceptions, disseminate fear, and create new "truths". Later the same day, the Doll sees the same security camera footage of herself and Tariq on another television channel, this time accompanied by a voiceover declaring, "'Police are fearful ... that two terrorists who escaped a midday raid at Potts Point may strike somewhere in Sydney any day'" (97). Thus, with just a single sentence, the media have altered the narrative so that the Doll has been transformed from an "accomplice" into a "terrorist" preparing for an imminent attack. The media's description of the police as "fearful" also serves to elevate the level of terror amongst the general public. With calculated use of rhetoric, the media create what media studies scholars such as John Fiske define as a "media event".[27]

In the days that follow, the media continue to use rhetoric and images to construct the Doll as a terrorist and create terror and paranoia amongst the citizenry. The novel contains far too many examples of media manipulations in the service of the rhetoric of fear to adequately address in this chapter, so I will focus here on a single detailed example. In the days after Gina's encounter with Tariq and Cody's invention of the story about her, which leads to her being labelled "The Unknown Terrorist", the television media create, revise, expand and continually replay a visual montage intended to convince the public of the Doll's involvement in the alleged attempted terrorist attack at the Olympic Stadium. In one scene, the Doll and Wilder watch an iteration of the montage together:

> they watched the same footage run again – the same bomb in the same kid's backpack; the same bad photograph of the same bearded man in Arabic-looking dress; the same slow-motion grainy images of Tariq and the Doll hugging each other ... The Twin Towers fell again; the same children's bodies were laid out once more in Beslan; the same man or woman dressed in black brandished the same machine gun; the Doll continued dancing naked. And there were new scenes – a murky London tube train moments after it had been bombed; the Sari nightclub burning after the Bali bombing; wounded being taken away from the Madrid train bombing, the montage culminating in a shot that zoomed in on the Sydney Opera House ... Osama bin Laden. George W. Bush. Missiles being launched. Men in robes firing grenade launchers. Great buildings exploding into balloons of fire. Women covered in blood. New York! Bali! Madrid! London! Baghdad! (159–60)

The inclusion in the montage of previous actual acts of terrorism, such as those that took place in New York, Beslan, Bali, London and Madrid, alongside images of Tariq and the Doll, serve to convince viewers of the legitimacy of the government and media's claims regarding the alleged terrorists, while simultaneously reminding Flanagan's readers of the ways in which the media and governments use the rhetoric and politics of fear in contemporary societies to advance their agendas and subjugate citizens.

Silvia Albertazzi argues that the constant broadcasting of the Doll's image by television media "creates a state of fear and anxiety around her face, which, with every new appearance, loses humanity and eventually becomes the face of evil itself".[28] In the novel's opening paragraph, the Doll is described by Flanagan's narrator as "A small, dark woman

---

27  John Fiske, *Media Matters: Everyday Culture and Political Change* (Minneapolis: University of Minnesota Press, 1994).
28  Albertazzi, "'And then I smiled'", 20.

... [whose] fine-featured face and almond eyes were set off by woolly black hair" (5). The Doll's physical features are used by the media to portray her in the eyes of the predominantly Anglo-Celtic public as "other". As Flanagan's narrator notes, "She had an open, oval face. It was exactly the wrong face for our age" (6), and thus the Doll is easily othered by the media, dehumanised, and presented as "the face of evil".[29]

In *The Spirit of Terrorism and Other Essays*, Jean Baudrillard discusses the importance and power of images in relation to terrorism. Baudrillard argues that "the sight of the images" has a profound impact on the viewers, and the "impact of the images, and their fascination ... [is] necessarily what ... [the viewers] retain".[30] According to Baudrillard, images "serve to multiply" an event "to infinity ... The image consumes the event, in the sense that it absorbs it and offers it for consumption ... it gives it unprecedented impact, but impact as image-event".[31] Likewise, in his discussion of the September 11 attacks on the Twin Towers in New York, Slavoj Žižek describes the attacks as an event staged by terrorists and produced by the media, arguing that the terrorists "did not do it primarily to provoke real material damage, but *for the spectacular effect of it*".[32] Like Baudrillard, Žižek emphasises the significance of the images, noting that for "the great majority of the public" the September 11 attacks "were events on the TV screen".[33] Žižek argues that the anthrax attacks in the United States in October 2001 gave the West its first post-September 11 experience of a "new 'invisible' warfare in which ... ordinary citizens ... are totally dependent on the authorities for information about what is going on ... [they] see and hear nothing; ... [everything they] know comes from the official media".[34] Flanagan's description of the use of images by the media in *The Unknown Terrorist* and the effects of images upon viewers aligns perfectly with Baudrillard and Žižek's arguments about the "image-event" and the spectacular effects of images. Moreover, Žižek's explanation of ordinary citizens' state of dependence upon the government and the media for information regarding terrorism is an apt description of the situation of the general public in Flanagan's novel.

In his article on terrorism in Australian fiction, Xavier Pons argues that terrorism "lends itself especially well to paranoid fears ... because its clandestine nature makes it eminently suited to all kinds of manipulation".[35] The "truth" about terrorist threats and activities is kept from the public by the government due to "national security" concerns, the government provides the media with carefully filtered and often limited information about terrorism, then the media disseminates the government's information to the public, often rewriting and manipulating the narrative in the process. Thus, it is impossible in such a situation for citizens ever to know the truth about the actual degree or imminence of danger, which in turn serves to heighten fear, terror and paranoia. Webb argues that Flanagan's novel illuminates the legal situation in Australia in relation to terrorism, "by drawing attention to the National Security Information (Criminal Proceedings) Bill 2004,

---

29  Albertazzi, "'And then I smiled'", 20.
30  Jean Baudrillard, *The Spirit of Terrorism and Other Essays*, trans. Chris Turner (2002; New York: Verso, 2003), 26.
31  Baudrillard, *The Spirit of Terrorism*, 27.
32  Slavoj Žižek, *Welcome to the Desert of the Real! Five Essays on September 11 and Related Dates* (New York: Verso, 2002), 11.
33  Žižek, *Welcome to the Desert of the Real!*, 11.
34  Žižek, *Welcome to the Desert of the Real!*, 37.
35  Xavier Pons, "Realigning the Spiritual Compass: Representations of Terrorism in Some Recent Australian Fiction", *Journal of the European Association for Studies on Australia* 1, no. 1 (2009): 25.

the Anti-Terrorism Act 2005, and similar legislative articles". According to Webb, when the legislation was

> first proposed in parliament, there was a flurry of media attention, but before long they faded into the background, leaving unobserved a staggeringly broad and excessive set of powers, whereby almost any ... [citizen] could be branded a terrorist or advocate of terrorism for the most innocent or trivial actions or words, with little or no legal recourse. In *The Unknown Terrorist*, these laws are brought to bear without evidence and without justice on the Doll and her friend Wilder, and their lives are lost (the Doll) or damaged (Wilder) in the process, without publicity, remedy or recourse.[36]

Similarly, Pons argues that Flanagan focuses closely on "the social and political context" in the novel because it "is not about terrorism" per se, "but about how the fear of terrorism is exploited by media personalities, law enforcement officers and politicians to manipulate the citizens".[37]

In Baudrillard's essays on terrorism, he describes what he terms "a negationist society", a society in which "No event is 'real' any longer. Terror attacks, trials, wars, corruption, opinion polls – there's nothing now that isn't rigged or undecidable".[38] Thus, Baudrillard and Flanagan both seem to suggest that all "events" (especially terrorist attacks) can be constructed by the government and the media, then manipulated in order to control citizens through fear, terror and paranoia. Ultimately, the government in Flanagan's novel seeks to create a passive public that can easily be controlled and manipulated, just like the citizens of Oceania in George Orwell's *1984*.[39] Furthermore, Flanagan's sharp critique suggests that the Australian government during the Howard era had the same agenda. Baudrillard goes so far as to argue that the increased security measures implemented by Western governments after the attacks on the United States on 11 September 2001 are "merely extensions of terror" and contends that "the real victory of terrorism" is that it has forced "the whole of the West" into an "obsession with security", creating "a veiled form of perpetual terror".[40] Similarly, Webb concludes (quoting John Frow) that Flanagan provides a depiction of Western governments that are not "defenders of freedom or protectors of the rule of law", but entities that exhibit a "'contempt for the rule of law and for rational policy formation'".[41]

In his work on Flanagan's novel, McCann reaches conclusions akin to those of Baudrillard, Žižek, Pons and Webb, arguing that "the novel is ultimately about the violence of an administered society and the processes of marginalisation and exploitation it rationalises in the name of self-defence".[42] Finally, American critic Theodore F. Sheckels argues that *The Unknown Terrorist* presents a rather bleak message:

> the world, with its racism and its sexism, will not change. People at-large accept all that the police, the government, and the media tell them about the terrorists in their midst

---

36  Webb, "Distant Context", 8–9.
37  Pons, "Realigning the Spiritual Compass", 31.
38  Baudrillard, *The Spirit of Terrorism*, 61.
39  George Orwell, *1984* (1949; New York: Signet Classics, 1950).
40  Baudrillard, *The Spirit of Terrorism*, 81.
41  Webb, "Distant Context", 5.
42  McCann, "Professing the Popular", 51.

without question; people at-large voice ugly comments about those who are ethnically "other" and accept, uncritically, all of the conclusions offered about Gina's danger based solely on her sexual behavior ... And what is perhaps the strongest evidence that people will not change their racism, their sexism, or their knee-jerk response to the terrorist threat is that Gina herself knows full well that she was just like these people before becoming the victim of both their ugly thinking and their un-thinking.[43]

In *The Unknown Terrorist*, Flanagan not only succeeds in constructing a realistic narrative regarding the effects of government and media manipulation of Australian society through the creation of terror, fear and paranoia, he issues an urgent, prescient warning concerning the need for citizens to resist media manipulation, government overreach, and the politics and rhetoric of fear in order to preserve and maintain free, democratic societies. In contemporary Western societies confronted by governments intent on eroding civil liberties, wielding propaganda against their own citizens, and manipulating the deepest fears of society in a "post-truth" media and political environment, Flanagan's novel and its call for resistance remains as relevant and important now as it was upon its initial publication in 2006.

## References

This chapter draws in part on a previous essay of mine, "Government, Media and Power: Terrorism in the Australian Novel Since 9/11", in *From Solidarity to Schisms: 9/11 and After in Fiction and Film from Outside the US*, ed. Cara Cilano (Amsterdam: Rodopi, 2009), 295–315.

Albertazzi, Silvia. "'And then I smiled': Recent Postcolonial Fiction and the War on Terror", *Le Simplegadi* 15 (April 2016): 16–23.
Ashby, Michael. Review of *The Unknown Terrorist*, *Eureka Street* 16, no. 15 (17 Oct. 2006): 23–4.
Baudrillard, *The Spirit of Terrorism and Other Essays*. (2002) Translated by Chris Turner. New York: Verso, 2003.
Bennett, Bruce. "Of Spies and Terrorists: Australian Fiction After 9/11", *Asiatic: IIUM Journal of English Language and Literature* 2, no. 1 (2008): 10–20.
Carr, Richard. "A World of ... Risk, Passion, Intensity and Tragedy: The Post-9/11 Australian Novel", *Antipodes* 23, no.1 (June 2009): 63–6.
Fiske, John. *Media Matters: Everyday Culture and Political Change*. Minneapolis, Minnesota: University of Minnesota Press, 1994.
Flanagan, Richard. *The Narrow Road to the Deep North*. New York: Knopf, 2014.
———. *The Unknown Terrorist*. New York: Grove Press, 2006.
Grattan, Michelle. "A Dangerous Web". *Age*, 26 December 2008. http://bit.ly/2H5z6jU.
Hage, Ghassan. *Against Paranoid Nationalism: Searching for Hope in a Shrinking Society*. Annandale, NSW: Pluto, 2003.
———. *White Nation: Fantasies of White Supremacy in a Multicultural Society*. (1998) New York/Annandale, NSW: Routledge/Pluto, 2000.
Jaivin, Linda. *The Infernal Optimist*. Sydney: Fourth Estate, 2006.
Lawrence, Carmen. *Fear and Politics*. Carlton North, Vic: Scribe, 2006.

---

43 Theodore F. Sheckels, "Gendered Terrorism: Intertext, Context, and Richard Flanagan's *The Unknown Terrorist*", *Antipodes* 24, no. 1 (2010): 37.

McCann, Andrew. "Professing the Popular: Political Fiction Circa 2006", *Australian Literary Studies* 23, no. 2 (2007): 43–57.

McGahan, Andrew. *Underground*. Crows Nest, NSW: Allen & Unwin, 2006.

Moorhouse, Frank. "The Writer in a Time of Terror", *Griffith Review* 14 (Summer 2006/7): 11–60.

O'Reilly, Nathanael and Jean-François Vernay, "Terra Australis Incognita? An Introduction to Fear in Australian Literature and Film", *Antipodes* 23, no. 1 (June 2009): 5–9.

Orwell, George. *1984*. (1949) New York: Signet Classics, 1950.

Pons, Xavier. "Realigning the Spiritual Compass: Representations of Terrorism in Some Recent Australian Fiction", *Journal of the European Association for Studies on Australia* 1, no. 1 (2009): 23–34.

Sheckels, Theodore F. "Gendered Terrorism: Intertext, Context, and Richard Flanagan's *The Unknown Terrorist*", *Antipodes* 24, no. 1 (2010): 35–9.

Weaver, Rachael. "Histories of the Present", *Overland* 187 (Winter 2007): 81–5.

Webb, Jen. "Distant Context, Local Colour: Australian 'Post September 11' Fiction". In "Common Readers and Cultural Critics," edited by Monique Rooney and Russell Smith. Special issue, *JASAL: Journal of the Association for the Study of Australian Literature* (2010): 1–14.

Žižek, Slavoj. *Welcome to the Desert of the Real! Five Essays on September 11 and Related Dates*. New York: Verso, 2002.

# 10
# Sydney, a City without Love: The Unknown Terrorist in *The Unknown Terrorist*

*Theodore F. Sheckels*

This chapter is about Richard Flanagan's 2006 novel *The Unknown Terrorist*. It pursues what I think is an unusual course: rather than focus on what the novel says about civil liberties in a post-9/11 world, the chapter will focus on what the novel says about the city of Sydney. The impetus for this exploration is the fact that the novel is so very tied to the city – its streets, its neighbourhoods, its structures. The chapter's more immediate impetus, however, is well outside the book, so I want to begin by discussing an often-forgotten 1982 film directed by Gillian Armstrong.

The upward trajectory of Armstrong's career began with the masterful *My Brilliant Career* (1979). It won multiple awards for the cast and creative team, but it also threatened to label Armstrong a "period piece" director. At a point in Australian film history when films labelled "the AFC [Australian Film Commission] Genre" by Dermody and Jacka were winning most of the – at least international – acclaim,[1] Armstrong was expected by many to follow up *My Brilliant Career* with another "classic", perhaps based on another revered work of Australian literature. She did not. Instead, she directed *Starstruck* (1982). Both *My Brilliant Career* and *Starstruck* featured a strong heroine trying to make it in the arts, but would-be pop star Jackie Mullens is a far cry from Sybylla Melvyn. And, more to the point here, the contemporary urban scene of Jackie's quest is a far cry from the late nineteenth-century rural settings of Sybylla's.

That urban scene is so striking in *Starstruck* that the city of Sydney seems to be a character in the film. With Jackie, we roam about the city, but two scenes are dominant: the Sydney Opera House and the traditional pub in The Rocks that Jackie lives above. These scenes are iconic, representing the new city and the old city. Uniting them is another icon: the Sydney Harbour Bridge. It not only is near the two sites, literally looming above one, but is the backdrop within the two for memorable musical numbers that occur on the hotel bar and the Opera House stage. The film, then, is not just a campy story of teenage success against the odds but a paean to Sydney. The film's climax has Jackie performing in a New Year's Eve competition at the Opera House *and* the older patrons at the pub dancing along there while watching the Opera House performance. Jackie performs before a stage backdrop representing the Harbour Bridge; the "olds" dance before a bar, behind

---

[1] Susan Dermody and Elizabeth Jacka, *The Screening of Australia*, vols 1 and 2 (Sydney: Currency Press, 1987–8).

which is a backdrop representing the Harbour Bridge. The climax celebrates both Jackie and the city. Reactions to *Starstruck* have varied, both when it was released and in critical commentary since. It was too campy for some; it was too Hollywood for others. Felicity Collins found the use of Sydney "shameless";[2] I, on the other hand, found it celebratory. Either way, Sydney is very much a part of the film, not just its setting.

The city of Sydney is also a character in *The Unknown Terrorist*, but its depiction is quite different than in Armstrong's *Starstruck*. After establishing how present Sydney is in Flanagan's novel, as if it were itself a character, I will argue that the city is depicted in negative and, ultimately, apocalyptic terms. Such a depiction is not unprecedented: it is common in feature films (other than the upbeat *Starstruck*). What this motif suggests is that *The Unknown Terrorist* is less about potential 9/11 style attacks but, rather, about a morally polluting force that has poisoned the urban environment, a force that may well be the eponymous "unknown terrorist". The novel, then, although not rural in setting, does fit the Flanagan oeuvre more than initially seems to be the case. It also fits insofar as it is just as philosophical as it is political. The author was undoubtedly drawn to comment on post-9/11 hysteria, but he was just as drawn to talk about a broader lack of love in the world that lurks behind the polluting force. He insinuates that theme into the novel in subtle ways that may surprise the reader who has been drawn into what may seem to be a popular fiction story featuring intrigue and sleaze.

### Sydney in the Novel

Flanagan is, of course, an artist with some international acclaim. Given this, it is indeed odd that he would pen a novel that seems to presuppose familiarity with a setting that few readers outside Australia – perhaps, outside Sydney – would have. Sections of metropolitan Sydney are referred to without much by way of explanation. Some are iconic: Bondi Beach, Kings Cross and Circular Quay; others have been in the news, such as the Olympic Stadium in Homebush. Others perhaps require some exposition for international readers: Darlinghurst, Manly, Woolloomooloo, Elizabeth Bay, Double Bay, Darling Harbour, Redfern. Then, there are the numerous references to sections of the city to its north, its east and its west. Although the significance of these directions is referred to in the novel, their full meaning is assumed. Readers are assumed to know that the direction of the particular suburbs from the Sydney CBD makes a world of social difference – stereotypically, snobs to the north, those arrogantly well-off to the east, and the markedly ethnic lower-middle-class masses, with their materialism and their prejudices, to the west. Readers are especially assumed to know what being a "Westie" means. Sydneysiders do; most Australians probably do; those outside Australia probably do not.

Sydney streets are referred to as if readers all knew them: Oxford Street, Victoria Street, William Street, George Street, Pitt Street, the Cahill Expressway, Martin Place. So are Sydney train stations: Circular Quay, Town Hall and Central. One who has walked the length of Pitt or George Street from The Rocks out to Central Station can visualise the business stretches, the commercial stretches, and the borderline seedy stretches. As an occasional foreign visitor to Sydney who possesses a keen sense of urban geography and a love of maps, I am familiar

---

2   Felicity Collins, *The Films of Gillian Armstrong: The Moving Image* 6 (St Kilda, Vic: Australian Teachers of Media, 1999), 7–98.

with the references. Would other foreign readers be? Would all Australian readers? If it is not safe to assume that most readers have this familiarity, what do we then make of Flanagan's choice to foreground Sydney so? It certainly enhances the novel's realism, but it also compels readers to get into "the head" of the city in much the same manner as they are typically asked to get into "the head" of a character. The novel, then, offers us a city that, like many characters, is a puzzle. What do these streets and these places really mean? And what, if we probe even more deeply, do these streets and places hide from one's initial, superficial view? Just as we dissect a novelist's characters for surface meaning and, then, deeper meaning, we are compelled by *The Unknown Terrorist* to dissect Sydney.

Sydney is, to the tourist's gaze, a beautiful city. Dominant among the sites are the iconic Opera House and Harbour Bridge. From out on that harbour (or atop the bridge), the view can be stunning. A character in the novel, thinking about sailing on the harbour, notes "how beautiful Sydney was and how so few people really get to see its full charms".[3] Roam farther afield, to the north and east, there is more that is stunning to see: "avenues of European cars", "grand refurbished ... mansion[s] on the top side of a street that commanded views of the harbour and city", "the harbourside mansions splendid" (126-7). The "vision splendid" has been transformed from natural landscape to posh cityscape. Early in the novel, the central character, Gina or "the Doll", goes off to Bondi. Water (especially the beachfront) is important to Sydney's ethos, and she glories in the cooling water there. But the novel also notes the city's sewage pouring into this water, with Gina "smelling suntan oil and wet sand and air salty from the sea and acrid from the outfall sewage frothing to a latte on distant points" (11). True at Bondi; equally true at Manly, where "shit ... floats past" bathers (39).

What else is characteristic of the Sydney that Flanagan offers us? I would point to seven characteristics, increasingly ominous. First, there is the stifling late-summer heat, described as both "intense" (277) and "stinking" (274). Second, the air, described as both absent (that is, "airless" [177]) and "a brown, prickling rug" and a "smog spread[ing] a gritty fug over the city" leaving "a burning taste in the Doll's mouth" (214). Third, noise. There are "car horns and sirens wailing", and "cries and shouting" (201). There is the "screeching noise of tyres breaking too quickly, then the abrupt sound of colliding metal and shattering glass" (266). Cities, of course, are not quiet places, but Flanagan chooses to accentuate Sydney's harsh sounds.

Fourth, traffic, which Flanagan refers to incessantly throughout the novel. Sometimes, he notes it, as if it is a constant vibration. Sometimes, it is described as jammed or clogged, issuing the "sweet smell of fumes" that distract Gina from "the sour stench" of a beggar on the footpaths (124). At other times, it is described as speeding with a "violent rumbling" (143). It is "infernal" (178) and inescapable in the city.

Fifth, there are the battered bodies of "street people". There is the aforementioned stinking beggar Gina gives money to; there are Aboriginal beggars that no one gives money to. And, late in the novel, near Kings Cross, there is a man, maybe a beggar, maybe a drunk, being kicked by "Westies": his "body on the ground moved with their blows like a heavy mattress ... The body – its rags, its crumbling bomber jacket, the plastic shopping bags stuffed with trash that lay spilled around it – was clearly that of some beggar or another" (278). He is left, by the "Westies" and by Gina, "[h]is face ... covered in blood and filth" (279).

---

3   Richard Flanagan, *The Unknown Terrorist* (New York: Grove, 2006), 272-3. All subsequent references are to this edition and appear in parentheses in the text.

Sixth, there is sexual exploitation, with Kings Cross its obvious centre: "the brothels and sex shows and streetwalkers of the Cross – an area chiefly known for a dying retail line in old world sleaze" (18). There, you find "Centrefolds Sex Show", "Club X", the "Spice Bar," and "Fuck hotels. The World Famous Love Machine. The Pleasure Chest Cruise Area. Madonnas" (299–300). And, at the classy end of the sleaze, the Chairman's Lounge, where Gina nightly strips nude. A less obvious site?: "the Chinese brothels operating in anonymous CBD tower blocks, the chicken coops where Chinese girls, smuggled into Australia, lived and worked" (42). To a walker's gaze, shiny, tall corporate buildings with boutiques on the ground level, but, within, an unimaginable hell.

Seventh, there is slavery of different sorts. There is the sex slavery already noted. There is a more general slavery, begun when Asians are shipped into the country, hidden in containers of whatever goods. Many slaves do not survive the importation, resulting in "corpses floating in the harbour" (75), the body of water "where so many [of the] other secrets of Sydney lie hidden" (177).

Flanagan makes it very clear that Sydney was not always this way. Martin Place, with its posh shops, seems eventually to Gina to be "as empty and strange as the ruins of an ancient city" (179). The lustre is gone. The train ride from Redfern into the city depicts the place as dirty and decaying: "the train continued past green goods trains, shopping centres as bleak as penitentiaries, rusting corro roofs, concrete walls weary with graffiti, billboard after billboard" (223). The lustre is long gone. As the novel ends, Bondi, the beach and the sea there, are described as "the last things left in the city that reminded people that the measure of all things was not man made" and subject to decay (316). But even that beach has oozing sewage at its edges. Bondi is not a place of redemption any longer; the city is not a place of beauty. "The city," the novel tells us, "was no longer the most marvellous of human creations, but the most oppressive" (316). Once it was a place of dreams, but the dream has died. In this atmosphere, even the Opera House is not the magnificent structure it once was: "The opera house's school of dorsal fins sat on the breast of the city like a brazen brooch on an old tart" (78).

## The Evil Within

Once readers have discerned what the Sydney of Flanagan's novel is now like, the next logical question is, how did the city get this way? The answer stressed in the text is the city's – perhaps the nation's – intense materialism. With the rich to the north and the east, the materialism shows up in the opulence of their dwellings; with the would-be rich to (or from) the west, the materialism shows up in their obsession with money. Consider the following two passages in the novel:

> As though it meant something or everything, so that they would feed her money, the Doll tried to entice them to tip … everything the Doll did, every word she said, every gesture she made, everything she revealed and the many more things she so carefully hid, all of it, she told herself, was about money, to get and to keep money, for all the things that money could buy and for all the things that money made her feel. (34)

> With her cash back at her flat there was freedom, possibilities, hope. And just thinking about all her money there, imagining the feel of those hundred-dollar notes on her body

and her body once more relaxed and comfortable beneath them, made the Doll feel better. She didn't know what she was going to do with the money, but she knew money could buy a lot of things, and the more money, the more you could buy: time, space, people. But without the money she would be lost. (151)

The dominant word is "money" – five times in the first passage, five in the second, and that not counting synonyms. Coupled with that drive for "money" is an ugly prejudice against those who lack that vital fuel. This prejudice is almost always "coloured" – against those with darker skin than the "true" Anglo-Celtic Australians.

Sydney is not alone in being presented in these negative terms. Flanagan makes it clear that Melbourne is no different: "She found the same city, the same streets, the same dead stares, the same filth, the same indifference, the same grand decay, the same hive-like energy, bursting and building, killing and destroying, robbing flowers and fertilizing flowers for no point other than to continue" (241). Flanagan also makes it clear that Gina is just as poisoned by materialism and prejudice as the city she lives in. From early in the novel, we come to understand how much she delights in the expensive goods money can buy. We do not need the scene of her covering her nude body with currency in her Darlinghurst apartment, a scene that evokes Frank Norris' novel *McTeague* (1899) and the movie *Greed* (1924) based on it, to get the point. And, although she tries to rise above the ethnic prejudices of her fellow "Westies", she does not free herself. Even after she becomes coloured herself by the suspicion that she is a radical Islamic terrorist, she still looks down upon those who have crowded into Australian cities after the "White Australia" policy ended. Her being a political outcast does not keep her from still looking down upon the many social outcasts.

## The Apocalyptic: in the Novel, in Film

Sydney and Gina, then, are much the same as characters. It therefore makes narratological sense that they suffer their demise together. So, as the novel concludes, a fierce, surreal hailstorm strikes the city. It pounds on the taxi Gina is riding in; it crashes the cab's windows, as well as those of other vehicles driving along William Street. Even though the hail is piled up on the sidewalks of the Cross a foot deep, Gina makes it to the Chairman's Lounge, a stolen Beretta in her bag. She shoots the sleazy journalist who has been intent on ruining her life to earn himself fame, and a police officer, who has been intent on saving her life, shoots her dead instead. That demise returns me to film, not to *Starstruck* but to another minor but culturally resonant Australian film.

The director is another famous name from the "Australian New Wave", Philip Noyce. Judy Davis, the lead in *My Brilliant Career*, does play the lead role. In this 1982 film, *Heatwave* (together with John Duigan's 1981 *The Winter of Our Dreams*), Davis prevents the industry from stereotyping her as a "period piece"/"AFC genre" actress. *Heatwave*, like *Starstruck*, is a very Sydney-focused movie. It is centred in Kings Cross, where an urban development scheme has attracted protest and, likely, murder. Davis' character is probing that murder, and doing so has led to many plot complications. Although some of the complications are romantic – after all, it is a feature film - most involve money, with characters and groups of characters trying to find ways to profit, despite human costs. These complications are realistic but fictitious; the murder that haunts the film is that of anti-development activist Juanita Nielsen. It lurks in the background of the slightly earlier (1981) *The Killing of Angel Street* by Donald Crombie; it emerges out of the background in Noyce's film when the body of Mary Ford (the film's version of Nielsen) washes up among the footings on a new construction site. This emergence is possible because all of the film's action culminates in a melodramatically violent New Year's Eve thunderstorm, filmed with apocalyptic fervor. Kings Cross is bombarded in this film just as it is in Flanagan's novel. And, coincidentally, a climactic shot is fired at a posh New Year's Eve party, by a Kings Cross stripper, who is then gunned down by guards. The narratological rhythms of Noyce's film and Flanagan's novel climax in somewhat similar scenes.

Noyce's *Heatwave* is an interesting film but far from an Australian classic. However, it fits a motif that we can see in many Australian films. There is a sense of the apocalyptic in more famous films such as Peter Weir's *The Last Wave* (1977) and all four Mad Max films (*Mad Max* [1979], *Mad Max 2* [1981], *Mad Max Beyond Thunderdome* [1985] and *Fury Road* [2015]) created by George Miller (and others). In Weir's film, we envision the destruction of Sydney as the film ends, despite the wave itself being a cinematographic disappointment; and, at least in the third Mad Max film, we see the broken remains of Sydney as Captain Walker flies the "lost children" overhead as the motion picture concludes. In a large number of Australian films, then, Sydney is presented, not in the positive terms of *Starstruck* but in apocalyptical ones. The motif of apocalypse is, of course, not restricted to either Australia or film. Both Michael Titlestad in *Safundi: The Journal of South African and American Studies* in 2013 and Emily Apter in *American Literary History* in 2006 have described the motif's operation, especially as an outgrowth of paranoia, in global writing.[4] My point, however, is that Flanagan's use seems not so much a reflection of a recent global trend as a symbolic plot device used in conjunction with Sydney in films beginning in the early 1970s.

In *Starstruck*, Sydney is depicted realistically if campy. A similar realism – with sensual and slick added to campy – is evident in *The Unknown Terrorist*. But, in both works, Sydney functions as a synecdoche for Australia and, beyond that, the world. In *Starstruck*, all is well: generations unite, music blares, and Jackie Mullens performs triumphantly on the Opera House stage. In *The Unknown Terrorist*, the world has turned bad: there is division, throbbing techno replaces good ol' rock-and-roll, and Gina Davies, "the Doll", performs her final act just off to the side of the stage on which she once dance naked.

Sydney is a character in both. In Armstrong's film, Sydney is triumphant – the hero of the piece. In Flanagan's novel (as in Noyce's other films), Sydney is apocalyptically dying. Its death is not due to terrorism, and it is not due to the mania global terrorism is producing. Rather, the point of Flanagan's depiction of Sydney is that the greed and prejudices that cause humankind to forget that the names tossed about in the terrorism drama are human beings set the stage for the mania. The unknown terrorist in the novel, then, is not Gina Davies, but the many people who have embraced an ideology that renounces love and commodifies all, humans included. The unknown terrorist is within the crass ideology that has seized Sydney, Australia, the world. Flanagan is far from unique in using the city in this manner: it is a common trope. Norris' *McTeague* (1899), subtitled "A Story of San Francisco" has already been mentioned. Theodore Dreiser uses Chicago

---

4   Michael Titlestad, "The Logic of the Apocalypse: A Clerical Rejoinder", *Safundi: The Journal of South African and American Studies* 14, no. 1 (2013): 93–110; Emily Apter, "On Oneworldedness: Or Paranoia as a World System", *American Literary History* 18, no. 2 (2006): 365–89.

in much the same manner in *Sister Carrie* (1900). Earlier than these turn-of-the-century books is Charles Dickens' London in *Bleak House* (1853); later is Tom Wolfe's New York City in *Bonfire of the Vanities* (1987).

## Flanagan's Serious Message

My impression is that many who study Australian literature – and, more particularly, Flanagan – found *The Unknown Terrorist* an odd book: it was so rooted in Sydney, not Tasmania; it was so urban, not rural; it raised political questions, not environmental ones. And the book seemed to be targeted at a popular audience, not the more elite one Flanagan – and international authors of his ilk – usually write for. There was, perhaps, an initial tendency to dismiss the novel, to treat it as an aberration from the emerging Flanagan canon. It was reviewed rather negatively by James Ley in the Melbourne *Age* and David Marr in the *Sydney Morning Herald*.[5] The *Guardian*'s Peter Conrad described the novel as a retreat on Flanagan's part to the "safety of convention"; the *New York Times*' Michiko Kakutani described the novel as "not as ambitious" as the author's previous work.[6]

If one focuses primarily on what the novel has to say about post-9/11 Australia, then some of this critical "dismay" might be in order. If one focuses on what the novel has to say about Sydney and how the novel uses the city as synecdoche, then what might seem superficially political becomes, instead, a profound indictment of a world that has become so corrupted that it is now a fertile seedbed for all of the hysteria we see depicted in the novel. If Flanagan is thought to be a pro-environmental writer, then *The Unknown Terrorist* is his "Inferno", the hell that the neglect of the environment might spawn. But that neglect is not simply the endless pouring of concrete and the spewing of sewage; it goes deeper. Within that environmental neglect is a disregarding of life and love that finds people chasing money and material goods while, seen but not seen, beggars are beaten, dead bodies pop up in the harbour, and young girls serve as sex slaves. Walking the streets of Sydney, then, are not the happy, quirky Jackie Mullens and her cousin Angus from *Starstruck*, but many, many unknown terrorists who have helped create an environment that destroys many who are unwittingly complicit victims, as well as many who are innocent victims.

There is another oddity in Flanagan's novel besides its urban location and departure from the author's usual themes. This is a structural oddity. Chapter 2 begins, "THE DOLL WAS A POLE DANCER" (5) and spends pages talking about the central character and her nude dancing at the Chairman's Lounge in "the Cross". The chapter boldly (well, all caps) and loudly takes us to the sleaze of Sydney. But Chapter 2 is preceded by a strikingly different Chapter 1. It is a brief one. It begins by raising "THE IDEA" of "LOVE" and declaring that it "IS NOT ENOUGH" (1). The chapter evokes Jesus as a madman who desperately wanted love to prevail and Nietzsche as a madman who sadly knew that evil would instead. This chapter, only two pages long, sets up a novel very different in content

---

5    James Ley, "*The Unknown Terrorist*", *Age*, 4 November 2006, http://bit.ly/2se340v; David Marr, "*The Unknown Terrorist*", *Sydney Morning Herald*, 28 October 2006, http://bit.ly/2Jdsu81.
6    Peter Conrad, "Days of Thunder Erupt Down Under", *Guardian*, 8 April 2007. http://bit.ly/2J10PUK; Michiko Kakutani, "A Misunderstanding, and a Simple Life Descends into a Nightmare", *New York Times*, 8 May 2007, https://nyti.ms/2L6DKAw.

and tone from what follows. We expect a text that is philosophical, perhaps sombrely so, but what we get, at least initially, reads more like a "popular novel" (whatever that is) than a "serious work of fiction" (whatever that is). This move on Flanagan's part evokes the theorising about a wide range of texts in John Schilb's *Rhetorical Refusals* (2007).[7] Schilb suggests that there are many reasons why artists defy expectations, but, in general, they all involve compelling the reader to see things he or she might not otherwise see.

In the case of *The Unknown Terrorist*, the text – that is, Chapter 2 and onward – does indeed read at times like a book that one might pick up at an airport newsstand to pass the time during a long transcontinental flight. The expectation is an exciting story with, maybe, a touch of sex thrown in. And Flanagan's novel, Chapter 2 and onward, meets this genre's requirements – so much so that many readers, after finishing the book, probably have forgotten that Chapter 1 was in a very different key. That this seemingly "pop" novel has a political message is not a shock: that a "pop" writer would also often have a theme to present is not surprising and, in the post-9/11 context, the theme seems timely, especially from the perspective of an American reader. Chapter 1 could then be forgotten, but, if one recalls it and recalls how it did not fit what followed, one is compelled to ask why Flanagan starts off on one note, only to shift to another. I would suggest two reasons: first, to compel readers to think about the novel's focus not being post-9/11 fears run amok, but a world without the love that produces a lack of respect for the rest of creation, human and not; second, to compel readers to realise that beneath actions, be they in fiction or in life, there are attitudes both profound and, in this case, profoundly wrong. The second, much as the texts examined long ago in Stanley Fish's early work on seventeenth-century literature, pushes readers to be better readers.

In the foregoing I have used the terms "key" and "note". This musical language was deliberate because what joins Chapter 1 and the rest of the novel is Chopin's mysterious Nocturnes, specifically the Nocturne in F Minor. It is Gina's chosen music, not the techno-rock she strips to; and it provides the eerie background for the novel. Oddly, this very piece is part of the score of the political thriller *The Peacemaker* (1997) by US director Mimi Leder. Although it stars Nicole Kidman, it is not an Australian movie. Rather, it is Hollywood fare about terrorism. In fact, the Chopin Nocturne in F Minor is the music the film associates with the Yugoslavian terrorist Dušan Gavrić. This coincidence probably has more to do with the music itself. According to Chopin biographer James Huneker, the piece is "neat in its sorrow".[8] And according to Mieczysław Tomaszewski, the piece "bears a melancholy that is deepened by the almost obsessive repetition of the initial melody". That melody "is contrasted with a brief counter theme: music that escapes for a moment into a realm of brighter sonorities (A flat major), though it does so in vain".[9] The mood fits a story of lost love, and the rhythm matches the plotline. The Institute says more about the rhythm: "It takes the form of a collision between the violent octaves of an aggressive recitative and the calm strength of the chords that stand opposite". Similarly, in the novel, Gina tries to stand strong against the waves of police and media aggression that batter her.

---

[7] John Schilb, *Rhetorical Refusals: Defying Audiences' Expectations* (Carbondale: Southern Illinois University Press, 2007).

[8] James Gibbons Huneker, *Chopin: The Man and His Music* (1900; Mineola, New York: Dover Books, 1966).

[9] Mieczysław Tomaszewski, "Nocturne in F minor, Op. 55 No. 1", the Fryderyk Chopin Institute, http://bit.ly/2Lc1S4X.

In music and novel, "The tumult leads to a climax, a watershed", then, "the narrative", as the Institute describes it, "[goes] back into melancholy aura" with an ironic "ray of hope" as F minor becomes F major in the Nocturne, as the Chairman's Lounge's manager Ferdy declares, "'It's time we all got back to dancing'" (320).

The mood and rhythm of Chopin's Nocturne fit the story, but nocturnes are usually thought to be about love. And so *The Unknown Terrorist* is, but it's not the love between Gina and Tariq, or Wilder and Nick; rather, it is the love that "humanity has for centuries" sought as "the greatest force on earth" (1). That love is lacking in the Sydney – in the world – of the novel, and its lack is the unknown terrorist Flanagan wants us to begin to see.

### References

Apter, Emily. "On Oneworldedness: Or Paranoia as a World System", *American Literary History* 18, no. 2 (2006): 365–89.

Collins, Felicity. *The Films of Gillian Armstrong: The Moving Image* 6. St Kilda, Vic: Australian Teachers of Media, 1999.

Conrad, Peter. "Days of Thunder Erupt Down Under". *Guardian*, 8 April 2007. http://bit.ly/2J10PUK.

Dermody, Susan and Elizabeth Jacka. *The Screening of Australia*, vols. 1 and 2. Sydney: Currency Press, 1987–88.

Flanagan, Richard. *The Unknown Terrorist*. New York: Grove, 2006.

Huneker, James Gibbons. *Chopin: The Man and His Music*. (1900) Mineola, NY: Dover Books, 1966.

Kakutani, Michiko. "A Misunderstanding, and a Simple Life Descends Into a Nightmare". *New York Times*, 8 May 2007. https://nyti.ms/2L6DKAw.

Ley, James. Review of *The Unknown Terrorist*. *Age*, 4 November 2006. http://bit.ly/2se340v.

Marr, David. Review of *The Unknown Terrorist*. *Sydney Morning Herald*, 28 October 2006. http://bit.ly/2Jdsu81.

Schilb, John. *Rhetorical Refusals: Defying Audiences' Expectations*. Carbondale: Southern Illinois University Press, 2007.

Titlestad, Michael. "The Logic of the Apocalypse: A Clerical Rejoinder", *Safundi: The Journal of South African and American Studies* 14, no.1 (2013): 93–110.

Tomaszewski, Mieczysław. "Nocturne in F minor, Op. 55 No. 1". The Fryderyk Chopin Institute, 2003–8. http://bit.ly/2Lc1S4X.

# 11

# "Fireless flame gone amorous": War amid Love in *The Narrow Road to the Deep North*

Nicholas Birns

Richard Flanagan's *The Narrow Road to the Deep North* (2013) garnered international acclaim for its eloquent and austere portrayal of a World War Two veteran, Alwyn "Dorrigo" Evans, as he copes with the trauma of having been a prisoner of war in Japanese-occupied Burma. Yet it could be argued that the emotional heart of the novel is just as much the strange love story between Dorrigo and his uncle's wife, Amy Mulvaney. This chapter will explore how Flanagan, astonishingly, makes even war seem an interruption of the mysterious quest for love. As a secondary argument, I will trace Flanagan's imagining of war amid the rest of life by noting affiliations and affinities within a specifically Australian context of writing about war, while also noting Flanagan's debts to the larger canon of world literature.

This larger canon prominently foregrounds the question of the relation of war and love in imaginative literature. Since Tolstoy and, going far back, Homer, writers have been balancing stories of love and war, using them to counterpoint each other. Very early on in *The Narrow Road to the Deep North*, Flanagan openly alludes to Tolstoy: the aphoristic, "A happy man has no past, while an unhappy man has nothing else", alludes to the opening line of *Anna Karenina*.[1] And almost as early, he refers to Homer's *The Iliad* ("the Greeks, the Trojans, what's that all about" (11)), referencing quickly two writers who place war and peace in counterpoint. Yet here there is less counterpoint than contradiction; the radical privacy and idiosyncrasy of the Amy story is in a different key from the sober and responsible story of Dorrigo's war. That the Tolstoy allusion is not to *War and Peace* but to the far more domestic *Anna Karenina* is symptomatic here. Moreover, the quasi-incestuous aspect of the romance brings up issues of blood and kinship that are also found in the revelation that Darky Gardiner, Dorrigo's fellow soldier who is brutally tortured and killed by the Japanese, is both Aboriginal and Dorrigo's own nephew. It is tempting to look upon World War Two as an era of moral certainty and to construct the contemporary era as having drifted from this moral clarity. But Flanagan in fact reveals the individuality and strangeness of the people who serve in the war, a strangeness that we are in danger of sentimentalising and standardising now that, as Susan Lever has put it, "any direct experience of these war veterans is now receding into the past".[2]

---

1   Richard Flanagan, *The Narrow Road to the Deep North* (2013; New York: Knopf, 2014), 4. All subsequent references are to this edition and appear in parentheses in the text.
2   Susan Lever, "Heroes, Certainly", *Sydney Review of Books*, 26 November 2013. http://bit.ly/2J1WksQ.

Flanagan also emphasises the Asian setting of the war. It is notable that, though people lack information about World War Two as the twentieth century's first genuinely global war (World War One possessing African and Near Eastern action, but very little in Asia, and mainly being fought in Europe), in fact the war is very much divided in a binary way between the European and Pacific fronts, which also effectively marks the division between those areas where the war bleeds into the Holocaust and those where it is more involved with the fate of an Asia over which Europe is rapidly losing control. Though Flanagan gestures to the Holocaust through his epigraph, "Mother, they write poems", from Paul Celan, the book nonetheless recognises the way in which the Asian front raises issues distinctive to Australia's regional identity, echoing previous novels such as David Malouf's *The Great World* (1990) and Shirley Hazzard's *The Great Fire* (2003), even as it considers Asian literary forms more than either of them. Furthermore, the fact that the Australian and other POWs were "the slave of the yellow man" (246) undermines white privilege; even after the defeat of the Asian power, there is a sense that the era of European hegemony outside Europe is over. But there is the danger here of making sense of the novel through adept sociological generalisation. Indeed, I will argue that what is most central to the novel is not its treatment of war as such, but the love plot: Dorrigo's lifelong passion for Amy Mulvaney, a woman he meets in a bookshop off Rundle Street in Adelaide and then next runs into when she is married to his late aunt's husband, Keith Mulvaney. Amy remains the love of Dorrigo's life despite his subsequent marriage to Ella, an aristocratic, refined woman whose balefulness does not reach the level of the basically similar Enid Wheeler in Willa Cather's World War One novel *One of Ours* (1922), but who similarly is portrayed as an inadequate life partner for the protagonist. Though Ella has told him Amy has died, in the mid-1960s Dorrigo sees Amy alive in Sydney, leading him to realise his wife has lied to him. Though the two former lovers do not talk, the near-miraculous chance meeting is visible proof of how essential their connection remains to each of them even though they are permanently separate.

In a novel dominated by the grave atrocities of twentieth-century warfare, the love plot, poignant as it may be, may risk appearing merely subjective and personal. James Bradley describes the novel as "a work of remarkable economy in which everything – love, family, the illusions of nationhood and honour – is revealed as a deception, leaving the characters without consolation". Bradley adds, however, that if "the novel has a fault it is its occasional tendency to tacitly endorse old pieties about the ordinary Australian soldier".[3] I would argue, though, that reading the novel as lapsing into such pieties is only possible if one overlooks how much it is about beauty, and not just the beauty that is ruined in wartime but that which remains in spite of it. When Dorrigo first reads Tennyson's "Ulysses" and first looks lovingly at Amy, he realises that these two things are "the first beautiful thing" he has ever known (14). And it is that beauty that remains through both his POW experience and a bitter, unfulfilling marriage.

The love plot is not superfluous to the novel; it is needed to keep the war plot from facile redemption. That the novel embraces Japanese literary influences such as haiku even while exposing the sadistic wartime conduct of the Japanese soldiers addresses a paradoxical mystery that finds resonance in the bittersweet and confounding nature of the love plot. This came up in the strange variance between two readers of the novel

---

[3] James Bradley, "Booker Prize Shortlist, Now Open to Americans, Offers Few Surprises", *Australian*, 11 October 2014. http://bit.ly/2xuGA07.

## 11 "Fireless flame gone amorous": War amid Love in *The Narrow Road to the Deep North*

whose reactions to it reached far beyond the sphere of book reviews and routine literary discussion. When the 2014 Prime Minister's Literary Award for fiction was jointly bestowed on *The Narrow Road to the Deep North* and Steven Carroll's *A World of Other People* (2013), Les Murray, a member of the judging panel, claimed that then Prime Minister Tony Abbott supervened the decision of the judging panel to award the prize to Carroll's book alone.[4] Murray further commented that he was "thunderstruck to see the Tasmanian pop up", the appellation of "the Tasmanian" somewhat resembling how an Ivy League hiring committee in the 1950s might describe a candidate from a state university.[5] What is fascinating here is that this was unquestionably a quarrel among the right. Murray has long been perceived as friendly to Coalition policies, though not an explicit supporter of Abbott per se. Moreover, the reactions of both men to the book indicated a tacit reading of it. Abbott read the book as praise of Australian wartime bravery: he was reading the book patriotically. Although Flanagan makes clear there is humanity (and inhumanity) on both sides, the novel is not revolutionary with respect to the historiography of World War Two or of the Australian POW experience. Most readers of the book would, like Abbott, understand it as mainly about the suffering and sacrifice of the prisoners.

Murray, though, read it differently. Calling it "pretentious" and "stupid", he saw in the novel fundamentally disturbing currents.[6] And here it could well be that the reader who disliked the book actually had a greater insight. Whereas Murray's verse novel, *Fredy Neptune* (1999), gives in its compelling final section, "Lazarus Unstuck", a vision of cathartic forgiveness and transcendence of the twentieth-century ordeals suffered by its titular character, Flanagan's novel insists that Dorrigo has exhausted his public persona as "a war hero, a famous and celebrated surgeon, the public image of a time and a tragedy, the subject of biographies, plays and documentaries. The object of veneration, hagiographies, adulation" (17).

But while Dorrigo is alienated from his public persona, he suffers perhaps from the opposite malady from Murray's Fredy, who is burdened by his inability to feel: Dorrigo feels too much, and especially for Amy. The Amy plot makes *The Narrow Road to the Deep North* more than the war novel Abbott takes it for, and closer to what Murray suggested was the novel it should have been. Though many readers, including this one, do not share Murray's negativity about "the Tasmanian" and his work, his comments are nonetheless highly perceptive about identifying what Flanagan was trying to express. It is just that from his own ethical and aesthetic perspective, Murray simply did not care for it. It is indeed fascinating that Flanagan's novel, which, given its subject, could be expected to have received dutiful and ceremonious reviews for its commemoration of the suffering of POWs, instead received extremes of both adulation and excoriation. It won not only the Prime Minister's Literary Award but also the Man Booker, by far the most prestigious prize in the Anglophone world, but the novel was not only reviled by Murray, Australia's greatest living poet, it also received a scorching review by the well-known British poet, critic and translator Michael Hofmann in the *London Review of Books*.[7] Hofmann went so far as to say that the winner of what was

---

4  Les Murray cited in Stephen Romei, "Les Murray Claims Abbott 'Swifty' on Richard Flanagan Book", *Australian*, 11 December 2014. http://bit.ly/2svJo7M.
5  Les Murray cited in Susan Wyndham, "Undercover: The Year of Richard Flanagan", *Sydney Morning Herald*, 12 December 2014. http://bit.ly/2kB50fd.
6  Les Murray cited in Romei, "Les Murray".
7  Michael Hofmann, "Is His Name Alwyn?", *London Review of Books*, 18 December 2014. http://bit.ly/2xzSgiu.

essentially that year's award for the best book in the English language should not have been published at all, that Flanagan should have set fire to his draft of the book.

Hofmann, amidst his contumely, makes this remarkable observation: "The war passages have a bullying automatism that leaves Flanagan quite at sea in the rest of the book. The war won't settle, and it doesn't help. It either matters or it doesn't". Hofmann's comment is actually perceptive, although one might see the "bullying automatism" not as a flaw of the writer but an aspect of war itself, and the unsettling Hofmann speaks of one of the extraordinary achievements of the book, since it could be said to be considering the relationship of war to the rest of life in a new way. Hofmann's comment, and Flanagan's novel, reveal that war literature, as a category, is almost inherently a contradiction in terms. In writing about the antiwar poems of Elizabeth Bishop, Susan Rosenbaum has argued that we under-read these poems if we see them as just a critique of something – war – that can be represented from a distance, rather than acknowledging that modern writing about war, no matter how perceptive, has representational limits, and that the distance between observer and observed is always collapsing, so there is no determinate subject.[8] This is even more the case with twentieth-century total war, which truly became, in words made famous by Carl Schmitt via Giorgio Agamben, a "state of exception".[9] If war – no matter how justified, as clearly Flanagan believes that this war, as far as Australia and its allies are concerned, *was* justified – is a state of destruction whose aim is the extermination of other lives in the service of ideology, then it is apodictically anti-literary. Any literary representation of war, as Rosenbaum argues, thus pulls at the very limits of language. And such a representation, as Rosenbaum observes of Bishop, needs "sentimental inheritances" that connect war to the life of affect, not ironise it from an ostensibly superior distance.[10]

This observation explains two issues in the role of war in twentieth-century literature. The first is how war poetry and fiction, as seen in canonical works of scholarship such as those by Samuel Hynes and Paul Fussell, are so often segregated from modernism or any discussion of literary innovation, as if the sheer business of war literature were transparently to testify to war, and the self-interrogation of literary structures that in fact was percolating all around both world wars was simply ornamental frippery.[11] Flanagan addresses this issue by having Dorrigo's first, intense meeting with Amy in the Adelaide bookstore coincide with a reading by Max Harris, the leader of the Angry Penguins movement, the target, notoriously, of the Ern Malley hoax, and the fount of deliberate modernist experimentation in Australian literature at the time. Dorrigo's instinctual tastes in literature incline towards a Tennyson that "no one reads" (18), as a result of the modernist and avant-garde revolutions in taste. Yet Amy, the emotional heart of his world, is placed in ironic conjunction with the closest Australia in the 1940s came to a self-conscious avant-garde. Dorrigo's own word-obsessiveness is not exempted from a general literary mobility and slipperiness. His role as a soldier does not lead him to insist on referentiality or on a literature that has to mean something concrete and palpable. This

---

8   Susan Rosenbaum, "Bishop's Theater of War", in *Reading the Middle Generation Anew: Culture, Community, and Form*, ed. Eric Haralson (Iowa City: University of Iowa Press, 2006), 53–82.
9   Giorgio Agamben, *State of Exception*, trans. Daniel Attell (Chicago: University of Chicago Press, 2005).
10  Rosenbaum, "Bishop's Theater of War", 53.
11  Samuel Hynes, *A War Imagined: The First World War and English Culture* (London: The Bodley Head, 1990); Paul Fussell, *The Great War and Modern Memory* (New York: Oxford University Press, 1975).

# 11 "Fireless flame gone amorous": War amid Love in *The Narrow Road to the Deep North*

assumption is just what undergirds the traditional separation of wartime writing from modernism.

The second issue is that war literature – especially that of World War Two – often insisted on its subject too much. This was partially a regressive reaction-formation, precisely because it was here that the link between language and representation really frayed. One can see this in the translation of *The Aeneid* by Robert Fitzgerald, the American poet (not to be confused with the Australian poet R.D. Fitzgerald). Fitzgerald renders the first line of Virgil's epic, "*Arma virumque cano*", most familiar in English as "Arms and the man I sing", as "I sing of warfare and a man at war". This phrasing not only doubles the "war" referent, it introduces the modern concept of "warfare" as a state into the reader's experience of the poem.[12] Fitzgerald, who served in the US Navy in the Pacific during the war, was doubtless drawing on his own experience of war as something absolute and horrible. But, instead of acknowledging that precisely because war is such a state, literature cannot adequately represent it, Fitzgerald presses down on the referentiality of warfare. He tells the reader that Aeneas is a man of war twice over, leaving the reader to be surprised to see that in the actual story Aeneas is in three very different relationships with three very different women: that, in other words, even *pius Aeneas* has a private life.

This issue also comes up in one of Australia's two great poems on World War Two, David Campbell's "Men in Green":

> Oh, there were some leaned on a stick
> And some on stretchers lay,
> But few walked on their own two feet
> In the early green of day.
>
> They had not feared the ape-like cloud
> That climbed the mountain crest;
> They had not feared the summer's sun
> With bullets for their breast.
>
> Their eyes were bright, their looks were dull,
> Their skin had turned to clay.
> Nature had met them in the night
> And stalked them in the day.
>
> And I think still of men in green
> On the Soputa track
> With fifteen spitting tommy-guns
> To keep a jungle back.[13]

Campbell was a true war hero, a decorated Royal Australian Air Force veteran, and the regularity of his incantatory quatrains conveys all the more vividly and viscerally that war destroys soldiers, even those who survive it. But there is an undeniable monologism here,

---

12  Virgil, *The Aeneid*, trans. Robert Fitzgerald (New York: Vintage, 1990), 1.
13  David Campbell, "Men in Green", in *Poetry of Australia, Vol. II*, ed. Douglas Stewart (Berkeley: University of California Press, 1965), 112.

as also seen in comparable American poems such as Richard Eberhart's "The Fury of Aerial Bombardment". The men in green, like Fitzgerald's Aeneas, are defined exclusively as men at war: what they lived for, what kept them sane through the fighting, what they hoped to be in their lives, is unimagined. Notably, Australia's other great poem of the war, Kenneth Slessor's "Beach Burial", not only begins, in almost an apotropaic anti-monologism, "softy and humbly", but speaks of the dead warriors' "last signature" and as equally "in search for the same landfall".[14] In Slessor's poem there is a mystery in the experience of the dead, a knowledge that their definition as dead does not recapitulate their definition in life, that goes beyond Campbell's poem. It is indeed significant that Slessor, after this sly, self-effacing and susurrant war poem, remained totally silent poetically for the remaining quarter century and more of his life, suggesting that after war, there can be no poetry. This is the reverse of insisting on war as an adequate and self-sufficient poetic subject, as Campbell's poem, for all its achievement, does.

An even more unorthodox response to the war is that of Kenneth "Seaforth" Mackenzie. In his poem "Searchlights", Mackenzie sees the beacons:

> splitting the moonlight,
> coldly caressing each other deep in the zenith
> of almost-midnight, loving one another
> like chill blue hoses of fireless flame gone amorous.[15]

The poet goes on to use this uncanny light to find the shape of his beloved, who, in another departure from orthodoxy, is most likely, given what we know of Mackenzie's sexuality, another man. But the pertinence to Flanagan's novel lies in the way Mackenzie's poem sees the language of love as piercing and overlapping that of war; that the narrative of war cannot be restricted to war alone.

Flanagan follows Slessor and Mackenzie in showing both mystery and silence at the end of war. Every soldier has his or, as possible in our era, her own inwardness; what is important is that there is inwardness. In Flanagan's novel, Lizard Brancussi survives not just his tenure as a POW but as a slave labourer in Nagasaki when that city was the target of a nuclear bomb by his nation's own ally, the United States. He survives the prison camps and the devastation of thermonuclear attack inspired by a "pencil sketch of his wife" (247) that Rabbit Hendricks had drawn for him in Syria. For him, amid pain and devastation, Maisie was "the one thing in the world that was not this" (292). Arriving home, though, he finds Maisie has married another man. Lizard Brancussi disappears and presumably dies. In war, the good guys may have won; in love, they do not. This is not just a lesson in irony or a contrast between war and the home front. It is an argument that the counter to the abnormality of war, the way it is a "state of exception", cannot just be humdrum, everyday normality, but an equally uncanny "state of exception" on the other side – that is, love.

The exceptionality of war is difficult to formulate because war is a public event. One may have different experiences of war or different views about the origin, purpose or tactics of war, but the identity of war, as an ontological fact, is apparent to all. This is

---

14   Kenneth Slessor, "Beach Burial", in *The Broadview Anthology of Poetry*, ed. Amanda Goldrick Jones and Herbert Rosengarten (Peterborough, Ontario: Broadview Press, 1993), 526.
15   Kenneth Mackenzie, "Searchlight", in *The Poems of Kenneth Mackenzie* (Sydney: Angus & Robertson, 1972), 15.

especially true of World War Two because of its historical centrality, its notoriety, its status as what Samuel Hynes, a veteran himself and an opponent of many of the mythologies about the conflict, has yet termed "everybody's war".[16] We can see this in the reception of Flanagan's *The Narrow Road to the Deep North*, in sharp contrast to the subjects of his earlier fiction, set in Tasmania, and, in the case of *Gould's Book of Fish* (2001) and *Wanting* (2008), during the colonial period. In the reviews there was no sense of discovery about the experience of the wartime POWs; indeed, the suffering of Burma prisoners was very familiar to Western audiences, in part because of the success of David Lean's 1957 film *The Bridge on the River Kwai*. Unlike Flanagan's earlier Tasmanian subjects, there was nothing odd or boutique (for an international readership) about the subject, setting, and, in consequence, effective readership of *The Narrow Road to the Deep North*.

Many reviewers and readers see the novel as constellating around the story of the wartime prison camps. And certainly Flanagan's critique of the Line – the Japanese marshalling of the POW column and the railroad itself – tacitly argues that wartime atrocities – and this could by extension include the Holocaust and even Hiroshima and various acts of internment – were specific instances of a general dehumanisation. *Gould's Book of Fish* and *Wanting* had linked this process with regimes of the Enlightenment and colonisation, but certainly this sense of dehumanisation was particularly prevalent in the era of modern totalitarianism. The danger here, however, is to assume that, simply because a public event is the cause of dehumanisation, the impact of this dehumanisation can be registered by restricting the imaginative gaze only to the public event. Flanagan instead makes the novel's maximal emotional thrust private and amorous, featuring Dorrigo's thwarted and yet still radiant love for Amy. The paradox here is that, even though everyone's love life is equally, in Tolstoyan terms, unhappy – in other words, has equal potential for unhappiness, is liable to the risk of emotional attachment – and even though love is inherently a private emotion, inexplicable and unchangeable, private, idiosyncratic love is all we have. We may all have read historical accounts of the Burma ordeal but that shared knowledge cannot bind us, as it is merely generic, something that we can know about, or try to know about, by reading or hearing about it as Flanagan himself did. It is only the shared knowledge of, perversely, what is secret – love – that can bind us.

In a bracing passage, Flanagan asks us to face the fact that private life can be a way of evading public responsibility; that private life can try to become "a secret life" but is in fact never "free of the world" (345). This is in the first place relevant to the Japanese officer Nakamura's attempts to live a private life after the war in Japan, evading trial as a war criminal under legal norms whose jurisdiction he does not admit. Yet Flanagan insists on equivalence between Japanese and Australian private lives, and suggests that, in both cases, to use the public to exculpate the private, or vice versa, is self-deluding. Flanagan indeed sees public and private life as fully interpenetrated, so war can never fully be war, nor love fully love, though I would argue that love knows this failure in its grain as war does not. Yet the "failure" of love – Amy and Dorrigo do not fulfil their destinies with each other – is both symptom of and antidote to the failure of war, because the failure of love and the failure of war are two different kinds of failures. Love fails because, even if two people are mutually happy, no one outside the relationship can ever understand why; war fails because war is never, in any meaningful human terms, comprehensible. What we are

---

16   Samuel Hynes, *The Soldier's Tale: Bearing Witness to Modern War* (New York: Viking, 1997), 22.

left with is "the secret life" (299) that cannot just be closed off as private, that Flanagan asserts will always be a part of the world.

This would be banal and obvious when discussing almost any other possible subject for literature. But war literature, by being wrapped in seriousness and referentially, has too often hovered outside of this truism, and therefore been rendered involuntarily minor. The problem at mid-century, as Mark Greif has recently argued in *The Age of the Crisis of Man* (2015), is that many thinkers reacted melodramatically by proclaiming a ponderous and hypertrophied humanism, a defence of man which shortly after its enunciation became burdened with all the embarrassments of being a period style, not the eternal wisdom it had presumed itself to be.[17] The responses to the perceived crisis of man, Greif argues, were so rhetorically inflated that they failed to address the underlying issue. Flanagan discerns the same threats to humanity as the discourses Greif chronicles, but makes sure not to respond with reactive, stentorian inflation.

Flanagan's characters proclaim their humanity not by rhetorically asserting it but by intimate displays of solidarity. One of the central incidents in *The Narrow Road to the Deep North* – whose importance is discerned, for instance by Thomas Keneally in his *Guardian* review of the novel – occurs in Nikitaris' fish shop.[18] Here, a group of the ex-POWs breaks the window in honour of their slain comrade, Darky Gardiner, and the role Nikitaris' shop played in his entertaining stories. The men go to Nikitaris' shop, smash the window and free the fish trapped in the tank, but then feel remorse. They go back to the shop's proprietor and apologise, prepared to take their punishment or at least pay for the window. When they apologise, though, Nikitaris, pausing to take in the situation, asks, "He was your cobber?" (97) – the migrant using the Australian slang, and using "cobber" rather than the more anodyne "mate", speaks volumes. Nikitaris, instead of getting angry, unexpectedly invites the men for a meal as his guests, offering them red wine and his finest fish. It is eventually revealed that Nikitaris' son died in New Guinea. The way Nikitaris is "strange and welcoming at the same time" (253) is a moving, uncanny gesture of solidarity amid loss. It is also, though, an act of love on the part of the Greek restaurateur, as he transfers his love for his missing son to the other returned soldiers even though they have damaged his property.

Nikitaris' fish shop constitutes an intermediate space between the POW camp and Dorrigo's domestic routine with Ella, as well as portraying the struggle of postwar living for the entire group of men in the camp, not just Dorrigo. Flanagan provides a moving portrait of the men's incomplete adaptation to resumed civilian life, pertinent to veterans of more recent wars. But, just as in one way the Nikitaris incident is linked with Homer by the fish-shop proprietor's ethnicity, in another it is linked with the Amy plot by the way that in both cases, love for one person can extend beyond that person, can illuminate an entire way of life.

If Dorrigo's relationship with Ella is "an unshared life shared" (223), both the Dorrigo-Amy relationship and Nikitaris' relationship with the soldiers who had damaged his property are examples of how lives shared only in brief instances can create meaningful emotional connections. Although the Nikitaris scene does not involve romantic, sexual or

---

17  Mark Greif, *The Age of the Crisis of Man: Thought and Fiction in America 1933–1973* (Princeton, NJ: Princeton University Press, 2015).
18  Thomas Keneally, review of *The Narrow Road To The Deep North*, *Guardian*, 28 June 2014. http://bit.ly/2LIjSoq.

erotic love, it is motivated by a form of love, of *philia*, of a bond that, however undergirded by the tragic events of wartime, is deeply private and idiosyncratic. It can be seen as partially remedying the "ultimate failure" of wartime male bonding that Joanna Bourke describes as lurking underneath the "spurious rhetoric of wartime comradeship".[19]

In the novel's stress on secret loves amid inconspicuous lives, *The Narrow Road to the Deep North* solicits two radically different Australian peers, Patrick White and Gerald Murnane. The chance glimpse between Dorrigo and the presumed-dead Amy on the Sydney Harbour Bridge evokes – far more lyrically and romantically than its original – Waldo Brown's meeting with his old now-married love Dulcie Saporta in the street in White's *The Solid Mandala* (1966). Amy's backing of Old Rowley to win the Melbourne Cup "because he *was* one hundred to one" (125) evokes the linkage in Murnane's oeuvre between the risks and randomness of horseracing and that of interpersonal affection. In each instance above, love and loss are not unrelated.

Yet, although it may have literary precedents, the rendition of the Amy plot in *The Narrow Road to the Deep North* is almost deliberately unliterary. It might be tempting to see the poetry in Flanagan's novel as an ally to love and as a remedy for war. But although Dorrigo is what Iris Murdoch would call a "word child", reading is not presented as redemptive. Nakamura can read great literature (Bashō) with malignant intent, and there can also be bad texts tout court, as witnessed by Rooster MacNeice's reading of *Mein Kampf*. Yet, after Dorrigo, as an old man, is fatally injured driving through Parramatta and is brought to a hospital, he remembers a favourite poem, preceded by a dream of light "flooding a church hall in which he sat with Amy" (325). After a flashback to the war years and his hellish experiences there triggered by the trauma of his hospital stay, Dorrigo poignantly recalls his favourite poem by Tennyson, of a man willing to die satisfied because he has had a complete experience of life, yet seeking ever more:

> For my purpose holds, he whispered –
> To sail beyond the sunset, and the baths
> Of all the western stars until I die. (330)

The "he whispered" is key, not just to Dorrigo's failing personal strength but to the way his word-obsession has never been rhetorical, elocutionary or public. Instead, every pore of the novel is muted, deflective, whispering. After he finishes reciting Tennyson's celebration of passionate effort in the face of circumstance, Dorrigo feels nothing but "shame" and "loss" (331): an overall inadequacy. Words cannot redeem. Words can reflect emotions, or tell us what emotions are, but having poetry beloved on the part of all the war's combatants makes it a shared dialogic conversation between them, valued artistically, if not morally privileged. Nakamura's love of Bashō even while he is torturing the prisoners is counterbalanced by Dorrigo's and Flanagan's own love of haiku – Flanagan told Ramona Koval, in an interview at the Wheeler Centre, that he had considered writing the novel as a haiku sequence.[20] Flanagan's naming of Keith Mulvaney's Adelaide pub "The King of Cornwall" (74) is a clear allusion to the story of Tristan and Isolde, in which, as in Flanagan's novel, Tristan's uncle is

---

19  Joanna Bourke, *Dismembering the Male: Men's Bodies, Britain and the Great War* (Chicago: University of Chicago Press, 1996), 136.
20  Richard Flanagan interviewed by Ramona Koval, *The Monthly Video*, 24 July 2014. http://bit.ly/2sqIfyd.

also Isolde's husband and Tristan's rival for her love. But words – not even Flanagan's – cannot redeem or even describe life. Thus there is a convergence between the novel's refusal to claim that it can conclusively represent war – or that war is conclusively representable – and its insistence on the secret life of love. This does not have to do exclusively with Amy. Dorrigo's childhood epiphany, after which nothing "would ever be as real to him" (9), occurs before he meets Amy. Moreover, Dorrigo's late-in-life affair with his friend's wife, Lynette Maison, is at once shameful and important to him, and even his relationship with Ella gains significant depth when Dorrigo rescues her and their children from danger. Amy is not the exclusive sign of Dorrigo's mysterious life in the book. But she is the definitive symbol of a life from which war cannot take all.

One could see Flanagan's discernment of an inner life within war as a luxury of a man and largely a generation that did not have to fight in wars – as younger, more emotionally expressive people simulate or are at least able to express the private life their fathers could not. Yet the incipient counter-tradition epitomised by Slessor and Mackenzie and limned above disputes that. So does "Mario and Jessica", a late (2008) poem by John Millett, a man born in 1921, still alive at age ninety-five at the time of the writing of this chapter, and perhaps the last surviving Australian literary figure of significance to have fought in the war:

> Mario, a critical mass, has the power to cripple
> the blind aces of other man – but now, touching
> Jessica so, he becomes something never before existing –
> and she, touching him, becomes so much more than
> she was not, a thermal wind, swallows flow down, onto
> the face of the river, to touch water asleep – as he and
> she sleep in the undercurrents of each other's breath.[21]

Mario, in Millett's poem, has the physical capacity to destroy, but, renouncing this through love, he becomes something "never before existing", as does Jessica – an amplification that is also a vacancy, a blank shape. Though the love of Millett's protagonists is far more realised than Flanagan's, they both speak to how war can be understood in the same field as love, while simultaneously adamantly refusing to see love as redemptive or dialectically reassuring. Interestingly, an American account of the wartime years in Australia, Herbert C. Jaffa's novel-memoir *Townsville at War*, is at its heart about a love affair between the author and an Australian woman.[22] Popular assumptions about Millett's, Slessor's, Mackenzie's and Dorrigo Evans' generation have denied them a private life. If that is restored, as Flanagan is attempting, maybe the balance between public and private in later generations will be more even, and war writing, in the purest sense, will no longer be sustainable, even if wars themselves, alas, continue.

Indeed, *The Narrow Road to the Deep North* could be seen as somewhat of a redress petition for private life in wartime. Just as, in World War Two narratives by Westerners, Asian cultural agency is usually denied, equally so is private life muted or set to the side. Thus the importance that Nakamura, in many ways a vile and appalling figure, is still given a private life and an ability to love art, even if he is blind to his own terrible flaws. Thus the

---

21 John Millett, "Mario and Jessica", in *Circles of Love* (Port Adelaide, SA: Ginninderra Press, 2008).
22 Herbert C. Jaffa, *Townsville at War: A Soldier Remembers* (Townsville, Qld: Foundation for Australian Literary Studies, 1992).

resemblance – in books with otherwise little in common tonally or aesthetically other than being by Australians and set in wartime in Asia – between *The Narrow Road to the Deep North* and Shirley Hazzard's *The Great Fire* (2003), because both insist on the erosion of European cultural primacy, and a radical and inscrutable private tenor at the heart of lives even lived on the most public canvas.

If, as was mentioned in responses to the book, World War Two was an unusual subject for Australian fiction, this can be only because the late eighteenth century and the nineteenth century have been so hegemonic. The predominance of the pre-1900 era, as in Kate Grenville's recent colonial trilogy, *The Secret River* (2004), *The Lieutenant* (2008) and *Sarah Thornhill* (2011), could be because the crucial issues of Australian settlement, and the usurpation of the Indigenous people, first unfolded then. It could be, as in the global recreation of the work of Peter Carey, both because pre-Federation Australia gives the world what seems to be the most distinctively Australian, and, conversely, because this era was when Australia was most tied to Great Britain, a country with far greater visibility in discourses of world literature. The World War Two setting depicts an Australia that is an autonomous nation-state with an increasing involvement in Asia, something far closer to the reality of the twenty-first century than the Australia seen in the novels most often exported internationally, but for reasons explained above less marketable in a literary sense.

Yet Flanagan's novel is not alone in recent Australian fiction in embedding war within larger networks of memory, relationships and representation. Thomas Keneally's oeuvre is the giant exception to the generalisation above about pre-1900 historical fiction and that depicting the twentieth century, as Keneally's historical fiction has bisected the 1900 divider more or less equally, and he is most famous for his works depicting twentieth-century history. David Malouf's *Ransom* (2009), another book that is in some ways a response to 9/11 – Flanagan told Ramona Koval he began his novel shortly after 2001, as Malouf did his – is surely present when Flanagan explicitly or tacitly refers to Homer.[23] Brenda Walker, in *The Wing of Night* (2005) (subtitled, evocatively, *A Novel of Love and War*) and Delia Falconer, in *The Lost Thoughts of Soldiers* (2006), have shown how soldiers' personal lives have impacted their battlefield experiences, and how to demarcate those out as separate subjects is not only a distortion but an injustice.[24] Three slight, imperfect, but suggestive novels by Australian men of letters – Thomas Shapcott's *Mona's Gift* (1993), Nicholas Jose's *Paper Nautilus* (1987) and Geoffrey Dutton's *Flying Low* (1992) – are all set in World War Two, although of the three writers only Dutton was of an age to serve.[25] They depict not just the war itself but also the reverberation of the war, its resonance and aftermath, the way it permeates and is surrounded by the swathe of ordinary life and private feeling. One can see this going back even further in Australian war writing, to Frederic Manning's *The Middle Parts of Fortune* (1929), which depicts men dwelling in the trenches of the Western Front in World War One, living as far as possible a sort of ordinary life there amid the constant thrum of daily vulnerability to death.[26]

---

23   David Malouf, *Ransom* (New York: Vintage, 2011).
24   Delia Falconer, *The Lost Thoughts of Soldiers* (New York: Counterpoint, 2009); Brenda Walker, *The Wing of Night: A Novel of Love and War* (Melbourne: Penguin Australia, 2005).
25   Geoffrey Dutton, *Flying Low: A Novel* (St Lucia: University of Queensland Press 1992); Thomas Shapcott, *Mona's Gift* (Ringwood, Vic: Viking Australia, 1993); Nicholas Jose, *Paper Nautilus* (Ringwood, Vic: Penguin Australia, 1987). Dutton's novel was first published in an alternative version as *Andy* (London: Collins, 1968).
26   Frederic Manning, *The Middle Parts of Fortune* (1929; London: Vintage, 2014).

*The Narrow Road to the Deep North* is a greater achievement than any of these works, but it builds upon their precedent in suggesting we should no longer speak of love amid war – of love as a respite from the horrific but discernible horrors of war – rather than of war amid love. No matter how stern and battle-scarred Aeneas is, he has Creusa, Dido and Lavinia, in all their divergent destinies, in his story as well. For love, however private and radically individuated, makes sense in its own terms, even if that sense cannot be directly communicated to others; whereas war can be nothing but inherently nonsensical. *The Narrow Road to the Deep North*, by perceiving the trauma of prisoners of war through the filter of the overall dimensions of their loves, depicts, in Mackenzie's words, a fireless flame with the possibility to go amorous.

## References

Agamben, Giorgio. *State of Exception*. Translated by Daniel Attell. Chicago: University of Chicago Press, 2005.
Bourke, Joanna. *Dismembering the Male: Men's Bodies, Britain and the Great War*. Chicago: University of Chicago Press, 1996.
Bradley, James. "Booker Prize Shortlist, Now Open to Americans, Offers Few Surprises". *Australian*, 11 October 2014. http://bit.ly/2xuGA07.
Campbell, David. "Men in Green". In *Poetry of Australia, Vol. II*. Edited by Douglas Stewart. Berkeley: University of California Press, 1965.
Dutton, Geoffrey. *Flying Low: A Novel*. St Lucia: University of Queensland Press, 1992.
———. *Andy*. London: Collins, 1968.
Falconer, Delia. *The Lost Thoughts of Soldiers*. New York: Counterpoint, 2009.
Fussell, Paul. *The Great War and Modern Memory*. New York: Oxford University Press, 1975.
Greif, Mark. *The Age of the Crisis of Man: Thought and Fiction in America 1933–1973*. Princeton, NJ: Princeton University Press, 2015.
Hofmann, Michael. "Is His Name Alwyn?", *London Review of Books*, 18 December 2014. http://bit.ly/2xzSgiu.
Hynes, Samuel. *The Soldier's Tale: Bearing Witness to Modern War*. New York: Viking, 1997.
———. *A War Imagined: The First World War and English Culture*. London: The Bodley Head, 1990.
Jaffa, Herbert C. *Townsville at War: A Soldier Remembers*. Townsville, Qld: Foundation for Australian Literary Studies, 1992.
Jose, Nicholas. *Paper Nautilus*. Ringwood, Vic: Penguin Australia, 1987.
Keneally, Thomas. Review of *The Narrow Road to the Deep North*. *Guardian*, 28 June 2014. http://bit.ly/2LIjSoq.
Koval, Ramona. Interview with Richard Flanagan. *The Monthly Video*, 24 July 2014. http://bit.ly/2sqIfyd.
Lever, Susan. "Heroes, Certainly". *Sydney Review of Books*, 26 November 2013. http://bit.ly/2J1WksQ.
Mackenzie, Kenneth. "Searchlight". In *The Poems of Kenneth Mackenzie*. Sydney: Angus & Robertson, 1972.
Malouf, David. *Ransom*. New York: Vintage, 2011.
Manning, Frederic. *The Middle Parts of Fortune*. (1929) London: Vintage, 2014.
Millett, John. "Mario and Jessica". In *Circles of Love*. Port Adelaide, SA: Ginninderra Press, 2008.
Romei, Stephen. "Les Murray Claims Abbott 'Swifty' on Richard Flanagan Book". *Australian*, 11 December 2014. http://bit.ly/2svJo7M.
Rosenbaum, Susan. "Bishop's Theater of War". In *Reading the Middle Generation Anew: Culture, Community, and Form*, edited by Eric Haralson. Iowa City: University of Iowa Press, 2006, 53–82.
Shapcott, Thomas. *Mona's Gift*. Ringwood, Vic: Viking Australia, 1993.

Slessor, Kenneth. "Beach Burial". In *The Broadview Anthology of Poetry*, edited by Amanda Goldrick Jones and Herbert Rosengarten. Peterborough, Ontario: Broadview, 1993.
Virgil, *The Aeneid*. Translated by Robert Fitzgerald. New York: Vintage, 1990.
Walker, Brenda. *The Wing of Night: A Novel of Love and War*. Melbourne: Penguin Australia, 2005.
Wyndham, Susan. "Undercover: the Year of Richard Flanagan". *Sydney Morning Herald*, 12 December 2014. http://bit.ly/2kB50fd.

# 12
## "Out of the tear-drenched land": Transnational Sites of Memory in *The Narrow Road to the Deep North*

Liliana Zavaglia

In 2014, Richard Flanagan made Australian literary history when he joined a select group of only three other Australian writers to be awarded the Man Booker Prize for his novel *The Narrow Road to the Deep North* (2013). Later that year, in a controversial intervention, the conservative Prime Minister Tony Abbott overruled his own literary awards panel to ensure that the novel became a joint winner in the Prime Minister's Literary Awards for Fiction, along with the panel's own recommendation, Steven Carroll's *A World of Other People* (2013). Such was Abbott's regard for the novel that his choice prevailed, even though Flanagan (an outspoken environmentalist) had only months previously attacked the prime minister publicly for his coal mining policies, speaking of his shame at being an Australian.[1]

The prime minister's esteem for *The Narrow Road to the Deep North* was by no means singular. The novel garnered high praise from prominent literary reviewers, with Geordie Williamson of the *Australian* lauding its "immense achievement"[2] and likening the author to William Faulkner,[3] while Morag Fraser in the *Sydney Morning Herald* suggested the novel was one of "mordant gusto, lyricism and astonishing tenacity".[4] Yet in an incendiary review, which became almost as well known as the novel itself, the *London Review of Books* literary critic Michael Hofmann dismissed its panoramic scope, which draws intertextually and transnationally from both classical literature and popular culture. In contrast to the Australian reviewers, he suggested the novel was in "an advanced and showy state of dissolution", its form "exploded", consisting of "rubble, fragmentary junk, debris".[5] A number of critics have noted that Flanagan's novels regularly produce divided opinions

---

1   Stephen Romei, "Tony Abbott Overruled Panel to Insist Critic Richard Flanagan Shared Award", *Australian*, 10 December 2014. http://bit.ly/2L92oRb.
2   Geordie Williamson, "Poetry without a Shred of Pity", *Australian*, 28 September, 2013. http://bit.ly/2J2NICq.
3   Geordie Williamson, "Flanagan's Path to Tasmania Passed through Faulkner's Mississippi", *Australian*, 18 October 2014. https://bit.ly/2LgC6jl.
4   Morag Fraser, review of Richard Flanagan's *The Narrow Road to the Deep North*, *Sydney Morning Herald*, 12 October 2013. http://bit.ly/2IZUMUa.
5   Michael Hofmann, "Is His Name Alwyn?" *London Review of Books*, 18 December 2014. http://bit.ly/2xzSgiu.

of this nature, "often quite sharply",[6] perhaps suggesting that they exceed their limits to become "populist approximations to the idea of the great novel".[7]

Within the academy, a number of deeper engagements with the novel have produced similarly contradictory results. Susan Lever suggests the novel is one in which the "ideal of the fair-minded Australian" results in a work of "filial and national piety",[8] while Robert Dixon reads Flanagan's novel in light of the author's long-held commitment to the project of materialist historiography, arguing that it operates as a counter-discourse to the linear progress narratives that underpin the national project, speaking critically from the margins, and bypassing the site of the national altogether. Rather, in its focus on the "constellations" of violent histories, the novel transcends the national scale, circling back and forth from regional Tasmania to global sites of international violence.[9]

In this chapter I diverge from critiques of the novel's form and discourse to argue for a more considered reading of the ways in which Flanagan's novel interrogates the past. Engaging with Dixon's argument of the novel's transnational scale, my reading will trace the novel's cross-cultural resonances with the literature of Holocaust witness, while also locating within it a discourse embedded with the residues of a particularly national concern which has materialised in the postcolonial particularisation of liberal whiteness after empire.[10]

In the novel, the lingering problems of race in Australia emerge in the recollections of the prisoner-of-war experience, which raise memories of the Jewish experiences of the Nazi death camps, producing configurations in which colonialism, imperialism and the Holocaust are brought together. It is from this transnational site of suffering that Flanagan stages a belated return of Indigenous memory in the figure of the Indigenous soldier Darky Gardiner. Flanagan uses the trauma and victimhood on the Thai-Burma Railway to challenge the national myth of the Australian soldier-hero, revealing in the process the ways in which white narratives of nation are closely connected to the marginal histories they suppress. Rather than reinforcing conventions which "simplify" understandings of the past,[11] I argue that the novel offers an insight into its unresolved nature, about which questions must continually be raised. This effort to keep the past open to ongoing interrogation offers a view of history that repudiates simple resolutions. As historian Bain Attwood suggests, to interrogate "the complex messiness of the past" can yield productive "political and social outcomes" that simplified histories refuse.[12] In the novel, this effort to question the past unravels the monolithic sites of white Australian memory to reveal the intimacies that flow between "seemingly opposed traditions of remembrance".[13]

---

6   James Ley, "Elusive Nobility", *Australian Book Review*, October 2013: 12.
7   Peter Craven, "The Booker May Well Kick a Book Along, but There's No Guarantee It'll Become a Classic", *Australian*, 2 August 2014. http://bit.ly/2sqhutK.
8   Susan Lever, "Heroes, certainly", *Sydney Review of Books*, 26 November 2013. http://bit.ly/2rZ8qfM.
9   Robert Dixon, "Communications from Below: Scalar Transformations in Richard Flanagan's *The Narrow Road to the Deep North* (2013) and Steven Carroll's *A World of Other People* (2013)", *Antipodes* 31, no. 1 (June 2017): 184–205.
10  Alfred J. Lopez, "Introduction: Whiteness after Empire", in *Postcolonial Whiteness: A Critical Reader on Race and Empire*, ed. Alfred J. Lopez (Albany: State University of New York Press, 2005), 1–30.
11  Lever, "Heroes, Certainly".
12  Bain Attwood, "*The Law of the Land* or the Law of the Land?: History, Law and Narrative in a Settler Society", *History Compass* 2, no. 1 (2004): 3, 19.
13  Michael Rothberg, *Multidirectional Memory: Remembering the Holocaust in the Age of Decolonisation* (Stanford: Stanford University Press, 2009), 7.

In a number of interviews discussing his biographical sources, Flanagan has spoken of a pivotal conversation with his father Arch Flanagan that would have consequences in the final days of his father's life. Arch Flanagan was himself a prisoner of war during World War Two, a survivor of the Thai-Burma Railway prison camps. It is his experiences, documented and co-authored with his other son Martin Flanagan in *The Line: A Man's Experience; A Son's Quest to Understand* (2005), and those of his fellow soldiers, that inspired the novel. In the course of his research for the novel, Flanagan met his father's former prison guard, Lee Hak Rae – a Korean soldier despised by both his fellow Japanese soldiers and the Australian prisoners he brutalised. After relaying the details of the meeting to his father, Arch Flanagan experienced a dissociative episode and lost all memory of his time on the Death Railway. His son's reflections – that although Lee and the other guards he interviewed had not been "necessarily entirely honest", yet seemed to carry some "regret and shame" at their treatment of Australian prisoners of war – produced the now well-documented contours of a classically traumatic response in his father.[14] As founding trauma theorist Cathy Caruth observes, such responses reveal not only the "repeated suffering of an event" but also "the continual leaving of its site".[15] Flanagan suggests that while his father understood he had been in the camps, he could no longer recall it in any detail.[16]

Flanagan's novel is not, however, biography but rather a fictional exploration of wartime experiences and their lingering effects in peacetime, taking into account the narratives of both Australian soldiers and their Japanese captors. As Susan Lever notes, Flanagan's father is not the central character, but most likely "the basis for one of the minor characters",[17] Jimmy Bigelow. Like Flanagan's father, Jimmy also loses his memory of the camps in old age: "he realised he could remember none of his time as a POW at all … he knew he had once been a POW as he knew he had once been a foetus … At the age of ninety-four he was finally a free man".[18]

The novel's principal character, Alwyn "Dorrigo" Evans, is a doctor and former prisoner of war, who has achieved late fame as a somewhat ambivalent war hero. In peacetime, he contends with the dissonance between his heroic public image and his private sense of a pervading inauthenticity. "I am become a name" (19), he says, melancholically invoking that other jaded soldier of English literature, Tennyson's Ulysses. In the narration that follows, stories of both love and war interlock in a tapestry which threads itself through small towns, states and nations, culminating in the cataclysmic events of World War Two.

Arch Flanagan was one of the group that had been called "Dunlop's Thousand", led by the famed army doctor Lieutenant-Colonel Edward "Weary" Dunlop. Dunlop is, at least in part, one of the inspirations for Dorrigo Evans. Flanagan points out that Lee Hak Rae was known to Dunlop and his fellow prisoners of war as "the Ivan the Terrible" of the camp, a guard whom the Australians called "The Lizard". Drawing on the details of Lee Hak Rae's

---

14  Richard Flanagan interviewed by Ramona Koval, *The Monthly Video*, 24 July 2014. http://bit.ly/2sqIfyd.
15  Cathy Caruth, "Trauma and Experience: An Introduction", in *Trauma: Explorations in Memory*, ed. Cathy Caruth (Baltimore: John Hopkins University Press, 1995), 10.
16  Koval, "Richard Flanagan".
17  Lever, "Heroes, Certainly".
18  Richard Flanagan, *The Narrow Road to the Deep North* (North Sydney: Random House, 2013), 452. All subsequent references are to this edition and appear in parentheses in the text.

brutalising victimisation as a colonial subject of the Japanese, his eventual conscription into the Japanese Imperial Army and his own sadistic treatment of his Australian captives, Lee is fictionalised as "The Goanna". Flanagan has explained that Lee was the only man he had ever heard his father speak of "with violent intent" and has noted that Weary Dunlop himself once waited on a pathway to beat him to death with a rock. Fortuitously for Lee, on that occasion he did not pass by.[19]

Lee Hak Rae, who was sentenced to death for his war crimes, was subsequently released in an amnesty in 1956. In his dotage, he appeared to Flanagan to be "a courteous, kindly and generous old man". In a synchronistic event which turbulently unfolded during Flanagan's meeting with Lee, an earthquake hit Tokyo and the writer was able to observe the old man's fear as "the whole room pitched around like a bobbing dinghy in a most wild sea". Flanagan's encounter with his father's wartime tormentor profoundly affected him, definitively unravelling moral categories of individual good and evil as the locus for the horror the Japanese inflicted in the camps. For Flanagan, who during that meeting perceived that "whatever evil is, it wasn't in that room with us",[20] the realisation produced a more complex transnational interrogation of history in *The Narrow Road to the Deep North*, which eschews questions of individual or national evil and resituates Australian experiences of war at global sites of collective violence and traumatic memory.

## Literatures of Witness

In his final work, *The Drowned and the Saved* (1986), the Italian Jewish Holocaust survivor Primo Levi forensically explored the conditions in the Nazi camps, which broke down the threads of humanity amongst its victims. In 1944, Levi was deported from Turin to Auschwitz, where he worked as a slave labourer in the Monowitz camp until the Soviet liberation of 1945. In the chapter titled "The Gray Zone", Levi describes the cultural tendency to simplify history as a Manichean structure of binary opposites "which shuns half-tints and complexities" and is "prone to reduce the river of human occurrences to conflicts and the conflicts to duels – we and they ... because the good must prevail, otherwise the world would be subverted".[21] A careful distinction needs to be drawn in this excerpt from "The Gray Zone". Levi's chief concern relates to the ethical ambiguities generated in the victim hierarchy of the camps. However, he extends his considerations to a Nazi officer who ordered the murder of a young girl who had somehow survived the gas chamber. While Levi notes that the officer was rightly sentenced to death after the war for his crimes, he suggests that even his culpability was not a "monolith", and that had the man lived in any other period, he may have behaved like any other ordinary person.[22] Levi's examination of the cultural desire for the binary formulations found in simplified history resonates with Flanagan's insights into the complexities of the past, which also render such oppositional categories redundant.

---

19　Richard Flanagan, "Freeing My Father", *Sydney Morning Herald*, 21 September, 2013. http://bit.ly/2sqCh04.
20　Flanagan interviewed by Ramona Koval, *The Monthly Video*.
21　Primo Levi, *The Drowned and the Saved* (1986; New York: Random House, 1989), 37.
22　Levi, *The Drowned and the Saved*, 57.

In *The Narrow Road to the Deep North*, the movement away from these simplifications is best illustrated through Dorrigo Evans' inability to convince the commander of the camp, Major Nakamura, to stop Darky Gardiner's senseless beating. In this central scene of horror, around which so much of the novel pivots, Dorrigo realises that he is powerless to change Nakamura's mind because the reason for the beating is not located in the present, but in what Dixon calls the deep-rooted historical "constellations of violence" that have coalesced and become a relentless, unstoppable force:

> Nakamura no longer seemed to Dorrigo Evans the strange but human officer he had played cards with the night before, not the harsh but pragmatic commander he had bartered lives with that morning, but the terrifying force that takes hold of individuals, groups, nations, and bends and warps them against their natures, against their judgements and destroys all before it with a careless fatalism. (305)

Rather than offering a simplified account of Japanese atrocities in wartime within a moral framework of good and evil, the novel's exploration of this "careless" and "terrifying" force is examined at a transnational site of collective memory. For Flanagan, the cultural accretions of militarism, nationalism, biological racism and the "poisonous" forms of religion to which any faith can turn, can bring about the conditions through which these sorts of atrocities might occur. As Flanagan explains, "It's always wrong to focus on the moment of violence, and think that tells you the whole story ... Any society can go down that path ... By the time you're building a railway through a wilderness with a quarter of a million slave labourers, it's a little too late to expect the jailers to behave with any humanity".[23]

These insights become particularly resonant when they are cross-referenced to the conditions that gave rise to the Holocaust. In his chapter in this collection, Robert Dixon cites Michael Rothberg's conceptual model of "multidirectional memory" as a useful one in any consideration of Flanagan's work. According to Rothberg, "multidirectional memory" describes the ways in which "remembrance of the Holocaust" can intersect with "the legacies of colonialism and slavery and ongoing processes of decolonization". Flanagan's imaginative project in *The Narrow Road to the Deep North* reveals the nature of this "multidirectional" dynamic by which different historical memories can contribute to each other's recognition. Against arguments that suggest Holocaust memory blocks other "historical memories from view", which he calls "competitive memory", Rothberg contends that it contributes to their articulation in a mutual exchange of cross-cultural reference. As Rothberg points out, it was in this way that Holocaust memory itself emerged in the late 1960s, in dialogue with "the dynamic transformations and multifaceted struggles that define the era of decolonization".[24]

Geordie Williamson was one of the first reviewers to find this dynamic at work in the novel, likening it to the "literature of witness" and to "the Auschwitz testimony of Primo Levi", among others.[25] In his interviews, Flanagan's reference to "The Lizard" as the "Ivan the Terrible" of the Thai-Burma Railway does the interesting work of operating through the novel's epitexts, those devices and practices located in the social space outside the book,

---

23  Flanagan interviewed by Ramona Koval, *The Monthly Video*.
24  Rothberg, *Multidirectional Memory*, xiii, 3, 6–7.
25  Williamson, "Poetry without a Shred of Pity".

such as interviews, promotional dossiers and blogs, that "mediate a book to its readers", ensuring its "presence in the world".[26] In this way, Lee Hak Rae's moniker of "Ivan the Terrible" mediates the novel for its readership, orienting it away from the monolithic site of Australian national literature towards a field of writing relating to the collective memory of the Jewish Holocaust. The identity of the man known as "Ivan the Terrible" has never been confirmed. He was thought to be Ivan "John" Demjanjuk, a Ukrainian prisoner of war who volunteered in the Nazi extermination camps, most notably the Sobibòr death camp in Poland. In the course of judicial investigations, many survivors identified "Ivan the Terrible" as the concentration camp guard who, in the course of operating the gas chamber, was known to take pleasure in hacking off ears or breasts, or splitting skulls with an iron pipe.[27] His nickname, taken from the Russian imperial history of a mentally unstable Tsar who murdered his own son, reflects the ways imaginative connections between "different histories and social groups"[28] can be formed to offer mutual recognition in "multidirectional" transfers of memory.

## The "Abomination"

Yet in the novel, the attempt to understand the motivations of this Korean "Ivan the Terrible" within a traditional framework of transcendent binaries is discarded as an inadequate model to explain his brutality: "he was the devil himself – inexplicable, unavoidable, pitiless … But as no-one up there on the Line believed in God anymore, it was hard to believe either in the devil. The Goanna just was" (192). Metaphysical meaning ruptures in the brutality of the camps and Manichean binaries are rejected in the observation that there is no meaning to be found in the moral chaos of the Line.

Christianity as a bulwark against the camp's degradations also collapses as a centre of meaning, in the physical and psychological ruination of the solider Tiny Middleton. Tiny is described as a preternaturally powerful "muscular Christian" (190), who sets new work records on the Line, much to the anger of the other Australian soldiers who are forced to keep up with his efforts. In his account of the Nazi death camps, Primo Levi explains how prisoners attempted to survive through the avoidance of hard labour. Yet he notes that one young prisoner, who had been broken by the camp system, lacked even the "rudimentary astuteness of a draught-horse". Levi describes how the young man worked himself to the state of exhaustion. Because of his inability to discern his predicament, he was considered to be a dangerous co-worker and was avoided by the other prisoners.[29] On the Thai-Burma Railway, the Australian prisoners also avoid Tiny, trying "to go slow, to do less, to save their diminished energies for the necessary task of survival" (191). But Tiny's zealous faith blinds him to the precarious realities of the Japanese camp, which he believes he can overcome through divine intervention. He is a "devout gospel-haller" who believes his body has been given by "The Lord … to work with, to rejoice in". When Darky suggests that his efforts

---

26  Robert Dixon, "Tim Winton, *Cloudstreet* and the Field of Australian Literature", *Westerly* 50 (November 2005): 246.
27  Joe Nickell, *Unsolved History: Investigating Mysteries of the Past* (Lexington: The University Press of Kentucky, 2005), 38.
28  Rothberg, *Multidirectional Memory*, 18.
29  Levi, *If This Is a Man* (1947; London: Abacus, 1987) 48–9.

will be the death of the soldiers, he assures him that "The Lord will see us right" (190). Yet illness and beatings reduce Tiny both physically and psychologically, and in a pivotal scene he breaks down weeping, clawing at himself in an attempt "to beat the shadows away" (193). Like the demise of the many prisoners Levi describes in his experience of Auschwitz, Tiny is "killed in [his] spirit", long before his death.[30] His end is an ignominious one, as Dorrigo comes upon his emaciated corpse lying on "the Wailing Wall" (230), an Australian vernacular term for the teak log upon which sick soldiers are lain down. The scene of the Australian Christian who dies against the metaphorical Jewish wall of lamentation is a powerful one in the novel, forging links to the Jewish experience of victimhood, and its similar rupture of metaphysical systems of meaning during the Nazi genocide.

In the extermination camps, Primo Levi (himself an atheist) also rejected this transcendent framework with his observation that because "Auschwitz existed, no one in our age should speak of Providence".[31] In his first autobiographical work, *If This Is a Man* (1947), the inadequacy of such frameworks to provide either solace or meaning is made clear following a Nazi selection for the gas chambers. Watching an old man praying aloud because he has been spared, Levi is incredulous: "Kuhn is out of his senses … Can [he] fail to realize that next time it will be his turn?"[32] In his rocking prayers of gratitude, Kuhn ignores those around him, who have themselves been selected for the gas chambers. For the usually detached Levi, condemnation is uttered through emotive biblical cadence. The selections are the "abomination" for Levi, exposing the profanity of prayer in Auschwitz. Their existence ensures that "no propitiatory power, no pardon, no expiation by the guilty … nothing at all in the power of man can ever clean again".[33]

In *The Narrow Road to the Deep North*, the collapse of metaphysical surety also takes on these contours when Dorrigo must give a service at the burning of a number of dead soldiers. Their ragged and emaciated bodies are piled together on bamboo logs, and the violent crackling and explosions of flesh consumed by fire are shot through with the overarching images of the furnaces in the Nazi death camps:

> As the flames leapt higher and the air filled with smoke and gyrating cinders, Dorrigo Evans took a step back. The smell was sweet and sickening … [The body of] Rabbit Hendricks sat up and raised both arms, as though embracing the flames that were now charring his face, then something inside him popped with such force that they all had to jump backwards … The bamboo pyre transformed into an ever more ferocious fire … There was a loud bang as another of the corpses exploded, and everyone ducked. (261–2)

The word "holocaust" emerges through French and late Latin, from the Greek word "*holocaustom*". The term appears in the Old Testament, and signifies a sacrifice wholly consumed by fire or a great destruction of life, especially by fire.[34] While its use has not been without controversy due to its religious connotations as a sacrifice for sin,[35] after the war it was adopted as the seminal term by which the Nazi genocide came to

---

30  Levi, *If This Is a Man*, 61.
31  Levi, *If This Is a Man*, 163–4.
32  Levi, *If This Is a Man*, 135–6.
33  Levi, *If This Is a Man*, 136.
34  "Holocaust", *Oxford English Dictionary Online*, http://bit.ly/2sjPW9Z.
35  See Giorgio Agamben, *Remnants of Auschwitz: The Witness and the Archive* (New York: Zone Books, 1999), 28–31.

be known. For Jimmy Bigelow, who must play "The Last Post" through diseased lips and tongue, the senselessness of the scene makes him feel as if his "whole body" is also "aflame", and his "music of death" spirals out towards a "shared dream of human transcendence that perished in the same sound". Jimmy does not understand what the music means, but is certain that it does not mean "that the soldier could now rest … How could anyone rest?" (257–9), he wonders. It is a question which was asked by many survivors in the wake of the Nazi genocide, and records the way in which the funeral pyre of exploding corpses becomes as incomprehensible for the Australian prisoners of war on the Thai-Burma Railway, as the Nazi selections were for Primo Levi in Auschwitz.

In a conversation with a fellow soldier, Dorrigo also indicates his disgust in his mouthing of religious sentiment at the dead soldiers' service: "Talking about God this and God that. Fuck God, he had actually wanted to say … fucked be His name, now and for fucking ever … fuck God for not fucking being here and for not fucking saving the men burning on the fucking bamboo". The "toad of disgust that rolled around his mouth" (260–1) after the service operates through the " multidirectional matrix",[36] linking itself to the sacrilege of prayer in Levi's Auschwitz. Both historical experiences reflect the transnational memory of many survivors across different national sites: the inevitable extinguishment of the transcendental signified in the selections and mass burnings of the death camps.

The memory of Levi's *If This Is a Man* is made explicit in Flanagan's novel in a conversation between Nakamura and his commanding officer, Colonel Kota. The discussion again concerns a rejection of binary systems of meaning, in which the lethal intent of the "concentrationary universe"[37] of the Holocaust arises. Kota rejects Nakamura's suggestion that the prisoners are humanised in their recitation of "Waltzing Matilda". He reminds him that the railway is no less a battlefield than the frontline. A corrected Nakamura concurs: "Exactly … One cannot distinguish between human and non-human acts. One cannot … say this man here is a man and that man there is a devil". The deterministic conclusion reached by Kota is that "war is beyond such things" (120–1). Yet in this implicit naming of Levi's chronicle, a subtle shift takes place. The rejection of God and devil as a framework to explain evil has been replaced with the binary of *human* and *non-human*, as Japanese ideology connects to Nazi ideology in a transnational interlacing. As Levi observes, the Nazi camps were a "great machine", which attempted to reduce men to "beasts",[38] and Flanagan's insights reflect Levi's, in mutual recognition.

The novel's exchange of memory with Holocaust literature of witness is further developed in the novel's dedication to Flanagan's father as *"prisoner san byaku san jū go (335)"*. Flanagan has explained that this is the number to which Arch Flanagan answered in the camps, and by which he became known.[39] The simple dedication to a number, rather than a name, also gestures to the ways in which men were stripped of humanity on the Thai-Burma Railway, invoking with it one of the most prominent images of the

---

36　Rothberg, *Multidirectional Memory*, 34.
37　The Holocaust survivor and writer David Rousset coined the term *"l'univers concentrationnaire"* in 1947 to describe the Nazi camp system. For Rousset, the camps were 'a universe apart, totally cut off, the weird kingdom of an unlikely fatality', unable to be depicted in all its scope. See Lynn Gunzberg, "Down among the Dead Men: Levi and Dante in Hell", *Modern Language Studies*, 16, no. 1 (Winter 1986): 10.
38　Levi, *If This Is a Man*, 47.
39　Koval, "Richard Flanagan".

Holocaust: that of the concentration camp tattoo by which the victims and survivors of the Holocaust were identified. Here the memory of the "concentrationary universe" emerges once more in the Japanese prisoner number of Arch Flanagan. Indeed, in Levi's account of his internment at Auschwitz, it becomes one of the earliest symbols of the Nazi dehumanisation program. With his name expunged by a number, he understands he is no longer Primo Levi: "I have learnt that I am a Häftling [prisoner]. My number is 174517; we have been baptized".[40] According to Isabella Bertoletti, the numbering of prisoners in the camps was the beginning of a process, which both Levi and Flanagan emphasise as the imperative of the camps: "the systemic destruction of the individual" until he was "nothing more than flesh, mere matter".[41] This is the condition of "bare life" described by the philosopher Giorgio Agamben in his influential study *Homo Sacer*. "Homo sacer", or sacred man, is a person divested of political and legal status that exists beyond the law and no longer lives under its protection. "Homo sacer", a figure taken from ancient Roman law, is analysed by Agamben as a feature of the Nazi camp system, where the prisoners' existence was "reduced to a bare life stripped of every right by virtue of the fact that anyone can kill [them] without committing homicide".[42]

Flanagan's epigraphic fragment of the poem by Paul Celan that follows the dedication ("Mother, they write poems") signals the literary vehicle by which the novel will link itself to Holocaust memory. Celan was another Holocaust survivor whose poetry of interiority resists facile interpretation. According to the writer Gail Jones, writing which displays an obvious intent cannot effectively testify to great suffering. It is in poetry such as Celan's, where the hidden nature of the image attests to the inexpressible, that Jones imagines the effective "conditions for justice" taking place.[43] In *The Narrow Road to the Deep North*, Celan's insight represents one of the novel's central paradoxes – that oppressors, along with their victims in both the Jewish Holocaust and the Japanese camps – appreciated the beauty of classical literature and art. For Dorrigo, the literature of Shakespeare, Tennyson and Kipling holds value because, like Gail Jones' observation of Celan's poetry, "all the words that did not say things directly – were for him the most truthful" (11).

## A "Gush of Dark Blood"

For the Japanese officers, the poetry of Bashō, Buson and Issa reinforces a sense of lethal national pride. It offers the justification, in literary terms, for their nation's imperialist program of expansion and domination. Here, they can experience "the higher side of themselves and of the Japanese spirit – the Japanese spirit that was soon to daily travel along their railway all the way to Burma, the Japanese spirit that from Burma would find its way to India, the Japanese spirit that would from there conquer the world" (131). Yet this is no simplistic critique of Japanese imperialism. Rather, it emerges from a transnational consideration, for the memory of British imperialism is also raised in the ambitions of the

---

40   Levi, *If This Is a Man*, 33.
41   Isabella Bertoletti, "Primo Levi's Odyssey: *The Drowned and the Saved*", in *The Legacy of Primo Levi*, ed. Stanislao Pugliese (New York: Palgrave Macmillan, 2005), 108.
42   Giorgio Agamben, *Homo Sacer: Sovereign Power and Bare Life*, trans. David Heller Roazen (Stanford: Stanford University Press, 1998), 183.
43   Gail Jones, "Speaking Shadows: Justice and the Poetic", in *Just Words? Australian Authors Writing for Justice*, ed. Bernadette Brennan (St Lucia: University of Queensland Press, 2008), 78.

Japanese project. In the preceding century of colonial expansion, the imperial tracks across Burma and India had already been laid by the British Empire, whose own national literature was to justify it. As Leigh Dale observes, it was Shakespeare – England's national poet – who became an identifying feature of empire, signifying the "English people, their language, and their literature in their most complete and distinguishable form". Transported to the colonies, the "ideal England, with Shakespeare at its centre, was the very heart of Empire".[44] The memory of British imperialism arising in the invocation of "the Japanese spirit" is made explicit in the novel, in Nakamura's response to Dorrigo's request for a prisoner rest day: "Your British Empire … You think it did not need non-freedom, Colonel? It was built sleeper by sleeper of non-freedom, bridge by bridge of non-freedom" (77).

Japanese and British imperialism also connect to the lingering traces of a particularly modern Australian discourse in a cross-cultural exchange of meaning. In the Indigenous soldier Darky Gardiner's dying thoughts, he angrily observes how systems of brutality become normalised and then forgotten:

> All this would go on and on and only he would be gone. Everywhere he looked, he could see the most vibrant world of life that had no need of him, that would not think for a moment of his vanishing, and it would have no memory of him … and in ten years or twenty years perhaps those who survived would be slaves in some new Japanese empire. And after fifty or a hundred years everyone would accept it as perfectly normal, and none of it would be better or worse than anything now. (271)

Through Darky's rage at his own impending death, Flanagan raises the subaltern histories of Australia's Indigenous peoples. Darky's observation, that "after fifty or a hundred years everyone would accept it as perfectly normal", reflects the modern white Australian disavowal of its own violent imperialist origins. This was made explicit by the conservative Prime Minister John Howard, who at the Reconciliation Convention of 1997 reduced the entire history of brutal colonial expansion in Australia to a "blemished chapter" in the overall story of Australia's great achievement.[45] Rather than reinforcing national myths, the novel thus engages with transnational sites of memory to rupture their hegemonic discourse in its cross-cultural explorations of imperialist ideology.

In his analysis of the Anzac myth, the historian Mark McKenna has traced the ways in which Australians in the twenty-first century have come to embrace "the Anzac legend as their most powerful myth of nationhood".[46] For fellow historian Marilyn Lake, the militarisation of Australian history has been central to this "reshaping of public memory" through a story of nation that defines "military values" as particularly "Australian values". She reveals the political and cultural motivations in this reshaping, suggesting that the public contestations which came to be known as the "History Wars" were, during the 1990s, the key motivation for the intensifying popular and academic focus on twentieth-century military history. As Lake observes, it was John Howard who was particularly

---

44  Leigh Dale, *The English Men: England's Colonial Grip on Australian Universities* (Toowoomba: Association for the Study of Australian Literature, 1997), 193.
45  John Howard, opening address to the Australian Reconciliation Convention, Melbourne, 26 May 1997. Transcript at Austlit, http://bit.ly/2kCkEXR.
46  Mark McKenna, "Anzac Day: How Did it Become Australia's National Day?", in *What's Wrong with Anzac?: The Militarisation of Australian History*, ed. Marilyn Lake and Henry Reynolds (Sydney: University of New South Wales Press, 2010), 111.

eager to redirect the focus from the history of Indigenous dispossession and frontier slaughter that had emerged from these debates. Howard promoted an alternative story of national cohesion in the reshaping of the Australian identity in international wars, encompassing not only the foundational Anzac landing at Gallipoli, but also Australian participation in every subsequent military conflict of the modern era. As a result, "the relentless militarisation of Australian history has effectively marginalised other stories, different historic sites and other conceptions of national values".[47]

If Anzac has now been installed as the white myth of nation, which disremembers the more confronting sites of marginalised Indigenous histories, then *The Narrow Road to the Deep North* counters that reification in the character of the Indigenous soldier Darky Gardiner. Lever's argument that the narrative voice is "conventionally patriotic" is thus complicated by Flanagan's choice to race the "fair-minded Australian"[48] who suffers the most in this novel as Indigenous, rather than white. In this way, Flanagan does not so much celebrate national mythology as contest it, revealing how an enduring Indigenous presence continues to shape the contours of white national memory.

In the novel, Darky Gardiner's mother is the haunting trace of a subaltern history and her absence, as presence, is a recurring theme in Dorrigo's memory. One of Dorrigo's earliest memories reveals how marginalised history is intimately connected to national history and is laid out by Flanagan in a series of symbolically resonant images. As the young Dorrigo's mother attends to a blood blister that has formed on his thumb, he hears his neighbour Jackie Maguire crying over his wife's disappearance. His mother listens to Maguire's woeful story as she inserts the tip of a heated knife into Dorrigo's cuticle to relieve the pressure of the blister: "She's vanished off the face of the earth" (3–4), insists Jackie Maguire, iterating in his anguish one of Flanagan's central concerns. As Robert Dixon observes, Flanagan's "suspicion of narratives of progress", emerges from a commitment to concepts found in the historical materialism espoused by Hannah Arendt and Walter Benjamin. These concepts resist the sequential linearity of historical determinism that occludes the subaltern history of oppression. Dixon traces this commitment through Flanagan's earliest works and it also emerges as a concern in *The Narrow Road to the Deep North*.[49] For the young Dorrigo, in this scene the "smoke" of the hot blade gives way to a "small gush of dark blood" as the "pain of his blood blister" subsides (4). The novel's denouement of Jacky Maguire's wife as an Aboriginal woman whose illegitimate son is placed with white adoptive parents reveals the ways in which Flanagan's imaginative project recovers the suppressed subaltern history that preoccupies national formulations of memory. Dorrigo's memory of this moment mingles with others across the novel, creating a mystery which circles around Mrs Maguire. In another scene, she is described as a "small, intense woman of exotic darkness", as Dorrigo spies his brother Tom kissing her in an erotically charged embrace. Thereafter, she remains a recurring memory:

---

47 Marilyn Lake, "How Do Schoolchildren Learn about the Spirit of Anzac?", in *What's Wrong with Anzac?: The Militarisation of Australian History*, ed. Marilyn Lake and Henry Reynolds (Sydney: University of New South Wales Press, 2010), 138–9.
48 Lever, "Heroes, Certainly".
49 Robert Dixon, "Circles of Violence: Historical Constellations in *Death of a River Guide* (1994) and *The Sound of One Hand Clapping* (1997)", this volume.

> For many years, Dorrigo often thought about Mrs Jackie Maguire, whose real name he never knew, whose real name was like the food he dreamt of every day in the POW camps – there and not there, pressing up into his skull, a thing that always vanished at the point he reached out towards it. And after a time he thought about her less often; and after a further time, he no longer thought about her at all. (7)

The meaning of Mrs Maguire is made clear at the deathbed of Dorrigo's brother Tom. Speaking of Jackie Maguire, he tells Dorrigo, "His wife was a blackfella, you know?" Dorrigo recalls her as a "long dormant memory – a memory that had in some way troubled and shaped him far more than he knew" (423). In Tom's admission that she gave birth to his child, the precise meaning of Dorrigo's remembering and forgetting of the woman is made clear:

> She had the baby in Launceston. A boy. And they sent it to Hobart. That day ... she held me ... And told me about the baby. She had just found out what happened to it ... I was the bloody father ... A family called Gardiner was bringing the kid up. Well-to-do people. It upset her. Upset me. But what could you do? Not that it was being looked after, but that we weren't doing the looking after ... It was just one of those things you had to live with. (426–7)

The "smoke" of Dorrigo's early childhood memory is transformed here into the metaphoric smoke of progressive "linear history", which obscures the connections interlacing Indigenous and white culture. The "small gush of dark blood" also operates as a metaphor for the return of the subaltern other, now intimately linked in a familial relation to Dorrigo. Using the literary practice favoured by Celan, Flanagan employs the shrouded nature of the image to excavate the occluded connections between black and white cultures, raising with it the traumatic memory of the deleterious Australian government policies and practices of Indigenous child removal that led to the Stolen Generations. In his review of *The Narrow Road to the Deep North*, James Ley suggests the revelation of this familial connection is "cheap from a narrative point of view" because its presence in the novel cannot be justified in a "thematic sense".[50] Yet in contradistinction to Ley, Kerryn Goldsworthy stresses its importance, arguing that Darky "personifies the rejection of 'black and white' as a clear opposition or dichotomy: the story of Australia, going centuries back, is a story of a population many of whom who have both indigenous and Caucasian relatives and family, acknowledged or otherwise, by marriage, birth, or adoption".[51] As Goldsworthy points out, it is precisely by revealing the hidden connections between Indigenous and white cultures that one of the novel's important thematic preoccupations emerges.

Dorrigo's gradual forgetting of Ruth Maguire suggests the ways in which this racial history of the nation is regularly disremembered. Yet Flanagan is at pains to point out that it is a history that nonetheless continues to "trouble" and "shape" the nation, in much the same way the memory of Ruth Maguire "troubles" and "shapes" Dorrigo. As Chris Healy argues in *Forgetting Aborigines*:

---

50  James Ley, "Elusive Nobility", 13.
51  Kerryn Goldsworthy, "*The Narrow Road to the Deep North* by Richard Flanagan", *Australian Book Review*, 22 April 2016. http://bit.ly/2H6aXtxn.

The pre-eminent mode in which indigenous people are remembered in Australia is as absent. The evidence of this trope and its dominance is ubiquitous. We can find in continental metaphors – a silent country with a dead heart – more broadly in the poetic and visual imagining of Australian space; and most powerfully in the found faith of colonisation of Australia, that the land was there for the taking.[52]

By exploring the phenomenon of disremembering that characterises the Australian nation in the wake of colonialism, Flanagan illustrates how the persistence of Aboriginal presence in white disremembering inevitably delineates its form as a haunting presence. Drawing attention to this process as it unfolded in Tasmania, Flanagan notes that Van Diemonian history was one not only of colonisation but also of "indigenisation", in which the " white underclass" incorporated many aspects of black culture and ways of living. Yet in the 1856 renaming of Van Diemen's Land as Tasmania, he suggests, a deliberate remaking of history took place, erasing "not only what was worst about [Tasmanians] as human beings, but also the possibility of what might be better".[53]

Flanagan's insight also finds resonance with Judith Brett's examination of John Howard's use of the word "blemish" at the Reconciliation Convention:

> It is … a more revealing word than Howard realises, one of those words Freud was so interested in where the forbidden, repressed thoughts of the unconscious insinuate themselves unnoticed into our conscious … In choosing "blemish" … Howard reveals the repressed thoughts the word is designed to deny – the role that skin colours played and continue to play in Australia's history.[54]

### Recalling The Saved

In her reading of *The Narrow Road to the Deep North*, Susan Lever demonstrates the ways in which Dorrigo "holds onto Tennyson", among other poets, in order to suggest that literature can "provide psychological strength". In the novel, Tennyson's "Ulysses" does offer this uplift and, at least in part, serves as the literary benchmark that attests to the resilience of the human spirit to strive and endure. Accordingly, Dorrigo is heroic and self-sacrificial on the Line, and can be seen to be offering, as Lever suggests, visions of "Australian manhood engaged in a kind of Christ-like self-sacrifice and suffering".[55] This is made explicit in a scene that links Dorrigo to the Christian messiah. Offered the rare commodity of a stolen piece of meat, his mouth waters at "the most desirable, extraordinary thing in the universe". But like the tempting of Christ in the desert, he angrily refuses an orderly's offer of the meat three times, so that it can be shared among the sick soldiers. Dorrigo understands the steak to be "a test he had to pass, a test that would become a necessary story for them all". He realises these are feats of endurance that demand "witness", in order to reinforce the Australian ethos of mateship as the last

---

52 Chris Healy, *Forgetting Aborigines* (Sydney: University of New South Wales Press, 2008), 11.
53 Richard Flanagan, "Van Diemen's Land", in *And what do you do, Mr Gable? Short Pieces by Richard Flanagan* (North Sydney: Random House, 2011). Kindle edition.
54 Judith Brett, "Why John Howard Can't Say Sorry", *Arena Magazine* 50 (2000–2001): 39.
55 Lever, "Heroes, Certainly".

defence against the degradations of the camp. Yet while he dislikes the soldiers' growing adulation of him as "The Big Fella" (53–4), it is through episodes such as these that Lever has interpreted him as "a hero in the self-effacing Australian mode". She suggests that while Dorrigo's ironic disregard for his own heroics operates to critique "public hero worship", this only makes him all the more admirable. Thus for Lever, the novel performs a double movement that criticises "the superficiality" of hero adulation, while still "celebrating the hero".[56]

While I agree that Dorrigo's "self-effacing" heroism can be read as a sacralisation, rather than an interrogation, of the myth of passive Australian masculinities in wartime, it is nonetheless a characterisation that can be complicated and enriched when relocated from the *national* site at which Lever analyses it, and reinterpreted through a transnational consideration of the legacies of survival and the difficulties of witness at the global scale of the Holocaust.

Tennyson's Ulysses is himself an ambivalent figure who has been interpreted in varying ways across the Western literary canon. Thus, while he has been understood as the epitome of human endurance and tenacity, he has also been read, as E. Warkwick Slinn notes, within a discourse of "absence and loss". Like Dorrigo, the Ulysses of Tennyson's poem is unfulfilled in the present and remains an incomplete figure, having returned home to Ithaca after many adventures and a long war. He forever yearns for "the elusive margin" that fades before him, whilst knowing that its fulfilment would lead to death. In his lament that he has "become a name" there lies "a textual trace", for Warwick Slinn, which suggests he is never himself, but "always other". His identity has dissolved into "part of all" he has met. The poem therefore can also be read through a continuing dialectic of "death in life" that characterises the condition of living, "not just as past loss or future limit, or as the goal of world weariness, but more pertinently as present process, as a psychology of human consciousness".[57] This reading of Tennyson's "Ulysses" finds resonance with Martin Flanagan's insights into the character of Weary Dunlop, one of the inspirations for Dorrigo Evans: "One way to understand Weary Dunlop as a character is to read Tennyson's poem 'Ulysses' … I came to sense that he was the loneliest man I had ever met. Loneliness was the shadow that fell across the face of the mountain but was never mentioned".[58]

Primo Levi, who also invokes the literary figure of the Dantean Ulysses in *If This Is a Man*, suggested that his memoir – like Flanagan's novel – "did not follow the chronology in which the events took place but poured out according to the logic of an overwhelming inner urgency".[59] The logic of "inner urgency" in *The Narrow Road to the Deep North* is driven by the recurring memory of Darky Gardiner and the manner of his brutal death. In peacetime, Dorrigo's life becomes one of melancholic aporia in the midst of this heroic adulation, which begins on the Line, and which he describes in the novel as "one monumental unreality". For Dorrigo, "To have been part of a Pharaonic slave system" leads him to conceive of "unreality" thereafter "as the greatest force in life" (400).

---

56  Lever, "Heroes, Certainly".
57  E. Warwick Slinn, *The Discourse of Self in Victorian Poetry* (Charlottesville: University Press of Virginia, 1991), 64.
58  Arch and Martin Flanagan, *The Line: A Man's Experience; A Son's Quest to Understand* (Camberwell East, Vic: One Day Hill, 2005), 100.
59  Levi cited in Bertoletti, "Primo Levi's Oddyssey", 106.

Dorrigo's engagement with this dialectic of "death in life" is made explicit in his experience of a modern Australia which, after the war, he no longer understands: "The Australia that took refuge in his head was mapped with the stories of the dead; the Australia of the living he found an ever stranger country" (80). The trauma theorist Dominick LaCapra describes this "death in life" experience, in its Freudian formulation, as a melancholic stasis: "an arrested process in which the depressed, self-berating, and traumatized self, locked in compulsive repetition, is possessed by the past, faces a future of impasses and remains ... identified with the lost object".[60] While Dorrigo Evans exhibits many of the heroic characteristics of Tennyson's Ulysses, they are, postwar, subtended by this form of aporia. After the war "There was, he knew, within him ... a great slumbering turbulence he could neither understand nor reach, a turbulence that was also a void, the business of unfinished things" (402). The "void", for Dorrigo, is the meaninglessness of Darky Gardiner's death and his struggle to approach it in the novel; it also reflects the dilemma faced by survivors of the Holocaust, how witness might be borne to events which escape normative systems of meaning.

Early in the novel, an aged Dorrigo sets about writing an authoritative introduction to a book of sketches by the wartime artist Rabbit Hendricks. Dorrigo's introduction details the history of the Thai-Burma Railway, but is prefaced by a meta-textual passage, which attests to the inadequacy of language to capture the true horror of the camps: "Horror can be contained within a book, given form and meaning. But in life horror has no more form than it does meaning" (24). Yet even so, Dorrigo is unable to locate that form and meaning when it comes to the incomprehensibility of Darky's death and so he excludes the "most important detail":

> he felt it was one more failed attempt by himself to understand what it all meant ... His tone, he felt, was at once too obvious and too personal ... His head was full of so many things, and somehow he had failed to realise any of them on the page. So many things, so many names, so many dead and yet one name he could not write. (26–7)

Through Dorrigo's difficulties to ethically witness the full meaning of Darky's death, Flanagan is entering into a transnational contemplation on the vexed issues of ethics, representation and art after the Holocaust. One of the most famed dictums on this subject came from the philosopher Theodor Adorno, who stated that "to write poetry after Auschwitz is barbaric".[61] As many critics have observed of this much misunderstood declaration, Adorno was not suggesting the impossibility of poetry after the Holocaust, but rather was referring to the tension that arose between ethics and aesthetics inherent in an art that "reproduces the cultural values of the society that generated the Holocaust".[62] For Lynn Gunzberg, Adorno's statement asks culture to consider if the taming of the moral chaos of the Holocaust into an aesthetic form ultimately justifies "that chaos in aesthetic terms".[63] In reply, she quotes the German poet and author Hans Magnus Enzenberger, who

---

60  Dominick LaCapra, "Trauma, Absence, Loss", *Critical Inquiry* 25, no. 4 (1999): 713.
61  Theodor W. Adorno, "Cultural Criticism and Society", in *Prisms* (1967; Cambridge, MA: MIT Press, 1983), 34.
62  Anna Richardson, "The Ethical Limitations of Holocaust Literary Representation", *Borders and Boundaries* 5 (Summer 2005): 1.
63  Lynn Gunzberg, "Down among the Dead Men: Levi and Dante in Hell", *Modern Language Studies* 16, no. 1 (Winter 1986): 10.

reportedly responded to Adorno's statement with a warning that silence in the face of Nazi atrocity would only be a "surrender to cynicism" which, by implication, would concede to the very forces that created Auschwitz.[64]

In Dorrigo's inability to adequately capture the horror of Darky's beating in writing, we might also trace certain aspects of these important debates. In a discussion with his lover, Lynette Maison, Dorrigo cannot recall the number of soldiers who beat Darky and he berates himself: "What sort of witness am I?" he asks. His admission that, while the historical facts of his introduction were accurate, they were nonetheless not truthful (58), marks the limits of representation and explains his lapse into silence: "There was no meaning" in Darky's beating and death, for Dorrigo, "not then and not now, but you can't write that, can you? … Darky Gardiner died and there was no point to it at all. And he wondered why he could not write something so obvious and simple" (16, 58). Dorrigo's inability to witness effectively thus reflects the insight in Gunzberg's observation of Holocaust writers as ones who faced "on the one hand, the urgent need to communicate and, on the other, the daunting aesthetic problem of reconciling the conventional world to which they had returned with the tightly regulated but irrational world they had outlived".[65]

For Primo Levi, the difficulties were insurmountable. The "true" witnesses were not the survivors, but rather those who perished:

> The worst survived, that is the fittest; the best all died … we, the survivors, are not the true witnesses … we are those who by their prevarications or abilities or good luck did not touch bottom. Those who did so, those who saw the Gorgon, have not returned to tell about it … [they are] the submerged, the complete witnesses, the ones whose deposition would have a general significance. They are the rule, we are the exception.[66]

In *Remnants of Auschwitz*, Giorgio Agamben explores the dilemma presented by the impossibility of complete testimony that Levi describes. Levi calls the victims who did not survive "The *Muselmänner*" of the camps, whom he suggests were those "in decay". Using the literary language of Dante, he names these the "drowned" of Auschwitz – an "anonymous mass" of "non-men", rendered insensate by Nazi dehumanisation, and as such, they plodded unknowingly to their deaths.[67] Levi's insights imply an inability in the survivor to bear full witness. Agamben suggests this signifies the presence of "a lacuna" in survivor testimony – an absence of the "complete" knowledge held by those that perished. This distinguishes it from other forms of testimony that traditionally draw on "consistency and fullness". Yet for Agamben, the true value of Holocaust testimony by its survivors "lies essentially in what it lacks", at the site of the lacuna:

> at its centre it contains something that cannot be borne witness to and that discharges the survivors of authority. The "true" witnesses, the "complete witnesses" are those who did not bear witness and could not bear witness … the drowned. The survivors speak in their stead, by proxy as pseudo-witnesses; they bear witness to a missing testimony …

---

64 Hans Magnus Enzenberger cited in Lawrence L Langer, *The Holocaust and the Literary Imagination* (New Haven, CT: Yale University Press, 1975), 2.
65 Gunzberg, "Down among the Dead Men", 11.
66 Levi, *The Drowned and the Saved*, 82–4.
67 Levi, *If This Is a Man*, 96.

> Whoever assumes the charge of bearing witness in their name, knows that he or she must bear witness in the name of the impossibility of bearing witness.[68]

For Agamben, this alters the value of Holocaust testimony in definitive ways, making it necessary to find meaning in "unexpected areas". He suggests the manner in which language gives way to "non-language"[69] in survivor testimony, reveals the task at hand is to interrogate or, more precisely, "to listen to the lacuna".[70] Dorrigo's failure to record Darky's death, expressed through his internal dialectic of "death in life", is an instance of Agamben's insight of the survivor bearing witness to *the very impossibility* of bearing witness. In the lacuna of Dorrigo's witness, Darky's absence resonates through Dorrigo's non-language in "the one name" he cannot write. Through another multidirectional exchange of memory, Darky becomes analogous to those Levi called "the drowned" in his writings. He has also seen "the Gorgon", and so cannot return to tell the tale. His ending, by drowning in a sewer trench, designates him as one of the "true witnesses", in Levi's terms, which leads Dorrigo to the same insight as that recorded by Levi in *The Drowned and the Saved*:

> there were for [the survivors] … only two sorts of men: the men who were *on the Line*, and the rest of humanity, who were not … Or perhaps, in the end, even this is inadequate: Dorrigo Evans was increasingly haunted by the thought that it was only the men *who died on the Line*. He feared that only in them was the terrible perfection of suffering and knowledge that made one fully human. (27)

*The Narrow Road to the Deep North* reflects similar aspects of the Dantean world to those that Levi invokes in *If This Is a Man*. Both the novel and the memoir suggest the train journey to the respective camps as the voyage of the damned to the mouth of the Inferno. In the novel, Dorrigo and his soldiers are loaded into a train where they are crammed together in a "sweat-wet slither", and they sway "in each other's arms and legs" in a long journey across borders into the heart of the jungle. When they arrive, a Japanese officer thanks them for their journey to help the Emperor build the railway. "Being prisoner great shame", asserts the officer, "Redeem honour building railway for Emperor. Great Honour" (42–3). The "Asian hell" (292) emerges in the many images of the soldiers on the Line, where the vision of "groups of near-naked men appearing and disappearing into smoke and flame" (43) provides a literary rendering that forms a nexus with the Dantean hell of Levi's Auschwitz.

In Levi's memoir, a similar train journey across countries is described with "men, women and children pressed together without pity, like cheap merchandise, for a journey … down there, towards the bottom". Upon arrival, a German soldier who asks for money and jewellery is likened to Dante's Charon, whose appearance is also notable in Dorrigo's dreams and eventual death scene, and who ferries the damned to the mouth of hell. As they enter the camp, Levi takes note of a sign above the door: "*Arbeit Macht Frei*, work gives freedom".[71] As Nicholas Patruno observes, this sign echoes the words chiselled into the rock at the entrance of Dante's *Inferno*: "Lasciate ogni speranza, voi che entrate

---

68 Agamben, *Remnants of Auschwitz*, 33–4.
69 Agamben, *Remnants of Auschwitz*, 39.
70 Agamben, *Remnants of Auschwitz*, 13.
71 Levi, *If This Is a Man* (23, 27–8).

(Abandon all hope, you who enter)".[72] A transnational site of remembrance is formed in *The Narrow Road to the Deep North* and the respective journeys and entries into the camps, where the Japanese assertion of work redeeming honour and the Nazi assertion of work offering freedom, meet in a meaningful exchange. Both Flanagan's novel and Levi's chronicle summon the image of the Dantean Inferno, where the imperative is not one that announces the possibility of freedom or honour through labour, but rather the abandonment of hope for all who enter.

The ambivalent figure of Ulysses in *The Narrow Road to the Deep North* can also offer a transnational contemplation when it enters the multidirectional dynamic to exchange memory with Primo Levi's chapter, "The Canto of Ulysses", from *If This Is a Man*. As Michael Rothberg and Jonathan Druker observe, many Levi scholars agree that Levi's employment of Dante's Ulysses is pivotal to any reading of his chronicle, but they disagree on "the implications of invoking a literary inferno to describe an actual place". While some readings have suggested Levi was attempting to transcend the degradations of the camp through epic poetry, later readings are more critical, tracing the use of Ulysses as a figure that reveals the violence by which culture is formed.[73]

"The Canto of Ulysses" concerns Levi's attempts to recite *The Inferno*'s Canto XXVI to his young friend, Jean, during a walk to the kitchens for soup. Levi tells Jean to "open [his] ears and [his] mind", to understand for his sake the significance of Virgil's imperative to Ulysses in the *Inferno*:

> Think of your breed; for brutish ignorance
> Your mettle was not made; you were made men,
> To follow after knowledge and excellence.[74]

It is a moment of poetic epiphany for Levi, which Jean asks him to repeat. Levi suggests Dante's words are for "all men who toil", but are of importance to Jean and himself in particular, "who dare to reason of these things" in the Auschwitz camp.[75] As Jonathan Druker observes, Levi's act of recalling Dante's Ulysses "affirms his [and Jean's] humanity by audaciously challenging irrational, inhuman forces greater than himself", thus allowing an interval in which there is a momentary liberation for the degraded prisoners in their sense of affinity with Ulysses.[76] Here, Levi resists the purpose of the Nazi "Lager", which he has earlier described as a great machine designed to reduce men to beasts. Thus, for Levi, Dante's Canto of Ulysses is the literary vehicle through which his assertion that "we must not become beasts"[77] is momentarily realised in the face of the camp's dehumanisation.

However, Druker's reading also takes into account Ulysses' standing as the "prototypical fascist hero", thus recalling Adorno's warning on art after Auschwitz and highlighting the dangers of Holocaust writing set within a humanist framework. For

---

72   Nicholas Patruno, "Primo Levi, Dante, and the 'Canto of Ulysses'", in *The Legacy of Primo Levi*, ed. Stanislao Pugliese (New York: Palgrave Macmillan, 2005), 35.
73   Michael Rothberg and Jonathan Druker, "A Secular Alternative: Primo Levi's Place in American Holocaust Discourse", *Shofar* 28, no. 1 (Fall 2009): 116–17.
74   Levi, *If This Is a Man*, 119.
75   Levi, *If This Is a Man*, 120.
76   Jonathan Druker, "The Shadowed Violence of Culture: Fascism and the Figure of Ulysses in Primo Levi's *Survival in Auschwitz*", *CLIO* 33, no. 2 (2004): 144.
77   Levi, *If This Is a Man*, 47.

Druker, who cites Horkheimer's and Adorno's critique of the deadly aspects of the mythical Ulysses, Levi's use of the Dantean Ulysses risks collusion with "the murderous master narrative of fascism" that it seeks to challenge.[78] Yet for Nicholas Patruno, and many others, Levi's attempt to recall the Canto of Ulysses in *If This Is a Man* does quite the opposite: it becomes for Levi the assurance that the "Nazi scheme to dehumanise" him had ultimately failed.[79]

While Levi's use of Ulysses has therefore been the subject of much critical debate, perhaps the last word should be left to the survivor himself. Writing forty years later in *The Drowned and the Saved*, Levi suggested that "culture" had periodically "served [him] well and perhaps it saved [him]". Thus for Levi, Dante's words

> Then and there … had great value. They made it possible for me to re-establish a link with the past, saving it from oblivion and reinforcing my identity … They elevated me in my own eyes and those of my interlocutor. They granted me a respite, ephemeral but not hebetudinous, in fact liberating and differentiating: in short, a way for me to find myself.[80]

Shot through with memories of Levi's Dantean Ulysses, Dorrigo Evans' heroic aspects take on greater resonance. They are transformed at a transnational site where different historical remembrances illuminate each other in mutual recognition. Rather than reinforcing militaristic myths of the Australian soldier-hero, the "multidirectional matrix" reveals Dorrigo's Ulyssean characteristics and his recourse to high literary culture as an endeavour to affirm his own (and his fellow soldiers') humanity in ways which recall Levi's use of epic verse in the death camps. On the Thai-Burma Railway, they become yet another resistance to a dehumanising "machine" which also inexorably ground men to "beasts".

## "No Sacred Face will help thee here"[81]

In *The Narrow Road to the Deep North*, however, such exceptional qualities are not limited to Dorrigo Evans. If glimpses of the Messianic trope are observable in the characterisation of Evans, then Flanagan ensures that they are fully realised in the novel's other central character, Darky Gardiner. In a Syrian village, where Dorrigo first meets him, Darky is pictured sitting in the middle of a main street in "an opulent armchair … upholstered in blue silk brocaded with silver fish". He is characterised as having a "kitbag" which is half the size of the other soldiers' kitbags, but from which there regularly appears "a seemingly inexhaustible supply of foodstuffs and cigarettes – traded on the black market, foraged or stolen – small miracles that had led to his earning of his other name of the Black Prince". It is from this kitbag that Darky throws Dorrigo Evans "a tin of Portuguese sardines" (36). On the Line, Darky "steals tins of fish from the Japanese stores to keep the living from dying" (48). His character is often depicted as saintly. Like St. Francis of Assisi, he is associated with the patronage of animals; he empathises with the sodden monkeys in jungle downpours (236), and as a result of his sufferings as an incarcerated slave-labourer

---

78 Druker, "The Shadowed Violence of Culture", 158, 160–1.
79 Patruno, "Primo Levi, Dante, and the 'Canto of Ulysses'", 39.
80 Levi, *The Drowned and the Saved*, 139–40.
81 Dante cited in Levi, *If This Is a Man*, 35.

on the Line, longs to return to Tasmania to set free the fish which are held in the tank of his favourite fish and chips shop: "I never thought how that's their prison", Darky tells his fellow soldiers, "Their camp. And I feel sick now thinking about those poor bloody fish in Nikitaris's tank" (241).

Like Dorrigo, Darky's resilience and tenacity are also foregrounded. Through deft thievery and bargaining he can locate other "small miracles" of boiled duck eggs and condensed milk. In the dank humidity of the jungle, Darky feels "the breeze as a form of hope" (187-8), and when Tiny grows ill, Darky offers him half of a remaining duck egg. Tiny receives it in cupped hands, "as if it were a sacrament" (195). Darky is regularly associated in the novel with the figure of the fish, a symbol of the Messianic in Christian theology. His character is also one that finds resonance with the sacrificial characteristics of his commanding officer. As Dorrigo refuses the meat because he knows the men require such heroism to endure in communal survival, Darky offers his duck egg to Tiny to keep him alive: "courage, survival, love – all these things didn't live in one man. They lived in them all or they died and every man with them" (195).

Yet illness and a sequence of ruinous events lead to Darky's demise, and Levi's memories of Auschwitz emerge through the novel's descriptions of his decline. Darky's incorrect folding of a bed blanket results in a savage beating by the Goanna, who thrusts a "rifle butt into the side of Darky Gardiner's head" (208) during a morning inspection of the huts. According to Levi, this was also an aspect of the "useless violence" of the Auschwitz camp system, in which bed making became a "sacral operation to be performed in accordance with iron rules" or punished by a public and savage beating.[82] Darky's snagging of his boot during his labours also portends his death, in a cross-cultural exchange with Levi's testimony. *The Narrow Road to the Deep North* records that "Without boots or shoes most men struggled to last long" (235), reflecting Levi's observation of their importance at Auschwitz: "And do not think that shoes form a factor of secondary importance in the life of the Lager. Death begins with the shoes".[83]

Darky's demise through a prolonged beating also links itself to Holocaust memory in the Nazi death camps, where Primo Levi records a death by hanging in the following terms:

> To destroy a man is difficult, almost as difficult as to create one: it has not been easy, nor quick, but you Germans have succeeded. Here we are, docile under your gaze; from our side you have nothing more to fear; no acts of violence, no words of defiance, not even a look of judgement.[84]

For Lawrence L. Langer, nowhere is the meaning of Levi's title of *If This Is a Man* more clearly invoked than in this passage.[85] The victim who was hanged was thought to have participated in a revolt at Auschwitz-Birkenau, where members of the *Sonderkommando* blew up one of its crematoria in a courageous rebellion. Levi, who had watched thirteen such hangings, was until this day immune to the usual "pomp and ruthless ceremony" of such events. But, as he suggests in his memoir, "Today is different". He records how, in the inhumane conditions which had sought to reduce men to non-men, a "few hundred

---

82  Levi, *The Drowned and the Saved*, 117.
83  Levi, *If This Is a Man*, 40.
84  Levi, *If This Is a Man*, 156.
85  Lawrence L. Langer, *Preempting the Holocaust* (New Haven, CT: Yale University Press, 1998), 32.

men at Birkenau, helpless and exhausted slaves like ourselves, had found in themselves the strength to act, to mature the fruits of their hatred".[86]

Not unlike the Australian prisoners who are forced to watch Darky's beating, the Jewish prisoners are forced to watch the excessive cruelty that constitutes this hanging. And also like the Australians, the Nazi victims remain passive, "as the cry of the doomed man" pierces through them: "'*Kamareden, ich bin der Letz!*' (Comrades, I am the last one!)", he shouts. Yet there is no response to the man's cry:

> I wish I could say that from the midst of us, an abject flock, a voice rose, a murmur, a sign of assent. But nothing happened. We remained standing, bent and grey, our heads dropped ... at the foot of the gallows, the SS watch us pass with indifferent eyes: their work is finished and well finished.[87]

Back at the hut, Levi cannot look at his friend Alberto. He acknowledges that they are "broken" and "conquered" by this act: "even if we know how to adapt ourselves, even if we have finally learnt how to find our food and to resist the fatigue and cold, even if we return home".[88] As Langer observes, "Being a helpless spectator to the murder of others" will thus remain for Levi "a constant reminder of personal defeat, a source of shame that nothing can erase".[89]

On the site of the Thai-Burma Railway, this defeat and shame is reflected in the Australian prisoners of war as they watch Darky's beating:

> they did not want to be here. They stood in the middle of the parade ground, a hundred or so prisoners ... to witness Darky Gardiner, a man who pitied wet monkeys, being beaten by the Goanna for a crime he had not committed ... While one of the guards slapped Darky's face back and forth and a second one punched him in the torso, some of the prisoners tried to be happy in their memories of roast pumpkin and roast lamb and plum pudding with beer washing it all down. And though they would carry the memory of Darky's beating to their own deaths six days or seventy years later, at the time the event seemed no more within their control, and therefore no more within their consciousness, than a rock falling or a storm breaking ... Help! Darky Gardiner moaned. Help me! ... So they saw, but they did not see; so they heard, but they did not hear; and they knew, they knew it all, but still they tried not to know ...Their empty and emaciated faces grew only more emaciated and empty the longer the beating went on ... these men who were not men, humans unable to be human. (295–8)

Here, Flanagan forms another connection to the title of Levi's memoir in his reference to the ruined "men who were not men", again transcending the national scale to bind together "diverse spatial, temporal and cultural sites"[90] in a transnational consideration of wartime suffering and trauma.

---

86  Levi, *If This Is a Man*, 154–5
87  Levi, *If This Is a Man*, 155–6
88  Levi, *If This Is a Man*, 156.
89  Langer, *Preempting the Holocaust*, 32.
90  Rothberg, *Multidirectional Memory*, 11.

In the world of the camp, where transcendent meanings of understanding have perished, the words of Christ in Mark 4:12 are also inverted: "they may be ever seeing but never perceiving, and ever hearing but never understanding", to register the prisoners' traumatic response to Darky's beating.

The mobilisation of Christian imagery in what might be interpreted as the rehearsal of a passion play raises pertinent questions. Does this development undermine Flanagan's earlier depiction of the collapse of metaphysical surety in the camp, and give rise to charges of Christian exceptionalism at work in *The Narrow Road to the Deep North*? Can the depiction of Darky Gardiner's death be understood as a "secularised reworking of a theological trope", which undergirds and, indeed, reinforces the Christian master narrative of salvation through suffering and atonement?[91] As I have noted elsewhere,[92] the appearance of the Christian Messianic trope in Australian narratives of reconciliation is a problematic development in imaginative works dedicated to unearthing subaltern histories, for it reinvests in the themes of redemption and progress that submerge those histories, and which Flanagan has eschewed in his own literary practice. However, *The Narrow Road to the Deep North* does not record the restoration of wholeness or hope that attends the trope of Christian renewal, but rather refuses it in a strategy that decentres and fragments the progressivism underpinning the eschatology of Christian belief.[93]

It is in Darky Gardiner's own disavowal of religious faith that Flanagan's intent is made clear: Darky "did not believe, as Tiny Middleton had … He did not believe he was unique or that he had some sort of destiny. In his own heart he felt all such ideas were a complete nonsense. Life wasn't about ideas. Life was a bit about luck" (234–5). Darky's belief in "luck", rather than "destiny", echoes Levi's rejection of "providence" after Auschwitz, and his observation that "good luck" was one of the deciding factors in the arbitrariness of survival or death in Auschwitz. Transcendence is also denied in Darky's meaningless death, and thereafter there can be no restoration in the lives of the men who are forced to watch it. Rather, they are psychically deformed by the experience and Flanagan records their extinguishment of hope in a multidirectional exchange with that "kingdom set apart" in Levi's *If This Is a Man*.

Levi proposes the many stories of the victims and survivors of the Holocaust were, like the stories of the Bible, "incomprehensible". "Are they not themselves stories of a new Bible?",[94] he suggests. Flanagan also offers this reflection, reshaping Christ's words of religious unbelief in Mark 4:12 into newly forming traumatic contours that attest to the inability to believe in anything thereafter. For Dorrigo also, Darky's beating obliterates belief. Powerless to act, he watches "three hundred men watching three men destroying a man whom they knew, and yet they did nothing … and Dorrigo was the first among them" (307).

This is "the most important detail" omitted from Dorrigo's introduction to Rabbit Hendricks' sketches: the incomprehensibility of the camp's moral chaos, which reduces the human to non-human and thus lies out of normative systems of meaning. For Primo Levi,

---

91  Danielle Celermajer, "Unsettling Memories and the Irredeemable", *Theory and Event*, 19, no. 2 (April 2016). https://bit.ly/2mowJ3L.
92  Liliana Zavaglia, *White Apology and Apologia* (Amherst, NY: Cambria, 2016) 59, 102, 170.
93  Danielle Celermajer suggests *The Narrow Road to the Deep North* explores "the ruthlessness of a political form whose theological structure is messianic". See Danielle Celermajer, "Unsettling Memories and the Irredeemable", *Theory and Event*, 19, no. 2 (April 2016). http://bit.ly/2xtzskF.
94  Levi, *If This Is a Man*, 72.

the hanging death of this rebel had profound effects and led to the realisation that "there are no longer any strong men among us, the last one is now hanging above our heads … The Russians can come now: they will only find us, the slaves, the worn-out, worthy of the unarmed death which awaits us".[95] Levi was liberated soon after, but suffered effects for the rest of his life until his presumed suicide in 1987 at the age of sixty-seven. In his final work, *The Drowned and the Saved*, Levi recorded his postwar experience as one of guilt and shame:

> Are you ashamed because you are alive in place of another? And in particular, a man more generous … worthier of living than you? You cannot block out such feelings: you examine yourself … It is no more than a supposition, indeed the shadow of a suspicion: … that each one of us (but this time I say "us" in a … universal sense) has usurped his neighbour's place and lived in his stead.[96]

It is in Jimmy Bigelow's postwar relations to his children that the bleakest of cross-cultural exchanges takes place, finding resonance with Levi's postwar experiences of shame:

> He would feel some nameless terror that was beyond him to explain – a confusion they too would carry with them for the rest of their lives that was both love and fear … He knew they didn't understand … They knew none of it … How could they know that their father was desperately trying to protect them from the unexpected smash of a rifle butt … But sometimes it was just there: staring out an open window to see little Jodie look up and wave to him with the biggest smile … shocked to know he had been lucky enough to live … And he would watch his children playing outside in the sun. Ashamed. Amazed. It was always sunny. (313–14)

In Dorrigo's dying memories, the contours of the Dantean "tear-drenched" Inferno,[97] which also frame Levi's chronical, emerge through a final connection to Holocaust witness. On the Death Railway, he is forced to make the harrowing decision of selecting those prisoners who are least ill to join the Japanese soldiers in a retreat to the Burmese front. Flanagan records this selection as "a death march" in which Dorrigo understands he is condemning his men to death. He chooses "those men he thought might best cope" but "who would most likely die nevertheless" (460). As Levi was "broken" at Auschwitz as "the last one" died, so this event ends in Dorrigo's devastation. In a novel which begins with the observation that in the world of Dorrigo's youth, "No one cried, except babies" (1), the deleterious effects of his wartime experiences are made powerfully obvious at the close of this scene:

> At its end, Dorrigo Evans stepped back and dropped his head in shame. He thought of … Darky Gardiner, whose prolonged death he could only watch. And now these hundred men … When it was done, he walked off into the jungle at the side of the parade ground and wept (460).

---

95  Levi, *If This Is a Man*, 156.
96  Levi, *The Drowned and the Saved*, 81–2.
97  Dante Alighieri, *The Divine Comedy Vol I: Inferno*, trans. Mark Musa (New York: Penguin, 1971), 93.

Dorrigo's agonising selections for the Japanese withdrawal recall the memory of one of the Nazis' most infamous acts. In the final days of World War Two, thousands of victims, emaciated and reduced, were forced to leave the extermination camps in a retreat from the oncoming allied forces. This event became known collectively as the "Nazi death marches", and Levi's chronicle also details its calamitous effects. In *If This Is a Man*, Levi records another impossible decision, which was made under duress: whether to join with those prisoners leaving the Auschwitz camp, or to take the option of remaining behind. Either decision could have led to death and Levi, who was ill with scarlet fever, chose to stay. His closest friend, Alberto, was well and was forced to leave with the Nazis. Levi, who never saw his friend again, was liberated only days later but records that some twenty thousand disappeared "almost in their entirety" during the death marches. "Perhaps someone will write their story one day", Levi mournfully suggests in his memoir.[98] Richard Flanagan, at another transnational site of suffering and trauma, responds with an imaginative rendering of those who were lost on the Thai-Burma Railway. It becomes a powerful cross-cultural exchange of mutual remembrance between the two writers, punctuated with the deep poignancy of Levi's loss in the closing days of World War Two.

While my chapter has focused on the war theme in *The Narrow Road to the Deep North*, it is notable that Dante's influence extends to the novel's interconnecting love story. In Canto V of *The Inferno*, Dante the pilgrim meets the historical lovers Paolo Malatesta and Francesca da Rimini. The aristocratic da Rimini, who was a contemporary of Dante, had engaged in an extramarital affair with her husband's brother, Paolo. The couple were murdered by Francesca's husband, Gianciotto Malatesta, when he discovered them in the act of adultery. In what is probably the most famed episode of *The Inferno*, Francesca lays the blame for her affair on the reading of a chivalric romance, suggesting the lovers were overcome with passion through the power of literature. Dante places this notorious couple in the Circle of the Lustful, where their punishment, or *contrapasso*, is to be eternally fused to each other, lashed constantly by stormy winds and only able to move as one. Like Paolo and Francesca, Dorrigo and Amy are related by marriage, and also fall in love while reading classical literature in a bookshop in Adelaide. Pertinently, Amy's notion of love involves a desire for oblivion with her lover, which recalls Paolo and Francesca's punishment in the *Inferno*: "She wanted ... Not comfort, but the inferno ... exploding within one human being ... annihilation" (162, 164).

Following Dorrigo's death at the close of the novel, the final pages involve a return to the scene of the camp. When read through an intertextual exchange with Dante's classic, the novel's conclusion strikes a hopeful note, as Dorrigo bends down to find "a crimson flower" in the muddy track – a symbol linked to Amy who wears a red flower in her hair at their first meeting (68). Although Dorrigo has been informed through his wife's letter that Amy has died in an explosion, he suggests that "the love story will go on forever and ever, world without end" and that "He would live in hell, because that is love also" (466–7). Here in the inferno of the camp, which may be read as a metaphorical form of afterlife following Dorrigo's demise, Flanagan stages another inversion of religious verse – in this instance, the doxology of *The Gloria Patri*: "As it was in the beginning, and now, and ever shall be, world without end". With this refashioned prayer also recalling the eternal conjoining of Paolo and Francesca in hell, Flanagan attests to the transcendence – not of God, but of human love. After finding the "small miracle" of the flower, the novel's final words record

---

98   Levi, *If This Is a Man*, 161.

Dorrigo "contin[ing] on his way" down the track, thus reflecting the beginning of Dante's journey into hell, in Canto I of *The Inferno*.[99]

As I noted at the beginning of this chapter, Michael Hofmann dismissed *The Narrow Road to the Deep North*, in part, because he considered its form "exploded", its parts made of "rubble, fragmentary junk" and "debris". Yet these descriptions, which disparage the novel in no uncertain terms, perform an interesting insurrection of their own. They recall the images employed by Walter Benjamin in his critique of linear history:

> A Klee painting named "Angelus Novus" shows an angel looking as though he is about to move away from something he is fixedly contemplating. His eyes are staring, his mouth is open, his wings are spread. This is how one pictures the angel of history. His face is turned toward the past. Where we perceive a chain of events, he sees one single catastrophe which keeps piling wreckage upon wreckage and hurls it in front of his feet. The angel would like to stay, awaken the dead and make whole what has been smashed.[100]

A "storm" Benjamin calls "progress" propels the angel backwards into the future. Yet he continues to look at the past "while the pile of debris before him grows skyward". Similarly, Richard Flanagan resists the pull of linear, homogenous history in *The Narrow Road to the Deep North* in order to focus on this "debris" – the subaltern stories the "storm of progress" leaves behind. Resonating cross-culturally with Levi's witness, the novel thus refuses to endorse the militaristic myths of nation that rely on this progressive linearity, offering in its place transnational insights of rupture, which retrieve marginalised history through meaningful exchange with Holocaust memory.

## References

Adorno, Theodor W. "Cultural Criticism and Society". In *Prisms* (1967). Cambridge, MA: MIT Press, 1983), 17–34.
Agamben, Giorgio. *Remnants of Auschwitz: The Witness and the Archive*. New York: Zone Books, 1999.
——. *Homo Sacer: Sovereign Power and Bare Life*. Translated by David Heller Roazen. Stanford: Stanford University Press, 1998.
Alighieri, Dante. *The Divine Comedy Vol I: Inferno*. Translated by Mark Musa. New York: Penguin, 1971.
Attwood, Bain. "*The Law of the Land* or the Law of the Land?: History, Law and Narrative in a Settler Society", *History Compass* 2, no. 1 (2004): 1–30.
Benjamin, Walter. "Theses on the Philosophy of History". In *Illuminations: Essays and Reflections*. Edited by Hannah Arendt. New York: Schocken, 1968, 253–64.
Bertoletti, Isabella. "Primo Levi's Odyssey: *The Drowned and the Saved*". In *The Legacy of Primo Levi*. Edited by Stanislao Pugliese. New York: Palgrave Macmillan, 2005, 105–18.
Brett, Judith. "Why John Howard Can't Say Sorry", *Arena Magazine* 50 (2000–1): 35–41.
Caruth, Cathy. "Trauma and Experience: An Introduction". In *Trauma: Explorations in Memory*. Edited by Cathy Caruth. Baltimore: John Hopkins University Press, 1995.

---

99  See Dante, *The Divine Comedy, Vol 1: Inferno*, trans. Mark Musa (New York: Penguin, 1971), 67–71, 110–13; For an intricate exploration on the importance of the love theme to *The Narrow Road to the Deep North*, see also Nicholas Birns, "'Fireless flame gone amorous': War Amid Love in *The Narrow Road to the Deep North*", this volume.
100  Walter Benjamin, "Theses on the Philosophy of History", in *Illuminations: Essays and Reflections*, ed. Hannah Arendt (New York: Schocken, 1968), 257.

Celermajer, Danielle. "Unsettling Memories and the Irredeemable", *Theory and Event*, 19, no. 2 (April 2016). http://bit.ly/2xtzskF.
Craven, Peter. "The Booker May Well Kick a Book Along, but There's No Guarantee It'll Become a Classic". *Australian*, 2 August 2014. http://bit.ly/2sqhutK.
Dale, Leigh. *The English Men: England's Colonial Grip on Australian Universities*. Toowoomba, Qld: Association for the Study of Australian Literature, 1997.
Dixon, Robert. "'Communications from below': Scalar Transformations in Richard Flanagan's *The Narrow Road to the Deep North* (2013) and Steven Carroll's *A World of Other People* (2013)", *Antipodes* 31. no. 1 (July 2017):184–205.
———. "Tim Winton, *Cloudstreet* and the Field of Australian Literature", *Westerly* 50 (November 2005): 245–60.
Druker, Jonathan. "The Shadowed Violence of Culture: Fascism and the Figure of Ulysses in Primo Levi's *Survival in Auschwitz*", *CLIO* 33, no. 2 (2004): 143–61.
Flanagan, Arch and Martin Flanagan. *The Line: A Man's Experience; A Son's Quest to Understand*. Camberwell East, Vic: One Day Hill, 2005.
Flanagan, Richard. *The Narrow Road to the Deep North*. North Sydney: Random House, 2013.
———. "Freeing My Father". *Sydney Morning Herald*, 21 September 2013. http://bit.ly/2sqCh04.
———. "Van Diemen's Land". In *And what do you do, Mr Gable?* North Sydney: Random House, 2011. Kindle edition.
Fraser, Morag. Review of "Richard Flanagan's *The Narrow Road to the Deep North*". *Sydney Morning Herald*, 12 October 2013. http://bit.ly/2Lbtwz0.
Goldsworthy, Kerryn. "*The Narrow Road to the Deep North* by Richard Flanagan", *Australian Book Review*, 22 April 2016. http://bit.ly/2H6aXtx.
Gunzberg, Lynn. "Down Among the Dead Men: Levi and Dante in Hell", *Modern Language Studies*, 16, no. 1 (Winter 1986): 10–28.
Healy, Chris. *Forgetting Aborigines*. Sydney: University of New South Wales Press, 2008.
Hofmann, Michael. Hofmann, "Is his name Alwyn?" *London Review of Books*, 18 December 2014. http://bit.ly/2xzSgiu.
Howard, John. Opening Address to the Australian Reconciliation Convention, Melbourne, 26 May 1997. Austlit, http://bit.ly/2kCkEXR.
Jones, Gail. "Speaking Shadows: Justice and the Poetic". In *Just Words? Australian Authors Writing for Justice*, edited by Bernadette Brennan. St Lucia: University of Queensland Press, 2008, 76–86.
Koval, Ramona. Interview with Richard Flanagan. *The Monthly Video*, 24 July 2014. http://bit.ly/2sqIfyd.
LaCapra, Dominick. "Trauma, Absence, Loss", *Critical Inquiry* 25, no. 4 (1999): 696–727.
Lake, Marilyn. "How Do Schoolchildren Learn about the Spirit of Anzac?". In *What's Wrong with Anzac?: The Militarisation of Australian History*, edited by Marilyn Lake and Henry Reynolds. Sydney: University of New South Wales Press, 2010, 135–56.
Langer, Lawrence L. *Preempting the Holocaust*. New Haven, CT: Yale University Press, 1998.
———. *The Holocaust and the Literary Imagination*. New Haven, CT: Yale University Press, 1975.
Lever, Susan. "Heroes, Certainly". *Sydney Review of Books*, 26 November 2013. http://bit.ly/2rZ8qfM.
Levi, Primo. *The Drowned and the Saved*. (1986) New York: Random House, 1989.
Ley, James. "Elusive Nobility", *Australian Book Review*, October 2013: 12–13.
Lopez, Alfred J. "Introduction: Whiteness after Empire". In *Postcolonial Whiteness: A Critical Reader on Race and Empire*, edited by Alfred J. Lopez. Albany: State University of New York Press, 2005, 1–30.
McKenna, Mark. "Anzac Day: How Did It Become Australia's National Day?". In *What's Wrong with Anzac?: The Militarisation of Australian History*. Edited by Marilyn Lake and Henry Reynolds. Sydney: University of New South Wales Press, 2010, 110–134.
Nickell, Joe. *Unsolved History: Investigating Mysteries of the Past*. Lexington: The University Press of Kentucky, 2005.
Patruno, Nicholas. "Primo Levi, Dante, and the 'Canto of Ulysses'". In *The Legacy of Primo Levi*. Edited by Stanislao Pugliese. New York: Palgrave Macmillan, 2005, 33–40.

Richardson, Anna. "The Ethical Limitations of Holocaust Literary Representation". *Borders and Boundaries* 5 (Summer 2005): 1–19.
Romei, Stephen. "Tony Abbott Overruled Panel to Insist Critic Richard Flanagan Shared Award". *Australian*, 10 December 2014. http://bit.ly/2L92oRb.
Rothberg, Michael. *Multidirectional Memory: Remembering the Holocaust in the Age of Decolonisation*. Stanford: Stanford University Press, 2009.
Rothberg, Michael and Jonathan Druker. "A Secular Alternative: Primo Levi's Place in American Holocaust Discourse", *Shofar* 28, no. 1 (Fall 2009): 104–26.
Slinn, E. Warwick. *The Discourse of Self in Victorian Poetry*. Charlottesville: University Press of Virginia, 1991.
Williamson, Geordie. "Flanagan's Path to Tasmania Passed through Faulkner's Mississippi". *Australian*, 18 October 2014. https://bit.ly/2LgC6jl.
———. "Poetry without a Shred of Pity". *Australian*, 28 September, 2013. http://bit.ly/2J2NICq.
Zavaglia, Liliana. *White Apology and Apologia*. Amherst, NY: Cambria, 2016.

# Contributors

**Bill Ashcroft**, FAHA, is Emeritus Professor of English at the University of New South Wales. A renowned critic and theorist and founding exponent of postcolonial theory, he is co-author of *The Empire Writes Back* (1989), the first text to offer a systematic examination of the field of postcolonial studies. He is author and co-author of seventeen books and over 180 articles and chapters, variously translated into six languages, and he is on the editorial boards of ten international journals. His latest work is *Utopianism in Postcolonial Literatures*.

**Salhia Ben-Messahel** is Senior Lecturer in English at the Université de Toulon. She is the author of *Mind the Country: Tim Winton's Fiction* (2006) and *Des Frontières de l'Interculturalité* (2009). She is currently completing a monograph on recent Australian fiction, *Globaletics and Radicant Aesthetics in Australian Fiction*, to be released with Cambridge Scholars Publishing.

**Nicholas Birns** is Associate Professor at the Center for Applied Liberal Arts, New York University. He is the author of *Understanding Anthony Powell* (2004) and the co-editor of *A Companion to Australian Literature Since 1900* (2007), a CHOICE Outstanding Academic Book for 2008. His other books include *Theory After Theory: An Intellectual History of Literary Theory from 1950 to the Early 21st Century* (2010), *Barbarian Memory: The Legacy of Early Medieval History in Early Modern Literature* (2013), and *Contemporary Australian Literature: A World Not Yet Dead* (2015). He has contributed to *The New York Times Book Review*, *The Hollins Critic*, *Exemplaria*, *MLQ*, and *Partial Answers*. With Nicole Moore and Sarah Shieff, he co-edited *Options for Teaching Australian and New Zealand Literature* (2017).

**Joseph Cummins** has published widely on Australian literature and popular music. His first book, co-written with Ashley Barnwell, is *Reckoning with the Past: Family Historiographies in Postcolonial Australian Literature*.

**Marc Delrez** teaches literatures in English, old and new, at the University of Liège, Belgium. His research interests include Janet Frame, New Zealand literature, and Australian studies. He recently edited, with Gordon Collier, Geoffrey V. Davis, and Bénédicte Ledent, a volume of essays in memory of Hena Maes-Jelinek entitled *The Cross-Cultural Legacy* (2017). He is a former chair of the European Association for the Study of Australia (EASA).

**Robert Dixon**, FAHA, is Professor of Australian Literature at the University of Sydney. His recent books include *Photography, Early Cinema and Colonial Modernity: Frank Hurley's Synchronized Lecture Entertainments* (2012); *Alex Miller: The Ruin of Time* (2014); and, with Brigid Rooney, *Scenes of Reading: Is Australian Literature a World Literature?* (2015). He is general editor of the Sydney Studies in Australian Literature series.

**Margaret Harris**, FAHA, is Challis Professor of English Literature Emerita at the University of Sydney. Her principal area of research is Victorian fiction, especially the works of George Eliot and George Meredith. Major publications include *George Eliot in Context* (2013) and *The Journals of George Eliot* (with Judith Johnston, 1998). She also publishes on Australian nineteenth- and twentieth-century fiction, and is the literary executor for Christina Stead.

**Ben Holgate** is a Leverhulme Early Career Fellow at Queen Mary University of London in the Department of Comparative Literature. Previously he was an associate lecturer at the University of York in the Department of English and Related Literature. Ben's first monograph, which is about magical realism as environmental discourse, will be published by Routledge in 2019.

**Nathanael O'Reilly** teaches Australian, British, Irish and postcolonial literature at Texas Christian University. His books include *New and Selected Poems of Anna Wickham* (2017); *Tim Winton: Critical Essays* (2014), co-edited with Lyn McCredden; *Exploring Suburbia: The Suburbs in the Contemporary Australian Novel* (2012); and *Postcolonial Issues in Australian Literature* (2010). He is the author of many journal articles, book chapters and reviews, a past president of the American Association for Australasian Literary Studies (AAALS), and a widely published poet.

**Theodore F. Sheckels** is the Charles J. Potts Professor of Social Science at Randolph-Macon College, Ashland, Virginia. The author of *Celluloid Heroes Down Under: Australian Film 1970–2000* (2002), he has more recently published *The Political in Margaret Atwood's Fiction* (2012) and, with Carl Hyden, *Public Places: Sites of Political Communication* (2016). He has published essays on novelists Richard Flanagan and John Marsden, and filmmakers Peter Weir and Rachel Perkins. He is founding editor of *Margaret Atwood Studies*.

**Laura A. White** is Associate Professor of English at Middle Tennessee State University. She is also affiliate faculty with the Women's and Gender Studies Program. Her scholarship has appeared in journals such as *ISLE: Interdisciplinary Studies in Literature and Environment* and *The Journal of Commonwealth Literature*. Her current book project, *Ecospectrality*, will investigate how Anglophone novelists deploy ghosts and hauntings to cultivate an environmentalist epistemology.

**Liliana Zavaglia** is a sessional lecturer in Australian literature at the University of Sydney. She has previously published in literary journals and an edited collection on Alex Miller. Her book *White Apology and Apologia: Australian Novels of Reconciliation* (2016) was published by Cambria.

# Index

9/11 (terrorist attacks) 9, 15, 156–167, 170, 176, 189; *see also* "War on Terror"

Abbott, Tony 181, 193; *see also* Prime Minister's Literary Awards
activism 6, 31, 52
Adams, Jenni 44–45
Agamben, Giorgio 110, 182, 201, 208
Ahmed, Sara 14, 74–75, 79
"airport novel" 158, 176
Alexander, Alison 139, 142
alienation 52, 75, 96
altermodern 15, 103, 111, 114
Ankersmit, F.R. 92
anthropocentrism 50, 52, 53, 56
apprehension 22, 23, 25–29, 36, 37; *see also* crystallisation
Arendt, Hannah 12, 22–23, 29, 33, 37, 203
Armstrong, Gillian 169, 170, 174
Asturias, Miguel Ángel 49

Bashō, Matsuo 113, 187, 201
Baucom, Ian 39
Baudrillard, Jean 165–166
belonging 4, 13–15, 45, 73, 80, 81, 85, 103, 112
Benjamin, Walter 2, 12, 21–28, 36, 38, 39, 203, 217; *see also* philosophy of history
biofictions 12, 119–122, 124, 128
Blake, William 4, 30, 89
Bock, Thomas 10, 143–144
Bourriaud, Nicolas 103, 107, 111, 116
Boyce, James 5, 47
Bradley, James 180
Brenner, Neil 6, 31
Butlers Gorge 33, 33–37

Campbell, David 183–184
capitalism 33, 35, 38, 51
Carey, Peter 49, 121, 147, 189
Carroll, Steven 181, 193
Celan, Paul 180, 201, 204
Chakrabarty, Dipesh 39, 50, 88
Christer, Nikki 8
cinematic narrative 25–27, 37, 137
circle and the line, the 4, 11, 21, 29–30, 35; *see also* constellations
Clarke, Marcus 7, 63–64, 68
class 27, 75, 106, 111, 157, 170
  white underclass 47, 49, 51, 205
Clendinnen, Inga 120
colonisation 6, 14, 26, 47–51, 90, 95, 137, 205
conservation movement 75, 78, 85; *see also* environmentalism
constellations 12, 13, 21, 22, 28–32, 36–38, 136, 194, 197; *see also* circle and the line, the
convicts and the convict system 7, 14, 28, 47–48, 51, 55, 77, 80, 82–83, 94, 95–97, 101, 127, 130
  penal history 7, 38, 51, 56, 95, 128; *see also* Port Arthur, Sarah Island
Cousins, Geoff 9
crystallisation 22, 23–28, 32, 38; *see also* apprehension

dams 7, 34, 35–38, 48, 51, 80, 108
Dante Alighieri 17, 109, 111, 206–217
de Heer, Rolf 7
Deleuze, Gilles 61, 62, 104, 110
Delrez, Marc 31, 46, 105
Derrida, Jacques 45
desire 10, 13, 88, 135, 137–138, 140, 149

Dickens, Charles 10, 13, 130–131, 135–138, 141, 145–151
dispossession 47, 139, 203
Dixon, Robert 12, 16, 136, 194, 197, 203
Dombrovskis, Peter 6, 31, 78
Dunlop, Edward "Weary" 10, 112, 122, 127, 195, 206

ecocriticism 14, 43, 50, 53, 55
"edge, the" 9, 13, 17, 22, 28, 36, 116
environmentalism 9, 14, 39, 50–53, 74, 79, 85, 175; *see also* conservation movement
exile 15
explorers 75, 78, 121, 137, 140, 146

Faulkner, William 6, 8, 89, 113, 193
fear 15, 75, 79, 80, 82, 155–158, 159, 160, 162–164, 165, 167
  politics of fear 155, 160, 163
Federation 27, 28, 31
Flanagan, Arch 2, 10, 109, 195, 200
Flanagan, Martin 10, 195, 206
Flanagan, Richard
  *A Terrible Beauty: History of the Gordon River Country* 2, 14, 51, 73–76, 79, 82, 85
  *Death of a River Guide* 3, 5, 13, 21, 25–32, 33, 39, 46–56, 61, 63–65, 77, 78, 80, 84, 103–107
  *First Person* 4
  *Gould's Book of Fish* 6–9, 12, 43, 46, 52–56, 65, 67, 77, 82–85, 87–101, 124–126, 127–130, 185
  *Narrow Road to the Deep North, The* 1, 10, 16, 29, 39, 103, 105, 109–113, 122, 126, 179–190, 193–217; *see also* Man Booker Prize
  "Out of Control: The Tragedy of Tasmania's Forests" 9
  "Parish-Fed Bastards": A History of the Politics of the Unemployed in Britain, 1884–1939 2
  *Rest of the World Is Watching: Tasmania and the Greens, The* 2
  *Sound of One Hand Clapping, The* 7, 21, 32, 39, 59, 61, 65–68, 103–106
  *Unknown Terrorist, The* 9, 15, 122–123, 155–167, 169–171, 174–176
  *Wanting* 10, 13, 61, 65, 67, 121, 130–131, 135–151, 185
  "Writing Landscape" 4
Flinders Island 39, 59, 131, 143
Flinders, Matthew 7, 140
Franklin, Sir John and Lady Jane 10, 68, 130, 135–148

Franklin River 4, 26, 34, 51–52, 56, 64, 78, 104–107
fundamentalism 156, 162

genocide 33, 38, 90, 98, 199
genre 45–46, 92, 119–121, 131, 158
globalisation 1, 3, 114
Glotfelty, Cheryll 50
Goldsworthy, Kerryn 204
Gordon River 31, 51, 80
Gothic, the 60, 63–64, 66, 142
Gould, William Buelow 7–8, 46–49, 52–57, 65, 67, 82–84, 89, 91–93, 94–101, 124–125, 127, 129; *see also* Flanagan, Richard: *Gould's Book of Fish*
Grenville, Kate 120–121, 189
Grossman, Vasily 32, 38
Guattari, Felix 62, 104, 110
Gunew, Sneja 114, 116

Hage, Ghassan 156
haiku 30, 112–113, 116, 126, 180, 187
Hazzard, Shirley 180, 189
Healy, Chris 204
Hegerfeldt, Anne 44–45
historical fiction 13, 21, 37, 136, 189
History Wars, the 17, 101, 120, 122, 202
Hitt, Christopher 55
Hofmann, Michael 181
Holocaust, the 16, 22, 29, 32, 38, 180, 185, 194, 196–201, 206–210, 212, 214
Homer 16, 179, 186, 189
homogeneity 23, 25, 27, 122, 131, 217
Howard, John 155, 156, 166, 202, 205
Huggan, Graham 49, 50
Hydro-Electric Commission *see* Tasmanian Hydro-Electric Commission

Ihimaera, Witi 43
"imagined sound" 14, 60, 61, 64, 66, 68, 69
  noise 61, 62, 68–69
  the scream 61, 65, 66–67
  the song 61, 64–65, 67
immigrants 7, 36, 109, 155
imperialism *see* colonisation
Indigenous Tasmanians 2, 14, 47–49, 55–57, 65, 139, 202–205; *see also* dispossession
  culture 49, 54
  history 14, 51, 64, 90, 194
  knowledge 13, 14, 43, 61
islands and islandness 7, 13, 34, 61, 63

# Index

Jaivin, Linda 155, 158
Japan
  during World War Two 10, 38, 110, 113, 127, 185, 195–202, 209, 215
  literary influence of 30, 113, 126, 180
Jones, Gail 121, 201
Jones, Jo 8, 125, 127

Kellner, Hans 90, 92
Keneally, Thomas 39, 186, 189
Koval, Ramona 144, 187, 189

Lackey, Michael 119, 127
Lai-Ming, Tammy Ho 144
landscape 4–5, 35, 44, 47, 63, 76, 103, 115
Lennon, Paul 9
Lever, Susan 11, 179, 194–195, 203, 205
Levi, Primo 17, 196–201, 206–216
linear narrative 4, 12, 21, 28–30, 100, 125, 204, 217; *see also* circle and the line, the, constellations
love and war 11, 16, 84, 109, 195
Luckhurst, Roger 34

Mackenzie, Kenneth "Seaforth" 16, 184, 188, 188, 190
magical realism 3, 9, 13, 43–47, 49–51, 53–57, 122, 124, 132
Malouf, David 120, 180, 189
Man Booker Prize 1, 10, 39, 85, 105, 181, 193
Marx, Karl 23, 82, 88
Mathinna 10, 68, 130–131, 135, 137, 142–145, 147, 151
McCann, Andrew 15, 123, 158, 166
McGahan, Andrew 155, 158, 159
McKenna, Mark 120
McMahon, Elizabeth 7, 34, 54
metamorphosis 46, 52–54, 56, 100
metaphysics 125, 132, 198, 214
migration 4, 59, 64, 103, 108
modernism and modernity 6, 9, 12, 33, 38, 49, 88, 97, 110, 182
monoculturalism 6, 15, 31
Moorhouse, Frank 156
multiculturalism 103, 107, 114, 115, 156
multidirectional memory 12, 16, 28, 32–34, 38, 197, 200, 209–211
Murray, Les 181

nationalism 6, 11, 31, 36, 60, 94, 114, 115, 131, 156
  anti-nationalism 6, 25

natural world, the 2, 4, 14, 27, 32, 43, 50–56, 59, 63, 66, 78
Nixon, Rob 5, 35

occluded histories 11, 24, 26, 204
oral histories 4, 12, 21, 30

philosophy of history 2, 22–25, 39, 131
politics 2–3, 8, 15, 108, 112, 122–123, 155–164, 166, 176
Pons, Xavier 89, 99, 165–166
Port Arthur 39, 73
  massacre 32, 36
postcolonialism 1, 14, 46, 50, 60, 64, 73, 90, 114–114, 120, 194
postmodernism 8, 25, 89, 119
Prime Minister's Literary Awards 11, 181, 193
prisoners of war *see* Thai-Burma Railway
Pybus, Cassandra 2, 83
Pynchon, Thomas 8

realism 14, 29, 45, 50, 122–124, 132, 171, 174; *see also* magical realism
Reynolds, Henry 17, 121, 140
rhetoric 12, 15, 36, 68, 87, 89, 90, 147, 155, 164
Rhodes Scholarship 2, 21, 122
Ricoeur, Paul 92, 97
Robinson, George Augustus 121, 130, 137, 140, 143, 149
Robson, Lloyd 139, 140
Romei, Stephen 1
Rothberg, Michael 12, 32–33, 38, 197, 210
Rushdie, Salman 1–3, 25

Sarah Island 7, 28, 51, 54–55, 59, 89, 92–97, 101, 124, 128
Schama, Simon 5
Schmitz, Aron Ettore *see* Svevo, Italo
settlers 14, 48, 54, 75–76, 83
Sheckels, Theodore F. 16, 166, 169
Slemon, Stephen 46
Slessor, Kenneth 16, 184, 184, 188, 188
Slovenia 30–39, 59, 108
sound *see* "imagined sound"
Svevo, Italo 31
Sydney as a literary setting 16, 106, 122, 158–164, 169–175

Tasmania 6, 13–14, 59–61, 76–79, 85, 205
  as a literary setting 30, 33, 59, 63, 64, 135, 185

as separate from mainland Australia 1, 13, 31, 34, 39, 54, 69, 132, 140; *see also* islands and islandness
history of 2, 5, 7, 27, 30, 40, 47, 63, 88, 132, 139–140
Indigenous heritage 31, 38, 48, 54, 76, 98, 145
wilderness of 2, 31, 43, 52, 54, 73–76, 85, 103, 108, 115, 135
Tasmanian Hydro-Electric Commission 32, 34, 36, 51
teleological form *see* linear narrative
Tennyson, Lord Alfred 180, 182, 187, 195, 201, 205
Ternan, Ellen 149–151
terrorism 10, 15, 174–176
Thai-Burma Railway 29, 35, 39, 105, 110, 112, 122, 194, 197, 207, 211, 216
Tiffin, Helen 49, 50
Tolstoy, Leo 16, 179, 185
Tomalin, Claire 149
totalitarianism 11, 21–23, 33, 38, 185
tourism 14, 73–74, 76–80
tourists 14, 52, 56, 79–83, 85
transnationalism 8, 16, 31, 33, 37, 193–202, 206, 210, 211, 213, 216

trauma and the trauma novel 21, 34, 39
Truchanas, Olegas 6, 31

Van Diemen's Land *see* Tasmania
Virgil 183, 210

"War on Terror" 9, 15, 124, 155, 157; *see also* 9/11 (terrorist attacks), terrorism
Webb, Jen 159, 166
White, Hayden 12, 87, 89, 92
White, Laura A. 52, 122, 124
White, Patrick 121, 187
wilderness *see* natural world, the; *see also* Tasmania: wilderness of
Williamson, Geordie 1, 6, 193, 197
Winton, Tim 106, 112
World War Two 11, 32, 69, 109, 179–181, 183, 185, 189, 195, 216; *see also* Thai-Burma Railway
Wright, Alexis 43, 49

Yentob, Alan 4, 9

Zavaglia, Liliana 16, 111
Žižek, Slavoj 123, 165

www.ingramcontent.com/pod-product-compliance
Lightning Source LLC
Chambersburg PA
CBHW081419230426
43668CB00016B/2283